*Mind: An Essay on
Human Feeling*

MIND: AN ESSAY ON HUMAN FEELING

VOLUME II

SUSANNE K. LANGER

THE JOHNS HOPKINS UNIVERSITY PRESS

BALTIMORE AND LONDON

The Johns Hopkins University Press, Baltimore, Maryland 21218
The Johns Hopkins University Press Ltd., London

Library of Congress Catalog Card Number 66–26686
ISBN 0-8018-1428-6

Library of Congress Cataloging in Publication data will be found
on the last printed page of this book.

Acknowledgments

Volume II

TO MOST of the colleagues and other friends who helped me as I was writing the previous volume I owe thanks again for their continuing kindness and interest; first of all to the Edgar J. Kaufmann Charitable Trust, for patient and faithful support of so long a work; also to Mrs. James R. Dunbar, who read the whole second volume in proof; and to Miss Helen Aitner, whose help has always gone far beyond any professional commitments. I would like, furthermore, to express my appreciation of Professor Sibyl Hausman's drawings from nature and from difficult photographs, which grace as well as clarify the text.

Contents

Contents

[ix]

Speech essential to social organization; animal communities not societies; most languages built on object-naming; Australian languages on action words; influence of language on earliest conception; Aristotelian structure imposed on perception; no socially inadequate language; early cerebral impairment of speech compensated by reorganization; origin of language an integrative process; sounds as parts of many activities; perhaps autistic for ages; development of speech and hand centers in man; many forms of memory in man, only hysteresis in animals; evolutionary advances not synchronous; imagination often ahead of other mental traits; subjective-objective dialectic; danger of excessive imagination; in civilized man, a childhood phase; flashback memory; sense of pastness a problem; feeling of reality; role of language in most memories; complexity of language shown in pathological losses; growth of language forms like biological advances; language and "dream work"; each language a system of feeling; communication of ideas the paramount source of intellect; all moral traits peculiar to man

List of Illustrations

[xi]

Part IV

The Great Shift

12

On Repertoire and Instinct

THE principles of life, and especially animal life, discussed under the heading of *Natura Naturans*—"Nature Bringing Forth"—extend from the simplest beginnings we can find, i.e., the proto-acts that belong to biochemistry, through the whole evolutionary theater to the inscrutable complexities of human brains that engender mythologies, mathematics and world-shattering overt actions. Every one of those vital principles, some of which have been only briefly introduced heretofore, consequently will figure again at some higher level, as we trace the unbroken course of our own history even across what seems like a break between a physical and a non-physical realm, but is really the sinuous line of a great reorganizing change, from which new phenomena emerge.

The most important concepts to bear in mind in dealing with the problematical issues of animal behavior are (1) the wholeness and typical form of acts, (2) the advance of situations, and (3) the fact that an organism always does everything it can do. These fundamental ideas have been employed, so far, mainly in relation to physical development, growth and organic function. But, as already stated in the previous chapter, primitive behavior is an extension of the internal functions, and is governed by analogous (though not identical) controls. In its simplest form it resembles the homeostatic interactions of organs, which is a dynamic system of stimulation and inhibition; stimulation by a perpetual stream of changes in the internal situation, constantly motivating new impulses, and inhibition of vast numbers of their presumptive enactments by stronger, rival acts or act products, so the somatic impulses which finally come to overt expression represent only a very small selection. The main difference between such intraorganic activity and the lowest forms of behavior is that the decisive conditions controlling behavior are external, the somatic elements being largely permissive.

A modulus of reactive behavior may be seen in the rising and sinking of plankton in adjustment to light conditions and to the day and night surface temperatures of the water. Several decades ago, A. C. Hardy made a factually and theoretically interesting study of locomotion in the animal plankton,[1] and found it to be dependent on drift horizontally but "voluntary" (I would prefer to say "facultative") vertically. "Medusae, siphonophores, chaetognaths and polychaete worms," he wrote, "crustacea of many groups, pteropods and pelagic tunicates: they all show the same general type of behaviour. The range of vertical migration of different species may be very different, and many of them climb hundreds of feet each day."[2]

"They are too small to swim far in a horizontal direction; but they have the power of sinking away from the upper layers. . . . Now waters at different levels are nearly always travelling at different speeds. An animal going down from the surface and remaining at another level for a few hours will come up again to the surface *at a different place.* . . . Vertical migration provides the plankton animal, otherwise drifting at the mercy of the environment, with the mechanism for *changing that environment for another"* (pp. 148–49).

Hardy treats this capacity to escape from an environment that is becoming too hot or cold, bright or dark, acid or alkaline, etc., as a power of choice, and perhaps it could be so designated; but before having proffered any definition or discussion of "choice," I would rather say that the animal had a behavioral option, because this option may be resolved very much like the millions of physiological options that make up the advance of organic existence. Certainly in these minute animals tropisms are dominating impulses, and behavior consists of immediate reactions. The creature moves to escape discomfort, not to reach a goal, and comes to rest where the conditions are tolerable, without knowing in advance where that will be. In this way its ambient is very widely extended, but never defined or organized. As Hardy observed, "Vertical migration in the drifting plankton . . . leads to the continual presentation of new environments. By dropping or climbing out of these, the animal itself has some, if limited, power of selection. . . . This must primarily be concerned with *change;* it is not a movement to a particular habitat; each migration brings it into a fresh environment, always unknown to it" (p. 158). This is a truly primitive form of behavior, induced by a general influence (temperature, light, chemical state of the water) on the tiny agent as a whole, which goes into the highest activity possible to it, either rising or sinking, according to its own chemical state. It has no goal, but comes to rest when its

[1] "Change and Choice: A Study in Pelagic Ecology" (1938).
[2] P. 146.

[4]

situation becomes sufficiently tolerable in some other medium; it was not enticed by better conditions known through previous experience. If it continued (say) to rise from dark depths higher than the level of its optimum illumination, the excess of light in the daylit surface water would send it down again. This is very much like the homeostatic influence of organs on each other by means of their respective products or activities, except that the two nocent extremes between which the congenial balance (not necessarily 50–50) obtains are external to the organism and motivate its counteraction as a whole, i.e., by locomotion or change of posture.

Aimless motility is the lowest form of behavior, but develops, of course, in concert with the vague ambient which it expands enormously by every specific act. Its forerunner is the all-important power of bodily extension and contraction which might be considered still on the biochemical level, save that it already shows the complexity of causal pattern here called "motivation."[3] The external cause operates as a stimulus, that is, through the matrix of activities which is the organism, to add its influence to the prevailing condition of that system. In a swarm of unicellular beings like the zooplankton, the effects of a stimulus are statistically predictable but not individually certain. The stimulus creates an option which, at this low level, the internal state of the agent decides. But even here the decision is between alternative acts of the typical form: impulse, rise, consummation, cadence, amid pressions that limit and shape the response and may distort or frustrate it. Protozoa and the simplest metazoa have only a few facultative functions with which they respond to a considerable number of inward and outward changes of situation. In the case of the minute animals, chiefly diatoms, that compose the pelagic plankton, rising or dropping must serve to evade excessive light, acidity, alkalinity, cold, warmth, and perhaps ultraviolet or other rays that we are not aware of. Those two simple acts are the only locomotory acts in the agent's repertoire. Their effect is unforeseen, probably often fatal, but because the acts are consummated as soon as they are no longer stimulated by adverse conditions they usually steer the organism into a tolerable zone where it then comes to rest.

The potentialities of a very small repertoire of movements, elicited by fewer kinds of influence than any animal's ambient contains, are graphically demonstrated in the cybernetic toys which perform an astounding number of moves under the particular circumstances to

---

[3] A higher development of this function, which clearly shows the indirect and non-linear causation characteristic of organic processes, may be seen in the action of sea anemones discussed by C. F. A. Pantin; cf. Vol. I, p. 269, n. 28.

which their actions are geared. Such a device is described by W. Grey Walter in his Maudsley Lecture, "The Functions of Electrical Rhythms in the Brain" (1950). The machine contains two electrical elements which are connected with just two receptors, one for light and one for contact, and two effectors, for rotation and progression, respectively, with interconnections that may be variously employed. Dr. Walter asserts that "with only two elements, behaviour is exceedingly complex and quite unpredictable when the device is operating in a normally irregular environment" (p. 3).[4] The sensitivity of the recording mechanisms and their connections with the equally controllable motile units in these experimental toys are certainly astounding. A slight contact with an object will override attraction to distant lights; very strong light repels the contrivance and prevents its bumping into a light source— as insects, not adapted to artificial illumination, generally do. The oscillations set up by contact cause it to push through minor obstructions and sidle past more massive ones. It shows some special behavior —unfortunately, not specified by Dr. Walter—upon meeting its own image in a mirror. Its internal couplings are so variable and labile that there are all sorts of possible combinations of actions under circumstances of various duration, and altogether the imitation of organic behavior is deceptively "life-like," though the internal action is, of course, not life-like at all. The device is powered by imported energy, not by the pervasive building up of unequal electrical potentials by its own constant metabolism in submicroscopic fluid structures; it is not biologically engendered, and will not divide, mate or procreate by internal processes of growth. The "self-repair" and "self-reproduction" of some cybernetic machines is a product of combinatorial logic, exemplified in achievements of small-current engineering, and does not in any essential way imitate the natural history of a plant or animal.[5]

[4] That it is empirically unpredictable even after fairly long-continued observation may well be; but of course it is calculable within a small margin of error if solid surfaces, volumes, distances, illumination and light reflections are measured before the machine is put into action, because the environmental conditions work through the recording mechanisms directly on the propulsive and rotatory units. There is no pattern of metabolic and hormonal activities, general or local, no matrix of autogenic rhythms in the robot to make exhaustive knowledge of its inward constitution impossible by the transience and fluidity of its acts and even its parts. It might require another machine to compute the variables, but with modern methods the actions of any engineered device under specified circumstances must surely be computable.

[5] This is not to belittle the scientific value of such constructions for the study of mechanical principles which may underlie the origination of life. A sober evaluation of their heuristic virtues is given by Lionel S. Penrose in "Self-Reproducing Ma-

What the model does demonstrate, however, with direct bearing on animal life, is how many acts may be compounded out of a very small repertoire. In higher animals a repertoire of behavioral acts is prepared, if not actually exercised, *in ovo* or *in utero*; and it is this fetal forerunner of adaptive behavior that furnishes the elements from which instinctive acts are formed, by much the same sort of process that engenders elaborate organic functions. There is, indeed, a continuity between somatically functional prenatal or neonatal behavior and the subsequent uses of the same inherited elements of overt action in the maturation of instinctive or otherwise adaptive behavior.[6] In many situations organic activities are normally supplemented by facultative acts ranging from probably unconscious responses, steered by simple though often variable stimuli, to clearly voluntary movements directed toward ends rather than away from external pressions.

A case of purely physiological activity which is, nevertheless, behavioral in character is the gemmation of sponges. As J. T. Bonner describes it, "instead of a special region of the sponge being cut off as a gemmule, the cells that make up the gemmule apparently aggregate to central collection points. Not only that, but other cells keep wandering in to provide the original cell aggregation with rich food reserves, and then to cap everything, a group of amoebae carry in the spicules which have been built elsewhere in the sponge and bring them to the surface of the gemmule and cement them in with military precision."[7]

Sponges are a very primitive phylum, and their asexual reproduction evidently is not clearly divided into central activities of growth and differentiation on the one hand and locomotory acts of relatively independent parts on the other. The parts still play a behavioral role in

---

chines" (1959), p. 114, following his lucid exposition of the mechanism he and Roger Penrose devised, where he says in conclusion: "It has been said that the fundamental mechanisms of the biological machine may perhaps be elucidated with the aid of theoretical models. The machines discussed here, however, are not models in this sense. They are machines in their own right, conceived for the specific purpose of self-reproduction. In some ways they may resemble living organisms and, in so far as this is so, they may help to explain how some primitive forms of life originated, maintained themselves and eventually developed into more complex and more stable structures.

"Self-reproductive chains of mechanical units may help to explain the way in which nucleic acids in living cells actually replicate. But they are more likely to assist in the understanding of systems of simpler character, like those that must have preceded the nucleic acids in the evolution of life."

[6] Cf. the preliminary discussion of this point in Vol. I, pp. 406–7.

[7] *Size and Cycle* (1965), p. 58.

forming new individuals, as they do in reconstituting an old one that has been minced by being forced through a sieve.[8] Their behavior is probably unfelt and certainly unaimed, motivated by chemical or electromagnetic forces which are not entirely understood at present. Their separate potentiality is relative to their degree of individuation during a given passage of their total history. When a migratory cell enters into a gemmule it gives up its individuation, and its behavioral competence is lost without being actualized. The significant aspect of such loose organization in pseudo-metazoan structures[9] is that it shows how elementary overt action is in animal life; wherever there is even transient individuation there are potential concerted acts of the individual as a whole. The amoeboid actions of slime mold cells, which finally compose an orthodox plant producing windborne spores, present another example; the influence exerted by *Fucus* eggs on each other, and even by a single one on itself, by means of "exterior hormones" illustrates the motivation of group activity by the products of individual members, singly and collectively.[10]

In the metazoa, behavior is essentially muscular activity, which arises with the development of muscular tissue just as the visceral functions

[8] Melvin Spiegel, in "The Reaggregation of Dissociated Sponge Cells" (1955), gives the following account: "Wilson (1907) first demonstrated that a sponge could be dissociated by pressing it through bolting cloth into isolated cells which would form a number of reaggregates within a day's time." (There are two kinds of cells in a sponge, amoebocytes, which move by pseudopodia, and choanocytes, or collar cells, which move by means of a flagellum. The division is not absolute in all species, but holds for most of them.) "The cells begin to move almost immediately, the amoebocytes moving at about 0.6 to 3.5 μ/minute and changing direction, apparently at random, roughly three times per hour. The cells generally coalesce upon coming in contact with one another. The cell surfaces of the apposed cells join together zipper-wise, proceeding from the area of first contact. After 5 to 10 minutes, the surface of union between any 2 cells is indistinct, and evidence . . . indicates that the outer hyaloplasm forms a common matrix for the inner granuloplasms, which remain separate and distinct from one another. . . . If one makes a mixed suspension of two species of cells, *e.g.*, *Microciona* and *Cliona*, . . . 24 hours after dispersal, the aggregates formed consist of only the one species or the other. . . . [But] this segregation is preceded by a temporary intermixture of cells of the two species, followed by a later sorting-out. After sorting-out has taken place, the aggregates, readily distinguished by the red color of *Microciona* and the yellow color of *Cliona*, are *never* a homogeneous mixture of cells of both species" (pp. 1056–58).

[9] Libbie Hyman, in "The Transition from the Unicellular to the Multicellular Individual" (1942), p. 37, says: "all that is needed to bring sponge development in line with other metazoa is the elimination of the inversion process." But the ontogenesis of the gemmule might be taken as another differentia.

[10] Both of these examples have been described and discussed in Vol. I, pp. 346–48.

arise with the development of cardiac, mesenteric, and other organ tissues. It may be myogenic, like the early fetal heartbeat or the movements of cilia, but in all more advanced structures or stages behavior is energized by nervous impulses and serves primarily for their enactment. Like the maturing organic functions, muscular acts arising endogenously may be adapted to the vital rhythms and even entrained to facilitate physiological activities. Robert Gesell has provided several illustrations in the paper he contributed to an international symposium on instinct, where he said: "Squirming of the leech in an acid environment, *e.g.*, is conceivably a respiratory device of considerable importance since it would move the individual into new opportunity for gaseous and nutritive exchange and by self-massage improve circulation within the individual itself. The pushing of the immobile gills of the mackerel through the water by the tail at a velocity proportionate to the oxygen requirements indicates a chemical regulation of breathing at nervous levels lower than the conventional respiratory center. A similar relation of locomotion is seen in the squid where the propelling jet ventilates the gills...."[11] Our own breathing apparatus is essentially muscular, facultative, though not completely voluntary, since facultative acts may fall under pressions that leave only one choice open—that is, necessity. But within limits we can control our breathing very precisely by voluntary muscles, as in speaking and singing, although for ordinary purposes of air intake, the activity of those muscles has been completely assimilated to the round of somatic processes.

In all the cases so far discussed it is the muscular exercise as such that is utilized to facilitate or even essentially implement vital functions. Such utilization may become quite complex, performing more than one organic service, as the peristaltic movement of the lugworm's esophagus, which G. P. Wells studied in detail, serves digestion and respiration by turns. Wells gives a concise account of this phenomenon in an article entitled "Worm Autobiographies" (1959)—somewhat cluttered, unfortunately, by the currently fashionable talk about "clocks" that are "built into" the pacemaking organs and "compel" the animal to act rhythmically, as though the clocks were something else than the animal; yet in a few straightforward passages in which nothing is ticking, ringing or being put into storage, the assimilation of one muscular activity to two different organic functions is thus simply described: "Under natural conditions the worm feeds in little bursts, each lasting

---

[11] A Neurobiological Analysis of the Innate Behavior of Man" (1956), pp. 463–64. Cf. the function attributed by Matveyev to fetal limb movement (Vol. I, p. 407, n. 75).

for a few minutes, with a rest of a minute or so between. In a glass tube of sea water with no sand to eat, the worms often make the same movements with about the same timing. If the . . . esophagus is removed from the worm and placed in a dish of sea water, it too exhibits this rhythm automatically. For a few minutes it is vigorously active, with waves of contraction running along it in regular sequence from the front end to the back; then it becomes quiet for a couple of minutes, and so on. One can show . . . that the behavior of the esophagus is the determining cause of the intermittent feeding of the intact worm. When the esophagus is active, its activity spreads through the nervous system to most of the muscles of the body, affecting them in various ways and producing the complicated movements.

". . . If the sand surface dries during low tide, the worms commonly cease to feed and defecate. The periodic excursions persist, however, and now serve as a means of aerial respiration, air being swept down into contact with the gills by the pumping motion. After a period of enforced oxygen lack, the excursions follow each other at unusually short intervals. But bascially the rhythms are intrinsic" (pp. 141–42).

The action of an esophagus might not be deemed "behavior," being a movement of involuntary muscles, nearly if not fully as automatic as the pulsation of a heart;[12] but it is on the borderline, since it is said to be the pacemaker for the nervously controlled feeding movements, which certainly constitute behavioral acts. Feeding, of course, has more than endogenous motivation because it has to be implemented by materials found in the external world. At the low activity level of plants, which is normally a purely somatic level, contacts with environmental stimuli motivate unequal rates of metabolism and mitosis, so roots grow vigorously toward a source of food, buds open fastest where light and warmth reach them most freely, etc. It is typical of animals, however, to unfold their behavioral acts particularly under the influence of external events, so that more or less acute outward changes are reflected in the motivation of overt acts, making those acts appear like direct mechanical effects of the stimulus. The fact that an isolated organ, dissected out of a living animal, often can be activated without any total bodily matrix to motivate its response supports this view. But this is really an interesting example of act contraction and expansion, appearing at the level of individual existence as the principle that mutilated organisms— each kind within its own limits—tend to reorganize their activities almost immediately on a new basis and adapt them to their new con-

---

[12] Indeed, the author suggests that the mechanisms may work on a common principle.

dition. Even an amputated part that continues to react to stimulation performs total acts, reorganized to express the simplified motivation which is all that is left to the extremely deprived organism it has become. As long as the preparation can perform enough acts of breaking down and resynthesizing its own substance, i.e., can continue its cellular rhythms, it lives,[13] and may respond to massive impinging stimuli; but as soon as its self-consuming metabolism stops, its structures disintegrate, and overt behavior ceases. While such macabre behavior lasts, it may look like a lifeless "output" of motion effected by the electrical or mechanical "input"; but it really represents an artificial heightening of endogenous processes, and fails when there are no more such processes to heighten.

If an individual from which a limb has been amputated or an organ excised is still capable of carrying on its life-sustaining functions, its remaining activities readjust themselves to form an unbroken round on a smaller scale, probably with reduced functional capacities, as a person who has had his gall bladder removed can carry on his digestive processes on a somewhat restricted diet. The ability to dispense with normally available limbs or organs differs widely in different creatures; many of the lower orders have powers of regeneration that range from the competence of many lizards to regrow their very fragile tails whenever they break off to some planarians' ability to regenerate a whole intact animal from body sections as small as one-tenth of the worm.[14] In these self-restoring animals it is the internal, trophic activity that is radically reorganized to fit the extreme situation. In others which cannot replace bodily parts yet can survive a crippling loss, there usually is a reorganization of behavior that allows the important acts of life to go on essentially unchanged. Thus Hans Thorner found that a truncated

[13] A similar condition obtains in nature when organisms are deprived of part of their substance not by mutilation, but by starvation. C. M. Child has discussed the differences among species in this respect in *Senescence and Rejuvenescence* (1915), p. 35: "Under conditions where the breakdown of material overbalances the increment, as for example in starvation, the higher organisms soon die with a considerable portion of their substance intact, but in many of the simpler forms the material previously accumulated serves to a large extent as a source of energy and the organism remains alive and active, but undergoes reduction until it represents only a minute fraction of its original size. Various species of the flatworms *Planaria* may undergo reduction from a length of twenty-five or thirty millimeters to a length of three or four millimeters with a corresponding change in other proportions before they die, and many others among the simpler organisms are capable of undergoing great reduction without death."

[14] See J. W. Buchanan, "Intermediate Levels of Organismic Integration" (1942), p. 50.

ringsnake (*Tropidonotus natrix* L.) moved in the same curves as an intact snake of the same length, instead of the curves it had described before operation. So, he observes, "the organism exhibits a tendency to readapt itself, upon mutilation, in such a way that it presents as a new whole." On the basis of this "neoplastic" tendency, as he calls it, he judges that nervous impulses excite the spinal cord as a whole, not by segments in strict couplings, and that to the total spread of an excitation there corresponds a particular form of movement which varies precisely with the extent of its field.[15]

The animal, in fact, tries at all times to use elements of its basic repertoire in any given situation; and situations comprise inner as well as outer conditions. There is a wide borderline where inner, homeostatic functions are complemented by behavioral acts or the two sorts of activity intersect, and where sometimes it is hard to classify an action quite certainly as one or the other: shivering, for example, is a muscular act, serving a purpose, yet involuntary and only slightly preventable (in human beings) by voluntary counteraction, i.e., tensing the muscles. Is it behavioral or entirely autonomic? And similarly: what of the gular flutter whereby many animals dissipate excessive body heat? It looks like a behavioral response, yet is probably as autonomic as shivering.[16]

In some animal species, true behavior has taken over certain homeostatic functions which in other species are entirely under physiological control. The implementation of such acts may still arise in some measure from the agent's own reflex mechanisms. An excellent example is

[15] "Die harmonische Anpassungsfähigkeit des verkürzten Nervensystems, untersucht an Schlangen" (1932), p. 13.

[16] See G. A. Bartholomew, "The Role of Behavior in the Temperature Regulation of the Masked Booby" (1966), p. 524: "The Masked Booby's most conspicuous mechanism for heat dissipation is strong, sustained fluttering of the gular area. The Masked Boobies nesting at Punta Suarez employed gular flutter almost continually whenever the sun was shining, and it appears to be a highly important mechanism for heat dissipation in this species." And further, p. 530: "The most obvious behavioural response of the chicks to heat stress is vigorous fluttering of the naked and vascular but unpigmented gular area. Gular flutter, unlike the shivering [which sets in only as the chick develops its downy covering], is present immediately after hatching. Chicks still damp from the egg showed a strong intermittant gular flutter when exposed to heat stress." See also R. C. Lasiewski and G. A. Bartholomew, "Evaporative Cooling in the Poor-Will and the Tawny Frogmouth" (1966), p. 258: "Gular flutter is a rapid vibration of the gular area, apparently driven by the hyoid apparatus. It differs from panting in that it does not involve trachea, lungs, and air sacs. Birds that use gular flutter can also respond to an increased heat load by panting. . . . Gular flutter is metabolically relatively less costly than panting, presumably because the thin floor of the buccal and pharyngeal cavities, and anterior portions of the esophagus, can be moved more easily than the thoracic cage."

the quokka's mode of allaying its discomfort in hot weather by giving itself a veritable tongue bath, which G. A. Bartholomew has described in a thoughtful as well as detailed study, wherein he observes: "The capacity of the quokka to control its body temperature is as great as, or greater than, that shown by most placental mammals of similar size. It employs the same general mechanisms of temperature regulation that are used by placentals—vasomotor changes, shivering, panting, copious salivation, and, presumably, changes in metabolic rate. However, in contrast to most medium-sized and large placentals, under conditions of severe heat stress neither sweating nor panting appears to be so important as copious salivation and licking. Under experimental conditions, when ambient temperatures equal or exceed body temperature, quokkas salivate heavily and lick their front and hind feet, tails, and sometimes bellies until these parts are dripping wet, while at the same time, the feet and tail experience a general vasodilation.... This mechanism would be less useful to a rapidly moving cursorial mammal, such as the large kangaroos of the genus *Macropus*, than either sweating or panting because it is not just a physiological response but an elaborate behavioral response which can be carried out effectively only by an animal at rest."[17]

This method of cooling the body is certainly instinctive, as it is developed *in utero*;[18] and it is a counterpart of a purely somatic activity, for the substrate, saliva, which the animal's behavior requires is a product of its own organs. The action of the salivary glands is probably stimulated by the tongue action, in a dialectical cycle that differs from more familiar homeostatic processes mainly in having a behavioral phase.

A further step in the external supplementation of internal balancing mechanisms is taken by animals that seek out places with comfortable microclimates in the midst of generally adverse conditions. The advance, however, is not simply associated with evolutionary advance. Like most vital principles, the rise of behavioral control of ambient conditions may be found operative at all metazoan levels; an excellent example of active, responsive adaptation engaged the attention of C. M. Bogert as he studied the habits of lizards in the wild. "Lizards belonging to

[17] "Temperature Regulation in the Macropod Marsupial, Setonix brachyurus" (1956), pp. 35–36.

[18] P. 39: "The licking response to heat stress is established months before the young leave the pouch. The temperature regulatory capacity develops steadily during their sojourn in the pouch and is essentially at the adult level prior to their first voluntary and temporary departure from the pouch."

different genera," he reports, "may live side by side in the same habitat, but by behavioral thermoregulation maintain significantly different thermal levels in the body.... Behavioral control of body temperature in reptiles implies a rather high degree of sensitivity."[19] He holds, in fact, that endothermy was developed from a particular coincidence and integration of mechanisms which had been separately elaborated for behavioral control of temperature in various reptile species.[20] This hypothesis fits well with the conception of shifts of function through over-elaboration of mechanisms which, becoming somewhat trammeled by their own complexity, allow a different, simpler action to emerge and perform their function on a higher level of organization.[21] But I am inclined to doubt that the basic processes of homoiothermy have been evolved from behavioral thermoregulation. The mechanisms to which functions shift when their old mechanisms become unadaptive are usually far removed from the old. Genes that have long been suppressed can come to expression in effective impulses when more anciently established operations, which have long inhibited them, give way for any reason. Then the repertoire of the stock seems to show new elements, out of which apparently new acts can be formed; but the potentiality may have been there from primitive ages, only held in abeyance by the prior development of competing activities.

The change to endothermy must have begun in a steadily increasing and statistically more evenly distributed rate of energy production, and led to the remarkably constant consumption of the excess energy as body heat. The result is not so much a liberation from behavioral methods of adaptation—for warm-blooded creatures seek comfortable temperatures just as much as cold-blooded ones—as independence of the level of behavior from climatic conditions. A poikilothermic creature slows down in cold surroundings and is activated by increased warmth. A homoiothermic one can hold its rate of activity steady for a long time because its internal organs are kept at an even temperature under widely varying climatic conditions. This steady interior state allows the agent to counteract external heat loss by muscular exercise, so that to

[19] "Thermoregulation in Reptiles, a Factor in Evolution" (1949), p. 209.

[20] P. 206: "Offhand it might appear difficult to account for the acquisition and perfection of the mechanism for internal heating by endothermic vertebrates. Presumably this had its antecedents in their ectothermic reptilian ancestors, and the ability of some existing reptiles to maintain high, relatively constant, body temperatures when active, provides information of value in accounting for the evolution of the separate elements involved in the mechanisms of thermoregulation in birds and mammals."

[21] For a preliminary discussion of this principle see Vol. I, pp. 441 ff.

some extent the influence of ambient temperatures is paradoxical, encouraging active behavior rather than suppressing it. The innovation, though probably very slow, was nevertheless radical, for it affected the very matrix of any stock that attained it, and gave an entirely new freedom to the central nervous system, the basic source of voluntary action, from the autonomic nervous system which had held much closer control over it theretofore. Such a new tendency could arise only with a steady and great elaboration of tissues, creating more interfaces between units of different electric potential and perhaps more complex or more rapid biochemical changes. Its effects might well make some traits of "cold-blooded" animals—for instance, the ability to survive in a comatose state, needing no food and little oxygen and water, through long inclement seasons—obsolete or rare in the higher forms of life.[22] But there is no indication that the new mode of living arose as a higher development of former ways. It is much likelier that an independent physiological advance overtook some reptile species and motivated the entire new complexes of behavior appropriate to avian and mammalian life.

The gradual complication of inner conditions is the phylogenetic process that engenders the hereditary basic behavioral repertoire of each kind of animal. Some repertory elements are common to many taxa, even to several phyla; others are species-specific. In either case they may differ from one individual to another, either as extreme deviations from the norm for the stock, or as a first appearance of a mutation; in the latter instance, of course, the new behavioral competence would not remain individual, unless the hereditary line came to grief forthwith. The neural potentialities of response to changing external conditions seem to develop on the same principles as the neural controls of somatic functions; that is, they develop to varying degrees *in utero*, and sometimes express themselves first in forms which may or may not look like

[22] At least one bird and a fair number of mammals show variable degrees of homoiothermy, the lowest bordering on poikilothermy. The hibernating bird is the poorwill, of which Jean Dorst, in *The Migrations of Birds* (1962), pp. 279–80, says that several birds of this species (*Phalaenoptilus nuttallii*) were found in winter in the Colorado desert in California "huddled in rock crevices, their heads turned towards the wall, . . . in a state of complete lethargy! No breathing or heart beat could be detected, and a bright light focussed on the eye produced no reaction. Furthermore, the rectal temperature was very low, between 64° and 68° F. (the temperature of the air was between 63° and 75° F.), whereas . . . the internal temperature of this bird when it is awake is usually 106° in summer. This poorwill evidently hibernates, just like some mammals, in response to falling temperatures." He remarks subsequently that this is the only bird for which hibernation has been scientifically established.

the behavioral acts into which they are destined to enter postnatally. Not every stereotyped response of extrauterine life necessarily has a recognizable intrauterine precursor; the characteristic pattern may be engendered only in the radical ontogenetic shift of situation at birth (or hatching, metamorphosis, etc.), or in later stages, for in most of the higher animals the process of maturation continues through a period known as "youth."[23] An act may also be so composite that the innate factors are masked by mutual modification, or eclipsed by the much more evident external factors to which they are adapted in practical use. But I think there is convincing evidence to be found—though only on close study and reflection—that all animal behavior below the level of concept formation is instinctive; and the conceptual level is very high on the evolutionary ladder, not far short of human mentation, if short of it at all.[24]

The building up of instinctive behavior from the matrix of trophic and somatic activities is not a simple ascent; behavioral acts may supplement autonomic processes, as the quokka's licking instead of sweating heavily and the poikilotherms' selection of suitably air-conditioned stations; or the advance may proceed on the opposite principle, such troublesome methods being gradually obviated by the development of physiological mechanisms, like internal temperature controls, which automatically and constantly perform the necessary functions. In evolutionary progressions, just as in taxonomic classes, there are no simple patterns and definite constant directions. The course of progress from lower forms of organization to higher ones is zigzag, and, like categorial divisions, is sometimes blurred; there are no sharp lines between organic specialization and competence for behavior, between reflex action and behavioral action, repertoire and instinctive acts. Most biological processes are, in fact, dialectical; that is to say, they go forward as an interplay of opposed but mutually determined phases. The essential forms of vitality repeat themselves on all levels of life, from metab-

---

[23] Nikolaas Tinbergen, in *The Study of Instinct* (1951), p. 143, states that ducklings respond at a very early age to the dummy of a hawk, while goslings respond only to the parents' alarm cry at the sight of the same dummy. In reporting his own experiments, he says: "When, at an age of several weeks, the goslings began to react to the dummies themselves, the natural conclusion would be that they had been conditioned to them. However, rearing the goslings in isolation revealed that the sensitivity to the dummy appeared at the same age; this proved that the sensitivity was innate but that it developed much later than in ducks."

[24] Some psychologists hold that abstract conception and symbolic thinking occur in pigeons, rats, and even bees. Their claims seem to me to rest on anthropomorphic interpretations which are not necessary. But this problem will be met later, in a broader connection.

olism to ratiocination. Sometimes they are most apparent in elementary functions, sometimes in very high, superimposed attainments. The principle of dialectic was originally discovered by Plato as the pattern of philosophical thought. It is also the basic biophysical pattern, the principle of cyclic concatenation of acts, whereby the cadence of each consummated act is the preparatory phase of the repetition of the act. This is the dynamic form known as "rhythm."[25]

Homeostasis, long recognized as the source of "steady states" under conditions of constant biochemical activity, has its analogue on the behavioral level in the interactions of impulses with their coordinated "inhibitors" and "releasers" (inhibitors of the inhibitors). In organic behavior (breathing, peristalsis), inductor and inhibitor substances, which can evoke or block the muscular acts involved in each cycle, are fairly well known, even with respect to their origination in the body. In reflex action, specific stimuli and selectively responsive sensory organs, as well as many of the neural paths and plexūs over which the stimulated impulses are conducted, have been found; and in organisms of relatively simple structure, such as most arthropods, the inhibiting "centers" (e.g., abdominal ganglia) which hold the reflex activities in check can be located by excision experiments which release unlimited mechanical movements.[26]

In higher forms of animal behavior, too, there are stereotypic actions, sometimes of considerable complexity, that show very little variation from one individual to another within a species, but great interspecific differences. They are the actions that are generally referred to as "instincts." Their endogenous nature is evident because the first time an animal attempts them it executes them in typical fashion, just as it carries out its first breath, yawn or whimper without "trial and error." The course of the act, which may be an elaborate series of movements, is prepared by the creature's developing anatomy. The chief difference between the operation of an "instinct" and of organic behavior is that the former is fitted to external conditions and requires extraorganic substrates or means. Its distinction from reflex action is that it is pre-

[25] Cf. Vol. I, Chapter 9 *passim*, esp. pp. 324–27, for the previous discussion of rhythm.

[26] In the mantis, the subesophageal ganglion is—among other things—the organ that holds the "center" for sexual activity, the terminal ganglion of the ventral cord, in check. A fairly full account of mantis mating behavior, in the course of which the head and prothorax of the male are frequently eaten by the female, is given by Kenneth Roeder in *Nerve Cells and Insect Behavior* (1963), pp. 132–41. According to his description, as soon as the controlling ganglion is removed, the remaining body of the male goes into "intense and continuous sexual movements," which go on for hours, and produce a normal spermatophore.

pared by related acts, or "appetitive behavior" which culminates in the consummation of the total act, i.e., in a subact, quite properly called the "consummatory act." As usual, the distinctions between subacts, and even the contours of the total action, are not sharp; many consummatory acts have a reflex character, for instance, the final swallowing that ends every form of eating, or the culmination of the male sexual act, sperm emission. Other reflex elements, too, may be contained in the instinctive performance: erection of the penis is as truly reflexive as emission. Consummatory acts are the most stereotypic movements, but also least peculiar to any taxonomic division below the largest, e.g., class or even phylum. It is mainly "appetitive behavior," and the less noticed cadence which follows consummation, that are species-specific, and provide the defining characteristics of the various "instincts."

The naturalists who call their pursuit "ethology" (a discreet evasion of the fully anthropomorphic term "ethnology" in speaking of animals) have built their new "-ology" on the study of such particulate items of overt animal activity, and have listed a considerable number, though not really an impressive one, by way of empirical data. Konrad Lorenz, who is the inspirer and, with Nikolaas Tinbergen, the leader of the school, has stated the facts on which it is built, saying: "Whitman and Heinroth, independently from each other, ... discovered the fact that behavior patterns could be used as taxonomic characters.... They are predictable, not only for a species, but for a genus, an order, or even a larger taxonomic unit. It is, for instance, predictable with supreme certainty that any new species belonging to the order of Columbidae will drink in the manner just described ['they drink water by sucking it up with a peculiar peristaltic movement'] or that any species of Anatidae will take oil from the oil gland by rubbing its head on it in a rotatory movement."[27]

---

[27] "The Objectivist Theory of Instinct" (1956), p. 52. Later (p. 57), he makes bold to say, "All the Oscines which I know (and also all those which I do not) do this by taking oil from the gland with the tip of their bill." In view of the strange exceptions to characteristic physiological activities found, sometimes, in a single subspecies or race—as, for instance, the excretion of uric acid by Dalmatian dogs, but by no other dogs (see Vol. I, p. 260, n. 6)—a categorical statement about what will be found in new species, or is true of all those species of a genus which one does not know, is a risky extrapolation. Its only justification might be that the behavior pattern is used as a criterion, in which case any species which does not exhibit it is *ipso facto* excluded from the taxonomic unit it characterizes, so the trait, then, will indeed be "predictable with supreme certainty" of any included species.

But Professor Lorenz has gone beyond the facts themselves, and postulated the existence of a special neural "center" for each instinctive action, solely responsible for the performance of that complete action.[28] This made his theory a neurological hypothesis; and since neurologists so far have not reached the point of watching the embryonic formation of nuclei in the brain, his commitment to that hypothesis makes him unwilling—because unable—to think of hereditary behavioral responses as complexes of more elementary impulses arising in the course of fetal and early postnatal development. His position, naturally, brought him into conflict with the embryologically oriented animal psychologists whose watchword is "learning," and whose ambition is to carry their notions of learned behavior back into the ontogeny of instinctual elements. The resulting dispute has wasted much time and energy that should have been spent on research, since bouts of mutual disparagement can neither reveal the presence of mechanisms in the brain nor demonstrate any "trial and error" preceding the performance of species-characteristic acts.

Nikolaas Tinbergen, in his serious but still largely speculative book *The Study of Instinct*, formulated the "ethological" doctrine. Like Lorenz, he accepted as "instinctive" those elementary acts that culminate in a complex but integral movement—pecking, gaping, preening, etc.; and he centered his speculation on the relation between those final, consummatory phases and the freer, adaptive subacts which normally lead up to them. In summary, he conceives the pattern of a total instinctive act to be an inverted hierarchy of movements which descend step by step from the most variable performance, guided by perception, to the most automatic, invariant, final one, the consummation.[29] Corresponding in reciprocal order to the sequence of acts, he postulates a

[28] In "The Comparative Method in Studying Innate Behavior Patterns" (1950), p. 248, he postulated not only act-specific neural structures, but even act-specific kinds of energy. Energy does, of course, appear in different forms, e.g., as light, heat, motive power, but kinetic energy that will drive only one sort of mechanism and no other is unknown to physics. Fortunately this unscientific fancy is not needed in its author's instinct theory.

[29] See p. 107: "It seems ... that the centres of each level of the hierarchical system control a type of appetitive behaviour. This is more generalized in the higher levels and more restricted or more specialized in the lower levels. The transition from higher to lower, more specialized types of appetitive behaviour is brought about by special stimuli which alone are able to direct the impulses to one of the lower centres, or rather to allow them free passage to this lower centre. This stepwise descent of the activation from relatively higher to relatively lower centres eventually results in the stimulation of a centre or a series of centres of the level of the consummatory act, and here the impulse is finally used up."

[19]

chain of "centers" in the brain stem, ranging from the spinal cord through medulla and pons and terminating in the hypothalamus,[30] each center activated by the somewhat less rigid one above it. Finally, he proffers a definition of "instinct" that goes beyond Professor Lorenz's concept of "innate species-specific behavior," and lets the term denote a permanent physical mechanism, a series of "centers" (nuclei?) constantly primed to go into action, but normally prevented from doing so by other neural structures, "inhibitors," which hold the "instincts" in check until an "innate releasing mechanism" ("IRM") inhibits the inhibitors. "I will tentatively define an instinct," he says, "as a hierarchically organized nervous mechanism which is susceptible to certain priming, releasing and directing impulses of internal as well as external origin, and which responds to these impulses by coordinated movements that contribute to the maintenance of the individual and the species."[31]

One embarrassing feature of this instinct theory is that it leaves us at the hypothalamus. If appetitive behavior is guided by perception, why are the activities of the optic thalamus relegated to the vague higher levels of "certain priming, releasing and directing impulses" beyond the instincts? What of the work of the entire neopalium? Where is the line drawn between instinctive and non-instinctive processes, and why just there? Does "external origin" mean "external" to the brain (e.g., arising in peripheral organs) or to the organism? What are non-instinctive impulses "of internal origin"? Responding "by coordinated movements" presumably means "by activating coordinated movements" in motor mechanisms. And so on; the whole neurological picture is highly schematized, simplified, and yet fuzzy.

One should perhaps remember that it was projected when micro-electrode studies had just been begun and Dr. Tinbergen's factual supports were chiefly the experiments of W. R. Hess, and the early ones of E. von Holst. Since then, a great deal of work in this field has been done. That stimulation of various spots in the brain stem, if it is effective at all, usually elicits well-formed behavioral responses is an established fact. But the chains of "centers," each performing a phase of the response and leading to a lower and more rigidly automatic "center," have not been found; not even any areas permanently related to a particular action have been identified. One could easily admit, of course,

[30] P. 109: "While the spinal cord and the medulla seem to control only certain components of the instinctive patterns, the hypothalamus contains the highest centres concerned with instinctive behaviour."
[31] P. 112.

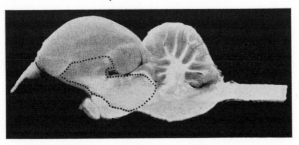

Figure 12–1. Sagittal Section of Chicken Brain (dotted line demarcates diencephalic field tested)

the self-same area would yield (apparently in random succession) now this, now that unit of instinctive behavior

(After Erich von Holst and Ursula St. Paul, "Vom Wirkungsgefüge der Triebe," *Naturwissenschaften*, XVIII [1960].)

without disturbing the basic conception, that a "center" might have some variety of possible responses, according to the strength of the stimulus input; that would accommodate the findings of Hunter and Jasper, which apparently had not come to the author's notice in time to be used by him.[32] But the later work of Von Holst and some of his collaborators calls the theory of instincts as locally fixed organic structures into question much more radically. In experiments he conducted together with Ursula Saint Paul, the investigators found that from the diencephalic field shown in the accompanying figure, "practically all those familiar movements can be elicited which serve orientation and bodily needs, or relate to enemies, rivals, sex partners and offspring;

---

[32] J. Hunter and H. Jasper, in "Reactions of Unanaesthetized Animals to Thalamic Stimulation" (1948), reported experiments with implanted electrodes in the thalamic reticular system, whereby they found that moderate charges of low frequency (6–10/sec.) produced "arrest," either in frozen pose, or lying down as if to sleep. Increased intensity at the same frequency caused twitching of the face or body jerks. "With a slightly higher frequency (20 or 30 per second) running, search and climbing responses were produced. In some animals (cats) a fixed posturing of a constant pattern was produced, sometimes associated with turning and coordinate movements of the forelegs, similar to hemiballismus." Higher frequencies (50–200) produced "sham rage"; the current may have reached subthalamic structures. They conclude: "It appears that local stimulation of the thalamus in the region of the massa intermedia may produce either general inhibitory or excitatory effects, depending upon the frequency of the stimulating current" (pp. 171–72).

Cf. R. G. Heath, "Motor Activity and Inhibition from Identical Subcortical and Cortical Points" (1952).

also the vocalizations which are proper to them."[33] But often the locus of an electrode which had yielded one stereotypic act in response to a first stimulation produced a different one upon a later stimulation of exactly the same frequency and intensity; and, still more disconcertingly, if electrodes were left in place in a chicken's brain stem and the experiment extended for several hours, the selfsame area would yield (apparently in random succession) now this, now that unit of instinctive behavior—preening, cackling, fleeing or what not—with occasional intervals of no overt response.[34]

Such experimental results do not lend much support to a theory of act-specific centers as the mechanisms of instincts; rather, they point to a variable use of most, if not all, stations in the brain, a great versatility of its nuclei, as though they were junctures in circuits rather than fixed organs with specialized functions. The nearest to a fixed neural mechanism in control of overt acts is the spinal reflex arc, which, however, appears on close examination to be much less simple, far more involved with the brain, than its early investigators ever suspected.[35] The long and short of it is that we have as yet no physiological knowledge of the brain adequate to explain the phenomena of animal (let alone human) behavior.

The chief reason why the study of instinct has made so little headway, despite the wealth of empirical data which we owe largely to the patient field work of the ethologists, is its lack of usable basic concepts in terms of which problems could be framed and hypotheses mooted. Its weakness is philosophical; that is why research in its domain falls apart into antagonistic schools. A. N. Whitehead once remarked that the only ideas opposed schools of thought have in common are their tacitly accepted presuppositions, which are fallacious. Something like that holds for the instinct theorists and the learning theorists: what they hold in common is the concept of "behavior" as a reaction of a fixed mechanism, which may be a whole animal or a

[33] E. von Holst and Ursula Saint Paul, "Vom Wirkungsgefüge der Triebe" (1960), p. 410.

[34] P. 411: "Völlig ein Rätsel für den Histologen ist schliesslich das häufige Phänomen, dass der gleiche Weg der Elektrode, ein zweites Mal durchschritten, oft selbst bei gleichen Reizgrössen anderes Verhalten aktiviert.... Lässt man die Elektroden fest an ihrem Ort und dehnt den Versuch über viele Stunden aus, so kommt es nicht selten vor, dass zeitweise nichts, dann ein paar Mal etwas Davonlaufen, später Gackern, danach Gefiedersträuben, schliesslich vielleicht Sich-Putzen ausgelöst wird; alles vom gleichen Feld bei gleicher Reizspannung."

[35] See E. Eldred, R. Granit and P. A. Merton, "Supraspinal Control of the Muscle Spindles and Its Significance" (1953), passim.

special part within the animal, to a distinct stimulus or series of stimuli originating in the environment. As a phenomenon, this is what we find. But what one finds as an objective datum depends on one's units of thought; and units of thought have historical origins, but only pragmatic credentials. The main shortcoming of the stimulus-response unit is that it builds no large frame of biological thinking in which organism and organs, vegetative functions and strictly animalian functions, special mechanisms, reflexes, "conditioned" responses (which may be reflexes or not), sense impressions and guidance of behavior, instinct, adaptation, options, voluntary movement and learning all have some common denominator. The lack of such a common denominator, or basic conceptual unit, has made it seem necessary to study some major psychological phenomenon by a special approach, in its own special terms, and to treat all the rest of psychology as an extension and generalization of the concepts and principles used in that particular study. So we have "motivation theory," where "motivation" is by stimuli which activate "drives" and the animal's behavior is a process of "drive reduction"; but "motivation" in such a context is restricted to behavioral acts, so the study of psychology begins on the behavioral level. The "drives" might be regarded as impulses, except that they are to be allayed, removed, rather than realized or expressed.[36] This is an interesting conception; the phenomena to which it applies are voluntary acts, but by describing them in terms of drives which the animal obeys, the theorist creates a much simpler pattern of cause and effect than the indirect causal structure exhibited in the constant emergence of acts from the organism, motivated by its situation from moment to moment, and consummated in behavioral or in vital or covert mental acts. Impulse reduction could hardly figure as a goal of rhythmic internal activities; behavior, therefore, does not appear as a continuance in form as well as in power of vital processes (this, by the way, does not mean that reduction of excessive impulsion, i.e., of felt "drives" in a perfectly empirical, concrete sense, can never be the aim of voluntary acts, but only that such would be a special, not general, condition.)

Then, too, we have "instinct theory," another and not dissimilar sim-

[36] The crucial distinction is also implied in the proposition that some acts may not require any "drive." Thus A. J. Watson says, in "The Place of Reinforcement in Behaviour" (1961), p. 301 (the end of his article): "There remains the problem of the explanation of exploratory behaviour. It . . . seems unlikely that this type of behaviour is dependent on the operation of drives, and upon the reduction of these in a manner analogous to that in which, for instance, food-seeking behaviour has been held to be so dependent." The notion of an act not requiring any impulse for its origination would be hard to accept.

plification of cause-and-effect relations, assuming neural "centers" rather than a whole body of developing, mutually constraining action potentials as the sources of complicated, often species-specific behavior; and pitted most intently against that doctrine, we have "learning theory"— where "learned" may mean "conditioned," in the classical (Pavlovian) sense, or "established by trial and error," or "facilitated by repetition" (sometimes applied even to inanimate mechanisms with hysteretic properties[37]), or "suggested by observation" (i.e., imitated), or "discovered by new insight" (perception of a new gestalt), or even simply systematically changed due to development.[38] When D. O. Hebb claims that the synchronous firing of neurons to produce the large brain waves of infant sleep is "learned," being "established *in utero* as a result of the neural activity itself,"[39] it is hard to imagine what he would accept as a criterion of "unlearned." The precarious concept of instinct, therefore, is rendered doubly vague and ambiguous by the vagueness and ambiguity of its alleged negative, as a minted image would be by fuzziness and confusion in the die, the intaglio, that is its negative.

The basic failing of psychological theories, the fallacious assumption they all share in some measure, is that they must be based on some simple dyadic relation of cause and effect, in terms of which all psy-

---

[37] See, for example, Nicolas Rashevsky, "Learning as a Property of Physical Systems" (1931). All cyberneticists talk about "instructing" their machines rather than setting them; by implication, the computers must be able to learn.

A distinction between the hysteresis of machines and the betterment of human or animal skills by practice is insisted upon by Arthur Russell Moore, in *The Individual in Simpler Forms* (1945), where he says: "Reactivity of itself may introduce physiochemical changes in the central nervous system sufficient to modify subsequent reactions. For the individual, the most significant of these chemical changes is the formation of memory traces in the brain....

"As a term for this faculty of remembering J. Loeb has proposed 'associative hysteresis' which avoids personal and poetic connotations. 'Hysteresis,' as used in physical science, denotes an 'after effect' in substances such as glass, iron, colloids.... a new machine is bettered in its performance by use. Is this 'learning' in the sense that men and higher animals learn? Or is it not rather simple hysteresis in the physical sense? It is of course the latter, and we go further and discover similar effects in living systems." The fact that physical hysteresis occurs in organisms which also develop "associative hysteresis" shows the danger of using words metaphorically in new sciences.

[38] Thus an ecologist, M. J. Dunbar, asserts: "Ecosystems can compete, and evolution of the stable ecosystem can be looked upon as a process of learning, analogous to the learning of regulated behavior in the nervous systems of animals" ("The Evolution of Stability in Marine Environments. Natural Selection at the Level of the Ecosystem" [1960]).

[39] *The Organization of Behavior* (1949), p. 121n.

chological phenomena can be described. The first really automatic-looking and isolable item of behavior found somewhere in every sort of animal, including man, was the reflex. The concept of direct reflex movement is old; according to J. F. Fulton, the first experiment based on that concept was made in 1730, the terms "stimulus" and "response" were introduced soon afterwards, and the type of movement, effected by a sensorimotor arc without volition, was called a "reflex" by J. A. Unzer in 1771.[40] The term was soon extended to all acute critical events touching off very distinct, brief responses. The discovery of "conditioned" reflexes, and subsequently of much wider shifts from one item in a motivating situation to another, eliciting similar behavioral acts even of a non-reflex sort but classed as "conditioned reflexes," led to the sanguine hope of building up all psychology—animal and human—on the Pavlovian principles of stimulus and reflex, "conditioned" reflex, and compounding of stimulus-and-reflex patterns. This project soon proved to be all too simple; most psychologists, with exception of the official Russian school, have abandoned or radically modified it. But the stimulus-response concept has become so deeply ingrained in our thinking that it is the only pattern we look for in any situation or use in setting up psychological experiments. Consequently much of the old reflex concept is still incorporated in that of behavioral responses, although in the higher vertebrates—birds and mammals—the chief elements of behavior seem to arise from other than reflex movements. They arise from what Victor Hamburger has called "the motor action system," a system of autogenic activities which are not specific, precisely predictable reactions to equally specific stimuli, as reflexes are, but which derive from the growing musculature and its gradual innervation, under the constantly changing stimulation of metabolic and hormonal developments.

Dr. Hamburger has given particular attention to the differences in the developmental patterns of amphibians, fish, birds and mammals, respectively. In salamanders he found the growth of acts to be essentially a progressive development of reflexes; in the chick embryo, by contrast, before any reflexes appear, autonomous activity occurs in many muscles. "Observations and experiments on the chick embryo," he says, "demonstrate the existence of two behavior components that can be dissociated from each other on the basis of behavior characteristics. Beginning with the stage at which the first neuromuscular connections are established and continuing through the greater part of the incubation period, there

[40] *Physiology of the Nervous System* (2d ed., 1943), p. 51.

exists a *motor action system* with the following characteristics: (1) it is overt and spontaneous—that is, it discharges independently of reflexogenous stimulation; (2) it performs in motility cycles of regular periodicity, up to 13 days, and from then on almost continuously; and (3) it involves generalized motility of many or all parts that are capable of motility at a given stage. Independently of this system there develops the *reflex apparatus* which begins to attain functional maturity 3 or 4 days after the onset of spontaneous motility. . . .

". . . when the reflex system is structurally completed, it does not 'take over' or 'incorporate' the motor action system in the sense that the latter loses its identity as an operational unit. The motor action system has its own progressive differentiation and probably persists throughout life, as suggested by Coghill, Tracy, and others."[41]

J. D. Ebert writes in a very similar vein (referring to "vertebrates," in his context probably mammals, but possibly also chicks): "As soon as the first neuromuscular connections are established *an autonomous motor action system* begins to function. . . . In contrast to the heart, in which the early pulsations are *myogenic*, the spontaneous motility of the muscles we are discussing appears to be *neurogenic*.

"The *reflex apparatus* appears to develop independently, attaining functional maturity 3 or 4 days *after* the onset of spontaneous motility. . . .

". . . there is sufficient evidence to warrant the working hypothesis that autonomous motility is the foundation on which integrated behavior patterns are built."[42]

In insects, the development of behavior is quite different again. I think it may be doubted that there is anything comparable to the "motor action system" at all; but if there is not, then insect behavior is a wonderfully high systematic development of reflex activity, far beyond the highest that is found in any other phylum. Some insect actions look very much like instinctive ones of the supposedly "lowest" type, extremely rigid and senseless, yet adapted to circumambient conditions in a way simple reflexes are not;[43] taxes and tropisms may be con-

---

[41] "Some Aspects of the Embryology of Behavior" (1963), pp. 351–52.

[42] *Interacting Systems in Development* (1965), p. 203.

[43] I have watched worker ants in a jar containing a little food and a few grains— less than a dozen—of coarse sand. The ants picked up the tiny stones, carried them about, laid them down for other ants to pick up, and so forth. Despite adequate food and air, all the ants died within two hours. I do not know whether "joblessness" was the cause, but the frustration of their normal activities seemed to be the only stress they suffered. They had lived in a colony in captivity for three weeks.

sidered an intervening pattern of responses,[44] bringing the animal into situations where its reflex actions normally can negotiate the successive phases of its life cycle. The control of those actions seems to rest chiefly in a correlative system of "inhibitors," i.e., of active organs working against the reflexive responses unless particular, very powerful impulses overcome their inhibitive influence or something holds them in abeyance.[45] In any event, the instinctive acts of insects, if "instinctive" they are, have a different functional pattern from those of vertebrates, but it is a pattern capable of high development in its own direction apart from other evolutionary trends.

To find divergent lines of evolution springing from different anatomical possibilities, with consequently different principles of action, is disconcerting; none of the hypothetical cause-and-effect patterns can be expected to serve as a modulus in the systematic study of all forms of life. Certainly learning theory does not make a good approach to insect behavior; Tinbergen, in his thoughtful fifth chapter, "An Attempt at a Synthesis," concludes that the hierarchical organization of "centers" has been found in insects as well as in fish, birds and mammals;[46] but

[44] G. Viaud, in "Taxies et tropismes dans le comportement instinctif" (1956), p. 5, says: "Les *réflexes* ne sont pas, à proprement parler, des comportements. Sous leur forme la plus simple, ils sont des réponses partielles, segmentaires ou glandulaires, d'un organisme à une stimulation locale appropriée. . . . Mais ils entrent comme éléments dans des comportements complexes, tropismes et instincts.

". . . Les *tropismes* ou *taxies* sont, au contraire des réflexes, des reponses d'organismes entiers, des véritables comportements, faits de mouvements d'orientation, souvent aussi de locomotion, déclenchés et entretenus par des agents physiques ou chimiques externes" (He attributes this definition of "tropism" to Jacques Loeb.)

[45] See, for instance, the report of A. D. Blest on some behavioral developments in a large family of moths: "Work on a variety of insects (mantids, crickets, cockroaches and ants) has shown that while the excitation and maintenance of the reflex patterns of locomotion is mediated by the suboesophageal ganglion, the selection of activities is achieved by the pressure of patterned inhibition which the corpora pedunculata of the supraoesophageal ganglion exert upon it; it is the modulation of this inhibitory potential by incoming stimuli which is believed to be in part responsible for the selective release of items of overt behavior, the reflex units of which are mediated in the first place by the thoracic and abdominal ganglia" ("The Evolution, Ontogeny and Quantitative Control of the Settling Movements of Some New World Saturniid Moths, with Some Comments on Distance Communication in Honey-Bees" [1960], pp. 234–35). Cf. also the reference to mantis behavior above, p. 17, n. 26.

[46] *The Study of Instinct*, p. 110: "It is especially interesting that the hierarchical organization has not only been found in vertebrates but in insects as well. According to Baerends's results [referred to on p. 9 of his study] a wasp with a decentralized system of ventral ganglia and its relatively small 'brain' presents essentially the same picture as vertebrates."

Kenneth Roeder, who has given close study to the neurological structures in these different phyla, warns explicitly against such analogies, because the apparatuses are so different that convergence of their effects is more probable than parallel processes.

"When a full-fledged microelectrode study of an insect ganglion is eventually undertaken," he says, "it must not be based on the assumption that the situation will be similar to that in the mammalian spinal cord. To begin with, the anatomic relations of neurons in invertebrate ganglia are very different. Insect motor and internuncial neurons are monopolar, the cell bodies being on a side branch from the receiving and conducting parts. The cell body does not appear to be a site for the synaptic knobs and thus concerned directly in the integrating mechanism, but instead it lies together with others in the external layer or cortex of the ganglion.[47] Indeed, the whole insect nervous system is, even grossly, visibly different from the vertebrate (Fig. 12–2).

In exploring the several fields of animal life, especially for their men-

---

[47] Nerve Cells and Insect Behavior, p. 114. A very similar description is given by D. M. Vowles in "Neural Mechanisms in Insect Behaviour" (1961). Vowles says, at the outset: "The insect nervous system differs from the vertebrate at all functional levels, not least in the structure of its individual cells." He goes on, furthermore, to discuss the potentialities of the sense organs and the mode of innervation of the muscles which perform complex acts, all of which present a pattern altogether different from the vertebrate or even cephalopod or any other than the insect pattern. After describing the stringent limitations of the insect nervous system, he writes: "If the neurons of the insect C.N.S. are unable to deal adequately with numerous inputs, this ought to be correlated with the evolution of simple sense organs.... When one considers the size and complexity of insect sense organs, however, they seem to deride this expectation. The compound eyes are enormous, the antennae are covered with a thick felt of sensory hairs, as are the mouth parts and tarsi, the exoskeleton and its joints are well supplied with proprioceptors, and there are complex auditory organs in the legs, thorax and antennae. It is, however, important not to confuse physical elaboration with neural complexity, for the two may not occur together—indeed, in the human eye, where an optically poor image is moving continuously over the retina the nervous system compensates for the optical defects, suggesting that physical and neural factors involved in sense organs may be inversely related" (pp. 9–10). As for the effectors, "In insects ... the number of motor neurons controlling a single muscle is very small indeed, and may be as few as four or two.... every muscle fibre is innervated by most of the motor neurons, and most of the motor neurons innervate every fibre. Each neuron has several endings in each muscle fibre and the muscle, which has no effective action potential, contracts only around the regions of the active endings.... Inhibitory fibres have also been described.... It is clear, therefore, that the integration of excitatory and inhibitory processes is decentralized on to the muscle itself, and this could be taken to support the idea that the neurons themselves are incapable of sufficiently adequate integrations. It seems probable that the primitive type of control may be peripheral, and that insects have refined this to an extremely efficient system" (p. 15).

Figure 12–2. (*Left*) Bipolar Neuron of Vertebrate Central Nervous
System; (*Right*) Unipolar Neuron of Arthropod
Central Nervous System

*the anatomic relations of neurons in invertebrate ganglia
are very different*

(Kenneth D. Roeder, *Nerve Cells and Insect Behavior*
[Cambridge, Mass.: Harvard University Press, 1963].)

tal phenomena, any primary working concepts are acceptable as long
as they make research possible and fruitful. But to understand the evolution of instinctive acts from early forms to the amazing complexities
presented by advanced nesting and food-getting acts, one has to have
a more abstract and more inclusive conceptual scaffold. The conception
of animal life as an advancing stream of activity instead of a pattern
of overt acts induced by external stimuli or a fixed number of internal
"drives" suggests such a versatile treatment of instinctive behavior. It
does not contradict most of the generalizations which have been made,
often with great logical circumspection, from experimental findings
recorded in the traditional terms; rather, it tends to show their full
implications by shifting the emphasis to different aspects of the established facts. In such a conceptual framework the notion of a stimulus,
for instance, as a "trigger" needed to release a pre-set physiological

[29]

mechanism appears as a highly simplified mechanical model; for an actual "stimulus" is a crucial item that completes a situation which motivates the responsive act. The concept of physiological "triggers" or "releasers" is a valuable one in neurology, where its use is naturally limited to the study of particular nuclei and circuits, and in exactly such contexts it is legitimate and useful in psychology, too;[48] but it harbors a danger for the unwary imagination, namely, the suggestion of the mousetrap ready to close, but doing absolutely nothing until the trigger is released. No living mechanism is ever doing absolutely nothing. If its normal and special action is inhibited, something is covertly going on, there are changes with the maturing, proliferating or perhaps aging processes of the surrounding tissues; the inhibited complex is waiting, and waiting is a physiological activity.[49]

There are, in fact, several kinds of species-specific (which means, of course, hereditary) acts: (1) pure reflexes, elicited by particular acute stimuli, and requiring no conscious intent; (2) autogenous acts moti-

[48] Its great heuristic value may be seen in the serious works in which it has been freely employed, such as the articles collected by T. H. Bullock in *Physiological Triggers and Discontinuous Rate Processes* (1956). Even here, however, a tendency to extend the word to all inductive processes, whether they be quick and acute or more gradual completions of motivating situations, is already apparent; as, for instance, in H. A. Schneiderman's contribution, "Onset and Termination of Insect Diapause," where we are told that "in insects with facultative diapause, inactivation of the brain may be triggered by temperature, absolute or changing photoperiod, humidity, nutrition, etc.," and that "in most insects the triggering stimulus acts at an early stage in the life cycle while diapause is not manifest until much later" (p. 47). Here the metaphor of the "trigger" threatens to lose its value and leave only a vague image of some simple automatism, which does not suit living matter in any way.

[49] An excellent example of the inward aspect of an act which outwardly looks like a response directly induced by a stimulus is given by Sir Joseph Barcroft in his *Researches on Prenatal Life* (1946), Vol. I, pp. 130–31. Speaking of the reflexes which, on particular days in the course of gestation and early life, come to control the rabbit's heart, he says: "It might be supposed that the 32nd day for the repressor reflex and the 60th day for the carotid sinus reflex were the days on which the machinery finally reached that stage of development and assembly before which it could not be used. The facts are far otherwise, the development and assembly took place at a much earlier stage in both cases and the reflex machinery has been waiting there ready for the day to come when the body should make use of it." What is not complete in either case is the internal situation for the reflex act. An essential part of that situation is the arterial blood pressure; "the critical pressure for the depressor reflex at this age is 65 mm. and for the carotid sinus 80 mm. Hg.... Now, the rabbit is born with a much lower blood pressure—about 30 mm. As the days pass the arterial pressure rises and it is not until it has risen to the values of 65 and 80 mm. respectively that the reflexes appear."

vated by changes of internal situation, prenatal or postnatal; (3) direct responses to opportunities for action offered by the ambient, which are made in characteristic ways by different species—the typical movements generally recognized as examples of instinct; (4) special proclivities, such as the raccoon's to dip its food into water, the cat's to bury its feces; and (5) apparently purposeful, elaborate acts, like the sunfish's fanning his brood, the nesting and feeding habits of many birds, the astounding performances of sea otters, dolphins and apes.

These acts are all instinctive in animals. That does not mean that they are never done intelligently, nor that their performance is "unconscious" in the sense of being unfelt by the agent. Animal intelligence is the perception of opportunities to perform instinctive acts without suffering any harm—that is, with a weather eye for dangers; and animals differ widely in intelligence. But that subject belongs to the next chapter. Our present concern is with the organic substructure of behavior, which is the native repertoire developed by every individual according to its kind, not necessarily in very early youth, but by the gradual articulation of its organs, sufficient accumulation of their products, and perfection of muscular and other bodily mechanisms by growth and use before another instinctual element can come into play. Instinctive acts have their proper time of life, though some of their subacts may occur before or after that time, in other behavioral patterns or alone. Even in maturity, an animal may perform a new act in typical form at the first attempt, without guidance or example; sexual and parental behavior occur when the organism is ready, and are perfected by repetition, but are not changed to different ways.

No matter how cleverly the environment may be exploited to implement the actualization of animals' impulses, I submit that their acts are all made out of elements in the agent's native repertoire and steered by the current advance of the motivating situation, organic and ambient, from move to move. The sort of behavior classed above under the headings (4) and (5) can be traced to the native talents listed as (1), (2) and (3). (There may, of course, be other and better classifications; such schemes should never be taken too seriously.) The natural forces which cause the evolution of behavior are the same ones that cause the evolution of organs and their interacting functions, and spring from the formal structure of acts, which determines the peculiar organization of causal relationships here called "motivation." The same principles operate from the beginnings of life, at the borderline between chemical interactions and primitive organic activities, to its highest forms. The basic processes that build up elaborate behavior patterns have physiological versions in the activities of the simplest animals and of the organs of higher ones. For instance, the tendency of acts to perseverate unless repressed or disrupted by dominant acts appears in the continuous action of the frog's olfactory bulb and also pieces of the brain, even *in vitro*.[50] Even trophic processes—which are all composed of genuine acts and proto-acts—have the repetitious character which is behaviorally known as perseveration; its material record is the replication of structures.[51] The occasional supplementation or even replacement of organic processes by behavioral ones, discussed above (see pp. 12–13), shows one form of transition from somatic to voluntary action, and even closer relations may obtain between the ambient-sensitive autonomic system and the volitional, perceptive and conative acts of higher animals through the participation of that system in the balancing and grading of the energies spent in behavior.[52] The push

[50] J. Z. Young, in "The Evolution of the Nervous System and of the Relationship of Organism and Environment" (1938), p. 194, states that the olfactory bulbs of a frog continue to record waves of activity even when they are removed from the head; in his monograph, *Patterns of Substance and Activity in the Nervous System* (1946), p. 11, this same author writes that "rhythmical activity in the forebrain of the frog continues even in a piece of brain removed from the body altogether."

The perseveration of a nervous activity, once started, long after cessation of the stimulus was observed *in vivo* by G. H. Parker, who severed the autonomic (parasympathetic) nerves controlling the changeable color bands in the tails of killifish; Parker remarks, in conclusion, that "probably many nerves, medullated as well as non-medullated, may remain more or less continuously active for long periods, days in fact, after their severance from their centers" ("The Prolonged Activity of Momentarily Stimulated Nerves" [1934], p. 310).

[51] Cf. Brian C. Goodwin, "A Statistical Mechanics of Temporal Organization in Cells" (1964), p. 322: "Periodicities in time can generate periodicities in space by leaving a trace, as it were, of the rhythmic activity. In connective tissue there occurs a rather remarkable orthogonal layering of collagen fibres, one layer of fibres lying at 90° to the next. It is very difficult to imagine how this could occur during embryonic development if there is a continuous, steady release of collagen from chondrocytes. However, if collagen is released from these cells periodically with a well-defined rhythm, then one has a new variable with which to explain the physical periodicity.... Gross ... suggests that oscillatory behavior in embryonic cells may frequently underlie spatial periodicities in the morphology of the adult. The possibility of using time structure to generate space structure gives the developing organism a further dimension for morphogenesis."

[52] J. I. Lacey and B. C. Lacey, in their report, "The Relationship of Resting Autonomic Activity to Motor Impulsivity," propose that "autonomic discharges may have energizing, adaptive functions which adjust receptivity and reactivity to the needs of the moment, and, as well, free the organism from immediate and total dependence on environmental stimulation." Their final conclusion is that "the importance of autonomic nervous system phenomena does not lie solely or even mainly in the areas of emotion and stress. Autonomic measurements are not simply metered

to action comes from central sources, from the matrix, the organism as a whole, which is always doing all it can as energy is brought in or drawn in, bound in constantly self-restoring protoplasmic structures if its immediate expenditure is prevented (which is largely, and constantly, by action of the parasympathetic system), and meted out again in thousands of enacted impulses, whenever and wherever the ways are clear.

The complexity of animal life, certainly at the vertebrate level and perhaps in the highest invertebrate forms, is such that every behavioral act arises from a texture of activity which is full of gradients, summations, urgencies, inadequacies and abnormal substitutions. The intra-organic situation motivating an act is only statistically estimable, and our experimental control of it correspondingly crude.[53] The environment is more readily controlled; it is there that we establish thresholds of stimulus intensity and vary the "input" to elicit quantitative and qualitative variations of an animal's "output." Sometimes we change the internal situation in gross and abnormal fashion by injecting chemicals or excising parts of the organism, and by such methods a great deal has been learned; the extent to which mutilated animals can reorganize their functions, the participation of many mechanisms—including dispensable ones—in most facultative acts, the balanced round of hormone actions, the chemical unity and individuality of higher animals and relative divisibility and tolerance of lower ones and, indeed, nearly all the general physiological facts that serve to explain animal behavior have been established by cumulative series of experiments and the statistical tabulations of their various results. But the necessity of watching one controlled factor at a time, or at most two or three in

---

indications of affect; they reveal the operation of an activating or 'energy mobilizing' ... system. As such, they play a role in all behavior from sleep to the most intense and excited activity" (p. 202).

[53] Animal psychologists are generally aware of this difficulty inherent in their research material. R. A. Suthers, for instance, testing the visual perception of motion by bats, remarked it, saying: "Successful elicitation of optomotor responses depended upon the bat being in a proper psychophysiological state. It was therefore necessary to distinguish between absence of response because of lack of optical stimulation and absence because of a low degree of interest on the part of the animal.... The data presented ... are for the individual bat of each species that yielded the most consistent data. In some cases optomotor responses could be elicited from only one of the few individuals tested. A number of species ... gave no optomotor responses" ("Optomotor Responses by Echolocating Bats" [1966], p. 1103). Compare the similar finding, with respect to a much lower phylum, by C. F. A. Pantin, discussed in Vol. I, p. 269, n. 28.

conjunction, tends to obscure the fact that what is a factor in the scientist's picture is an element in the activity of his animal preparation. The superimposed records, especially when smoothed to a general curve, yield what looks like a direct causal correlation of "input" and "output," and for the purpose in hand that may be desirable. It must be remembered, however, that for the larger purpose of understanding animal life, the deviations from the norm, which the statistician properly ignores, are significant; for, while in an inanimate mechanism they would be trivial, caused by jarring or by uncontrolled changes of light or temperature which could be eliminated if greater accuracy were demanded, in an animate system they signify the underlying and largely inscrutable processes which motivate overt action or progressive changes in metabolic and organic activities such as hypertrophy or degeneration of tissues. The facilitation or inhibition of microscopic acts which summate or culminate in behavior is always a variable element in any individual preparation, affecting its every reaction; so the spectrum of deviations which are smoothed out of the statistical curve representing an experimental sequence is an index to the relative depth and complexity of the matrix on which the stimuli impinge.

There are gradations of intensity in acts as well as in the stimuli (bodily contacts, temperatures, lights, etc.) in a creature's ambient. The lowest level of activity is that of obscure impulses summating into a dense and constant potentiality but not coming to expression; this massive background of impulses is the field of options in which every consummated act—microscopic or macroscopic, overt or covert—determines by its own realization the abrogation of countless other incipient acts. It is lower in activity than the fabric of minute but realized somatic acts which constitute the tonus of a living body; even beneath the muscle tone and the metabolism that upholds it there is the continuous possibility of activation, whether for growth, internal change, cyclic functions or behavior. But that deepest stratum, the vitality that exists in dormant eggs, seeds and suspended lives generally, goes almost entirely unrecognized.

It is from this depth of potentiality that the history of an act should ideally be traced. But in seeking to construe and understand the data we actually have on any particular instinctive act form, such as a spider's web-spinning or a goose's way of retrieving a displaced egg, we have little hope of carrying back our study of its evolution to the earliest motivating conditions, and demonstrating step by step what elements have entered into its formation, so that now the behavioral pattern in question characterizes the stock which shares in that long life history. We have to begin with some hypothetical "primitive" stage of the stock, at an evolutionary level where it is recognizable as a probable forerunner of the animal in question. Surely some ancestors of a graylag goose looked more like lizards than like geese, and others even like modern tunicates, and still earlier ones like nothing that lives on earth now; but we cannot trace anserine history back to the origins of genes and physiological competence, we have to begin with geese and the ostensive present competence of the goose embryo. Yet it makes a great difference in the relative powers of psychological theories whether they are couched in terms that suggest and invite a biographical view of the structure as well as the action of living bodies, so the image of physiological mechanisms appears as a detailed picture in the context of a huge relevant whole, any part of which could be drawn in and handled in the same terms, or whether the terms suggest unphysiological mechanisms, such as industrial and communication machines, built out of independent parts and operated by a devised system of signals, triggers, couplings and prearranged emergency switches, while nothing in natural history corresponds to the designing, manufacture and setting up of the machines.

The best starting point in the study of instinctive behavior is probably *in medias res*: that is to say, with the organism's postnatal repertoire of acts which show some degree of stereotypic form the first time they occur. Such relatively simple, brief acts—pecking, sucking or gaping to receive food, and later preening or grooming, characteristic ways of drinking, sleeping, wriggling, etc.—are the hereditary behavioral traits which Professor Lorenz adduces as examples of instinct. They have species-specific form and generally predictable times of appearance in the course of the individual's life, without being preceded by any attempt to perform them in some different way. It is with their histories that instinct theory is directly concerned. Some of these activities are ready to function at birth or very shortly thereafter, so their whole preparation is prenatal, and they present as fully formed acts in the neonate's ambient. Human beings are born in a very helpless state, really still a fetal condition, yet H. F. R. Prechtl, who has made systematic studies of the earliest human actions, mentions the following abilities: "A newborn has a repertoire of specific motor patterns, such as sucking, head turning, crying, crawling,[54] eye movement, and athenoid movements of the fingers. If a baby lies on his back in the waking state, he alternately flexes and extends his limbs rapidly and turns his

[54] I do not know what this word is intended to denote; certainly not "creeping."

head more or less irregularly."[55] All these overt acts consist of many subacts which in themselves would hardly be appreciated as units, though they are recognizable in several different complexes, as distinct patterns of breathing may be seen in crying and in sleeping; and they in turn subsume overt and covert acts, some completely integrated in the larger whole, others partially entrained, borrowed elements of concomitant processes, down to organic acts like breathing, which in most animals is an autonomic activity rather than an instinctive performance.[56] Spinal reflexes, sometimes modified by intrauterine conditions,[57] provide ready-made movements to be incorporated in more precisely adaptable responses.

Every instinctive act is motivated by a situation that is deeply prepared in the organism, by gene-controlled stages, to produce massive impulses to muscular action, intrinsically patterned in hereditary forms. Those dynamic forms are products of evolution just as certainly as the taxonomic forms that characterize the agent, which means that they have a phylogenetic past and an ontogenetic course of individual progress, just like bodily structures. As long as vital acts are entirely internal, like heartbeat and peristalsis, involving mainly or wholly involuntary muscles and autonomic nerves, their status as evolutionary products is rarely questioned. But when they are directed outward, something

[55] "Problems of Behavioral Studies in the Newborn Infant" (1965), p. 86. Swallowing and defecating are really specific motor patterns too, more ostensibly so than the mere relaxation of the sphincter that permits urine to pass at intervals. The inventory could undoubtedly be further extended.

[56] A possible exception is the bottlenose dolphin, *Tursiops truncatus*, whose breathing seems to require voluntary control, so it ceases if the animal is anesthetized. W. N. Kellogg, in *Porpoises and Sonar* (1961), p. 82, ventures the opinion "that the centers controlling respiration probably lie in the cerebral cortex rather than in the brain stem, as is the case with man and other mammals.... If this is true, it follows that respiration in the bottlenose dolphin is a conscious or voluntary activity."

[57] See, e.g., Prechtl, "Problems of Behavorial Studies in the Newborn Infant," p. 85: "In infants born with breech presentations, we observed a direct correlation between the position of the legs during the last weeks before delivery, and the posture of the legs as well as the patterns of the flexion (withdrawal) and extension (magnet) reflex after birth.... Breech babies with extended legs ... not only keep the legs in extension spontaneously, but also extend the lower limbs after stimulation of the sole of the foot instead of flexing them.... The reverse is seen in babies after breech presentation with flexed legs. Here the withdrawal reflex is exaggerated and the magnet reflex ... is absent.... However, in cases diagnosed as breech presentation ... [and] turned successfully during the last 4–6 weeks before delivery, and then born with a vertex presentation, we observed normal leg postures, motility, and reflex patterns of the lower extremities."

more than self-perpetuating organic rhythms may enter in to determine their courses, namely, substrates to act upon and sometimes means to find or reach such implementing conditions. If the necessary environmental complement is directly given, the organic pattern of a hereditary act is scarcely modified; sucking, for instance, seems to be a complicated movement which occurs even without implementation; but restless head motions, generally called "search behavior," accompany or alternate with vacuous sucking, until the young one's mouth comes in contact with a milk-yielding teat and the purely organic sucking action becomes an instinctive "response" to the continuing lactation of the mother (or mother-surrogate). Swallowing, too, has been observed in several animal species well before birth.[58]

But not all neonate activities are so preformed that they need only to be spontaneously exercised to have a favorable effect on the agent's situation. The thrashing, kicking and other typical movements of newborn babies, though they may have physiological value in building muscle or aiding circulation, make no practical changes in the infant's surroundings. Yet it is interesting that from the start these muscular expressions are total acts; the avenues of impulsive discharge have been prepared *in utero*.

Such short, unadapted, but fairly well defined and repeatable motions are not strictly speaking instinctive acts, since they do not in themselves serve to negotiate the agent's life in his ambient, but they are the instinctual elements out of which true instinctive acts are made by gradual integration, maturation and the molding forces of pressions from within and without. Instinctual elements, rather than a collection of "instincts," compose a creature's basic behavioral repertoire.

To trace the highest developments of animal behavior back to their instinctual sources one has to abandon the common-sense standpoint from which they appear to have arisen in response to special needs, and ask from what beginnings such elaborate actions could have grown to their present complexity. Here we have, on the level of instinctive behavior, a problem already met on the lower level of metabolic action —how a sequence of acts could have evolved in which the earlier members serve only to prepare later ones which are going to be appropriate to a subsequently given situation. This question arose earlier with respect to molds and other autotrophic organisms which regularly synthesize chemical compounds from which they can ultimately pro-

---

[58] According to Davenport Hooker, "the guinea-pig fetus begins to swallow on about the 42nd day (gestation, 67–69 days)" (*The Prenatal Origin of Behavior* [1952], p. 112).

duce the metabolites they need for their living.[59] N. H. Horowitz speculated that such preparatory acts were not evolved in ascending order,
but in reverse, the final consummation being originally possible without
special preparation, but becoming more and more difficult until only
those mutant strains which synthesized the necessary metabolites could
survive. These strains, which soon became the whole continuing stock,
again and again met the same sort of situation through which they
alone had been able to pass; and there was another crisis and another,
at each of which the stock was nearly anihilated by exhaustion of an
essential metabolite, save that each time some mutant organism—in
molds, possibly just one, though in view of the astronomical numbers
of individuals probably more—synthesized the rare chemical and continued while millions of normal colonies perished. Gradually the vital
activity of such autotrophic organisms has become a stepwise process
in which only the last step is really metabolic.[60]

Such radical elimination of an old "wild type," still leaving a mutant
strain, is less likely in high forms of life than in *Neurospora*, yet there
are cases of it on record; Van Tyne and Berger, for instance, referred
to one such crisis in the life of a sea bird species, saying: "Cottam *et al.*
(1944) described the interesting case of the Brant (*Branta bernicla*)

[59] See Vol. I, p. 396n.

[60] Horowitz, in his important article, "On the Evolution of Biochemical Syntheses" (1945), pp. 299–300, presents the hypothesis as follows: "The species is at
the outset assumed to be heterotrophic for an essential organic molecule, A. It
obtains the substance from an environment which contains, in addition to A, the
substances B and C, capable of reacting in the presence of a catalyst (enzyme) to
give a molecule of A. As a result of biological activity, the amount of available A
is depleted to a point where it limits the further growth of the species. At this
point, a marked selective advantage will be enjoyed by mutants which are able to
carry out the reaction $B + C = A$. As the external supplies of A are further reduced, the mutant strain will gain a still greater selective advantage, until it eventually displaces the parent strain from the population. In the A-free environment a
back-mutation to the original stock will be lethal, so we have at the same time a
theory of lethal genes. The majority of biochemical mutations in *Neurospora* [bread
mold, the most popular laboratory material] are lethals of this type." When B
becomes limiting, "the population will then shift to one characterized by the genotype $(D + E = B, B + C = A)$." Finally, "long reaction chains can be built up
in this way." There may even be "symbiotic associations of the type $(F + G \neq C,
D + E = B)$ $(F + G = C, D + E \neq B)$."

These famous experiments have been repeated by Horowitz himself with collaborators, with similar results. See Horowitz *et al.*, "Genic Control of Biochemical
Reactions in Neurospora" (1945); also Harold Raistrick, "Reflections on Some
Present Tendencies in Microbiological Chemistry" (1939), which first revealed
mutability in synthetic actions of *Neurospora*.

when its usual winter food of eelgrass became drastically reduced. The population of the Brant decreased to one-tenth of its former number and the remaining birds changed their food habits, either by taking other marine plants or by eating true grasses on meadows 100 or more yards from water."[61] In that emergency, those birds which could live on other foods than eelgrass survived while the common run perished; between the lucky one-tenth and the rest of the stock there clearly was a physiological difference which was inherited by the descendants of the survivors, a mutant strain that might never have shown up if the eelgrass had not disappeared, since the members of the tolerant line (or lines) also preferred eelgrass when it was available.

Although the change here cited involved only a single step, it does indicate that biochemical variation, on which food tolerance and utilization depend, may occur on very different levels of life; and that all sorts of mutations may exist in a gene pool, to come into play when extraordinary pressions screen out the standard type. In this sense, and this kind of evolutionary change, one might say that the change occurred in response to a need; but the statement has a weasel character, since actually the change had already occurred in part of the stock, no one knows how many generations or eons ago, and a new need only made the existence of the genotype apparent as the phenotype proved to be preadapted. In a rather rapidly changing habitat where the historically young conditions (for instance, drying up, glaciation, new predator invasion) were inescapable such violent "natural selection" might even happen repeatedly, as in Horowitz's molds, and bring forth behavioral adaptations leading up deviously to implementation of basic vital acts —feeding, mating, protecting and finding protection. Most evolutionary novelties arise without total destruction of the older forms; hence the prevalence of species and varieties, related genera and even orders presumed to have common ancestors. But the great mutant forms that leave no representatives of their ancestral stock on earth may have taken evolutionary spurts under severe circumstantial pressions; many evolutionists, led to the problem of fast and slow phases of physical and behavioral change, have remarked that the most spectacular alterations and departures occur at low points in the phyletic history of a stock, when it is "defeated," and its individuals are small, few or precariously supported by their environment.[62]

[61] J. Van Tyne and A. J. Berger, *Fundamentals of Ornithology* (1959), p. 250. Their reference is to C. Cottam, J. J. Lynch and A. L. Nelson, "Food Habits and Management of American Sea Brant."

[62] See, e.g., A. Tumarkin, "On the Evolution of the Auditory Conducting Ap-

We do not know what goes on in the forming of each individual genome; but if one thinks of this essentially biochemical process as a dynamic system of organic acts, then each behavioral act appears to rise from the physiological matrix exactly as every heartbeat, breath or peristaltic contraction does, to take shape as an articulate directed impulse under the restraint of competing impulses, to find its implementation by ambient conditions, through preparatory preceding behavior and constant, concerted perceptual acts, and to be sustained by the dynamics of the act form itself—rhythmic perseveration, which in behavioral acts becomes facilitated repetition—elaboration, entrainment and integration, and especially an over-all tension that is resolved in consummation. These main aspects have been discussed in Chapter 8, and have only to be borne in mind; they dictate the working principles stated at the beginning of the present chapter, which seem to me to

---

paratus: A New Theory Based on Functional Considerations" (1955), p. 231: "Functional theory suggests that air-sensitive ears developed independently in Anura, Archosaurs, Squamata and Mammalia and that in each case the transition from the preceding bone-conducted hearing took place when the animals were defeated and were consequently tiny."

G. G. Simpson, in his excellent book, *Tempo and Mode in Evolution* (1944), says: "The earliest members of each mammalian order are smaller than the average for the later members, and a fair inference is that their unknown ancestors were as small or smaller. Among other vertebrates and among the invertebrates . . . also, it is the rule that in the higher taxonomic categories the earliest known representatives are relatively small individuals. . . .

"The ancestral type, at about the probable time of origin, is often well recorded and representative of probably abundant and widespread groups, while the first representatives of the new type are usually rare as fossils" (p. 110). And further; "among the more abundant fossils of generally ancestral groups, the precise line that represented the phyletic ancestry is usually rare or absent, as if these particular ancestors had been rare lines or locally differentiated small populations within abundant groups" (p. 111).

It is interesting that this tendency to speciation at a critical time in the life of a stock appears in plants as well as animals. For example, G. L. Stebbins, in *Variation and Evolution in Plants* (1950), states that "in most instances the origin of polyploidy involves a period of partial sterility which may last for several generations before the polyploids have become stabilized" (p. 355). "The chief external factor favoring the establishment of polyploidy is the availability of new ecological niches. . . . Polyploidy, therefore, may be looked upon as a process which is most effective as a means of enabling species groups which have reached a certain stage of depletion of their biotypes, and of sharp divergence of specific entities, to adapt themselves to new environmental conditions which arise relatively suddenly" (p. 358). "Polyploidy is now widely recognized as one of the principal methods for the formation of new species among the higher plants" (p. 359).

[40]

throw a different light on the tangled problems and exhibits of "instinct," "learning" and other cognate phenomena.

The most important principle for a biological interpretation of such behavior, and indeed of all animalian acts, overt or covert, is that an organism always does everything it can do at the time. Everything it does not do is precluded by what it does do or has done, or by lack of opportunity in its ambient. Its growth has created countless possibilities and limitations, its whole past underlies every situation that emerges for it from moment to moment. This raises an interesting question with regard to so-called "inhibitor" functions. Every voluntary muscle that goes into action inhibits its antagonist, but the inhibition is automatic, incidental to what the active muscle is doing; a muscle cannot simply inhibit another's act, without performing a rival function of its own. Similarly, every "center" in the nervous system that is found to be holding some specific act in check is probably doing something in the vital round, incompatible with the inhibited function. The "releasing mechanisms" postulated by Lorenz, Tinbergen and other students of instinct must then be thought of as yet further acts, motivated by outside stimuli or inner processes, which interfere with the normally present inhibiting activities. It is not necessary to postulate specific mechanisms; in the play of rival impulses, any physiological mechanism can act as an inhibitor, and its own inhibition would disinhibit any impulse or impulses now no longer prevented. This is, of course, just Sherrington's "principle of reciprocal innervation,"[63] explored and extended since his day by many physiologists and some psychologists. Several decades ago, G. R. Wendt opposed the concept of inhibition by alternative actions to Pavlov's hypothetical nervous process of pure inhibition. Though Wendt's article is entitled "An Interpretation of

[63] T. M. Sonneborn found the principle of reciprocal inhibition operative far below the zoological level of any innervation in *Paramecium*. Having derived six strains from one animal, each presenting a different antigen complex, he reported: "By exposure to dilute paralyzing antiserum, each of the six types could be transformed into one or more of the other five types. These transformations, induced in up to 100 per cent of the treated animals, are inherited thereafter. ... The types thus obtained can also be transformed back to the original type by exposure to antiserum that paralyses the newly acquired type. ...

"The data thus indicate that interference with, or suppression of, the multiplication of one of the antigen plasmagenes is followed by increase of another one.

"Altogether the results show that the diverse antigenic types ... have identical antigenic potentialities and support the hypothesis that the differences among them are the results of competition among a series of six possible antigenic plasmagenes, which are best adapted to different conditions" ("Beyond the Gene" [1949], pp. 43–44). Cf. Vol. I, p. 378.

Inhibition of Conditioned Reflexes as Competition between Reaction Systems" (1936), and begins accordingly with a study of reflex responses (nystagmus elicited by rotation), it ends with learned behavior that is not reflex at all (baboons opening a drawer upon signal). The generalization is certainly valid and strengthens his case. His statement of the thesis is the most succinct I have found, though—as he remarks on his first page—he was not the first to entertain it: "The extension of the Principle of Reciprocal Innervation to the inhibitions of complex behavior means that we must take the point of view that anything an animal may be doing at the moment, be it sleeping, playing, grooming, vocalizing, sitting quietly, or any other, is reciprocally related to anything it would otherwise have been doing at the same moment. The responses which are absent or inhibited are so when the animal is responding to other stimuli, or when some other response than the one in question is being made to its stimulus."[64]

The same essential condition of life that limits and inhibits growth and behavior by competition—namely, that an organism is always performing every act it can at any given time—also makes up the pervading opportunities of living things. Under the spell of orthodox, single-minded selection theory, some Evolutionists do not appreciate the fantastic lengths to which this opportunism may go. But it is really the obverse aspect of the "unoccupied niche"; the force that makes "niches" in the first place, the automatic trend of impulses toward implementation of their active expressions. This trend may be a constant shifting of central activities (perhaps a groping expansion in various directions) until implementing conditions for the act, or part of the act (subact), are met and the overt phase develops. Something like this must occur in the transition from impulse to behavior, or the many unusual adaptations could not have arisen; simply to note that they have survival value and were "selected" is not enough to account for their emergence in the first place; no physical trait and no action can prove valuable, and consequently be "selected" (i.e., be able to continue), until it has actually occurred.

The constant development of opportunities for the carrying out of incipient acts thwarted in their most direct paths to consummation,

[64] P. 278. An interesting footnote on p. 276 reads: "Author's correction in proof: Since writing this paper I have become convinced that the selection of the terms 'reaction system' and 'response system' was unfortunate, inasmuch as these terms imply the need of a *stimulus* to evoke the system in question. Since many such systems owe their maintenance or origin to central factors, the term 'behavior system' would be more accurate and would have greater generality."

and the fact that every consummated act provides some facilitation, however slight, for its repetition, probably work together to give hereditary changes of physique and behavior the tendency to develop more and more according to the openings they find in the surrounding world, which Simpson refers to as "oriented evolution."[65] The constant transformation of every environment by geological and meteorological causes, the rise and decline of floras, the coming and going of animals (think only of the Grand Banks built of minute exoskeletons of formerly innumerable creatures) make heredity and mutation only a moiety—though perhaps the greater one—of evolutionary advance. No being, and no living stock, can ever arise in maladaptation to a fixed environment and subsequently become adapted; but changes, slow or relatively fast, in an environment have to be matched by changes in the genotypes it supports. That is a generally accepted concept today: the evolution of ecosystems. What is less well known, perhaps (no study, so far as I know, has ever been made of it except incidentally), is the scope of individuation and aberration, the freedom of action permitted by a creature's place in the ecosystem which frames its existence. Undoubtedly some ecosystems are more exploitable than others, so they encourage the enlargement of at least some of the *Umwelten* they comprise. This highly variable factor, this leeway of life, is of prime importance in the origination of novelties, and in some respects certainly underlies the growth of instinctive behavioral acts and the ambients that expand with their growth.

[65] Cf. Vol. I, p. 397. Simpson is one Evolutionist who is fully aware of the part which special opportunity plays in nature.

13

Animal Acts and Ambients

IF WE would trace the rise of human life from its presumable animalian origins, it is necessary to have, first of all, some fairly exact idea of the scope and character of animal life. The scope is enormous, since the different taxonomic forms run into millions (think only of insects, not to mention protozoa!). Even in the vertebrates, which are our main concern at this point, there is a staggering variety. To find the differences that set man apart—as he certainly is set apart—from all non-human animals, one has to consider particularly those traits which all the relevant types of such animals share, which govern their lives, yet may prove not to govern his.

As already stated in the foregoing chapter, I hold that all animal behavior is instinctive, arising from organic sources as impulse seeking expression in motor action, and guided to direct or indirect consummation by acts of perception. To understand a creature's aims and methods one has to consider in what sort of *Umwelt* it lives, that is, what it is able and likely to perceive. The most natural thing is, certainly, to assume that animals—not only dogs, horses and other familiar kinds, but also birds, fish, insects, and all forms possessing eyes—see forms and colors much as these appear to us. Laboratory studies, however, have led most investigators to the belief that mammals with the exception of the primates have little if any color vision, whereas birds and fishes see colors as we do; insects, too, are credited with this "higher" ability, originally conceived, of course, in strict accordance with our own.

The investigations of Karl von Frisch on the mechanisms of insect vision challenged the traditional assumption that all animals see objects as fixed shapes outlined against a contrasting background, and led him to the hypothesis that the compound eyes of flying insects pick up the presence of objects not by seeing contours, but by seeing various patterns of flicker.[1] Further physiological and psychological studies added

---

[1] *Bees: Their Vision, Chemical Senses, and Language* (1950), p. 24: "The bees seem to notice whether a figure is very much broken or is compact. But they do not

evidence that the color spectrum of bees' eyes—and perhaps of most diurnal flying insects' eyes—is displaced toward the violet end, and seems to include utraviolet as a visible hue.[2] The bee, therefore, can probably see red objects—if it can see them at all—only as a color-blind person does, i.e., with whatever other colors, visible to the red-blind eye, the objects may have; whereas ultraviolet-colored objects have a quality for the bee that we cannot possibly imagine, for we, in our turn, see such objects only with their admixed colors of longer wave lengths, or else as white. The most convincing of Von Frisch's tests of the bees' visual upper range was made with white cards of different materials, some of which absorbed ultraviolet rays while others did not; the bees could be trained to the former and not to the latter; white without ultraviolet seems to be neutral, perhaps even invisible to them, whereas it is highly visible to us, but between the ultraviolet cards which attracted the bees and the other "whites" no human eye could distinguish.[3]

It has long been known that most mammals have a much keener sense of smell than men—probably as long as people have used dogs to follow scent trails, and have had to hide their own trails and their food stores from animals. The distance vision of hawks, the night vision of owls and nocturnal beasts are familiar examples of sensibility surpassing our own. But that there may be sensory qualities entirely unknown and unknowable to us is a sobering thought for a scientific thinker, who is of necessity an empiricist. Ultraviolet vision is only one such manifestation; its discovery was quickly followed by that of the bats' echoic hearing of their own squeaks in ranges which are supersonic for man,

perceive in what manner the patterns differ from one another in other respects. Thus their form perception is based on wholly different criteria from ours, a fact that may be related to the different optical arrangements of the compound eye of the insect on the one hand and the cameralike human eye on the other. But the chief reason may well be that the bees see the patterns during flight. Since a bee's eye is rigidly fixed on its head, a broken pattern probably gives a flickering visual impression as the bee flies past. In fact, recent experiments by H. Autrum have clearly demonstrated that this is actually the case."

[2] *Ibid.*, p. 9: "If we compare the color sense of bees and men, we find that the visible spectrum is shortened for bees in the red but that it is extended in the ultraviolet. In this way the visible region is merely shifted to shorter wave lengths. But a much more important difference is that the human eye can distinguish about sixty distinct colors in the visible spectrum, while the bee apparently sees only four different qualities of color: yellow, blue-green, blue, and ultraviolet." (The last inference seems doubtful to me, for the lack of behavioral distinction may easily be due to experimental conditions, which do not call for practical responses to differences that may, nevertheless, characterize the covert phases of the insect's perceptual acts. Negative findings are hard to substantiate.)

[3] *Ibid.*, p. 11.

whereby they seem to steer their courses in the dark among obstructions and track their flying prey.[4] This aural function is pragmatically so different from ordinary sound perception that one may wonder whether sound and ultrasound form one sensory continuum for the animals or two sensory modes. I suspect the latter, because the over-all result of a bat's high-frequency vocalization and echo reception is a spatial frame in which the animal acts, while its low-frequency hearing seems to be alertive, episodal and geared to the range of its own emotional utterance, like the hearing of most other mammals.

Still more recently, Yngve Zotterman brought experimental evidence that some animals, but not all, possess a taste organ which responds to pure distilled water; overt behavior as well as electrical recordings from the gustatory nerve indicate a taste reaction to water dropped on the tongue.[5] The most baffling aspect of these findings is that the ability to taste water neither rises nor declines with advance on the evolutionary scale. Frogs appear to have it, also pigeons and chickens; cats and dogs, but not rats; and most surprisingly, rhesus monkeys, but not men.[6] Again, we can form no idea of what pure water tastes like. The same researches make it very probable that some animals cannot taste sweet, some cannot taste bitter, and so forth. Also, a substance we find bitter, sour or sweet may excite, in another animal, the nerve fibers which characteristically respond to NaCl.[7] Every vertebrate so far examined appears to have some gustatory sense; with the high development of

[4] The pioneers in this field were above all Donald R. Griffin and Robert Galambos. See particularly their early articles, "Obstacle Avoidance by Flying Bats" (1940) and "The Sensory Basis of Obstacle Avoidance by Flying Bats" (1941). Those observations have led to extensive further studies by many investigators, well presented and evaluated by Griffin in *Listening in the Dark: The Acoustic Orientation of Bats and Men* (1958).

[5] See "The Nervous Mechanism of Taste" (1959). A brief summary of this report, in *Psychological Abstracts* (XXXVI, p. 46), says in part: "Besides sweet, sour, bitter and salty as taste classes, water taste may exist. Frogs have taste fibers that respond specifically to water. Using action potentials of the chorda tympani, the cat, dog and pig respond positively to water stimulation. The cat does not respond to sweet, only NaCl and water stimulate single fibers. Chickens and pigeons do not respond to sweet, but show water sense."

[6] Zotterman, "Studies in the Neural Mechanism of Taste" (1961), p. 215: "It seems to us rather odd that we should lack specific water fibers, whereas our next relatives the monkeys have such fibers. This fact does not make it easier to understand what physiological purpose the water taste fibers may serve."

[7] *Ibid.*, p. 209: "in our experiments 50 per cent of the pigeons responded positively to saccharine although they lacked fibers that responded to sucrose and quinine. In behavioral tests the pigeons reject saccharine, but they do not discriminate between quinine solutions and pure water. Thus it is not in jest that I venture to suggest that saccharine may taste salty to these birds."

smell, even very limited taste capacity may furnish a great variety of savors.

The discovery that many animals have percepts entirely unknown to us has naturally led to a wide search for still further senses which might explain the ability of many creatures, notably birds, to perform feats of migration and homing which are quite unaccountable in terms of human means of pathfinding. Some plausible hypotheses and some rather fantastic ones as to further non-human senses that might guide the travelers over thousands of miles of open sea or over land in darkness have been proposed and tested: use of polarized light,[8] radio waves[9] and radar signals,[10] Coriolis force,[11] magnetic currents from the earth,[12] inertial pressures[13] and perhaps other possibilities that never reached even the stage of a "preliminary report" in a professional journal. Experiments in such a field are hard to devise and carry out. So far, certainly, artificial conditions set up to establish special modes of per-

[8] K. C. Montgomery and E. G. Heinemann, "Concerning the Ability of Homing Pigeons To Discriminate Patterns of Polarized Light" (1952).

[9] Ingeburg Besserer and Rudolf Drost, "Ein Beitrag zum Kapitel 'Vogelzug und Elektrizität'" (1935).

[10] Rudolf Drost, "Zugvögel perzipieren Ultrakurzwellen" (1949); also A. O. Knorr, "The Effect of Radar on Birds" (1954). A group of French biologists repeated the experiments of Drost and Knorr with birds released in such a fashion that their flight would be abruptly cut across by radar waves; they failed to find any effect exerted by the waves. But they offer a possible explanation of the discrepancy, saying: "les différences notables entre les cas cités par les auteurs étrangers et nos expériences sont, d'une part, que les oiseaux observés étaient des migrateurs en vol ... et, d'autre part, qu'elles étaient effectuées au bord de la mer. On peut émettre alors l'hypothèse que les oiseaux se soient chargés d'électricité statique produite soit par la friction des ailes sur les molécules de l'air, soit par la charge statique de l'air. . . .

"Dans ce cas, l'oiseau en contact avec l'air ionisé par le radar se trouverait relié électriquement à la terre et perdrait une partie de sa charge à chaque impulsion, il recevrait une série de chocs électriques dont l'amplitude décroîtrait jusqu'à ce qu'il soit déchargé ou qu'il sorte du faisceau. Ces chocs pourraient expliquer les troubles du comportement signalés par les auteurs." But such disconcertment by radar beams does not suggest any guiding function of natural electronic charges (R. G. Busnel et al., "Absence d'action des ondes du radar sur la direction de vol de certains oiseaux" [1956], p. 20).

[11] W. J. Beecher, "On Coriolis Force and Bird Navigation" (1954).

[12] A. R. Orgel and J. C. Smith, "Test of the Magnetic Theory of Homing" (1954); also W. H. Allen, "Bird Migration and Magnetic Meridians" (1948).

[13] J. S. Barlow, "Inertial Navigation as a Basis for Animal Navigation" (1964). The most complete theory of bird "navigation," postulating the existence and usability of all these hypothetical sense data, has been proposed by H. L. Yeagley in two articles under one and the same title, "A Preliminary Study of a Physical Basis of Bird Navigation" (1947 and 1951).

ception by undiscovered sense organs or more diffuse bodily feeling have indicated no such sensory endowments.[14] There may, of course, be influences of local conditions that rise above the threshold of perception, as some human beings feel electric charges in the air before or in a thunderstorm, and a good many people feel low atmospheric pressure; but that does not mean that they can use such feelings to guide them from place to place.

All the other possible means of pathfinding that have been seriously contemplated are geographical—guidance by river valleys, shores, mountain ranges, etc.—or else celestial, the use of constellations and especially the sun as skymarks for the cardinal directions. Many theories have been based on possible (or supposedly possible) ways of steering by the sun's position in the sky, even involving extrapolation of its path from a short observation of its movement.[15] Excellent naturalists have credited birds with "true navigation" by heavenly cues, and even with maintaining a course under cloud cover by memory of compass points taken from such cues on a previous day.[16]

[14] See Jean Dorst's comprehensive book, *The Migrations of Birds*, chap. xii, for a detailed account and critique of all these hypotheses, especially the physical postulates and deductions of Yeagley. Dorst sometimes makes rather too short shrift of ideas he dislikes, relegating such terms as "instinct" to "the philosophers" (meaning vain talkers), but his accounts of major experiments and theories are good.

[15] See, e.g., G. V. T. Matthews, *Bird Navigation* (1955), p. 116: "Provided that a portion of the sun-arc can be observed and evaluated, the requirement that the bird should extrapolate to the highest point of the arc does not present much difficulty. Extrapolation of the path of moving objects is essential in birds feeding on moving prey, such as a plunging Gannet.... the 'good eye' of an expert player in ball games or of the crack shot depends upon an ability for extrapolation." The sun, however, is not seen as a moving object. It is seen in a place, except during the minutes of rising or setting, when it appears to move past the horizon line; but by its creeping into sight at sunrise no path is immediately suggested.

[16] *Ibid.*, pp. 64–65 (after recounting various experiments by Hoffmann): "These experiments have clearly demonstrated that direction finding, innate or learned, in the Starling is based on the sun.... The fact that migrants continue to pass over in the 'standard' direction when the sky is overcast is no real objection. The direction could well have been determined by an earlier view of the sun and maintained in the cloudy interval with reference to general topography.

"It is probable also that night migrants receive their primary directions from the sun.... The direction of the night's flight could be determined from the sun during the day, or about sunset, and maintained as well as possible throughout the darkness with reference to topography, and possibly some general guidance from the moon and star pattern."

Cf. also Ursula Saint Paul, "Nachweis der Sonnenorientierung bei nächtlich ziehenden Vögeln" (1953), and Klaus Hoffmann, "Die Einrechnung der Sonnenwanderung bei der Richtungsweisung des sonnenlos aufgezogenen Stares" (1953).

The great stumbling block to all the "sun compass" theories of animal pathfinding is the fact that the sun's position relative to any given spot on the earth changes with the day and the pattern of change itself changes with the seasons, so a bird using the "sun compass" would have to make allowance for very complicated spatiotemporal factors. We are so accustomed, today, to the engineering metaphors of "automation" and information theory that the notion of birds taking bearings and computing the distances and directions on long flights does not strain our credulity.[17] Most readers do not try to envisage any psychological or physiological process when they meet, for instance, the statement: "In its home the bird is familiar with the different solar characteristics, as its internal clock is regulated by solar rhythm. Placed in strange surroundings, the bird observes the sun and, after watching even a small part of its course, can project the whole curve. The measure of maximum altitude, the angle in relation to the horizontal, and a comparison with the circumstances at home give latitude; the sun's position in relation to its highest point and the home position, as revealed by the bird's internal clock, give details about longitude."[18] Yet the author himself remarks, at the end of the chapter: "No one knows what psycho-physiological processes are involved or how the bird gets its bearings. . . ."[19]

As there are, then, inexplicable animal abilities to challenge our powers of theoretical interpretation, so there are equally astounding and inexplicable blunders and apparent stupidities. Nikolaas Tinbergen wrote, in *The Herring Gull's World* (1953): "It is wonderful . . . to see a gull take a shellfish up into the air and drop it in order to crush it, and to know that this is an innate (or inherited and unlearnt) capacity, provided for in the nervous system. But it is equally astonishing to see that the bird never realizes that it has to drop the shellfish on something hard, and it may go on dropping it on soft mud again and again. It is wonderful, again, to see how a gull rolls a misplaced egg back into its nest, but it is amazing that it does so in such a clumsy way, by balancing it on the narrow underside of the beak, instead of by a simple

---

[17] Matthews (*Bird Navigation*, p. 74) remarks: "The idea of an animal performing a *mental* triangulation is no longer so bizarre since v. Frisch (1950) has clearly demonstrated that bees do this." But the bizarre conclusions of Von Frisch about the trigonometry of bees have lately been seriously called in question and fairly well disproved in repetitions of his experiments under different interpretational assumptions (see A. M. Wenner and D. L. Johnson, "Simple Conditioning in Honey Bees" [1966]).

[18] Dorst, *The Migrations of Birds*, p. 358.

[19] *Ibid.*, p. 370.

sweep of the wing, which would seem much easier. It is wonderful, again, to see how every parent gull learns to distinguish its own young individually after about five days, but it is disappointing to see that it never learns to distinguish its own eggs from those of its neighbour, however different their colour may be. These limitations in behaviour are not due to limitations in the sense organs, but to limitations in the nervous system. It never 'occurs' to the gull to drop shellfish only on rocks, or to roll an egg in with its wing."[20]

Such ineptitudes, however, are by no means the oddest. Much more puzzling is the obliviousness of many animals—insects, birds and mammals—to what we would consider the goal of behavior, when that "goal" is displaced or removed. With our natural, common-sense assumptions of what animals should be responding to, some of their behavior is flatly inexplicable. Donald Griffin, for instance, tells of a bat which F. P. Möhres and T. Oettingen-Spielberg kept in a cage hung from the ceiling near the center of a room: "When a door [of the cage] on one side was opened," he says, "the bat would fly out for a time, but later return to its favorite roosting place inside the cage. While it was out of the cage the experimenters rotated the cage 90° or 180° from its usual position. On several occasions the bat tried to fly in where the door had been, and only after many such errors would it find the door in its new position. In one experiment the cage was removed altogether, and the experimenters reported that the bat did its best to fly in through the space where the door had been and to hang itself up on the usual part of the non-existent wire netting."[21]

---

[20] P. 6 (page references are to the paperback edition of 1967). J. A. Bierens de Haan, in *Die tierischen Instinkte und ihr Umbau durch Erfahrung* (1940), pp. 210–11, states that the rhea, a South American relative of the ostrich, uses his wing to catch each egg as the female lays it and roll it safely into the nest. The rhea's wing is not used in flight, and so is left free to develop other functional impulses and feelings.

[21] *Listening in the Dark*, p. 165. There is a comparable report on the behavior of a greenfinch, "Abnormes Umweltbild eines Grünfinks," by H. G. Schmitt, which O. Koehler, reviewing volume VI of the *Zeitschrift für Tierpsychologie* (1949, pp. 271–74) wherein it appeared, summarized as follows: "A nestling female Greenfinch was reared in a cage. In five years of caged life the door has been open whenever people were in the room; the bird however has never been known to leave its cage. When the cage was removed and the floor plate with food cup and bathing saucer was left at its place on the table, the bird, when put near them, immediately went to them and used them without signs of restlessness. However, even then it never moved beyond imaginary boundaries enclosing a space around the cup and saucer of exactly the same size as its cage. A similar observation was made with a Sea Eagle kept at the Vogelwarte Rossitten" (*Behaviour* [1950], p. 319).

Bats, though they are placental mammals, are insectivores, and as such are rated low on the evolutionary scale; a higher animal with better sensory equipment might be expected to be above such absurd behavior. But the expectation is disposed of at once, by an equally authentic though much older record from the laboratory of E. L. Thorndike. This early systematic experimenter in animal psychology tells of cats which he had trained to open a door by pulling a looped string and let themselves out of a box in which they were confined. When the trick was well learned, they performed it as soon as they were put in, hungry, smelling the fish that awaited them outside. And he reports, quite incidentally (in the course of an explanation to which we shall return), that they went through the act of pulling the loop even if the door was open, and that "cats would paw at the place where a loop had been, though none was there."[22]

A similar observation has been made on a tern homing to its nest after its foraging flights. In the absence of the bird, the experimenters altered the location of the nest in various ways: raising it, much or little, on a stand, or displacing it horizontally. When the nest was lifted 6 to 10 inches above its original position, the tern flew to it and seemed only a little disturbed by the change; but a displacement of that same distance in a horizontal direction, on the open ground, elicited a most surprising response. The bird, returning with its usual sweep and landing tactics, did not head for the widely visible nest, but landed and sat on the spot where the nest had always been. To a human being, the nest raised on a pedestal looked far more radically altered positionally than the slightly shifted nest on the ground. But to the tern the appearance of the nest as an object in space did not seem to matter very seriously; though vertical displacement disturbed the bird somewhat, it was soon reoriented. The nest could grow tall, like Alice in Wonderland or Jack's beanstalk, without losing its identity so long as it remained exactly in its place. If, however, it was removed from its place even ever so little, it apparently did not belong to the end of the homing act any more. The old place directly beside it was still the terminal.[23]

[22] *Animal Intelligence* (1911; 1st ed., 1898), p. 119.

[23] John B. Watson and K. S. Lashley, *Homing and Related Activities of Birds* (1915), pp. 63 ff. This source has been cited, in paraphrase or excerpts of literal statement, so many times that the findings appear much simpler and more spectacular than they really were. These early experiments were, in fact, rather crude, no attention being paid at all to incidental traumata which may have affected the birds, e.g., fluttering tags at the nest sites, and big spots of paint splashed on the subjects themselves; the birds were often chased off the nests, and the latter were interfered with again and again at very short intervals. The second-hand and third-hand accounts, moreover, do not report the discrepancies in the records of the two

Tinbergen tells very much the same story of the herring gull. "One simple experiment," he says, "is sufficient to show how different the gull's reaction is from ours. When we take the three eggs out of the nest and put them at about a foot's distance in plain view, the returning gull usually goes to the empty nest, and, often after some hesitation, sits down in it. It may look at the eggs outside, it may occasionally roll one of them into the nest, but at this distance it often ignores them.

"Now to what extent is it the nest, and to what extent the site that stimulates the bird? When the empty nest is removed and the pit filled up with sand, the bird, although hesitating, usually sits down at the spot where the nest was, thus showing the nest-site to be the prominent element in the stimulus situation.

"But when in this same situation we make an artificial nest under the displaced eggs, the gull's choice is in favor of the eggs. The nest itself, therefore, is also of influence, for it strikes the balance in favour of the eggs."[24]

Before any of these observations on cats, bats and birds were recorded, beekeepers are said to have known that bees could be seriously disturbed by small turns or shifts of their hives; but Albrecht Bethe seems to have been the first scientist to have checked such allegations. The facts proved to be really as spectacular as they appeared in popular claims, and as they have often been retold. Bethe carried several bees in a cardboard box from a hive at the Physiological Institute (University of Gratz) to a stone quarry some distance away, and released them there. The following results are from his report: "All the bees rose, and most of them, after flying a few circles in the air, took a straight course back to the Institute. Two animals flew up to a height of about 3 meters, where they described several circles 4–5 m. in diameter and then shot down vertically on the box. I chased them up again. They flew in still larger circles around the point from which they had risen and came down again on the container. Now, after driving them

---

authors and the contradictions in some of their conclusions (which are all a bit too sweeping). Watson found "that considerable changes could be made in the vertical position of the nest without affecting the bird's reaction in the slightest." Lashley, repeating the experiments (as nearly as wild conditions ever allow repetition), concluded that "adjustment to changes in the height of the nest is not made any more readily than to changes in the horizontal position." Later field studies by more sophisticated experimenters have largely corroborated Watson's finding of a considerable difference in the effects of vertical and horizontal displacement.

[24] *The Herring Gull's World*, p. 175. Herring gulls and terns seem to differ somewhat in their respective fixations on their original nest sites; according to the above report, a gull would probably not sit down beside its slightly displaced nest.

off again, I took the box and set it on another quarry stone. The two bees rose so high that I lost sight of them; but after a few seconds they fell lower again and *headed straight for the spot where the box had been standing before.* Had they been guided by chemical or visual stimuli, they surely would have flown to the exactly similar stone, only 2 m. away, where the box was now standing. But they flew back to the point from which they had arisen.

"I repeated the experiment many times after this.... The bees, if they came back to the area of release at all, regularly came back to the exact spot.... Once I even observed that one of them sat down on the field, sucked some honey from a *Salvia praetensis* and then returned to the point from which it had risen. But the most astounding thing occurred when once I held the box high in the air as I opened it, and then, when the bees had all risen, stepped aside a few paces, still holding it. Four of the six bees returned, after some circling overhead, and flew, at a man's height, in tiny circles around the spot where I had held the box when I opened it."[25]

By all these examples of what animal psychologists today call the "place habit" or "position habit" we are really forced to the conclusion that animals do not live in the same sort of spatial milieu as man. There are several well-attested conditions which make that proposition plausible. The most important is that animal perception is more intimately bound to overt action than ours; in fact, it is established in the performance of instinctive acts, which are guided by feeling, both central and peripheral—that is, by felt impulses and felt sensory impingements, or sensations. Percepts are often very indirect deliverances of interacting sense impressions of mingled sorts.[26] The principle of their formation is selection, among all the elements in the external aspect of

[25] "Dürfen wir den Ameisen und Bienen psychische Qualitäten zuschreiben?" (1898), p. 93.

[26] J. J. Gibson, in *The Perception of the Visual World* (1950), gives full and often highly original recognition to this fact. See, e.g., p. 135: "The perception of voluntary locomotion, as distinguished from passive locomotion, is jointly determined by two sources of stimulation, stimuli from the retina [which he previously distinguished from stimuli *to* the retina], on the one hand, and from the muscles plus the inner ear on the other.... The product of these stimuli is something neither wholly motor nor wholly visual; it is locomotor action in a visual world." And further, p. 149: "The visual vertical and horizontal ... have reference to the direction of gravity.... These features of space are inseparable from the feeling of the ground under our feet and the feeling of standing up, or moving about, and of looking. The tactual and kinesthetic stimuli which arouse these feelings ordinarily co-vary with the visual stimuli and the product is something which is neither visual nor postural."

a situation, of those that will implement whatever acts are in progress. That includes evasion of obstacles, especially death-dealing ones. In other words, the primary characteristics which animals see are values, and all the qualities of form, color, shape, sound, warmth, and even smell, by which we would naturally expect them to recognize things, enter into their perceptual acts only as they enter into their overt behavior as values for action.[27] A young animal creeps under any living or non-living body that is warm and soft. A cat generally chases anything that runs or flutters. That does not mean that the young one would recognize a fur-lined boot in which it had slept as the same object if the boot were on someone's foot, or that the cat which had chased a roller skate that was pushed across the floor would pay any attention to it if the skate stood in a rack.

Jakob von Uexküll had startled the philosophers and psychologists of his day with his reflections on how different the *Umwelten* of infusorians and the lowest metazoans must be from those of higher animals, say, the mammals, but his insights were, after all, not hard to accept if one considered the sensory apparatuses of the little creatures he studied. Thorndike's cats were more baffling; it is much harder to believe that cats and dogs may not see chairs and tables, cage doors and corridors just as we see them. Yet Thorndike's experiments really supported that conclusion, which he expressed with surprise and hesitation in the then prevailing context of association psychology.[28] He even entertained the idea that animals do not perceive permanent, well-defined objects as human beings do. Like Von Uexküll, he was aware

[27] William James, with his great gift for unprejudiced observation, once remarked that to a broody hen an egg is not a smooth, pale object of characteristic form, but just "a most beautiful, never-too-much-to-be-sat-upon object."

[28] See *Animal Intelligence*, pp. 108–9: "The possibility is that animals have *no images or memories at all, no ideas to associate.* Perhaps the entire fact of association in animals is the presence of sense impressions with which are associated, by resultant pleasure, certain impulses, and that, therefore, and therefore only, a certain situation brings forth a certain act." All the representations supposed to be associated to form a memory of a past experience might not exist at all; so "this theory would say . . . that the sense impression gave rise, when accompanied by the feeling of discomfort, to the impulse directly, without the intervention of any representations of the taste of food, or the experience of being outside, or the sight of oneself doing the act." He himself, at that time, found this notion too radical to subscribe to at once, but the passage concludes: "the question of the utter exclusion of representative trains of thought, of any geninue association of *ideas* from the mental life of animals, is worth serious consideration. I confess that, although certain authentic anecdotes and certain experiments . . . lead me to reject this conclusion there are many qualities in animal behavior which seem to back it up."

that an animal's ambient is not what we imagine as its "environment." It may not see what we see, when it does not act as we would act.[29]

Five years after the appearance of Thorndike's book, Hans Volkelt published a monograph on representations (*Vorstellungen*) in animals' minds.[30] He had access to the facts collected by Thorndike, Watson and Lashley, Bethe and Von Uexküll, as well as to the interpretations those authors had offered, and like them he concluded that animals had no store of images and memories of past occasions, and that even their current perceptions were not of physically defined, permanent things, to be met with again and again under various conditions. But he pushed his very careful and well-grounded speculations beyond those of Von Uexküll and Thorndike to the problem of what non-human creatures do perceive. His first realization, based on a long, though chance-inspired, observation of his own, was that the crucial property of animal percepts, which apparently determined all their other properties for the perceiver, was their value in the current situation, and that this value depended on what activities were in progress or in readiness at the moment.[31]

The experimental setup that presented itself for his exploitation was that a tunnel spider had spread its radial web inside his room in a corner of the window sash, with its tunnel off-side, the heavy "signal strand" connecting its retreat and the center of the web. The spider lay in wait within its funnel-shaped lair until an insect caught in the web caused the signal cord to twitch; then it dashed out, paralyzed and partly ensnared its prey, dragged it into the lair and immediately began to suck its juices. If another insect was caught before the first was devoured, the spider interrupted its meal, handled the new catch, but instead of dragging it home and starting to eat it, fastened it temporarily somewhere in the web and returned to finish the previous morsel. So, evidently, the spider had an appropriately variable repertoire of acts to deal with the various situations it would normally meet in the course of its insect procuration.

[29] *Ibid.*, p. 120: "the fact that an animal reacts alike to a lot of things gives no reason to believe that it is conscious of their common quality and reacts to that consciousness, because the things it reacts to in the first place are not the hard-and-fast, well-defined 'things' of human life."

[30] *Über die Vorstellungen der Tiere* (1912). This important essay was Volkelt's doctoral dissertation.

[31] *Ibid.*, p. 9: "Erstens müssen wir wissen, wie sich das gleiche Tier zu eben dem Dinge, dem es jetzt gegenübersteht, in anderen Situationen zu verhalten pflegte. Wir kennen alsdann den 'Wert,' den dieses Ding unter gewissen Umständen für das Tier besass. *Zweitens* müssen wir wissen, ob dieses Ding auch jetzt den gleichen 'Wert' besitzt. . . ."

But now, the experimenter introduced an insect from the rear of the funnel-shaped lair and teased it to move forward toward the spider; the latter retreated further and further before the intruder until both animals were well out in the web. Here the insect deviated from its path and got into the finer threads, and only then did the spider run along the cleared signal strand back to its lair. Unfortunately, we are not told whether it subsequently made a normal attack on the entangled prey.[32]

How directly the perception of higher animals than spiders depends on centrally motivated acts has been demonstrated in various ways, but the original discovery of the close relationship of acts and percepts takes us back to Thorndike's cats and dogs. The problem that led to the experiments which revealed that relationship was a fairly obvious learning problem: how much could the animals learn about a practical act, such as opening a door, by watching a previously trained member of their species do the trick? The simplest test would be to compare the subsequent performance of subjects which had seen it done with that of others which had not. To this end, the pioneer experimenter confined hungry cats in boxes that could be opened by various means, such as pulling a looped string or hitting a button, all of which a cat would sooner or later discover accidentally by simply clawing and pushing to get out. Once a chance movement had opened the door, it never took long for the cat to repeat it, and very soon to use it regularly in escaping from the box, whereupon it received fish outside. The experimenter then confined inexperienced cats in another compartment of the apparatus which permitted full view of a trained animal's escape. Most of the time the ignorant cats did not watch the skilled perform-

---

[32] *Ibid.*, pp. 15–18. Later, reflecting on the spider's acts, he wrote: *"Die Annahme, der Fliege entspreche in jenen zwei verschiedenen Situationen annährend das gleiche dinghafte Gebilde in dem Spinnenbewusstsein, diese Annahme erweist sich aus ihren Konsequenzen als unhaltbar"* (p. 55). *"Im Spinnenbewusstsein wird die Fliege ausserhalb eines ganz bestimmten Umkreises von Situationen nicht durch das gleiche dinghafte Gebilde repräsentiert wie innerhalb. . . . Nur in einem sehr engen Umkreis von Situationen besteht Konstanz der dinghaften Gebilde"* (p. 56).

He goes on to analyze this *Umkreis*, or circumstantial context, and in so doing he arrives at the same notion of "situation" which I have found adequate to account for the rise of every act out of an active matrix, which is an agent in a motivating situation: "Dieser begrenzte Umkreis war nun im eigentlichen Sinn des Wortes ein Umkreis von 'Situationen' . . . der Umkreis war bestimmt *durch eine Anzahl von Gesamtsituationen*." Every situation involves a system of interrelated factors, the main ones being the completed parts of an act in progress, in their immediate extraorganic setting. So he concludes: "Wir sehen also: was wir 'Gesamtsituation' nannten, lässt sich durch genügend zahlreiche Momente in seiner Eigenart bezeichnen, wenn wir . . . zu der Situation auch den Handlungszusammenhang, in dem eine Teilhandlung des Tieres eingebettet ist, hinzurechnen" (pp. 60–61).

ance, so out of many trials only the few in which the supposed observer was quite certainly looking at the escapee—about seven out of thirty—could be used; but by dint of many experiments enough cases were collected to judge whether cats which had seen the door opened were quicker to learn the trick themselves when put into the test box than cats which had never seen it.

When the records were compared, it appeared that the "instructed" cats had not profited one whit by the example set for them. They acted exactly like their uneducated brethren.[33] So, ruling out visual teaching as a *gradus ad parnassum*, Thorndike undertook to test the effects of tactual and kinesthetic instruction. He put his animals into boxes from which they did not know how to escape, and after a minute or two, put his hand through the bars from above, took the cat's paw, and thus passively caused it to manipulate the loop on the string which opened the door; the cat walked out and was fed with fish. Yet even this direct teaching did not work; "the results," he wrote, "show that no animal who fails to perform an act in the course of his own impulsive activity will learn it by being put through it."[34] But what really clinched the ineffectiveness of such physical guidance was that when the cats finally learned by themselves to escape from the box, "it happened in all but one of the cases that the movement which the animal made to open the door was different from the movement which I had put him through."[35]

Fully half a century after these early demonstrations that animals do not perceive events and things in their surroundings apart from their own impulses and acts, some quite similar experiments[36] have shown

[33] *Animal Intelligence*, pp. 88–89.

[34] *Ibid.*, p. 103.

[35] *Ibid.*, p. 105. All the experiments on cats were repeated on dogs with exactly the same results. A very interesting parallel from human learning is given by P. Guillaume in *La formation des habitudes* (1936), pp. 154–55: "On peut distinguer une méthode passive et une méthode active pour apprendre. Dans la première, le sujet est conduit, guidé de manière à effectuer l'acte sous une forme aussi parfait que possible, exempte d'erreurs, semblable dès le début à sa forme définitive. Dans la seconde méthode, aucune assistance n'est donnée au sujet, qui devra, par ses initiatives et ses corrections, arriver peu à peu au résultat désiré.

. . . Une méthode d'initiation à l'écriture ou au dessin consiste à faire calquer aux enfants des modèles en pointillé qu'ils repassent en traits pleins. Gates et Tylor font travailler deux groupes d'enfants qui ne savent pas encore écrire; l'un calque des lettres, l'autre les dessins d'après modèle, mais sans calquer. Or il est impossible d'apprendre complètement à former la lettre au moyen d'exercices de calque; les enfants qui passent du calque à l'écriture libre se trouvent presque en présence d'un problème nouveau et ne tirent qu'un bénéfice restreint des exercices antérieurs."

[36] See R. Held and A. Hein, "Movement-Produced Stimulation of Visually Guided Behavior" (1963).

this principle to operate in even more radical ways: their surrounding space itself is perceptible to them only by means of their own activity in it. The inherence of their sensory acts in larger behavioral acts is clearly apparent from a series of learning experiments in which young animals (kittens) were prevented from using and seeing their own limbs, while they were passively transported through a territory which they could view in passage, as one watches the landscape from a vehicle one is not guiding. The apparatus was a circular track in which one kitten walked in a halter suspended from a rotary arm above, so it could walk only forward, while the opposite end of the arm moved a gondola with another kitten that could move but not see its limbs, and could not walk, as it was carried passively around the same track. It could look forward and somewhat laterally; the walking kitten wore a shield restricting its vision in the same way. The result, briefly stated, was that the passively transported kittens learned nothing about the terrain, though they could see it, while the walking ones easily learned to place their paws and move or stop as they wished. This, in itself, was not surprising; that paw placement would profit from visual and tactual feedback is reasonable enough. But the next experiment on the same pairs of kittens showed the full effect of autogenic action on the development of visual judgment.

The second test was on the so-called visual cliff, a path with an illusory drop on one side, a shallow shoulder on the other. Denoting the actively moving kittens by A and passive by P, the experimenters report: "All A's behaved like normally reared Ss.... each A descended to the shallow side of the cliff on every trial.... The P members ... were tested on the cliff on the same days as their actively exposed litter mates. They showed no evidence of discriminating the shallow from the deep side.... Following the 48 hr. period of freedom in an illuminated room [all the experimental animals had been reared in the dark], the P members ... displayed normal visually guided paw placement and performed all descents to the shallow side of the visual cliff."[37]

So it appears that space itself, as an animal knows it, is action space, and that even its visual presentation is not simply given, but made by

[37] *Ibid.*, p. 875. In an earlier study, "Adaptation of Disarranged Hand-Eye Coordination Contingent upon Reafferent Stimulation" (1958), the same authors discovered that human subjects, under the artificial condition of wearing prism glasses that displaced the retinal image to left or right, needed reafference to learn to guide their hands in the new visual field. This suggests that the same mechanisms govern human and animal orientation; but since the human subjects were adult and already had a "visual world," whereas the kittens were finding it for the first time, the human case is not entirely comparable to that of the young animals, especially with respect to the "visual cliff" experiment.

the agent's own exploitation of its possibilities; though this making, according to the laboratory experiences here discussed, is not the slow process which has been inferred by D. O. Hebb on the basis of form-learning by Lashley's rats[38] and by congenitally blind persons who received sight in adulthood or late childhood.[39] The immediate recognition of the "visual cliff" appearance by cats which had never made a descent, but had explored a track with paws and eyes, indicates that for cats at the age of walking and seeing any natural incentive to space perception suffices to start all the mental acts required for its further development from one moment to the next, that is, from one situation to another. The feelings of direction, distance, contact and progression seem to be extended almost at once from actual to potential movement.

Such learning does not exemplify any of the patterns recognized in learning theory or assumed in setting up the usual learning tests; yet here it is, demonstrated in the animal laboratory, and one cannot but wonder how it could have been recorded there without arousing any surprise that "incidental learning" should so far exceed the predicted effects of reafferent stimulation. The canons of scientific method require

[38] See K. S. Lashley, "The Problem of Cerebral Organization in Vision" (1942), p. 302: "for the rat, as for man, visual impressions consist of organized objects, seen against a less coherent background." And on the next page he asserts that figure and ground and similarities of form are "fundamentally the same for the bird, the rodent and man and it is very probable that the same general principles will be found to apply to insects and cephalopods, when these have been adequately studied." In the case of insects, the subsequent studies of bees' visual functions make the similarity of their vision to man's appear anything but "very probable."

[39] Hebb, *The Organization of Behavior*, chap. v, esp. the following statements: "From Lashley's experiments, it is ... evident that line and angle dominate the rat's perception of patterns. We may therefore consider that these things are among the elements from which more complex perceptions develop" (p. 81). "Lines and angles, then, can be treated as perceptual elements, not fully innate in perception, but partly so, and likely to be learned before more complex patterns are.... A triangle then is a complex entity in perception, not primitive. As a whole, it becomes distinctive and recognizable only after a prolonged learning period in which there is a good deal of receptor adjustment—head and eye movement ..." (p. 83). When a rat learns to see a triangle $a \overset{c}{\triangle} b$ "one or more intermediate stages would occur, such as an integration of a with b before that of ab with c.... I mention ab as the first stage, rather than ac, because the horizontal line ... seems of fundamental importance in human perception and certainly is so for the rat in the usual conditions of testing" (p. 97) [the italicized letters in his text actually refer to hypothetical neural acts correlated with the items perceived]. "The congenitally blind patient after operation at first sees any figure as an amorphous mass, but may be able with effort to count its corners.... Exactly the same sort of thing is implied by Lashley's inference that the rat successively isolates (*i.e.*, sees as figure) various parts of a unified pattern before making a response" (p. 99).

that animals be presented with specific, controllable stimuli which seem simple to the experimenter, such as black squares and circles and triangles on a white ground, or vice versa, white on black. It is possible to train rats, dogs, cats and various other animals to distinguish such shapes, but they are certainly—like Shakespeare's rustic actor—"exceeding slow of study." Hebb sums up the rat's limitations, saying: "He does not recognize the triangle he was trained to recognize if it is rotated by 60°, nor a black triangle on a white ground. He has, in fact, some considerable difficulty in seeing the difference between a triangle and a square when their base-lines are identical. . . . When some change in the training figure is made, such as making it larger, the rat's behavior is clearly disturbed, while man might be quite unaware of the change; and the rat often discriminates only part of as simple a figure as a triangle."[40] He even held, on the basis of his experiments, that the rat notes the basal corners of a triangle first and then progresses to the apex.

But it may be that animals trained to distinguish squares, triangles, etc., as black-and-white figures never see them as such at all; that they distinguish black holes from white obstructions, or even just see black holes, and see nothing noticeable at all (the white shapes on black) if the background does not look like a dark alley. In viewing the standard black triangle they may never notice the apex, but see only the equivalent of a trapezoid, which would be the part required to admit a rat's body, and would do so as adequately as a square or oblong aperture. The angle formed overhead by the sides is irrelevant, whereas the horizontal base is not. But neither a possible hole nor a white "thing" plays any part in the food-reaching act that involves a choice of doors. It takes long training in the unnatural, simplified setting of cage or apparatus to establish a visible "sign stimulus" for an animal that does not use such things in its normal ambient.[41] Pressing a lever to make a food

[40] *Ibid.*, p. 95.

[41] Hebb appears to have been quite well aware of the fact that no animal—not even an ape—naturally uses "sign stimuli" learned by purely contingent experience, i.e., without hereditary or at least infantile value. See *ibid.*, p. 93: "In discrimination training, the . . . method of training is to offer a choice of two alleys, or doors or windows, one of which leads the animal to food. He is also given a sign as to which one contains the food: the correct door has a black card on it, or a circle, say; the wrong one has a white card or a square. Food, and the sign of food, are sometimes on the right, sometimes on the left. But what the rat, dog, or chimpanzee persistently tried to find out is something different. . . . He wants nothing of the rarified intellectual problem of the signs the experimenter has put on the doors; it is only after repeated discouragement of the position habit—the attempt to find food in some one *place*—that one can get him to learn anything else."

pellet roll down is a different matter, and easily learned; to manipulate twigs or hit a vine to shake down small fruits is in a rat's behavioral repertoire. But it may never distinguish the shape of beech leaves from that of spicebush leaves, though to us the one indicates the likelihood of finding, now or at some other time, a harvest of beechnuts, and the other of finding pungent berries (which, by the way, rats and mice eagerly gather).

The findings here collected and many others like them corroborate the judgment which Volkelt based on the few cases he knew—Thorndike's cats, Bethe's bees, Watson and Lashley's terns: that animals have no *Vorstellungen,* and so can call up no images of things met in one situation to recognize the same objects in another. What animals perceive, according to his conclusion, is above all a qualitative character which Krueger (modeling his terminology on Ehrenfels' *"Gestaltqualität"*) called the *"Komplexqualität"* of a total situation.[42] Any change of some contained element in a total situation may change the *Komplexqualität,* or "complex-quality," of that situation, so the animal may change its behavior without being aware of any specific new stimulus. As Volkelt put it, "In animals, the relationship of perception and action is not that the presentation of a thing-like complex evokes a correlative act; nor yet that the act is correlated with an atomistic sense impression. The behavorial acts of a primitive organism are adapted to the presence of certain holistic complex-qualities which may comprise even the entire motor, visceral and emotive condition of the animal itself."[43]

Every past event, therefore, is assimilated to the agent's reactive scheme; instead of recalling former experiences and "associating" sights and tastes, smells and movements, with consequent pleasures and pains, and then imposing such remembered patterns on similar sense stimuli encountered thereafter, an animal relives its act with its whole previous qualitative complex; "all at once, the entire past experience is present

[42] See Volkelt, *Über die Vorstellungen der Tiere,* p. 84: "Es lässt sich zeigen, dass es eine Art von Synthese gibt, die viele Qualitäten zumal dann umspannt, wenn diese Qualitäten sich ... in hoher Ungesondertheit befinden. Diese merkwürdigen einheitlichen Qualitäten eines mehrheitlichen Komplexes ... werden in der neueren Psychologie beschrieben unter dem Namen 'Komplexqualitäten.' " And further, p. 95: "Ein jedes, auch das peripherste Ereignis, wenn es nur überhaupt den Sinnen zugänglich ist, vermag die Komplexqualität zu modifizieren, ohne in der Komplexqualität als relativ selbstständiger Teilinhalt zu figurieren. Die Veränderung eines Teilinhalts kann an sich ganz verborgen bleiben und dennoch, gleichsam heimlich, das Ganze in bestimmter Richtung verändern."

[43] *Ibid.,* p. 90.

again; for the earlier total experience affects the present one assimilatively; the old one virtually repeats itself. . . ."[44]

The literature is full of observations indicating that what we see as permanent, essentially unchanging objects may have no such qualitative stability for animals. Leyhausen, in his excellent study of the hierarchy of moods observable in beasts of prey, especially various species of cats (viverrines, ocelots, African genets, civets, African tiger cats, servals and others), noted how the appearance of a rat or a mouse, which the experimenter saw unequivocally as "prey" for his felines, seemed to change even from one subact of the killing process to another; and as a subact might be elaborated, even in the course of the usual totality, to draw in subacts of its own and become temporarily the dominant act in progress, there is a play of moods, a relative hierarchy of motivations at every moment, in which the prey animal is successively (or alternately) a target, a toy, a victim, a morsel or what not.[45]

A still more striking instance of the act-dependence of animals' perceptions of objects is given by Mathilde Meng in a study of the responses of the common European toad to a mealworm suspended and rotated by a thread. The toad would go through its preliminary acts of fixating the lure and getting into position to snap, at which point the worm was dropped and promptly snapped up; but if it was inadvertently dropped too soon, the toad took no notice of it.[46]

From these and many other examples it appears that if we would venture any guesses at what an animal perceives we should first study

---

[44] *Ibid.*, p. 117. The use of "assimilation" instead of "association" was also proposed by Krueger.

[45] Paul Leyhausen, "Über die Funktion der relativen Stimmungshierarchie dargestellt am Beispiel der phylogenetischen und ontogenetischen Entwicklung des Beutefangs von Raubtieren" (1965), p. 470: "Von den Beutefanghandlungen kann also *jede zur erstrebten Endhandlung* werden. . . . Jede kann auch innerhalb gewisser Grenzen jede andere in ihren 'Dienst' stellen, sie nicht nur zeitweilig unterdrücken, sondern auch als 'Appetenzhandlung' aktivieren, falls sie selbst . . . nur auf diesem 'Umweg' zu erreichen ist. Dies nannte ich 'Relative Stimmungshierarchie.' . . . Sie beherrscht und 'programmiert' nicht nur die Motorik, sondern auch die gesamten afferenten Mechanismen. Dementsprechend ist daher die Maus entweder ein Objekt zum Belauern, oder zum Haschen, oder zum Töten, oder zum Essen, . . . d. h. die Reizqualität der Maus ändert sich mit der Rangordnung der Appetenzen."

[46] "Untersuchungen zum Farben- und Formensehen der Erdkröte (*Bufo bufo* L.)" (1958), pp. 316–17: "Anfangs waren die Tiere sehr unruhig. . . . Nach etwa 14 Tagen hatten sie sich soweit eingewöhnt, dass ich vier Tiere an die bewegte Attrappe. . . . heranlocken konnte, wo sie einen Mehlwurm erhielten. . . . Bald liefen sie recht sicher auf die rotierende Attrappe zu; wenn dann der Mehlwurm versehentlich zu früh herunterfiel, beachteten sie ihn nicht."

the nature of its acts, behavioral and, as far as possible, organic; for all non-reflex behavioral acts are continuous with internal preparatory acts, and any intimate study of overt responses must reveal something of their total form before we can reasonably infer anything about their covert, psychical phases. A few general aspects of animal acts, which become apparent only through a wide survey of patterns in very many, very diverse species, may account in some measure for the basic differences between human and non-human perception and capacities.

Instinctive acts are behavioral wholes from their beginnings, i.e., their respective main impulses; and where an avenue of expression is free, they go through characteristic phases of development. In the most established act forms which have not become highly elaborated, such as a frog's or a toad's hunting pattern, the sequence of stages from the motivation of the impulse to the consummation can be fairly well seen and analyzed; more complex acts, by comparison, then corroborate the findings. One of these most general observations is that adaptation to external conditions is made chiefly at the commencement of the act. Dr. Meng, in the paper cited above, recorded this fact. The consummatory phase is the most reflex-like and, indeed, in the acts which she studied, involved reflex movements, for which all the voluntary behavior furnished the proper conditions. Once the preparation is made, the act may even be completed *in vacuo* if the implementing conditions suddenly fail—for instance, if the target flies away before the hunter leaps or lurches for it.[47] This increasing automatization has long been noted,

---

[47] See *ibid.*, p. 314: "Beim Beutefang nimmt die Kröte als erstes Richtung auf die Beute, dann nähert sie sich ihr und schnappt zu, oft genug taxisunabhängig (Schnappen ins Leere, Hinsches 'T-Phänomen'). Offenbar nützt die Erdkröte bei der Endhandlung das volle Sinnesvermögen des Auges gar nicht aus; das Zuschnappen scheint mit optischen Afferenzen nur locker verschränkt zu sein. Dagegen lernt nach Eikmanns die Erdkröte leicht, bestimmte Reize mit dem ersten Glied der Beutefanghandlung zu verknüpfen.... Offenbar merkt sich die Kröte beim Richten weit mehr Einzelheiten des Zielobjekts als beim nachfolgenden Fixieren und Schnappen." The reference to "Hinsches T-Phänomen" is to the phenomenon of carrying out the act of snapping quite long after the lure has been removed, sometimes even repeating the lurch and snap at the empty place. See G. Hinsche, "Ein Schnappreflex nach 'Nichts' bei Anuren" (1935). Hinsche was particularly struck by the persistence of the toad's attention to a spot once fixated if the act had not been completed. He writes (p. 116): "Nach Ausbildung des T-Phänomens wurde in etwa 10 cm Entfernung von der bewegungslos nach dem leeren Fleck starrenden Kröte ein zweiter ebenfalls am Faden gehaltener Mehlwurm bewegt. Die Ablenkung der Aufmerksamkeit von dem leeren Fleck auf das lebende Futtertier gelang in vielen Fällen nur schwer und mit einer gegen das normale Verhalten deutlich verlängerten Reaktionszeit."

and inspired the theory which Lorenz and Tinbergen hold of a hierarchy of neural "centers," each controlling a lower one, down to a reflex "center" which triggers the consummatory act. Their neurological picture may be somewhat too simple even for the anuran brain, since so far, at least to my knowledge, the series of "centers" has not been found (which does not imply that it doesn't exist); but certainly the characters of the earliest and the last subacts are patent, though the graduated order of automatization claimed for the intervening acts is more assumptive than demonstrable.[48] There is convincing evidence that in the lower animals, at least, the situation that obtains at the beginning of an instinctive act engenders the total performance, even a day-long succession of cycles, so that any modification of the course of the act has to be introduced very early, while the impulse is forming under the influence of extero-afferences. The preparatory phase is the phase of adaptation. So Tinbergen tells, for instance, how G. P. Baerends found that when a digger-wasp was working on several holes he could make her bring more food than usual to a hole by robbing it, and less than usual to another one by partly filling it. "But," he said, "these changes influenced the wasp only when they were made before the first visit. Any later change had not the slightest effect. The situation in the hole at the time of the first visit determined the wasp's behaviour for the whole day. On the basis of the situation she found in the three holes she was attending, the wasp chose the one she supplied during the rest of the day."[49]

[48] A full account of the "hierarchical" theory of instinct may be found in Tinbergen's *The Study of Instinct*, which also contains many valuable ideas and interesting facts that might support other interpretations. The theory in question, however, is most succinctly stated on p. 107: "It seems ... that the centres of each level of the hierarchical system control a type of appetitive behaviour. This is more generalized in the higher levels and more restricted or more specialized in the lower levels. The transition from higher to lower, more specialized types of appetitive behaviour is brought about by special stimuli which alone are able to direct the impulses to one of the lower centres, or rather to allow them free passage to this lower centre. This stepwise descent of the activation from relatively higher to relatively lower centres eventually results in the stimulation of a centre or a series of centres of the level of the consummatory act, and here the impulse is finally used up." His further treatment of the concepts suggested but not defined in this passage requires a reading of his book.

[49] *Ibid.*, pp. 9–10. The source of Tinbergen's account is in G. P. Baerends, "Fortpflänzungsverhalten und Orientierung der Grabwespe *Ammophila campestris* Jur." (1941). There are, however, gradations in the operation of this principle, which may indicate the relative lengths of single act-tensions in different animal species. In a study of the pyramid-building ghost crabs of northeastern Africa, "Konstruktion und Signalfunktion der Sandpyramide der Reiter-krabbe *Ocypode*

The fact that the first stage of a protracted or complex total act in a relatively simple nervous system is the decisive stage for adaptation to ambient conditions, as well as the "pacemaker" for all its own repetitions, shows the unitary nature of instinctive acts. The main impulse, once it has been perceptually directed, really initiates a rhythmic continuum, or activity, for the day. We human agents hold our acts together by a conception of purpose and means, involving causes and effects, which holds us to our original intention; and we survey the results of our total performance to judge whether it is complete, and whether it was appropriate. An imaginative presentation of the conditions we hope to effect is contained in the purposive concept. But that is a human method. In animal acts, the over-all tension is preformed in the impulse, and the act is apparently not controlled by an image of external conditions to be achieved, but by a constant internal pressure toward its consummation.[50]

The standard laboratory method of making long, repetitious series of experiments, tabulating the results simply in two columns, positive (the looked-for response) and negative (any other), and regarding a statistically significant percentage of positive results as proof of whatever hypothesis is being tested tends to obscure not only the fact that a

---

saratan Forsk. (Decapoda Brachyura Ocypodidae)" (1967), K. E. Linsenmair, describing the "building periods" of the crabs and the advance of their sand pyramids by distinct stages, remarks that if a pyramid is experimentally tampered with, reduced, increased or removed, the crab will adjust his acts to the condition of the structure, but only if he (all builders are males) finds the change at the commencement of a building period: "Eingriffe vor dem 'ersten Auftauchen' zu Beginn einer Bauphase ... lösten immer das dem Zustand der Pyramide gemässe Verhalten aus; dagegen liessen sich die Krabben durch Verändern ihrer Pyramiden *während* einer Bauphase oft erheblich stören...." So he concludes "dass der *Pyramidenzustand zu Beginn jeder Bauphase neu beurteilt* wird. Im gegansatz zur Sandwespe *Ammophila*, bei der ein vergleichbarer Primäreindruck während eines 'Inspektionsbesuches' starr festlegt, wieviele Raupen in eine Bruthöhle eingetragen werden müssen (Baerends), kann das Bauverhalten von *O. saratan* auch durch Sekundäreindrücke modifiziert werden" (p. 415). Evidently, the length of the total act of the ghost crab's building is intermediate between that of the wasp's day-long act and the toad's single feeding performance.

[50] Lorenz expressed this view long ago; Tinbergen, in *The Study of Instinct*, p. 106, refers to his scattered statements of it, saying: "Lorenz has pointed out ... that the end of purposive behaviour is not the attainment of an object or a situation itself, but the performance of the consummatory action, which is attained as a consequence of the animal's arrival at an external situation ... releasing the consummatory act. Even psychologists who have watched hundreds of rats running a maze rarely realize that, strictly speaking, it is not the litter or the food the animal is striving toward, but the performance itself of the maternal activities or eating."

rival hypothesis might be proved by exactly the same figures, but also the theoretical value which may lie in negative findings. It is not customary to study the statistics of failure with the same interest as the "positive" columns. Yet the nature of failures may be revealing; one rat-psychologist, at least, reached the conclusion that performance rather than practical effect is the aim of behavioral acts, by a critical interpretation of failures reported in an article by another experimenter. The procedures described in that article were intended to demonstrate the effects of "delayed reinforcement" on the discriminative responses of rats to a bar which had to be pushed one of two possible ways to obtain food with a delay of from two to thirty seconds. After each "correct" response the bar was withdrawn and the food, after an interval, was given. The results were in no wise unexpected; two to five seconds made no difference, thirty seconds proved too long. But what led Dr. Voeks to her reinterpretation of the rats' behavior was a footnote, which reported that in the original arrangement of the experiment the bar was withdrawn following any response, right or wrong, whereupon the right response was reinforced by feeding, the other not. This led to the odd result of frequent failure even with brief delay, or none, before food was given, "several animals having a food delay of two to five seconds showing no sign of learning the correct response. With some animals, several hundred incorrect responses were made in succession without . . . any food reward. . . ." Dr. Voeks concluded that the crucial element in closing the act is not the "reward" but the withdrawal of the bar, because this so changes the situation that the act is over: "the preservation of a response depends upon the removal of the animal from the situation following the response. . . . The response last made in the situation is fixed. . . ." If food is given, the animal starts a new act (the usual conclusion of a consummated one), "which behavior changes his whole pattern of proprioception." In long delay, the animal concludes the act involving the bar and then does other things which "extinguish" the bar response, whatever it was. The food appearing half a minute later belongs to another act.[51]

As the earliest overt phases of instinctive acts, which are continuous with covert ones in the realm of impulses, seem to be the most intense, and in low animals the only ones sensitive to impingements from the external world, so the last phase, the consummation, whether successful or abortive, also has its special character: it is the most fixed ele-

[51] Virginia Voeks, "What Fixes the Correct Response?" (1945), pp. 49–50. The article which led to her reflection was C. T. Perin's "The Effect of Delayed Reinforcement upon the Differentiation of Bar Responses in the White Rat" (1943).

ment of the total act. This fact was already evident to one of the earliest analysts of instinctive behavior, W. Craig, who pointed it out in an article which is still valued and referred to by the ethological psychologists: "Appetites and Aversions as Constituents of Instinct" (1918). The text is full of animals "seeking stimuli" and even stimulated to action by the absence of a stimulus,[52] but Craig no longer subscribed to the pure Pavlovian doctrine of animal action as compounded out of innate localized reflexes, direct or conditioned and/or concatenated; and in questioning that doctrine he noted the relative freedom of "appetitive behavior" in comparison to the standardized performance of the consummatory stage. "An appetite," he said, "is accompanied by a certain *readiness to act*. When most fully predetermined, this has the form of a chain reflex. But in the case of most supposedly innate chain reflexes, the reactions of the beginning or middle part of the series are not innate, ... but must be learned by trial. The end action of the series, the consummatory action, is always innate" (p. 92).

This is essentially the pattern of instinctive acts which Heinroth, Lorenz, Tinbergen, Kortland, Thorpe and many other observers have found. The beginning and the end of the act are its essential elements —impulse and consummation—spanned by a single arc of nervous tension. In an elementary stage of its evolution an act such as food-catching was probably motivated by contact of food substance with the animal's body, as it is for amoeboid forms whose integument undergoes a brief change at the touch of a food particle, admits the morsel and encompasses it. Then the emenation of soluble factors from the food substance, reaching the animal in advance of actual collision with their source, are enough to set up a taxis toward the particle: the first orienting reflex. The two parts of the total feeding act would then be likely to undergo different evolutionary changes, the processes of ingestion developing with the anatomical and physiological advances of the organism, the subacts of approach and contact-making perhaps more rapidly and freely, with environmental changes plus the increasing

[52] Craig defines an appetite as "a state of agitation which continues so long as a certain stimulus, which may be called the appeted stimulus, is absent. When the appeted stimulus is at length received it stimulates a consummatory reaction, after which the appetitive behavior ceases and is succeeded by a state of relative rest" (p. 91). This is, of course, the language of the then prevailing "mechanistic" view, of which Lorenz remarked that the chief fault of its originators was "that they conducted only such experiments as were beforehand destined to confirm the theory.... So the central nervous system, poor thing, never got the opportunity to show that it could do more than answer to stimulation" ("The Comparative Method in Studying Innate Behavior Patterns," p. 230).

bodily abilities; that is, with the evolution of the agent in its growing ambient. The consummatory act has its own subacts; in a protozoan the whole process may be comparable to that which, in most metazoa, takes place after the consummatory phase of "eating," i.e., after the swallowing reflex has made sure of the catch. Even internal, chemical and kinetic actions undergo great evolutionary changes; but in their phylogenetic courses they fall under the control of the autonomic nervous system, whereas the orienting acts fall to the motor action system, the voluntary muscles and their nerves. Behavioral impulses generally arise from the latter system. In some lower forms of life, such as anurans and urodeles, hunting consists of perceptual orientation and then an unguided leap or lurch with open mouth ready to close, on the prey or on emptiness. With the evolutionary advance to higher forms it comes to include many very elaborate subacts—tracking, digging, the various forms of fishing practiced by birds, bats, raccoons and even by water-shy cats.

The development of such behavioral acts is sometimes so astounding that many psychologists and almost all animal-loving laymen cannot believe that the animals' performances are still instinctive. Hoarding food in summer "for the winter" seems an act of true foresight; and some ways of storing and finding it, as for instance the methods of the Swedish nutcrackers (Nucifraga) have been cited as wonderful feats of memory and planning.[53] Still more extraordinary are the habits of the mound-building birds (family Megapodidae) in which the male builds a huge mound of leaves, then digs a hole in it some 18 inches deep, into which the female lays her eggs, whereupon he spends months tending the "incubator," which is heated by fermentation within and sunlight from above, and kept at a temperature of about 90° F. by his constant work of opening and closing the mound according to the temperature changes of the air.[54]

---

[53] See Van Tyne and Berger, *Fundamentals of Ornithology*, p. 244: "These large jaylike birds fly considerable distances (up to 3¾ miles) from their haunts in the evergreen-forested hills to gather hazelnuts in the lowland. Filling their throats with nuts, the Nutcrackers fly back to the evergreen forest, bury and carefully hide the load of nuts in a single hole which they dig in the ground, and then hasten for another load. This process is carried on with hardly a break from sunrise to sunset during two or three autumn months. Then all through the winter and early spring they feed on these nuts, digging down through as much as 18 inches of snow to recover them. Swanberg believes that in their very successful search for these caches (86 per cent, or better) they depend entirely on memory."

[54] A good account of this habit and its variations in different species, or in one species under different conditions, is given by S. C. Kendeigh, *Parental Care and*

Now, the respective characters of the first and last phases of a relatively simple instinctive act, such as a frog's fly-catching—the first essentially an act of perceptual orientation, the last so stereotyped that it simulates a reflex—together may long have constituted the whole act. Early aquatic ancestors of our amphibians probably moved without aim, as many fishes do, snapping at such food morsels as they might meet on bottom or by nosing along under the surface, or, perchance, in the body of the water. Then there was no introductory alerting and orientation; the feeling of contact, at best presaged by a small aura of scent, was so close to the consummatory snap and swallowing that there was hardly a moment of expectancy between them. But with the development of a live-insect diet and terrestrial habits, the beginning and the end of the feeding act moved apart; only those individuals that could withhold the snap long enough to fixate the prey, which is apt to make the fixated object or spot a terminal of motion (as every learner on a bicycle knows), escaped starvation. The act expanded into a sequence of perception, conative posturing, and finally the strike.

This hypothetical but very probable expansion of a basic instinctive act is reminiscent of the growth of somatic acts which N. H. Horowitz observed in *Neurospora*: a successive increase of preparatory chemical activities synthesizing metabolites essential to the plant, when the autochthonic supply of them was exhausted. The final metabolic act was old and generally unchanging; but its rise from the trophic impulse evolved as the cultures which could not perform it any more on their depleted substrate died, and left the field to the few mutant strains that synthesized the needed compound.[55]

One fact supporting the parallel between the evolution of instinctive behavior and the biochemical evolution in the molds is that several investigators of instinct have found the rising stage of such complex, species-characteristic acts the most plastic, and in higher animals most steadily and minutely guided by peripheral sense.[56] Tinbergen has also

---

Its Evolution in Birds (1952), pp. 193–94; also by H. J. Frith, "Breeding Habits of the Family Megapodidae" (1956). Frith has also written a more popular article, "Incubator Birds" (1959), with helpful illustrations.

[55] Cf. above, p. 38n.

[56] Paul Weiss, in an early article, "Tierisches Verhalten als 'Systemreaktion.' Die Orientierung der Ruhestellung von Schmetterlingen gegen Licht und Schwerkraft" (1925), observed the fixity of a total act of the insect, such as crawling up a wall under the influence of light and gravity which held it to a vertical direction, and the variability of its movements in adjustment to the surface: "Die Schritte sind bald grösser, bald kleiner, greifen einmal weiter nach rechts, einmal mehr links aus, überspannen kleine Löcher, übersteigen oder umgehen Unebenheiten und Hinder-

noted that young animals, showing immature forms of acts which belong to later periods of life, exhibit rudimentary forms of the consummatory act, whereas adult individuals in which the impulse to a complete act has not yet gathered full strength show incomplete preparatory behavior.[57] Also, a theorist whose basic attitudes are sharply opposed to Tinbergen's, Daniel Lehrman, has found similar indications that the hereditary elements in typical behavior, whether "innate" or peculiarly likely to be "learned" by a particular species, have developed their complicated sequences by the "Horowitz principle" of increasing preparatory steps.[58] The fact that here the ontogenetic development of a complex behavior pattern presents a model for a possible phylogenetic process demonstrates the pervasiveness of the act form in all vital phenomena and the recurrence of evolutionary principles on the most widely separated levels.

The capacity of some large acts to span long periods of time in waiting for the appropriate situations to develop which will implement their progress and consummation has also been observed in behavioral contexts,[59] as Dombrowski and others found it in the suspended somatic

---

nisse; was aber als Ganzes regelmässig zustande kommt, ist die 'Vertikalaufwärtsbewegung' " (p. 172). Elsewhere on the same page he said: "Diese *Plastizität* der Bewegungsfähigkeit eines Tieres ist sehr beachtenswert."

Tinbergen, in *The Study of Instinct*, p. 105, spoke similarly of "appetitive behavior"—the perceptually guided, orienting stage of instinctive acts: "Contrary to the consummatory action it is not characterized by a stereotyped motor pattern, but rather by (1) its variability and plasticity and (2) its purposiveness."

[57] *The Study of Instinct*, pp. 139–41.

[58] In a paper, "On the Organization of Maternal Behavior and the Problem of Instinct" (1956), read at the Paris Symposium on Instinct, Dr. Lehrman, speaking of the development of crop-feeding of young doves in the nest—a process of regurgitation, motivated in the parent birds by the squab's pecking at the parent's bill—explained: "It appears that they must already be sitting on the squab for reasons arising in another behavioral situation (i.e. incubation), in order for the squab to provide stimulation leading to regurgitation-feeding. Once the regurgitation has taken place, however, subsequent feeding episodes are more and more organized as behavior patterns leading up to the act of regurgitation. The head movements leading up to the feeding act, and the approach of the parent to the nest, become integrated into an organized motor pattern probably on the basis of selective learning" (p. 491).

[59] In a discussion following the reading of another paper at the aforementioned Paris symposium, Marc Klein's "Aspects biologiques de l'instinct reproducteur dans le comportement des mammifères" (1956), one of the symposiasts, M. Courrier, said: "Le phénomène de l'acceptation du mâle ... permet d'établir une sorte de hiérarchie parmi les espèces. Au sommet se placent les espèces à ponte provoquée.... Le plus souvent, la femelle est à ponte spontanée; néanmoins, elle n'accepte

activities of bacteria, though certainly on a different time scale. One of the most variable and often intricate performances in the mating of animals is courtship; this behavior, preceding copulation, has both internal and external difficulties to meet: inwardly, an abnormally high emotional tension with violent impulses pressing for enactment, and outwardly a need for concomitant, complementary acts of another individual. It is the frequent failure to find a partner momentarily ready to join the rising passion and implement the sexual act that motivates the evolution of courtship activities.

An extreme case of such elaboration, with a strong indication of its phylogenetic origin, may be seen in the behavior of the bower birds of Australia and New Zealand, which A. J. Marshall has described in all the detail he could gather about these little-known birds (some kinds are well known to ornithologists and also to woodsmen and campers, but many have rarely been observed).[60] Their most striking peculiarities are, of course, their so-called bowers, structures built by the male birds out of twigs, grass, fibers, etc., usually on the ground under a tree in the forest, fronted or sometimes surrounded by a cleared space on which the bird deposits various objects—green leaves or such as have pale undersides that he turns up, berries, bleached bones, flowers, snail shells, bottle caps, stolen keys and other bright objects. In this area he postures and jumps about, sometimes holding a colored or white object in his beak, while the female, often hidden in the bower, passively watches his antics. This may go on for weeks or even months. After copulation she goes away to build her nest and rear her young without his help; in most cases he remains at the bower and continues his display for some time. Some species, especially after the mating season, will gather in one large court and perform in company, but apparently each for himself, i.e., without reference to any other bird's acts.

The building of "bowers" (of which Marshall distinguishes three

---

habituellement le mâle qu'au moment où les oeufs sont libérés et peuvent être fécondés. Quant à la Chauvesouris, elle présente un comportement assez extravagant, car elle accepte le mâle en automne, de longs mois avant l'ovulation; fort heureusement, l'hibernation survient à temps, et les spermatozoides ... peuvent conserver leur pouvoir fécondant jusqu'au réveil printanier" (p. 341). Jean Benoit topped this example with one still more "extravagant," the case of *Salamandra atra*, saying: "Chez cette espèce vivipare, qui vit en haute montagne, la gestation peut durer quatre ans. Le froid qui sévit en altitude arrête la gestation après quelques semaines, ou moins, de son évolution. La gestation reprend l'année suivante, puis est de nouveau stoppée, et ceci plusieurs années de suite, jusqu'à son achèvement" (p. 343).

[60] *Bower Birds. Their Displays and Breeding Cycles* (1954).

general types) and the decoration of display courts are certainly habits unmatched in the rest of the avian order (the pyramids built by the male ghost crabs in connection with sexual display may present a functional parallel to the bower).[61] The most astonishing performance, however, is that of "painting" the inside of the bower with berry juice, charcoal-stained mud, green leaf pulp or other colorful material that can be made to stick on its surface. This is a somewhat individual practice; not all members of the species wherein it is found will do it.[62] Some birds collect charcoal, macerate green leaves or stems, and when the pulp is mixed with saliva, roll it into a pellet inside the bill and jab with it as with a juicy berry, leaving a spot at every contact. This action has often been cited as an example of tool-using by an animal, and even likened to using a paintbrush; but Marshall explicitly declares that the wad is not a brush,[63] and brings some evidence that the bird does not perceive it as a tool, since it does not even seem to see the little pellet as an object.[64]

This fantastic mode of avian courtship presents a magnified picture of the widespread normal form, with the source of its exaggeration quite in evidence, namely, a progressive phylogenetic lengthening of the sexual phase in the procreative act. The mating impulses of the male and the female, instead of being fairly well synchronized as in most animals, have somehow moved apart, probably by degrees through

[61] The same comparison occurred to Linsenmair, though I think he carries it in a wrong direction. See his article cited in n. 49 above: "Das Pyramidenbauverhalten, als *aktives, optisches Markieren des Kopulationsplatzes,* welches *dauerndes Signalisieren des Erbauers selbst überflüssig macht*—ist in dieser hochentwickelten Form eine—soweit bekannt—einzigartige Erscheinung im Tierreich. Am ehesten noch vergleichbar sind die Balzplätze der Laubenvögel. Doch erhöhen die Lauben nur die unentbehrliche Wirkung des sichtbaren ♂ und seiner artgemässen Balzweisen" (p. 449). Since the bower bird needs a support for his time-filling activity rather than a substitute to make it dispensable, the comparison rests on a wrong principle; the true parallel will engage us later.

[62] *Bower Birds,* pp. 51–52.

[63] In a popular article, "Bower Birds" (1956), Dr. Marshall wrote: "The bird first collects some charcoal—of which there is plenty available in a country periodically swept by forest fires—and grinds it up in its beak to a sticky paste. Then it selects a fragment of bark and fashions a tiny oval wad. Some observers have supposed that this implement serves as a paint brush, but in actual fact the bird uses it as a stopper which keeps its beak slightly open and allows the charcoal stain to ooze from the sides of the beak" (pp. 50–51).

[64] Cf. *Bower Birds,* p. 52: "The wads of bark, still saturated with charcoal and saliva, are often left discarded on the floor of the avenue. Decorations, on the other hand, are never placed within the bower, nor is a fallen leaf allowed to remain there an instant after the owner arrives."

centuries, so that all the male's impulses relating to procreation—nest-building, providing, feeding, song and all other ways of occupying territory—have yielded their repertoire elements to the protracted courtship we find today.[65]

As acts can be expanded, so they can also be contracted. On the somatic level, down to the cellular and even the molecular, this occurs in the higher forms of life between generations in the continuity of a stock;[66] but it may also take place in behavioral acts, where it appears mainly as a sort of "telescoping" of stages, together with some reduction in the spatial scope of movements. E. A. Armstrong remarks that a male wren's nest-invitation display may be curtailed if the female already knows that nest;[67] H. Hediger, whose main studies have been of mammals rather than birds, found that the successive phases of the procreative act: oestrous, coition, pregnancy, birth, lactation and again oestrous, could be "telescoped" to various degrees by curtailment of one phase through premature onset of the next.[68] Another example of

[65] Dr. Marshall has speculated in the same vein on this expansion of the courtship act in bower birds; see *Bower Birds*, p. 22: "The males ... produce spermatozoa months before the females ovulate. Although the male has often been potentially ready to reproduce for many weeks, ovarian development is slow in all species so far studied and ovulation seems to be delayed until the changing environment presents to the female exteroceptors a pattern—a 'species requirement'—to which she has an innate capacity to respond." And further, p. 53: "I believe that bower-plastering is essentially an extension of the courtship-feeding phenomenon that is so widespread in birds." On p. 64 he remarks that the "fierceness" of some display acts suggest "that in this species [the satin bird] display is basically closely allied to the general threat complex which the bird has developed as part of the protection of ... its territory.... It would seem that gestures originally evolved as part of a mechanism of aggression have become part of a display mechanism which is released during emotional excitement of a somewhat different kind." Finally, p. 171: "Both males and females of most birds possess an inherent urge to build nests. Today only female bower-birds (as far as is known) build nests. These are built of twigs. The males ... have taken to building twig structures on the display-ground ... which is the focal point of their activity and, along with the female, of their interest. Nest-building among females is controlled essentially by the seasonal liberation of hormones. The same is true of bower-building. Therefore, it would seem that bower-building may have originated as a displacement activity that is fundamentally allied to nest-building." Elsewhere (pp. 65–66) he observed (in "ethological" terms that go rather uncritically through his whole book): "These activities have flowed into the vacuum, so to speak, created by the female's unwillingness ... to exhibit the sign stimulus to which an innate releasing mechanism in the male is probably hereditarily attuned to respond."

[66] See Vol. I, p. 380.

[67] *The Wren* (1955), p. 124.

[68] In the discussion following Marc Klein's paper, already cited, "Aspects biolo-

act contraction, more strictly behavioral, is given by Noble and Bradley in their study of mating procedures in lizards.[69] These observations, by the way, revealed the astonishing facts that in the species investigated the females have no sexual "drive" (so that the frequent statement that the male's display "attracts females" is without foundation), and the male shows no sign of knowing females from males,[70] but will subject weaker males to his sexual passion as often as females; so it is only because of the constant activity of the males that probably all females become impregnated sooner or later. The authors list four phases of the one-sided courtship, ending with copulation ("Act IV"), and say prefatorily of the species in question: "*Ameiva chrysolaema* has a complex mating performance, which it endeavors to follow even under difficult circumstances." They then proceed to describe the four steps to consummation, the first of which seems to be a purely organic excitement on the part of the male.[71] The second step is seeking a mate. "He may follow either a male or a female of his own species about the cage and he may rapidly transfer his attention from one sex to the other. He takes a position directly over the back of his unwilling partner and walks or runs along with his belly lying along his partner's back. The rate of movement depends upon the activity of the partner.... If the partner is very active in trying to avoid him, he ... slips immediately into the next phase of the courtship."[72]

---

giques de l'instinct reproducteur dans le comportement des mammifères," Hediger asserted "dass man bei den verschiedenen Säugetierarten verschiedene Grade der Ueberschneidung der einzelnen Fortpflanzungsphasen findet. Als Norm kann gelten die Reihe: Oestrus, Begattung, Trächtigkeit, Geburt, Laktation, Oestrus. Diese Anordnung gilt etwa für viele Raubtiere oder Affen. Von rechts nach links kann es zu einer 'Teleskopierung' kommen, d. h. zu einer zunehmenden Ueberschneidung mit dem Ergebnis einer beschleunigten Geburtsfolge. Beim Pferd beispielsweise schiebt sich der Oestrus weit in die Laktation hinein, bis zum 11, 9., 7. oder sogar 3. Tag post partum ..." (p. 340).

[69] G. K. Noble and H. T. Bradley, "The Mating Behavior of Lizards; Its Bearing on the Theory of Sexual Selection" (1933).

[70] Or at least, no sign that he cares, for, speaking of no particular genus, the authors say, "A male never fights a female" (p. 60), implying that he does distinguish the sexes when it is relevant, but does not find it so for sexual gratification.

[71] "Sexual activity is always initiated by the male. He begins to rub his cloacal region from side to side on the ground. He repeats this performance at intervals ... and may continue the action for two or three minutes.... The male goes through his preliminary performance apparently without having seen the females in the cage with him, his eyes often being closed and his back turned to them. In no case was there the slightest evidence that a female stimulated the male to begin this performance" (p. 31).

[72] *Ibid.*, pp. 32–33.

The next phase is the most complicated, since the partner (male or female) is fighting the rapist, but their further acts need not delay us here. As the whole process nears its consummation, the intervening subacts are still adaptive, contingent on the behavior of the partner, who is gradually immobilized by a process of rubbing, which may be persuasive—that is, pleasant—or hypnotic, or paralyzing,[73] then suddenly all groping and guiding responses cease, and the stereotyped movements of copulation supervene.

The point illustrated by all these instances is that the large instinctive acts of animals arise from apparently quite massive impulses, so their tensions may hold over long periods of time from inception to consummation, tolerate a good deal of interference without breaking, accommodate if not entrain a great many lesser impulses (such as responses to concomitant sensory impacts), and expand or contract in adaptation to the progress of the ambient situation. Such a view of animal life is very different from any that one can formulate in terms of stimuli and responses. An organism activated from moment to moment purely by successive external stimuli, like the cybernetic toys Grey Walter described,[74] could never carry through large acts like some hunting techniques, procreative patterns or animal peregrinations. There is no reason why stimuli should arrange themselves so providentially that millions of organisms should find them well ordered to produce appropriate responses from moment to moment. Many creatures, and by no means "primitive" or "low" ones, do often react to entirely fortuitous details in their ambient, which may properly be called "stimuli." The result, however, is not a wonderful display of adaptive behavior, but an exhibition of senseless, rapidly shifting responses, usually in an anomalous situation.[75]

[73] In this process, "he drops his pelvic region to one side of his partner and stands on the hind and front feet of one side only. He keeps his other legs pressed against his partner's opposite side and rubs that side vigorously with his hind leg while pressing the upper inner portion of this leg against the skin of her flank just anterior to her thigh.... Since the partner usually makes a desperate effort to escape the courting male, the leg rubbing is ... kept up until the male finds that his partner is quiet. This may require three or four minutes of desperate rubbing by the courting male" (p. 34).

[74] See Chap. 12, pp. 5–6, above.

[75] K. S. Lashley, in his "Notes on the Nesting Activities of the Noddy and Sooty Terns" (1915), p. 63, said: "In all its activities, where reaction to a new situation is involved, the behavior of the birds has a peculiarly impulsive character. One group of stimuli seems to gain momentary control and determine the bird's reaction in spite of contradictory elements in the situation as a whole. If a chick is taken from its nest and put down among strange adults they are at once attracted by its cries

Under normal circumstances countless impulses touched off by casual peripheral impingements are overridden by current acts stemming from larger impulses. It is the nature of these large impulses, motor and locomotor, that really shapes the ambient of an instinctively enacted life. They have not been studied with anything like the attention that has been given to perceptions, yet they probably are as important to what various animals perceive as the sensory capacities themselves; for in the frame of instinctive impulses and their expressions percepts function otherwise than in the human sphere. If we would speculate on what an animal sees or fails to see in its environment, we must start from what it is doing; for it sees whatever will implement or frustrate its acts. Their implementations may be materials, special places, and above all vistas and avenues permitting an act in progress to continue, unfold from one move to another; that is, the creature has an eye for enticements, openings and options, perhaps not far ahead, but arising as they become relevant. In this serpentine, ever-developing ambient, impending frustrations of acts, ranging from small obstacles to threats of instant death, appear with the same continual emergence as the successive opportunities.

The reason why animals, operating without concepts or symbols, can function as effectively as men might do in similar situations, and sometimes more effectively than men could, is that their major instinctive acts are highly articulated, phylogenetically developed units, unconfused by any awareness of merely possible exigencies, possible errors, or thoughts of other possible acts. Their instinctual evolution has been as gradual as that of the agents themselves. Their successive stages are often physiologically expressed in a homologous pattern of hormone production in which one biochemical phase engenders, and merges into,

---

and crowd around it. Several of them attack it and immediately others rush forward to defend it. The fight becomes general. . . . After a time some of the adults are driven away and leave the victors to strut about. If one of these catches sight of the chick, he attacks it and the fight is soon renewed. I have seen the same bird alternately attack and defend a chick through a number of fights; the sight of the strange chick calls out movements of attack; the sight of an adult attacking a chick calls for defense of the chick. Young chicks, when attacked . . . sometimes force their way under the body of an adult. When this happens it practically always produces a marked change in the behaviour of the adult bird. His aggressive attitude drops away suddenly, he shuffles about for an instant, looks down at the chick, tucks it under him with his beak, and assumes the brooding posture. If he is at some distance from his nest this brooding reaction is of short duration; he soon grows restless, gets up and turns around several times, and finally returns and attacks the chick with renewed savagery."

another; it is through this pattern (today called a "code") that the species-specific forms of instinctive action are heritable. Such complete patterns are not found in human lives; all their elements may occur, but they have been fragmented by the pressions of conceptual processes so there is no automatic sequence nor order of detailed, unpremeditated action any more. That subject belongs essentially to Part V, but the reason for mentioning it here is that it explains our difficulty in imagining instinctive behavior as more than a simple "drive" to copulation, self-defense or participation in mass hysteria. The large instinctive acts of animals are not only "triggered" by impinging conditions—meteorological, seasonal, communal or what not—but sustained by the bodily changes these impressions motivate when a creature is otherwise ready for them: those changes are hormone actions. Most hormone actions are gradual, sometimes cumulative, so they may present a different hormonal pattern at each station of their development, and consequently can sustain a complex total impulse throughout its progressive phases.[76]

As the ambients of higher animals are made by their acts, their places are created largely by instinctive activities, and reflect those behavioral patterns. The fact that a sea bird may be momentarily confused by radical changes in the surroundings of its nest site, such as removal of trees or spectacular pieces of flotsam—stranded barrels, wreckage, etc. —or the addition of new objects, does not mean that these things make its memory image of the site whereby it finds its way back to its nest. The bird gives little evidence of having anything like the memory images whereby we would find a colony we had visited and a particular nest in it; but the fact that it can fit a fairly close repetition of a former act into the re-encountered scene makes this "the same place," one met with what may be the most important feeling for space-construction in animal life—familiarity. Human beings are so used to identifying "landmarks" that we tend to overlook the fact that in driving along a known road, for instance, we see all the unremarked stretches between such

[76] Cf. D. B. Lindsley's comments following C. T. Morgan's Nebraska Symposium paper, "Physiological Mechanisms of Motivation," pp. 38–39: "the ascending reticular activating system is not solely influenced by impulses feeding into it from classical sensory pathways or from corticifugal sources. . . . not only do visceral and nociceptive stimuli give rise to marked activation of the cortex and an enhancement of sympathetic tone, but a delayed humoral effect (adrenaline) causes a persistence of such activation. This . . . acts not upon the cortex directly, but upon the ponto-mesencephalic reticular activating system and then by neural influence upon the cortex. The significant thing here, I believe, so far as motivation is concerned is the sustaining quality of this humoral influence."

special markers with a nearly, if not wholly, subliminal sense of familiarity. In the birds which have amazed ornithologists by their apparent oblivion of visual cues, that general sense of *déjà vu* may be all the identification of objects that they need or make. The removal of an obstacle that used to require a special response does not affect the repetition of the original place-defining act; its absence does not frustrate the special response. Lashley, in the paper cited above, gives a perfect corroborating instance of this principle, namely, the case of a sooty tern whose movements he describes as follows:

"At the edge of the beach two piles of brush were thrown together in such a way as to leave a small overarched passage extending half way through between the piles and opening on the beach to the westward. A pair of sooties had their nest at the inner end of this passage. The bird studied alighted always at the southern end of the brush pile, walked around the southwestern corner, where there was another nest, and then followed the western side of the pile to the opening of the nest. The path was complicated by a dead bay-cedar branch, which projected from the face of the pile and forced the bird to stoop and turn out to the left. The bird was seen to follow this path accurately in five successive trips to the nest. I broke off the branch and removed it, leaving a clear path from x to z [SW corner to nest opening]. On the next two trips to the nest, the *bird went through exactly the same movements of stooping and turning out which had been required by the presence of the dead branch.*"[77]

Lashley, true to the association psychology of the day (1908), concluded that the tern's act was an exhibition of "motor habit."[78] Just what that means is not clear. If the bird had really formed a habit of performing a series of muscular exercises, it ought to have run a similar path wherever it happened to be on the beach, dunes or heath. There is no record of such a phenomenon. What it really did was to repeat the journey which had articulated its nesting place, as that place existed for it. The act, which seemed inappropriate to the human observer once he had removed the obstructing branch, still fitted the sooty's place. If the bird itself had removed the branch, it might thereupon have changed its homeward course.

The same interpretation may be given to the behavior of Thorndike's animals, and to the apparent vagaries of bats and birds that have

[77] "Notes on the Nesting Activities of the Noddy and Sooty Terns," p. 70.
[78] *Ibid.*, p. 72: "In many cases it is evident that after orientation is gained the path to the nest is determined largely by motor habits irrespective of the immediate visual stimuli."

adapted their whole round of life to one place, the confines of a cage. "Places" are not geographical regions, but pragmatic entities, locations of felt events; as such, they may expand or contract with the expansion or contraction of the life to which they belong, which may have several places—feeding, nesting, hiding, courting places—each with its unique, inherent feeling tone, and its own special sense of familiarity when it is revisited.

If, now, we consider this intimacy of an animal's local adaptation, springing from the mutual influence of acts on spatial configurations and of the evolving space on acts, and put it together with the evident need of locomotory acts for the establishment of "place" demonstrated by Held and Hein, we may gain a new possible interpretation of the puzzling process of "imprinting" in the young of many precocial birds and possibly some mammals.[79] Like most ethological terms, "imprinting" has been conceptually blurred almost from its very inception by the two chief malpractices that bedevil psychological theorizing: (1) applying the term beyond its original domain, to habituation, attachment and sundry other effects, and (2) defining it in words that carry a heavy load of dubitable assumptions which consequently are taken for granted—not only "inhibitors" and "releasers" and "sign-stimuli," but also more universally accepted ones like "filial responses" and "social conditioning." I shall use "imprinting" in its strict sense, to denote the frequently observed phenomenon, distinctive enough to deserve a name of its own, that a relatively large object moving at pursuable speed over the floor entices newly hatched chicks (the exact optimum age, in hours, varying with species) of many gallinaceous and anserine birds to follow it about.[80]

[79] On the latter, see E. H. Hess, "The Effects of Meprobamate on Imprinting in Waterfowl" (1957), p. 725: "Although studied mainly in birds, examples of imprinting have been reported in insects, in fish, and in some mammals. Those mammals in which the phenomenon has been reported (sheep, deer, and buffalo) are all animals in which the young are almost immediately mobile when born. Experimental work with mammals has, however, not been done within the framework presented here."

I. Eibl-Eibesfeldt, in "Angeborenes und Erworbenes im Verhalten einiger Säuger" (1963), p. 712, says of newborn agoutis: "Die Jungen stehen gleich nach der Geburt auf allen Vieren, laufen koordiniert.... Sie laufen sogleich jedem sich entfernenden Objekt nach, bei künstlicher Aufzucht auch dem Pfleger, vor allem nach Gesichts- und Hörreizen."

[80] In view of all the careless and vague uses of supposedly "scientific" words, it is a relief to read, in H. Moltz's "Imprinting: Empirical Basis and Theoretical Significance" (1960), p. 294: "The present paper ... will use the term imprinting to denote a particular experimental operation and *not* a process or a mechanism...."

We are so beset, today, by social problems, so aware of social relations, that we are inclined to look for their analogues in animal life wherever a behavior pattern suggests such a parallel. So the juvenile following of a moving object, observed in many walking or swimming birds, was no sooner generally known than it was hailed as a "mechanism" to "socialize" the chicks, attaching them first to their mothers and then to their kind. There are several surveys of the development of the concept, but the one that shows most succinctly the progress of the "social" interpretation is given by Moltz in the article just quoted:

"In 1873 Spalding reported that incubator hatched chicks tended to follow persistently the first moving object to which they were exposed. Heinroth (1910) subsequently . . . reported that graylag geese can be made to respond to humans in filial fashion in preference to adults of their own species if they are exposed to humans just after hatching. . . . Lorenz (1935) . . . extended the empirical basis of Heinroth's observations and provided a theoretical framework within which to interpret these observations. . . .

"Lorenz designated the process or mechanism involved by a special term—imprinting. . . .

"When a bird becomes 'imprinted' to a particular stimulus it will readily transfer its following response as well as other social responses to all members of the class to which that stimulus belongs. . . . Lorenz conceived of imprinting (as it operates in nature) as a method of acquiring a 'consciousness of species'; a method that insures that social behav-

---

Thus, imprinting will be defined as the procedure of visually presenting to an animal a large moving object during the first several hours of its life under conditions that insure that the object is not associated with such conventional reinforcing agents as food and water. This procedure has been found to evoke a close following of the object in such precocial avian species as ducks, geese, coots, moorhens, and domestic fowl. However, imprinting as defined above, has *not* been unequivocally shown to induce following either in passerine birds or mammals. . . . To broaden the definition of imprinting so that the present discussion might encompass these species and perhaps, in addition, include a greater variety of behavior patterns is not likely to prove theoretically salutary." The only detail of Moltz's definition with which I could quarrel is the stipulation that the lure must be visual, as some birds, e.g., wood ducks, appear to follow the parental call, and some fairly different calls, as readily as they follow an object, provided the call moves away. He himself writes in the same paper: "Collias and Collias found that young ducklings of several species will . . . move in the direction of a repetitive low-pitched sound even when the source of the sound is not visible. Fabricius and Boyd . . . reported that rhythmic repetition of a brief sound will elicit strong following whether or not it is associated with a moving object. Indeed, some of the ducklings responded more strongly to the retreating sound than to the moving object" (p. 307).

ior will extend beyond the parent but not beyond the species" (pp. 292–93).

Lorenz maintained, as a chief tenet in his theory, that imprinting is an irreversible process, and that a young animal once imprinted by an adult of another species will prefer that species to its own, so that it will not flock or mate with its own kind. But this broad assertion was based on very complicated conditions, mixing true imprinting experiments[81] with such different procedures as putting newly hatched birds under brooding adults of a different species, to grow up with their young.[82] Both the following of an adult and the attachment formed to foster parents (which might be human beings) have been named "imprinting."

Meanwhile, controlled experiments in field and laboratory have brought a good deal of evidence that calls the primarily "socializing" function of imprinting, *sensu stricto*, in question. If its motivation is really an impulse to be near a particular other animal, it is odd that chicks and ducklings will follow cardboard boxes, balloons and cylinders as readily as they will follow an adult bird, and that they may even be imprinted more readily by such socially absurd objects than by a life-like decoy.[83] I have so far learned of no case in which a chick imprinted

[81] Professor Lorenz has made some controlled experiments, which he describes with little accuracy but great charm and rollicking humor in *King Solomon's Ring* (1957; German original, ca. 1952), especially chap. v, which is unspoiled by anthropomorphic fancies.

[82] E. H. Hess, in "Imprinting" (1959), uses the term in the sense of "establishing 'social' relations," and says: "At the turn of the century, Craig, experimenting with wild pigeons, found that in order to cross two different species it was first necessary to rear the young of one species under the adults of the other. Upon reaching maturity the birds so reared preferred mates of the same species as their foster parents. . . .

"Lorenz was the first to call this phenomenon 'imprinting.'. . . He postulated that the first object to elicit a social response later released not only that response but also related responses such as sexual behavior" (p. 133).

[83] See Hess, "Imprinting," pp. 135–36: "Eight spheres approximately 7 inches in diameter in the colors red, orange, yellow, green, and blue and in achromatic shades of near-black, near-white, and neutral gray were presented to 95 young Vantress broiler chicks as imprinting objects. . . . The stimuli, ranked in their effectiveness for eliciting following during imprinting, from the highest to the lowest, are: blue, red, green, orange, grey, black, yellow, white. . . .

"In order to determine also form preferences in imprinting objects, we took the same spheres . . . and added superstructures of the same coloring, so that the spheres had heads, wings and tails.

". . . the plain ball was found to be the most efficient; the ball with wing and tail-like superstructures, less so; and the ball to which wings, tail and head had been

by a cardboard box extended its attachment to other boxes of "the same species" (presumably, the same brand and manufacturer's number), preferred them later in life to birds of its own feather and tried to mate only with a box.

It has taken good ornithologists and other animal observers a surprisingly long time to suspect that the impulse of young chicks to follow a moving object could be anything else than a "filial response."[84] It is, of course, normally exhibited in a complex of filial relations prepared by the parent's brood-raising act, but that does not make the isolable following response itself filial. The fact that it can occur quite apart from any possible "social" concomitants certainly suggests that its immediate motivation, at least, is something else than an affective attachment. W. H. Thorpe seems to have been the first to conceive the idea that imprinting had anything to do with territory, though he did not connect the following response with what he called "habitat imprinting," but, rather, likened the latter to Lorenz' affective imprinting by a species representative for the subject's entire life. He remarked "that the attachment to a home may be something of the nature of the very rapid and rigid type of learning which Lorenz has called imprinting, and that we may be justified in speaking in some cases of 'habitat imprinting.' Such habitat imprinting is certainly suggested by the behavior of some of the higher Hymenoptera which carry out exploratory flights, usually known as 'locality studies.' For instance, in the case of the wasps of the genus *Bembex*, it is suggested that the first locality study establishes the area and immediate surroundings of the newly emerged insect as 'home' for the rest of its life, and that this may be the basis of the quite extraordinary topographical conservatism persisting year after year in some of these colonies."[85]

---

added, least efficient. We even presented a stuffed brown Leghorn rooster to the chicks, and it was found to be the least efficient model of all in eliciting the following response."

[84] W. Sluckin and E. A. Salzen, in "Imprinting and Perceptual Learning" (1961), p. 66, say: "It seems likely, that a wide variety of moderately intense visual or auditory disturbances of the environment that are brief and repetitive in character are capable of eliciting filial responses in chicks and ducklings"; W. H. Thorpe, in "Some Problems of Animal Learning" (1944), p. 79, writes: "Imprinting, which differs in some respects from associative learning, results in the acquisition of the biologically 'right' object of social relations by conditioning them, not to one fellow member of the species, but to the species pattern as such." By following boxes and (preferably blue) balloons?

[85] "The Evolutionary Significance of Habitat Selection" (1945), pp. 67–68. The term "locality studies" for the circling flights of wasps is typical of the anthropo-

The chicks that follow inanimate objects are not becoming imprinted either by their own kind or by a lifelong home. The phenomenon Dr. Thorpe appears to have in mind can hardly be equated with the effect of the following response, which is, I think, something more immediate and more elementary. The imprint is temporary, serving only to keep the chick in contact with a particular leader while it develops its space feeling and spatial perception by locomotion. The tendency to follow is compounded of visual fixation, which may be momentarily learned, like foot placement, and of the drawing influence of a fixated point if it moves, that is, of a lure, which makes the pristine action-space a path. This explains Hess's finding that the longer the path traveled by the chick the more it seemed to be imprinted by its leader; the time spent in the process made no difference.[86] The further the chick moves behind its leader, the more its action-space becomes structured; wherever that space collapses into nothingness, the animal becomes lost and frightened; hence the ardent pursuit of the direction-giving lure. Muscular feeling seems to enter crucially into the space experience; Hess, working with ducklings, observed that "the strength of imprinting is related directly to the effort expended by the duckling in getting to or keeping up with the imprinting object."[87]

One of the facts which have puzzled students of the following response is that after a certain length of performance, different for different species, and under varying conditions, it wanes, no matter what stimuli are brought to its support.[88] Most of the experimenters have

---

morphizing language whereby the ethologists endow animals with human behavior such as studying, observing rules, winning trophies and handing on traditions—of which we will have more hereafter.

[86] "The Effects of Meprobamate on Imprinting in Waterfowl," p. 729.

[87] Ibid., p. 730.

[88] Cf. Sluckin and Salzen, "Imprinting and Perceptual Learning," pp. 72–73: "Repeated presentation of the imprinted stimulus may lead to an apparent loss of the following response. . . . when chicks were exposed singly to an intermittently moving box . . . they all began to follow in the first hour and stopped following after several hours. A warm hover with food and water was situated to one side of the alley and the chicks spent progressively more time in their vicinity. . . . they had become at least temporarily satiated with the stimulus."

Also Moltz, "Imprinting: Empirical Basis and Theoretical Significance," pp. 299–300: "Following appears to be somewhat more stable in coots and moorhens, for Hinde, Thorpe and Vince . . . observed that a decrease in response strength first became evident after four or five weeks of testing in moorhens and not until seven or eight weeks in coots. There was no doubt, however, that even the intense following of the coot began to wane and that 'by the end of the juvenile phase was lost altogether' " (he is quoting Thorpe's Learning and Instinct in Animals [1956]).

judged the adequacy of the response by the age to which it can be kept up, apparently supposing that this must affect its "socializing" value, and consequently have sought means of prolonging it. If, however, we view their findings from the standpoint of the interpretation here proposed, that the chick is building up its perception of space, those findings appear generally corroborative. Especially an experiment conducted by Moltz and Rosenblum, in which the environment was held invariant over successive trials for the experimental birds but varied for the control group, resulted as one might expect: the ducklings whose enclosure was unvaried, so it was thoroughly familiar after a few structuring sessions behind their leader (a cardboard cube), stopped following considerably sooner than the controls which found themselves and their cube in a new area every day.[89] Equally if not even more indicative are the means whereby following may be reactivated when it is already on the wane: at such a time, according to Sluckin and Salzen, "filial responses can be restored" by introducing strange objects, stationary or mobile, into the familiar place.[90]

The literature concerning imprinting is large and could furnish more examples, but these few may suffice to justify some doubt as to the "filial" nature of the following response. Under natural conditions it is, of course, normally made to a parent bird (in some cases the father, not the mother), so that species bonds should become established at the same time in which the young animal is articulating its action space and engaging its powers of perception. That perception develops gradually with maturation of organs and interested exercise is a generally accepted tenet; but only a few ethologists so far have suggested that orientation and visual learning rest on responses which are not filial, and consequently may be evoked by entirely unparental objects, though

---

Two other observers, F. A. Beach and J. Jaynes, in "Effects of Early Experience upon the Behavior of Animals" (1954), p. 251, describing field experiments on three species of ducks (tufted ducks, eiders and shovellers) report: "Birds that had been imprinted subsequently followed the experimenter [who was emitting an effectual call] whether he walked, swam, or rowed a boat, and paid no attention to adult ducks. After three weeks the following-reaction to humans gradually waned."

[89] The account here used is given by Moltz in the article previously cited (see n. 80 above); the experiment referred to is reported in H. Moltz and L. A. Rosenblum, "The Relation between Habituation and the Stability of the Following Response" (1958). Sluckin and Salzen, "Imprinting and Perceptual Learning," p. 73, make reference to another experiment, saying: "Moltz and Rosenblum have shown that if ducks are habituated to the testing enclosure, then they are less responsive to a moving box than birds not so treated."

[90] "Imprinting and Perceptual Learning," p. 73.

normally they belong to the situation in which filial responses—still more gradually—develop. Beach and Jaynes have remarked on it;[91] and Sluckin and Salzen have made a further distinction, based on J. J. Gibson's theory of vision, whereby they first separate the space-structuring function of the following response from its socializing function, and second—incidentally—throw light on the baffling preference which young chicks show for simple balls as against balls complicated by appendages. As they themselves state their reasoning:

"Gibson ... has suggested that a distinction may be made between the environment and the social components of the environment in terms of the nature of the physical stimulation which they provide. Briefly, in the case of vision, the environment is one of surfaces, whereas the social or animal environment is one of movement and deformation of surfaces. Gibson contends that these are the kinds of information that the organism receives and has to differentiate. We suggest therefore that the process of which imprinting is a part may be considered in these two divisions, i.e. perception of the inanimate environment and perception of the animate environment, and that the development of social responses is part of the second of these two categories."[92] From the very beginning of the chick's pursuit of the moving object, it is doing two things—establishing not only its lacework of paths, but also its visual object constancy. For the latter activity the plainest forms are best; for the spatial integration of vision and motion, one lure may be as good as another.[93]

The great intimacy of relationships between animals' perception and action, the way their space awareness seems to reflect not only the general act form of rising, culminating and being spent, but the special forms of particular acts, may also contribute to our solution of those other major mysteries of animal movements, migration and homing.

[91] See "Effects of Early Experience upon the Behavior of Animals," p. 258: "Quite distinct from the theory of retention in adulthood of the same overt responses learned in infancy is the hypothesis that certain types of early experience influence later behavior by structuring the individual's perceptual capacities. Practically all the studies we have cited in the fields of sensation and learning are based upon this view."

[92] "Imprinting and Perceptual Learning," p. 75.

[93] Cf. Moltz, "Imprinting: Empirical Basis and Theoretical Significance," p. 307: "Hinde, Thorpe and Vince ... found that a black box was somewhat more strongly followed than a moorhen model by both moorhens and coots. However, when all the objects employed were considered, they concluded that there was '... no indication that any particular characteristic, other than movement, was of especial importance.'"

These two phenomena may not be manifestations of the same principle,[94] though I think they are related, so let us consider, first, only the large and spectacular act of migration. The tendency to move periodically over relatively long distances, keeping a steady direction, is a trait that appears in animals of astoundingly diverse stocks—e.g., butterflies, bats, turtles, sea otters, lemmings, grasshoppers, eels, hummingbirds, geese. It is so widespread in the animal kingdom that it may be expected to appear in almost any phylum, class and family, in one genus and not another, and even in one, or a few, or in all but one, species within a genus.[95] The great and at the same time odd distribution of the migratory impulse, which is certainly a hereditary trait, makes it appear like the effect of a very ancient gene (or gene complex), perhaps lying unexpressed in vast numbers of creatures, and easily blocked by circumstances even in stocks in which it normally comes to expression. The inheritance of such a tendency is not hard to accept theoretically, since it is known to be linked with hormonal rhythms, and hormone patterns seem to be essentially gene-controlled. But the impulse is all that we can attribute to heredity; the question of how animals find their way when the spirit moves them to travel remains unanswered.

Migration, for obvious practical reasons, has been systematically studied mainly in birds, where it is most prevalent and observable, and research has centered largely on the problems of their navigation, their supposed memory of routes and apparently constant geographical orientation. All the speculations which have been made on avian means of knowing and keeping a desired course assume, quite unwittingly, a

[94] The careful work of G. V. T. Matthews has demonstrated the presence of two distinct elements in the homing process, namely, orientation, which he considers innate, and navigation, largely learned by experience. The former element probably figures in migratory acts, too, while several differences, largely motivational, distinguish the two phenomena. See his paper, "The Orientation of Untrained Pigeons: A Dichotomy in the Homing Process" (1953).

[95] A. D. Halser, in discussion at a symposium, in reply to a question concerning the migratory behavior of young salmon, said: "It varies with each species.... one has to, in each case, be quite specific about what species is being discussed because they are quite different" ("Underwater Guideposts for Migrating Fishes" [1967], p. 16). Similarly Dorst (*The Migrations of Birds*, p. 313) remarked: "Many authors think they can apply the conclusions they reached when studying one species to all migrants, but nothing is more erroneous. The physiology of a little song-bird and its annual cycle are not the same as those of ducks or sea-birds. In addition to these specific differences, important variations in migration behaviour are caused by environment; populations of a species differ, and there are even individual distinctions."

human concept of the space to be traversed, and consequently of the directional clues which might be found in it. A person flying, especially in a small open plane, as our earliest aviators flew, sees the landscape below him very much like a map; the sky curves not only above him but all around him. He has a basic notion of compass points, north, south, east and west, and of the points which may be determined between them to complete the compass rose. His movements in this frame are guided entirely by observation of objects with fixed or calculably changing locations: stars, sun, landscape (e.g., mountains visible from afar, rivers flowing in known directions and, at closer range, buildings, copses, etc.) or urban sites. It is natural for him to assume that a bird or any other flying animal uses similar means to find its way even over hundreds of miles—thousands, in some cases—from one place to another.

All speculations on avian means of orientation center on the uses of landmarks and skymarks. Birds do tend to follow river valleys, shorelines, etc.; yet many also migrate directly across the Gulf of Mexico, or fly from one point on a coast far out to sea and swing shoreward again to their destination. Any directional signs they could employ must be celestial. The sun is usually supposed to be their chief guide. But since many birds migrate by night, their alleged sun orientation has to be transferred to the night sky and translated into a code of constellations, governed particularly by the Milky Way. Then, to add to the scientist's vexation, they travel under cloud cover by day and by night, often in total darkness; their flight calls are all that tell us of their passage.

Celestial navigation, however, is the most generally accepted hypothesis to explain the fact that birds do find their way over sea and land when a human being would be hard put to it to figure out the course by his keenest observation, calculation and memory. Birds starting their northward or southward flights under cloud cover or at night are supposed to use their memory of the sun or of the sun arc in relation to objects in their familiar environment to depart in the proper direction. Frank C. Bellrose, for instance, describes the behavior of blue teal released from captivity on a sunless day in fall, and speculates as follows: "As a result of prolonged confinement in our outdoor pens, the teal had opportunity to associate compass direction with celestial, landscape, and wind cues. Prior to release under overcast skies, the teal had the opportunity to identify wind direction in relation to the compass rose through association of local landmarks about the pen. Celestial cues provided the teal with the prior knowledge of landmark-to-azimuth relationship. On the day of release, the teal were probably intuitively aware of wind direction even under overcast skies from their previous long association of pen landmarks with the sun."[96]

From all we know of animal perception and observation of physical objects which neither stimulate pursuit nor block locomotion, it is highly improbable that ducks in a yard would associate surrounding trees, fences, water-pans, etc., with celestial cues and wind directions to establish the compass rose, and carry that knowledge with them into the entirely different environment aloft. If the aerial scene, especially its outermost frame,[97] were very radically and suddenly changed—the sun displaced, areas of sea and land exchanged—the migrants might be seriously confused. But ordinarily all shifts of geographical relations and all sidereal motions are gradual, and so wholly assimilated to the flying bird's sense of motion that they are likely to be subliminal elements in perception.

If such navigational theories with regard to birds are implausible, their application to terrestrial and aquatic creatures verges on science fiction. Migration and homing guided by sun and stars, with due allowance for time of day and season, have been claimed for frogs,[98] sunfish,[99] salmon[100] and land turtles[101] (sea turtles' movements have received some interesting theoretical treatment, to be discussed below), and has been looked for in salamanders, though the investigator decided against it on the basis of his observations.[102] No one that I know of has so far even attempted a neurological hypothesis to explain how a frog's or fish's brain could perform any calculations at all, let alone astronomical ones; and the frequently met statement that "there must be

[96] "Orientation in Waterfowl Migration" (1967), p. 92.

[97] D. O. Hebb has brought some convincing evidence that what an animal knows as "place" is visually determined primarily by the most fixed characteristics, i.e., the remotest forms. See *The Organization of Behavior*, p. 92.

[98] For instance, by D. E. Ferguson in "Sun-Compass Orientation in Anurans" (1967). The principle whereby these animals are said to orient themselves "requires that the frog or toad possess three kinds of information: (1) a known shore position relative to a body of water; (2) a view of a useful celestial clue; and (3) a clocking mechanism phased to local time" (p. 22).

[99] Hasler, "Underwater Guideposts for Migrating Fishes," p. 11 ff.

[100] T. J. Hara, K. Ueda and A. Gorbman, in "Electroencephalographic Studies of Homing Salmon" (1965), p. 885, refer to "the stage of open-sea existence, during which salmon seem to navigate by a sun-compass mechanism."

[101] See Edward Gould, "Orientation in Box Turtles *Terrepene c. carolina* Linnaeus" (1957).

[102] See C. R. Shoop, "Orientation of *Ambystoma maculatum*: Movements to and from Breeding Ponds" (1965).

a mechanism which tells them ..." adds nothing whatever to our knowledge.

All explanations of animal pathfinding as navigation by celestial cues impute excessively high mental operations to birds, bats, cetaceans (which would be the strongest candidates) and fish. Yet the amazing acts are patently observable, and typically are carried through without much hesitation, trial and error, or apparent misinterpretation of signals. Clearly there is something more than a use of zodiac signs and sun readings involved in the original orientation of migrating birds. Perhaps our search for the basic navigation compass in their external world is a vain effort, because neither birds nor beasts steer their essential courses by any compasslike means.

In our thinking, the structure of space is so obviously a geometrical one, with north, south, east and west defined by effects of the earth's rotation, that any line of movement is to us a division of space into areas composing its total expanse. Also, we find it axiomatic that a directed movement is directed from one place to another, i.e., from a starting point to a goal, and when the goal is reached the locomotory act is finished. This human way of seeing space raises the questions, for us, how an animal stirred by the migratory impulse knows the direction of its goal, and how, having determined that, it keeps its course exactly in that direction; for a small deviation at the beginning of a very long journey would make a large displacement at the end.

If, however, animal space is built up by non-conceptual acts—which does not mean, as Bethe assumed, unconscious, automatic action[103]— and is essentially a complex of paths and actively evolved places, the possibility of instinctive migratory behavior may be given with the formal character of locomotory acts themselves. The conditions that motivate great or small seasonal movements, over seas and continents or merely from one altitude belt to another on a mountain, in a mass migration, or a partial one, some of the population staying behind or

---

[103] Albrecht Bethe, at the conclusion of his article "Dürfen wir den Ameisen und Bienen psychische Qualitäten zuschreiben?" declares: "Es scheint also, als ob die ganze Gruppe der wirbellosen Thiere ein reines Reflexleben lebte. Es scheint, dass diese Thiere *über keine Sinne, über keine Möglichkeit Erfahrungen zu sammeln und danach ihr Handeln zu modifizieren, verfügten, dass alle Reize unter der Schwelle der sinnlichen Empfindung und Wahrnehmung bleiben und dass diese Thiere rein mechanisch alle die oft so vernunftmässig erscheinenden Thätigkeiten ausüben.* Danach wären die ersten Anfänge psychischen Lebens erst in der Reihe der Wirbelthiere zu suchen" (p. 98). Why reflexes should all be unfelt is not clear; we ourselves have reflexes which we cannot control—vomiting, startle, wincing—which are involuntary but not unfelt.

settling along the way (as our robins do in winter), are so diverse that every species has to be considered on its own terms as to routes or flyways, mode of departure, resting places or uninterrupted through-travel, and so on; but one feature appears to be common to all the larger locomotory acts of animals, and that, I think, underlies their mystifying navigational powers.

As animals live in psychologically established "places" rather than locations, their movements beyond a familiar place are ventures which originate and terminate in that place; that is, their wider movements are excursions. This circular character is prone to appear whenever a departure is not complicated and masked by serving other acts such as search for food, pursuit, escape, standing at bay, hiding, or other practical behavior not in the creature's own territory. Young animals chasing each other may run a long course, but it is circular; it tends to repeat itself again and again, unless the pursued one is suddenly pressed into a deviation. Play is the least practically modified behavior, which might be expected to show a primitive basic pattern in its purest form. But wherever a relatively large locomotory act without a direct goal (e.g., a quarry) is performed, it tends to begin and end in an established place (not necessarily a permanent "territory" of the individual or group). A good example is provided by Hans Klingel,[104] who spent two years watching the behavior of zebras on the Serengeti steppe and the wide grazing grounds within the rim of the extinct Ngorongoro crater in Tanzania, where tens of thousands of the animals are often gathered. Contrary to the reports of more casual observers in the wild and studies on captive animals, he found these zebras (*Equus quagga*) to live by permanent family units consisting of a stallion and several mares and their foals, and by less permanent, yet distinct and cohesive stallion groups. They have no permanent territories, but establish themselves in such loosely constructed herds wherever the terrain is good at the time.[105] He followed and plotted the diurnal movements of one such herd, observing that as long as the zebras occupied the area their activity pattern was largely repetitive from day to day. The sketch map here reproduced from his report (Fig. 13-1) shows the cyclic form of the total itinerary, which underlies the varied activities of the individuals in their natural progress.[106]

---

[104] "Soziale Organisation und Verhalten freilebender Steppenzebras" (1967).

[105] *Ibid.*, pp. 528 ff.

[106] See esp. pp. 614–15: "An klaren, warmen Tagen brachen die Zebras mit Sonnenaufgang (6.30 Uhr) von ihren Schlafplätzen auf und wanderten in die Weidegebiete, die z. T. an die Schlafplätze angrenzten, zu bestimmten Zeiten des

Some very similar records have been obtained by S. Young and E. Goldman of wolf runways, which they describe as follows: "The shape of the runway is generally an irregular circle, the diameter of which may be between 20 and 60 miles. Its extent depends on the amount of food available. . . . Occasionally, one may find what might be termed scouting courses, where wolves make short detours from the main runway. These eventually join the main runway again, and are apparently deviations made in search of prey.

"While traveling their runways, which they generally do counterclockwise, wolves move with a slow, regular trot, as they do on cross-country travel."[107] They map a couple of such runs from the southwest (United States and Mexico), one of which, in Colorado, is shown here (Fig. 13–2).[108]

A most striking observation on the inherent circularity of animal excursions is offered by Dr. Günter Gaffrey, commenting on the behavior of an Afghan bitch. These dogs, as he remarks, were bred as hunters, and since their recent introduction to Europe have lost little of their wonderful vitality. "Their great urge to run may even, in absence of any quarry, break over into overt action [sich abreagieren] spontaneously, without any perceptible external cause, i.e., the dogs, taken on a walk, will suddenly rush away at top speed, and after running several hundred or even thousand meters will circle back to the starting point. During these runs . . . one can only elect to stand still on that spot and await their return, or . . . cut off their homing course, if that lies somewhat off-side, and thus bring them into calling distance and under human control once more. This form of behavior shows certain parallels with the hunting and fleeing flights which every field ornithologist knows. O. Koehler, in a letter, has commented on this subject, as follows: A Spotted Flycatcher flies up suddenly from its perch, and returns by a short loop to exactly the same spot. That may be repeated several

---

Jahres aber bis zu 13 km entfernt waren. . . . Die wandernden Gruppen zogen dicht aufgeschlossen in langen Reihen hintereinander auf ausgetretenen Pfaden. Auf der Tagweide verteilten sie sich, die einzelnen Gruppen waren deutlich voneinander abgesondert. Im Verlauf des Tages zogen sie zur Tränke. . . . Am späten Nachmittag kehrten sie zum Schlafplatz zurück, wo sie die ganze Nacht blieben. . . .

"Der Tagesablauf richtet sich nach den ökologischen Gegebenheiten und wird vom Wetter beeinflusst." See also p. 617: "Da die Zebras nicht territorial leben, sondern sich im Verlauf des Jahres in verschiedenen Teilen ihres grossen Heimatgebietes aufhalten, ändern sich auch die Aktivitätsfolgen im Verlauf des Jahres und passen sich den Bedingungen ihres jeweiligen Standortes an."

[107] The Wolves of North America (1944), Vol. I, p. 81.
[108] Ibid., p. 95.

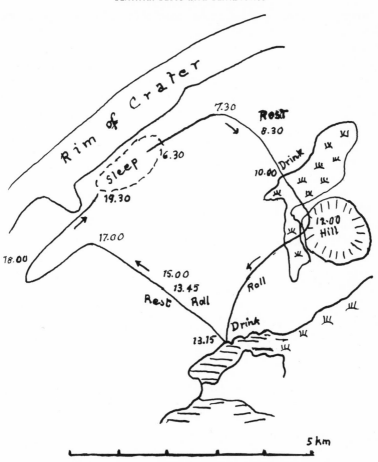

Figure 13–1. Daily Peregrination of a Zebra Family
*the cyclic form of the total itinerary, which underlies the varied
activities of the individuals*

(After Hans Klingel, "Soziale Organisation und Verhalten freilebender Steppenzebras,"
Zeitschrift für Tierpsychologie, XXIV [1967] [Berlin and Hamburg, Verlag Paul Parey].)

times, each circle started in the same direction and covering more or
less the same area as the first. Undoubtedly its purpose is food-catching;
with what success, could only be determined by observation.—Many
plovers and sandpipers show the same cyclic flight with considerably
greater radius and return sweep to the taking-off spot, if a beach stroller
nears the place where they are feeding in the littoral zone; quite similarly, in the breeding season, they fly from their nesting places. This is

their fleeing motion. If, on the beach, the stroller has passed their taking-off place while they were out at sea, they will resume their activity at precisely the same spot. If he has not reached it yet, they will sometimes drop down in amazingly close proximity to him and repeat the same maneuver several times, until he has gone by. On migration, to be sure, they may displace their landing after each flight,

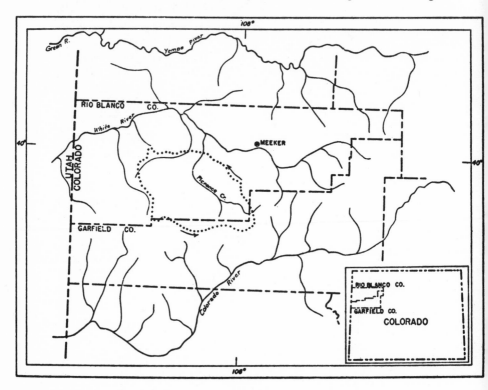

Figure 13–2. The Meeker Wolf Runway in Rio Blanco County, Colorado

'the shape of the runway is generally an irregular circle'

(From Stanley P. Young and Edward A. Goldman, *The Wolves of North America* [New York: Dover Publications, Inc., 1944]; reprinted through permission of the publisher.)

in the direction of their travel; that is something a non-migrating bird never does.' "[109]

The significance of this basic form of animal travel is that migration should, perhaps, be viewed as a round trip with "stopovers," rather than as a passage from one locality to another, with a known goal and a method of navigating by particular landmarks or skymarks.[110] The apparently purposive travel to better nesting grounds, climatic conditions, food supply or safer existence during an incapacitating molt of flight feathers[111] may have started with quite different motivation, from taxonomically much more disseminated, elementary impulses; nothing more, perhaps, than the very common hormonal disturbances that are reflected in the seasonal restlessness of many animals, known in birds as *"Zugunruhe,"* in man as "spring fever" or "itching foot"; Eibl-Eibesfeldt has remarked on the seasonal excitability of tame squirrels.[112] Since such restlessness in non-human creatures usually occurs at the commencement of the breeding season, it has been attributed without much question to the influence of the increscent sex hormones; Maurice Fontaine, however, found that in fish the effect may be concomitant with any state of the gonads.[113] His researches make it appear that any disturbance of the iodine balance inclines a fish to become restless, to venture into rapid or open water and to react to stimulating conditions—flood, moonlight or what not—and so start its journey, for

[109] "Ortsgebundene Scheinjagd bei einer afghanischen Windhündin" (1954), p. 144.

[110] The only suggestion of such a view that I have met is a brief but clear one in C. R. Carpenter's "Territoriality: A Review of Concepts and Problems" (1958), p. 237-38, where he says: "The Seal Island colonies ... represent spatial organization as one link in the annual cycle of movement that includes migration."

[111] See Dorst, *The Migrations of Birds*, p. 284, for an account of "molt migrations" performed by some ducks, which take long journeys to retreat into safe places during their complete molt of flight feathers, when they are helpless.

[112] "Angeborenes und Erworbenes im Verhalten einiger Säuger," p. 726: "Man beobachtet im Frühjahr oft Wutverhalten ohne erkennbaren äusseren Anlass: das ruhig dasitzende Eichhörnchen legt plötzlich die Ohren zurück und wetzt die Nagezähne."

[113] See his "Analyse expérimentale de l'instinct migrateur des poissons" (1956), p. 156: "la comparaison des observations faites sur le Saumon et l'Anguille permet, je crois, d'éliminer les hormones génitales du déterminisme de la migration d'avalaison.

"En effet, l'Anguille femelle migre alors que les organes génitaux viennent de commencer à se developper de façon notable. Au contraire, le jeune Saumon, le smolt femelle, migre avec les glandes génitales au repos. En ce qui concerne le smolt mâle, les états génitaux les plus variés peuvent être observés. . . ."

which it may otherwise be, physiologically, in greater or lesser readiness.[114] The thyroid activity starts a dominant behavioral act that overrides other tendencies, and suppresses whatever lesser acts it cannot entrain.

If, now, the fundamental form of animal peregrination is cyclic, that thyroid-inspired venture, whenever it occurs, is an excursion which normally will end where it began, no matter how protracted the "stopovers" (one or several) on its course may be. Fontaine worked with two families of migratory fish, eels and salmon. Of the latter he retails the following incident, in which the fish's performance certainly appears as a spectacular round trip: "Huntsman cites the case of a smolt marked in 1938 in the Northeast Margaree River in Canada; in June, 1940, it was retaken off the shore of Bonavista along the east coast of Newfoundland, more than a thousand kilometers away. It was marked again, and ninety-six days later was caught a third time, in the Northeast Margaree."[115]

Perhaps there is truth in a quip which Tinbergen attributes to Ernst Mayr—"that birds have got their wings not so much for the purpose of getting away to places but rather for the purpose of getting back into their territories."[116] One cannot generalize from fish to birds, but avian behavior provides its own versions of the "round trip" as O. Koehler's miniature examples, cited above, show clearly; a strong indication that migratory flights are legs of such a journey is given by the preparatory movements popularly known as "practice flights." These flock excursions occur while the impulse to migrate is building up, and many of its conditions are already complete, notably the high gregariousness and suggestibility that make each bird immediately follow suit if one launches itself into the air. The most telling aspect, however, is the circling form of the group action; as the birds rise together they also land together on the lawn or field from which they started. If one does not consider the natural circularity of animals' locomotion these flights

---

[114] *Ibid.*, p. 159: "Certaines années, les smolts descendent par petits paquets, et il semble ... que ces jeunes Saumons argentés descendent au fur et à mesure qu'est achevée leur préparation physiologique. Mais plus souvent encore, au printemps, pendant plusieurs jours ou plusieurs semaines ... nous n'assistons à aucune descente notable quand brusquement au simple signal d'une crue, même légère, c'est un veritable déboulé massif de dizaines de milliers de smolt. Il est difficile d'admettre que leur préparation physiologique à l'état de migrateurs a été terminée juste à cette heure H. ..."

[115] *Ibid.*, p. 161.

[116] *The Herring Gull's World*, p. 102.

seem purposely "organized," and as the purpose is not apparent, they are interpreted either as "practice flights" intended to train the young, or—more fashionably just at present—as "ritualized" acts with some symbolic social function.[117]

In phylogenetic history the rhythms of glandular activities have, of course, developed in mutual adjustment; no seriously disharmonious species could survive and, indeed, no extreme disharmony can develop, unless some impulse, otherwise held in check, can profit by the abnormality and give the whole system a new functional pattern; as the sexual display impulses in the bower birds, highly favored by a hormone asynchrony between the two sexes, have unfolded a potentiality no geneticist would ever have suspected, whereby the species is holding its own so far. The great wealth of unrealized possibilities in every being makes even the major activities adjustable to one another at every level of organic functioning. So, in those species which have a periodic urge to travel, this impulse and the procreative impulses have fallen into some mutually advantageous pattern, though not the same in all species—not even, necessarily, in closely related ones.

The elasticity of the "appetitive" stages of behavioral acts is what makes such large cycles as migration amenable to all sorts of elaboration. It also permits their progressive growth; and herein we may have a key to the mysteries of orientation and guidance. That migrations have evolved from small beginnings is certainly not a strange idea. It has been proposed many a time. Changes of season, coinciding with a mild restless period, would start a movement in the direction suggested by the warm appearance of the southern skies, or (where the discomfort is heat or drought) by the cool azure of the north. There may also be changes of climate. Such climatic changes are slow; if the animals had a strong "place habit," and their migration were gradually timed with the season of severest cold or heat stress, its circle might expand

---

[117] Similar anthropomorphic interpretations, as for instance that a *Bembex* circles round its hatching place in a "study flight" to learn the topography for future recognition (see above, p. 83) becomes gratuitous in the light of the cyclic nature of the excursions themselves. The same thing applies to an instance of animal behavior which Bellrose adduced as a proof that birds used terrestrial or celestial cues to steer their flight, in his "Orientation in Waterfowl Migration," pp. 91–92, saying: "A number of individual teal which exhibited a north-oriented flight when released 10 to 40 miles from our holding pens have returned to the vicinity of the pens. . . . It is evident that, at some time and place beyond our observation, these birds altered their course from north to one that would return them to the area of their previous residence. This performance indicates true navigation."

vastly. Environmental conditions, such as the lure of the new climate, would tend to encourage the expansion in a special direction and draw the cyclic excursion into a long ellipse such as we see in most avian migration routes; the plover's course here illustrated (Fig. 13–3)—swinging from arctic breeding grounds to the southeastern coast of South America and back—is typical, though few small birds make quite so long a journey.

It is on such extended flights, however, that the problem of navigation becomes acute; how do the migrants hold their course? There seems to be fairly general agreement among investigators that the sun somehow keeps them on it, though the difficulties presented by its own movements tend to call every sun-compass theory in question. Yet I think the sun may guide the long line of flight wherever guidance is necessary; the simplicity of birds' brains and the strength of their impulses make it possible, on a principle we have met with in lower animals of various kinds—wasps, crabs, toads—that the ambient conditions prevailing at the beginning of the act govern its entire performance. Perhaps the rising of the sun, which is always from the east, is enough to orient the flight, which then proceeds independently of subsequent changes of light or any other circumstances, until the energy of the travelers flags, and that subact of the total flight is finished. It may even continue under overcast, until the next clear sunrise starts and directs it again (for night migrants, sunset would play the same role). What is the length of an act (in *Bembex*, the day; in *Bufo*, the separate foray; in *Ocypode*, the "building episode") is not always easy to tell in the case of subacts of a long, overarching tension from a massive and complex impulse to its consummation, which, in the case of migration, is return to the starting place.

The main point, however, is that directional guidance along the migratory course of animals probably plays a minor role. The original direction was a circular excursion, perhaps with many stops, one of which was a long break at good feeding grounds when the *Wanderlust* was temporarily exhausted and almost as low as in the breeding season; as the act took shape in its multimillennial evolution, the great stopover and the narrowing of the flyway to and from it have made the single excursion look like two undertakings, each with a known goal and a course marked by navigation signals.

The direction, originally established on a small scale, is regularly reestablished with the start of the instinctive act. What long-past condition motivated it cannot be generally known, but would have to

Figure 13–3. Flyway of the American Golden Plover, *Charadrius*
[Pluvialis] dominicus dominicus

its circle might extend vastly . . . in a special direction and draw the
cyclic excursion into a long ellipse

(From J. A. Bierens de Haan, *Die tierischen Instinkte und ihr Umbau durch Erfahrung:*
Eine Einführung in die allgemeine Tierpsychologie [Leiden: E. J. Brill, 1940].)

be determined for each species or even population.[118] But once initiated, the excursion simply continues to occur, its form becoming more fixed and sure not only by repetition, but probably also by a concomitant increase in the hormonal activities—as processes encouraged by unrepressed enactment tend to increase—and thus, perhaps by favored micromutations, could gain some representation in the gene pattern. Differential elimination of the weaker migrants would play its usual major evolutionary role.

Opportunities always shape the growth of acts, for species as for individuals. The features of earth, sea and sky, although (to judge by the behavior of animals toward visible objects irrelevant to their acts of the moment) probably not specifically remarked, do have a subliminal familiarity value for the creatures moving among them; and as quickly as they offer support to a progressing act they are exploited. Such facilitating conditions have been observed and remarked in the study of some migration routes. So William F. Royce, for instance, speaking of the Pacific sockeye salmon, told a symposium audience:

"One characteristic of migration which we notice in the out-migration of the young salmon off northeastern Alaska and also most of the final migration of the adults back to the home stream (except during the very last part) is that the animals are going downstream with the ocean currents. Also, we can note that the ocean currents are such that with very little difficulty and with a series of decisions about crossing a current at an appropriate time, the salmon can spend most of its life in the ocean going downstream. Furthermore, this downstream migration

---

[118] An interesting and plausible theory of the evolution of the sea turtle's east-west migration from the entire bulge of Brazil to the breeding beaches on Ascension Island—a trip of at least a thousand miles, from points on an arc almost as long, converging on an island no more than five miles wide—has been advanced by Archie Carr, in his essay, "Adaptive Aspects of the Scheduled Travel of *Chelonia*" (1967). His theory involves the progressive separation of South America and Africa, gradually lengthening the trip which at first stretched between the continents with a stop at Ascension Island, but gradually became so long that the island became its eastern terminus. An interesting aspect of this hypothesis is that it carries the prehistory of the trait back to a time when the ancestors of any turtles were not yet recognizable as such—that is, "before there were turtles." A migration that probably was most conveniently implemented by geographical factors and the nature of the ocean current, so that nothing hindered its repetition even as the ocean widened in the course of eons, has every reason to have acquired a complex hereditary form including directedness (that is, its east–west orientation) as a genuine instinctual element. But if it does contain such an element, the fact that even today the oceanographic conditions could be regarded as optimal, and taken to account for the navigational feat, would mask the innate character of the animal's orientation for us. See *ibid.*, pp. 43 ff.

appears to be not a passive drifting but a positive ongoing swimming in excess of the speed of the currents."[119]

Several animal psychologists who have made observations under natural conditions have likened the sensory guidance of animals to the progression of a melody; as each movement furthers the motivating situation for the next, so the implementing situation advances from chance to chance, the creature progressing as its need is met. This is Santayana's "animal faith"—going on, using the moment, without knowledge of death at the end. Volkelt, at the close of his dissertation *Über die Vorstellungen der Tiere*, after concluding that animals possess no *Vorstellungen*, declared: "According to our view, the landscape which a carrier pigeon sees beneath it does not resemble a 'map,' but appears to the pigeon relatively unarticulated and diffuse. . . . The successive impressions do not compose an internally ordered series of mutually limited, distinct images, but present something like an optical melody. And likewise, what the carrier pigeon's memory contains is not . . . a vast sum of isolated impressions; but melody-like qualitative complexes, that will unroll at the touch of sensory impressions, constitute its available stores. By these optical melodies it finds its way from landscape to landscape, as a person reproducing a song finds his way from one tone to the next" (p. 126). In similar vein, most recently, J. J. Gibson pointed out that even in man's goal-directed, object-bound visual experience the underlying physiological activity of seeing proceeds in this same instinctive way.[120]

To construe animal acts in non-conceptual terms requires great care in wording not only statements, but questions, and consistency in interpretation to make systematic observation possible. The following chapter presents an attempt at such a coherent treatment of instinctive action, by offering possible alternative interpretations for the alleged "social," "rational" and "ceremonial" practices of animals in more animalian ways, as acts formed in impulses and guided by the melody-like passage and growth of sensible and emotive feeling, to consummation or failure.

---

[119] In the discussion following Hasler's "Underwater Guideposts for Migrating Fishes"; see p. 20.

[120] *The Perception of the Visual World*, pp. 158–59: "Successive excitations of the retina must be integrated by memory. . . . The kind of memory required to explain perception . . . is often called primary or immediate memory. It is the kind of memory which makes possible the apprehending of a melody. . . . Although the concept of primary memory has been derived from the study of auditory perception, it must apply with even greater force to visual perception, where successive integration is so complete that the observer can be wholly unconscious of his fixations."

14

On Animal Values

THE non-geographical, act-engendered nature of animals' space is so different from our visually given and implicitly relational space that it makes one suspect that their perception of events and their motivations may be equally different. To form any hypothesis of the evolution of human mind from its presumable animal origins, we need first of all a much clearer idea of animal mentality than we are employing in zoology and psychology today. What we ourselves are prone to feel or able to feel, objectively (i.e., as impact) or subjectively (as impulse and autogenic action) must have grown to its present developed stage from much less systematic, less coherent animal feeling. Without the benefit of protocol statements the occurrence of any psychical phases in animals can, of course, be only speculatively asserted, and any further conception of their nature must rest on what we know directly in human life; yet such conception need not be naïvely anthropomorphic if the significance of the differences between human and animal action be constantly kept in mind, and those differences themselves pursued and reflected on. The possibility of sensations may be largely inferred from physiological data; their actual occurrence or non-occurrence where one would expect them—for instance, the incidence of pain with gross bodily injury—may sometimes be experimentally tested on a basis of behavioral reactions.[1] But for the most part

[1] W. von Buddenbrock, in his *Vergleichende Physiologie*, Vol. I: *Sinnesphysiologie* (1952), reports the surprising discovery that large parts of many insects' bodies seem to have no pain reactions, so one can even, with scissors, cut off half of a wasp's abdomen without interrupting its feeding, whereas all mammals so far observed give behavioral evidence of feeling pain when injured. So he writes: "Das Schmerzgefühl ist beim Menschen von einer Reihe typischer Ausdrucksbewegungen begleitet, von denen der Schrei der markanteste ist, neben ihm ist die Hemmung anderer Tätigkeiten zu nennen, das Zurückfahren des vom Schmerz getroffenen Gliedes sowie eine Summe anderer, meist unzweckmässiger Bewegungen. Alles dies finden wir bei höheren Säugetieren ... in vollstem Masse wieder. Der Analogieschluss, ohne den eine wissenschaftliche Betrachtungsweise überhaupt unmöglich ist,

any psychological notions we can form of animal capacities, levels and modes of feeling must be theoretical constructions, working concepts. So far, however, the conceptual frame of our animal psychology is loose and flimsy. The "working concepts" do not work very well. Each set governs some area of the total field, but beyond that area may conflict with more systematically established facts, as the Lorenz-Tinbergen hypothesis of "act centers," "inhibitors" and "releasers" (inhibitors of inhibitors) does not fit into the fast-advancing neurological theories of total brain functions;[2] or the use of a basic hypothesis may be limited to artificially controlled phenomena, as the unquestionably true principles of reflex action and "conditioning" can only be applied in the insulated environment of the laboratory, so they give little explanation and certainly no constant guidance to the observer of creatures in the wild.[3] We have so far found no biological concepts on which to base

---

zwingt uns daher, diesen Tieren so gut wie uns selbst Schmerzempfindungen zuzusprechen" (p. 467–68).

"Dagegen kann mit Recht behauptet werden, dass die Arthropoden, insbesondere die Insekten, entweder gar keinen oder einen nur sehr mangelhaft entwickelten Schmerzsinn besitzen. Es folgt dies zunächst daraus, dass bei diesen Tieren die Hemmung anderer Handlung bei operativen Eingriffen häufig wegfällt. Bienen und Hornissen, die mit Trinken beschäftigt sind, kann man mit einer Schere einen Teil des Abdomens abschneiden, ohne dass sie mit Trinken aufhören. Ganz Entsprechendes hat Hase bei den Läusen beobachtet. Von gewissen Raupen ist beschrieben worden, dass sie, falls sie mit dem Maul zufällig an eine Wunde des Hinterkörpers kommen, den eigenen Körper ein Stück weit auffressen. Es erinnert dies an die häufig beobachtete Tatsache, dass Ratten nach Durchschneidung der sensiblen Wurzeln eines Beines sich an demselben gütlich tun. Die normale Raupe benimmt sich also genau so wie die denervierte Ratte" (p. 469).

[2] Especially the important phenomenon of nerves and nuclei standing in for each other is inexplicable by use of the model of hierarchically concatenated act centers. See, e.g., Gustav Hofer's study, "Zur motorischen Innervation des menschlichen Kehlkopfes" (1944), in which the author remarks that although from interruption of the superior external branch of the vagus nerve and the recurrens, or from bilateral section of the former, paralysis of the larynx results, in the case of unilateral section of the vagus branch "ersetzt offenbar der intakte Recurrens den Funktionsausfall vollständig, was bei doppelseitigem Ausfall jedenfalls nicht mehr möglich ist" (p. 790). There are many other instances of brain structures taking over functions of damaged neural mechanisms, for instance in the extensive recovery of abilities after a stroke, but it is rarely possible to tell what structure is acting vicariously, as in Hofer's cases.

[3] See T. A. Ryan, "Interrelations of the Sensory Systems in Perception" (1940), p. 662: "traditional investigations of perceptual problems have studied the localization of 'mere sounds' without much objective significance, the visual movement of dots and lines taken in isolation, and so on through more examples. Where meaning or significance has been met with it is thrown off as associative and thus brought under mechanical 'laws' of repetition, contiguity, and the like.

any indirect methods for the study of psychical phases in animal life. This leaves us with the direct, natural method of imputing an essentially human mentality to non-human agents, and two attitudes toward that practice: simple acceptance of its naïve anthropomorphism,[4] or a really equally simple, summary declaration that there is no way of finding out anything about animal feeling, so the best policy is to deny or at least ignore its existence. The first is a misguided approach, the second an acceptance of failure at the mere sight of the task. But the task itself is to find a means of using the natural approach and systematically correcting its errors; that is, assuming that animals' acts rise to psychical phases as ours do—a fairly safe assumption, on the ground that we are animals, and the general nature of acts is the same throughout the zoological realm—to discover how and why whatever other organisms feel might differ from what is felt by human beings. If the psychical moments of animal acts are different from ours, it means that the acts are different, perhaps from their very impulses to their consummations.

The best way to gain some understanding of the mentality of various high and low animals is, therefore, to discover step by step how their

---

"When we turn to the interrelations of the senses we find a similar approach. The effect of an auditory stimulus upon visual quality or spatial arrangement is also considered from this neutral point of view.... [But] the fact is that we do not spend our lives perceiving dots, lines, squares, and colors in a vacuum, but rather we perceive men, tables, chairs set ... in dynamic situations, affecting one another socially and physically, and this total situation is all perceived." The animal in a cage or a stand may provide data for the laboratory context, but the animal in its proper habitat acts in a total situation, and provides no usable data on reactions to colors and shapes. The field observer has to use other parameters. R. Jander and T. H. Waterman, in "Sensory Discrimination between Polarized Light and Light Intensity Patterns by Arthropods" (1960), reporting experiments on *Daphnia* and other tiny creatures, are careful to remark that "much of the experimental work on light reactions, particularly of aquatic animals, has been conducted under conditions which differ greatly from those typical of open air or open water. The present data suggest the possibility that quite unexpected patterns of behaviour may appear when the illumination of the experimental animal's surroundings is more natural."

[4] That this attitude is not restricted to sentimental persons who feel sure that they and their pets understand each other is made quite clear in Robert Stenuit's *The Dolphin, Cousin to Man* (1968): "In the fifteen years or so in which delphinology has been in fashion in the United States, the small world of the zoologists, neurophysiologists, psychologists and linguists has split up into supporters and opponents of the high intelligence of Odontoceti.

"As far as I am concerned, let it be understood once and for all that I am 'pro.' I am 'pro' without ever having dissected the smallest brain, or weighed a hypothalamus.... As I am not a scientist, I may confess, without jeopardizing my career, that I have taken sides mainly for sentimental reasons" (p. 59).

acts call our anthropomorphic image of their lives in question. They
will do so from almost each observation to the next, if we do not
overlook the small deviations from humanly specialized reactions, or
refuse to dwell on their significance in order to feel ourselves constantly
in rapport with the animal. All concern for maintaining an attitude,
whether a sentimental or a scientific one, for avoiding a conclusion that
would be theoretically disappointing or might lay us open to the charge
of espousing an obsolete "ism," is ruinous to research. Negative findings,
especially where the expected positive results seemed so certain that the
experimenter practically deemed his experiment a formality to satisfy
the demands of his methodology, are exciting mysteries, the first indications that familiar facts may need new interpretation. That is the route
of systematic correction which leads almost imperceptibly, stepwise, to
philosophically advanced standpoints, far from the naïve beginnings of
theoretical conception.

The previous chapter was devoted to this sort of study of animal space
perception and its role in shaping the ambients in which animals live.
When we discover how different their psychological space is from ours
we are led on to further questions: why is man's space experience geometric? And, if beasts have few or no permanently self-identical things,
how do we come to have so many, and to find and accept them so
readily that our world is given its structure primarily by physical
objects? Nothing is more natural to us than to think in terms of permanent, simple substances with variable attributes. If animals do not
perceive objects in this way, yet obviously deal with them, how do they
know what to do with them, when to seek and when to avoid them?
There must be differences between their object perception and ours, as
great as between their ways and ours of possessing space.

To discover and establish some coherent principles of animal perception and motivation requires, first of all, that we clear away such anthropomorphisms as we can easily recognize in current interpretations
of animal acts; for instance, the assumption that birds, beasts and even
fish[5] can imagine what they look like to other creatures, including human
beings, and how such observers would be likely to interpret their acts.
All claims that animals try to deceive, like the widely held belief that

[5] Hermann Härtel, writing of the feeding of a mouth-brooding fish, *Geophagus
jurupari*, stated that when enchytrae were put into the aquarium "they were at
once taken by the female, chewed and, *when she believed herself unobserved*,
ejected in a cloud together with the young. I could see the latter feeding in the
cloud" (quoted by M. J. Reid and J. W. Atz in "Oral Incubation in the Cichlid
Fish *Geophagus jurupari* Heckel" [1958] [italics mine]).

ground-nesting birds pretend to have a broken wing in order to decoy an intruder away from their brood, rest on that assumption. Otto Koenig, who has himself challenged popular attributions of motives to animals,[6] in this case accepts the intention of the birds quite at face value, and even says that the pretending actors will suddenly take off and fly away "as soon as they believe the foe to have been decoyed far enough away."[7]

The fishes and birds supposed to impute ideas and motives to other creatures are at least acting in the presence of their dangerous fellows, but the animal fable sometimes goes further than that; thus Klingel, in his sober and excellent report on the zebras of the Serengeti steppe, cites (without comment) E. Trumler's proposition that a stallion "marks" (i.e., urinates or defecates on) the excretions of a mare in oestrous, in order to hide her condition from other stallions.[8]

A much more widely disseminated, well-nigh universal assumption made by observers of animals in the wild and in captivity (zoos, farms, homes and even laboratories) is that animals communicate with each other by sounds and other "signals." To entertain even the possibility that animals have no social intercourse comparable to human language, no code to signal their demands, warnings or new discoveries to each other, is difficult for most people. Our very observations tend to be

[6] See his delightful book *Kif-Kif. Menschliches und Tierisches zwischen Sahara und Wilhelminenberg* (1962), p. 41, for his humorous account of a "snake-charming" act, with a realistic analysis of the motivations of man and snake, each acting from fear of the other.

[7] After observing that sick or handicapped animals are soon captured by predators, he writes in a tone of complete conviction: "Dieses ... Verhalten jagender Tiere machen sich viele Vögel zunutze, um Feinde von ihrem nest oder den Kindern abzulenken. Sie gebärden sich hinkend und flügellahm, flüchten scheinbar mühsam und äusserst linkisch, wodurch unweigerlich die Aufmerksamkeit des Jägers erregt wird.... Folgt ihnen der Feind, so halten sie gebührenden Abstand und fliegen urplötzlich, sobald sie den Gegner weit genug verleitet glauben, in alter Gewandheit davon" (p. 211).

This behavior is so generally regarded as a ruse to decoy a predator that a bibliography of reports calling it a "distraction display" or "injury-feigning" would run to scores of titles. I have quoted, above, a well-known naturalist to demonstrate that the histrionic designation is not simply a popular term applied to the act without being literally meant.

[8] "Soziale Organisation und Verhalten freilebender Steppenzebras," p. 620. (The reference is to E. Trumler's "Beobachtungen an den Böhmzebras des Georg von Opel Freigeheges für Tierforschung, e. V.: 1. Das Paarungsverhalten" [1958]): "Das 'Markieren' der Ausscheidungen rossiger Stuten durch den Hengst soll nach Trumler den Zweck haben, den Zustand der Stuten vor anderen Hengsten zu verbergen."

influenced by the facts that the noises produced by monkeys, mice and many birds sound like chatter, that a squirrel's excited vocalizing, with stretched neck and twitching tail, simulates scolding, and eager crowing, trumpeting or yapping at the finding of food, which often brings others to the feast, seems like calling them to share it. Popular and semipopular writing, even by notable ethologists,[9] strengthens this influence and effaces the differences between human language and animal utterances, and even more completely the entire psychological problem of "communication" in man and beast.

Communication is, in fact, such a problematical phenomenon that its exact meaning with respect to animals needs very careful statement. A correct formulation of the terms in which it is to be conceived is likely to hold implicitly the concepts that will automatically rearrange our empirical and theoretical views of mental evolution. The numerous inconclusive attempts to link human and non-human mentality in a continuum, which fill many serious books today, are perhaps all obstructed by the same weakness, the lack of adequate ideas of the animalian forms of perception and action from which our own development has taken off in its great expansion. A coherent view of animal mentality, without immediate reference to our own, might provide a foundation for surer insights into the fateful evolutionary shift that has taken place in the hominid stock.

To construct such a conceptual framework requires, however, the abandonment or at least shelving of practically all the basic notions in general use today; not only hypothetical entities such as the hierarchy of "act centers" in the brain stem, "inhibitor mechanisms," "innate releasing mechanisms," even the innocent-looking "sign stimuli" and "social signals," the older "memory traces" ("engrams") and "contents of consciousness," but also many slipshod generalizations embodied in words and phrases, that is to say, in the uncritically accepted ways we refer

9 See, for example, W. H. Thorpe, "The Language of Birds" (1956), in which it is said at the start that "bird songs and calls are not merely a spontaneous emotional outlet, that they are in fact the language in which the chirpers communicate with one another," and further: "the sounds that birds make have two main functions: to arouse an emotional state (by way of warning, wooing, etc.) and to convey precise information" (p. 129).

Also, Hubert and Mabel Frings, "The Language of Crows" (1959), p. 123: "Crows are great conversationalists, if we can assume that all their sounds have meaning." They subsequently distinguish assembly, alarm and distress calls. Once, having collected many crows with the assembly call, the authors displayed a stuffed owl; in this situation, they say, "the crows would then wait around, talking among themselves." Between a few significant calls and language that permits conversation lies the vast difference between man and animal, and neither science nor the layman's intelligent interest in it is aided by such "literary" flourishes.

to the objects of our descriptions and interpretative discussions: using "stimulus" for every motivating condition, specific or general, even for things the organism is expecting or seeking;[10] or talking about "mechanisms" where we really mean only functions and act patterns and have no idea whether these arise from special mechanisms or result from interactions of processes otherwise accounted for; and so on. In this way the key words of discourse lose their precision, and problems are sidestepped because they do not arise in the simplicistic scheme of "adequate stimuli" and correlated specific responses; while many challenges to analysis and scientific construction are met too easily with the assumption, "there must be a mechanism. . . ."[11]

But the most detrimental practice is the carrying over of words from anthropology and ethnology to ethology, with a radical change of meaning, which reflects back on their proper meanings in their proper places, and wipes out all conceptual accuracy in both contexts. Those words are, specifically, "symbol," "ritual" (or "rite") and "ceremony" (or "ceremonial"). To apply such terms to stereotyped animal movements requires their redefinition on the basis of superficial resemblances of such movements to human acts which have quite different motivation and really symbolic, ritual and ceremonial values. In the early years of anthropological research it was often critically remarked that the scholars in that new field knew too little of animal ways to trace human characteristics to their prehuman origins. Today we have the counterpart of that failing in the presently new study of animal behavior; our ethologists know too little anthropology to realize the inade-

[10] See, e.g., W. H. Thorpe's Introduction to Part III of Thorpe and Zangwill, *Current Problems in Animal Behaviour* (1961), p. 169: "Watson ... accepts Deutsch's conclusion that in both learning as well as in innate behaviour the animal is regarded as *searching for a cue* or for stimuli." A cue and a stimulus are very different things. W. Craig, in "Appetites and Aversions as Constituents of Instinct," p. 91, defines an appetite as "a state of agitation which continues so long as a certain stimulus, which may be called the appeted stimulus, is absent"; and a little later (p. 92) he remarks that sometimes, in performing an instinctive action, "the animal begins with an *incipient consummatory action*, although the appeted stimulus, which is the adequate stimulus of that consummatory action, has not yet been received." All too often a vague reference to "stimuli" stands proxy for the description of a real situation, which would be difficult; as J. A. King, in "Closed Social Groups among Domestic Dogs" (1954), explains that such a group of dogs will set upon a stranger "since he cannot provide the necessary stimuli to prevent the attack" (p. 335).

[11] For instance, when Eibl-Eibesfeldt, in "Angeborenes und Erworbenes im Verhalten einiger Säuger," disposes of the problem of relevance and fitness of instinctive acts, by saying: "Es muss sich ein rezeptorischer Apparat als stammesgeschichtliche Anpassung entwickelt haben, der dem Tier mitteilt, wann ein Verhalten seine biologische Funktion erfüllt" (p. 745).

quacy of their definitions of those key words in application to human experience, and to foresee how, in our evolutionary picture of the hominid stock, the differentiae that distinguish the genus *Homo* from other high primate genera are perforce obscured and made ineffectual for the understanding of human life.[12] Once "rites" and "ceremonies" are imputed to animals—not only to apes, but to gulls, ducks, lizards— all other distinctively human traits which actually underlie the occurrence of ritual performances by men are gradually ascribed to non-human creatures: symbols, concepts,[13] tradition,[14] superstition,[15] sham

[12] According to Lorenz ("The Comparative Method in Studying Innate Behavior Patterns," p. 243), Heinroth introduced the term *"Symbolbewegungen"* for visually striking but practically unimportant movements which have been established by "natural selection" as "social releasers." Since then there have been many claims that animals think and communicate symbolically, as even the titles of some articles show, e.g., Ruth Hunter, "Symbolic Performance of Rats in a Delayed Alternation Problem" (1941); L. Petrinovich and R. Bolles, "Delayed Alternation: Evidence for Symbolic Processes in the Rat" (cf. Vol. I, p. 39); and A. L. Kroeber, "Sign and Symbol in Bee Communications" (1952).

[13] This attribution may also be found in the titles of some papers, for instance, R. J. Herrenstein and D. H. Loveland, "Complex Visual Concept in the Pigeon" (1964), though concept formation is often treated as a problem. Perhaps the most serious claim for it is made by O. Koehler in "Sprache und unbenanntes Denken" (1956). This author not only credits animals with possession of wordless concepts, but also with thought, which men have inherited from animal ancestors; and toward the end of the article (p. 671) he declares: "Dieses tiermenschliche unbenannte Denken bildet Umweltbeziehungen und seelische Innenzustände so ab, dass arterhaltendes Vorausplanen künftigen Handelns, soziale Verständigung und manches andere dadurch möglich wird." And elsewhere, in a discussion at the same symposium, he spoke of "das *Symbolisieren*, das zweifellos auch weit in die Tierwelt hinabreicht" (p. 641).

[14] K. R. L. Hall, in "Observational Learning in Monkeys and Apes" (1963), speaks repeatedly about "traditions," but offers no evidence that species-specific behavior is continued by tradition; and even so careful a zoologist as S. C. Kendeigh, in his generally factual *Parental Care and Its Evolution in Birds*, makes the questionable statement, "In all cases, the young must be trained in the traditions of the species so there is a period in early life during which parental care is required." What traditions do wrens whisper to their young in the nest? As the fashion of anthropomorphizing animals grows, we are supposed to read without blinking about "cultural traits" of Japanese monkeys (G. W. Hewes, "Hominid Bipedalism: Independent Evidence for the Food-Carrying Theory" [1964], p. 417); and Hans Frädrich, in a long essay, "Zur Biologie und Ethologie des Warzenschweines (*Phagochoerus aethiopicus* Pallas), unter Berücksichtigung des Verhaltens anderer Suiden" (1965), p. 359, having described a wart hog's carrying a captured rag "as a trophy" after a fight, even notes its "vacuum" chewing motions as a *"Verlegenheitshandlung"* (embarrassment-gesture of a pig!).

[15] This fanciful term is used by a psychologist of high repute, W. N. Kellogg; see " 'Superstitious' Behavior in Animals" (1949); it was introduced by an equally

battles and tournaments,[16] punishment to correct the young[17] and even principles of exogamy[18] and special relations with aunts and uncles.[19] All these findings rest on the interpretation of animal acts, which are behaviorally convergent with human acts, in terms of human motivation. The convergences are not even always very pronounced; a superficial similarity, such as that of the posturing of animals which dare not attack each other to the prescribed moves of men in a fencing match, is enough to elicit the judgment that the non-human opponents do not wish to kill each other, but only to measure their relative powers in a conventionally limited contest.

The motive to such anthropomorphic psychologizing is the desire to find the evolutionary continuum of animal life, and especially mental life, from fish (if not from protozoon) to man. Charles W. Morris, many years ago, made the passing remark—as if calling attention to an obvious principle—that "no sharp line is to be set up in the evolution

---

respected laboratory scientist, B. F. Skinner, in " 'Superstition' in the Pigeon" (1948).

[16] See I. Eibl-Eibesfeldt, "Der Kommentkampf der Meerechse (*Amblyrhynchus crystatus* Bell.) nebst einigen Notizen zur Biologie dieser Art" (1955). Each example here given is selected from a large collection of its kind.

[17] Hans Kummer, in his observations on hamadryas baboons, *Soziales Verhalten einer Mantelpaviangruppe* (1958), writes "dass kleine Junge kaum je in der üblichen Weise von älteren Individuen bedroht werden. Der Extremitätenbiss [a bite in the front paw] . . . ist auf die 'Bestrafung' der kleinen Jungen beschränkt. Vor allem ältere Jungtiere werden öfters durch Spielversuche der Kleinen belästigt. In diesen Fällen ergreift das ältere Tier die Hand des kleinen Jungen, führt sie ins Maul und beisst—meist sachte—darauf. Im Gegensatz zu den heftigen Schwanz- und Genickbissen macht der Extremitätenbiss den Eindruck einer mehr symbolischen Zurechtweisung" (p. 57).

[18] Koenig, in *Kif-Kif*, p. 162, speaks of "die zur Vermeidung von Geschwisterehen so wichtige Neigung aller höheren Wirbeltiere, möglichst unbekannte Partner zu heiraten"; has anyone ever presented evidence for such a tendency in all—or even any—"higher vertebrates" except man?

[19] See, for example, R. A. Hinde, "Rhesus Monkey Aunts" (1963). The term "aunt" is there applied to any monkey that picks up or pays attention to another monkey's baby. The author speaks of "these females, which we refer to as 'aunts' with no implication of blood relationship" (p. 67). Evidently they need not even be females; in the discussion following the paper, one of the participants declared: "In the Santiago colony . . . there were one or two males which acted as aunts." According to Hinde's description, nothing in the behavior of the monkeys suggests the interest or helpful intention of a human relative. To call them "aunts" seems to have no purpose except to contribute another term to the anthropomorphic verbiage which is fashionable today. (Alison Jolly, in *Lemur Behavior. A Madagascar Field Study* [1967], p. 68, refers to such baby-sitting gentlemen as "uncles.")

of intelligence from the animal world to man."[20] The same assertion has been made by a great many writers, sometimes only implicitly; D. O. Hebb, in the *Organization of Behavior*, declared, "Emphasis on biological needs seems to limit animal motivation much too narrowly.... For example, children spontaneously avoid dark places even though no unpleasant event has been associated with darkness" (p. 179). Taking a child's experience as an example of animal motivation shows up, very clearly, how inadequate the non-human model is to the human phenomenon. Fear of darkness in children certainly does result from "unpleasant events," as I can remember all too well—the occurrence of uncontrollable imagery, not checked by the reassuring sight of familiar surroundings. A child's imagination, and memories elaborated by fantasies, run wild in the dark. The motivation of that fear is precisely what the child does not share with other animals; but the species-specific unrealism of mankind is often played down in favor of practical intelligence, which seems to be approached by some animals, or it is vaguely linked with stereotyped animal acts by calling the latter "superstitious behavior." That terminology suggests, of course, that the "superstitious" monkey, rat or pigeon, like a superstitious person, believes its formalized act to have a practical effect.[21] Such verbal vagaries and foibles, as well as the reading of symbolic intent into canine or simian gestures, are designed to eliminate the dividing line between animal and human existence.

Oddly enough, however, the various attempts to establish the continuity of animal life from the foot of the evolutionary scale to the present estate of man by removing that line militate against our finding the genuine continuity, because in nature every division is also a meeting line where the most intricate relations occur, so the smudging or masking of any crucial boundary obliterates the relations between

---

[20] *The Nature of Mind* (1929), p. 237.

[21] Klaus Foppa, in his article "Motivation und Bekräftigungswirkungen im Lernen" (1963), p. 655, adduces the behavior of Skinner's pigeons, isolated each in its cage and given bits of food at regular intervals regardless of what its behavior was at the time (though the food is called a "reward" and is thought to "reinforce" the casual behavior); the birds developed patterns of movement, each its own, repeated during the waiting periods between "rewards"; and the author assumes that they saw a causal connection between the antics and the "reward," as he says: "Diese komplexen Bewegungsfolgen unterscheiden sich von Versuchstier zu Versuchstier, je nachdem, welche Verhaltungsweisen die Belohnungen 'verursacht' haben, d. h. zufällig von Bekräftigungen gefolgt waren. Die zufälligen Kontingenzen führen offensichtlich zu objektiv falschen Interpretationen der Ereignisabfolgen und deshalb zu einer objektiv sinnlosen Selektion spezifischer Verhaltensweisen. Analoge Phänomene kann man nicht nur an Tauben sondern auch an Kindern und Erwachsenen beobachten."

taxonomic groups and the unity underlying evolutionary shifts. Therefore I shall follow a different method here by dwelling on the principles of animal motivation and interpreting the ethological data, which have beguiled many serious observers to see them in an ethnological light, as strictly and consistently as possible in non-human terms, up to the point where the "great shift" becomes imminent. Many first-hand observations in the field have been recorded which offer factual material for such an alternative treatment; sometimes they invite it by casting doubt on the alleged hierarchies, purposes or derivations of behavioral patterns.

Most of the principles of animalian impulse and perception which seem to underlie the evolution of feeling have already been discussed: the character of acts, especially their wholeness, their potential expansion and contraction, their comprisal, entrainment and induction or repression of other acts, and their constant competition, from the impulse level onward, for complete actualization. These basic properties of all acts produce the patterns of tensions which constitute the continuous lives of organisms. The courses which particular acts take, however, are of unsurveyable variety, starting in the thousands (indeed, millions) of specialized impulses—each specialized according to its moment in the progressing matrix—and running as they can through the fabric of circumstance to consummation in recognizable or hidden ways, or to repression, adding a new potentiality to the agent's cumulative past. It is in the covert stages of actualization that differences of motivation between human and non-human acts become effective, so that psychological experiments on animals with "stimuli" based on humanly conceived values sometimes have astonishing outcomes.

Yet to make really fundamental differences accessible to our theoretical imagination requires some hint of the alternative possibilities that lie open to an advancing act, either in very striking anomalies of practical behavior (such as a tern's detour "around" a branch which has been removed long ago) or else in some generally unrealized, chance-detected psychological experience of our own. A suggestive finding of this sort comes from the human psychology laboratory, where several experimenters have found that the recognition of words in tachistoscopic presentations seems often to be preceded by a subliminal reaction to their good, evil or mildly disturbing meaning. There is some premonition of value in the process of recognition which, in the case of negative value, retards the reading of the word.[22]

---

[22] J. M. Vanderplas and R. R. Blake, who used oral instead of tachistoscopic presentation, in their article "Selective Sensitization in Auditory Perception" (1949), p. 252, say of their predecessors in the investigation: "Although they did

Differences of recognition thresholds for various words presented to the same reader under the same conditions have long been observed, and given a generally valid explanation in terms of their relative familiarity or strangeness; certainly a driver on the highway may be expected to recognize "keep right" more quickly than "*Fahnenstock.*" Bruner and Postman found that an unfamiliar appearance in an otherwise familiar pattern evoked confused judgments of what actually had been seen.[23] But repeated experiments by these and other psychologists gave evidence that novelty and incongruity are not the only factors which hamper recognition; a "negative" value in the meaning of a presented word or the significance of an image also tends to delay or even distort perception.

This finding raises the problem, how a word, an image or any presentation can be evaluated before it has been recognized. That no response can be made to the character of an object before that object has been identified is an axiom of common sense.[24] When Bruner and Postman, in another joint article, broach the problem by asking: "In order to repress or negate a stimulus, must the subject not recognize it first for what it is?" the question sounds purely rhetorical, the answer "yes" being understood, as in a Platonic dialogue; but their perfectly reasonable reply is "no," which they promptly go on to explain, saying: "There can be tripped off, by the presentation of a stimulus, a multiplicity of response tendencies among which veridical reporting is only one, albeit a most important one. Other systematic reaction tendencies tripped off by the stimulus may be largely affective in nature and lead to various forms of avoidance responses. Each of these possible re-

---

not find a direct one-to-one relationship between value-score and the 'threshold of recognition,' the evidence seemed ample to permit the conclusion that there was a corresponding decrease in threshold for words associated with areas in which value was high and a generalized increase in recognition threshold for words associated with areas in which value was low."

[23] J. S. Bruner and L. Postman, "On the Perception of Incongruity: A Paradigm" (1949). These authors used playing cards, some of which were abnormal in that the colors of the suits were reversed, showing red spades or clubs, and black hearts or diamonds, among the familiar cards of the normal deck, as "incongruous" stimuli; in this case the tachistoscopic exhibits were not words, but basically familiar forms to recognize.

[24] R. S. Lazarus and R. A. McCleary, in an interesting study entitled "Autonomic Discrimination without Awareness" (1951), remark that to admit the negative value of "tabooed" words as a deterrent to recognition "places its proponents in the difficult position of having to postulate some process of discrimination occurring prior to the ability of the subject to report correct recognition." To find oneself challenging axiomatic assumptions is indeed to be in a "difficult position" (p. 114).

sponses has its own threshold, determined by characteristics of the stimulus and by the directive state of the organism. ..."[25]

This observation is certainly a great advance over the traditional treatment of perception as a passively and instantaneously received imprint. Yet the language of "stimulus and response," the trigger concept implicit in speaking of a stimulus as "tripping off" a whole cluster of "response tendencies" which are ready, in various degrees, for such activation, makes it somewhat difficult to see the "systematic" relations among those tendencies. Perhaps the situation could be more clearly described in terms of the perceptual act, consummated in human agents by the intellectual event of object-perception, but starting as a deep, complex, gradually gathering enactment of a total sensory impulse; an impulse elicited from the peripheral receptor organ by the impact of some ambient event, but propagated through the brain via many paths, and entraining all sorts of impulses—defensive, conative, or more vaguely emotive—as elements of itself along the way. Its psychical phase develops gradually, however fast its completion may seem; perception is not an instantaneous act followed by discrimination and evaluation, but is built up by processes of discrimination, each of which imposes some value on the ultimate form. The smallest element, going into its own psychical phase at its own time (as Bruner and Postman propose), may give the percept a cathexis stemming from the past of the organism before the intellectual phase of the sensory act is completed. But the earliest stages of perceptual as of behavioral acts are unfelt, cerebral preparations which may come to non-psychical expression, as Lazarus and McCleary ascertained in their study of galvanic skin responses registered in conjunction with subliminal sensory stimulations.[26]

The significance of these findings in human psychology for our necessarily speculative judgments of animal feeling, perception and motivation lies in the objective demonstration that value may be adumbrated before perception of forms is complete; indeed, the expectant, covert anticipation of the full percept appears to be an emotively tinged process, missed in our ordinary introspective analysis because of its minuteness and transitory character. The complexity of the human per-

[25] J. S. Bruner and L. Postman, "Perception, Cognition and Behavior" (1949), pp. 26–27. See, furthermore, the later corroborative experiments by N. F. Dixon and M. Haider reported in their paper, "Changes in Visual Threshold as a Function of Subception" (1961).

[26] "The results [of the reported experiments] indicate that at tachistoscopic exposure speeds too rapid for correct recognition, subjects are able to give discriminatory responses as measured by their galvanic skin response" ("Autonomic Discrimination without Awareness," p. 113).

ceptual act, which culminates in the recognition of a word, an image or some other closed form, allows earlier phases to be felt in other than cognitive ways, either as an uneasiness about the coming presentation or an eager expectation of it, growing as the percept emerges. This premonitory phase Lazarus and McCleary have named "subception." They define their new term to mean "a process by which some kind of discrimination is made when the subject is unable to make a correct conscious discrimination" (p. 113), and refer to it elsewhere as a distinct level of perceptual activity (p. 120).

If our recognition of sensory data builds itself up to a degree of intensity at which the receptor organ achieves focus and epicritical distinctions on a basis of lower but increasing motivation, it may well be that for other creatures the stage before such full cognitive action is the most important, perhaps undergoing elaborations for which it is given no time in man because the peripheral mechanisms overtake and entrain it (this subject will presently be discussed). In that case, animal perception might be normally a matter of locating situations for action, in which a center of highest value draws the agent's interest; that center—for us, the "object"—presumably has sensory properties which the animal recognizes without conceiving them descriptively, i.e., without distinguishing them as shapes, colors, surface feelings or even characteristic smells; recognition is not necessarily judgment.[27] Generalization is inherent in all acts, since perfectly identical situations do not occur, so "repeated" acts would be impossible if they could not allow for ambient changes within a fair range of conditions having similar implementing values; for instance, one kind of food or another for eating, one avenue or another for running. Heinrich Klüver has called this situational leeway "equivalence of stimuli."[28] One could equally well speak of "equivalence of consummations," since acts may also be successfully concluded in various ways: a rat's flight from a pursuer may end in finding a hole,

[27] Henri Wallon, in his excellent De l'acte à la pensée (1942), which I have had several occasions to adduce in corroboration of the principles adopted in Vol. I of this study, thinks of animal feeling in the same way that I have been led to do on the same basis. So he says: "L'effet n'est pas extérieur à l'acte; il est à la fois son résultat et son régulateur" (p. 67). And further: "Au lieu d'une intuition en quelque sorte instantanée, qui fasse saisir une relation directe et totale entre le but, les circonstances et les moyens, c'est une expérience d'abord confusée où les gestes possibles sont petit à petit mis en rapport avec leurs conséquences immédiates et le but final. Le resultat de cette sommation n'est pas encore un acte unique et irrévocable d'intellection; c'est le passage progressif d'un sentiment diffus et faible à la réalisation totale de la situation" (pp. 67–68).

[28] See "The Equivalence of Stimuli in the Behavior of Monkeys" (1931), passim.

climbing a tree, ducking under a stone or even plunging into water. Perhaps what is "the same" for an animal is the sense of satisfaction with substrates and aids to progress and with whatever situations emerge as successful acts are consummated; or, inversely, the sense of effort which may rise to desperation when an act is blocked.[29] Impulse and the feeling of passage are remembered in reenacting a performance, and how much of that remembrance is a psychical event and how much is effective without conscious recall may differ widely from one kind of animal to another, in conjunction with the relative degrees of intensity to which acts normally rise in each species and the height they may attain at their utmost concentration. An infusorian may not feel as much of its activity as an animal with a central nervous system, yet its acts show the same characteristics of facilitation by repeated successful performance, progressive sensitization to motivating conditions, abbreviation of the preparatory stages and, consequently, more rapid consummation, which makes the impression of purposeful aim at the usual result.[30] In the case of fleeing from diffuse noxious stimulation, however, there is probably no aim at all, no lure to any particular consum-

---

[29] Cf. J. A. Bierens de Haan, *Die tierischen Instinkte*, pp. 254–55, where he remarks "dass es ... nicht immer nötig ist, anzunehmen, dass das Tier das bei seinem Handeln Erlebte explizite aufbewahrt und später bewusst in seinen Geist zurückruft.... Es kann die Erfahrung auch in einer einfacheren Weise wirken, und zwar dadurch, dass der Ablauf oder das Ergebnis einer von dem Tier ausgeführten Handlung ein Gefühl der Befriedigung oder Unbefriedigung, von Lust oder Unlust sein wird.... Dieses sekundäre Gefühl nun (wenn wir das Gefühl, das das Streben auslöste, das primäre Instinktgefühl nennen wollen), verstärkt oder schwächt bei Wiederholung der Situation die Tendenz zur Wiederholung der vorherigen Handlung, und zwar dadurch, dass dieses Gefühl auf die ausgeführte Handlung zurückstrahlt und sie dadurch in der gegebenen Situation lustvoller oder weniger lustvoll für das Tier gestaltet.

"Wo nun durch Erfahrung die instinktive Bindung geändert wird, ändert sich auch dies, und bekommen die Gegenstände eine geänderte, sekundäre, Bedeutung (einen geänderten, sekundären Wert).... So 'sieht' für das Tier ein Gegenstand anders 'aus' als vorher, nachdem es durch eine Handlung gute oder üble Erfahrungen über ihn erworben hat."

[30] A good example of the facilitating effect of repetition on successive responses to similar motivating circumstances is given by L. L. Woodruff in "The Protozoa and the Problem of Adaptation" (1924), p. 63, where, after describing the effect of an infusion of carmine into aquarium water on a *Stentor* which ultimately leaves its site of anchorage to escape the noxious condition, he says: "The animal after attaining several times the relieving response by repeating a succession of movements, thereupon more quickly reaches the relieving response upon recurrence of the interfering condition. And sooner or later this reaction is made immediately to this interfering condition."

mation, but the act of escape goes over into its cadential phase as soon as the protozoan has reached a situation in which it can do something else—feed, digest, rebuild its energies. It is different, even at this low level, with creatures that gather at food sources or find host organisms; there the ambient presents lures to action and the diminutive agents orient themselves toward "goals"; surely without any prevision such as we have of true goals, but coming to rest where new opportunities are met. Whether such acts express entirely unfelt chemical "affinities" or have their moments of intensification in which they go into psychical phases we have no way of judging.

It is hard to conceive of perception and behavior without human ways of identifying and relating objects, first of all, by their attributes of color, shape, size, etc.; in spite of all theoretical realization that human standards do not apply to the mental acts of birds, beasts and fishes, we use them in judging their behavior as clever or stupid, random or purposive[31] and even egoistic or altruistic.[32] When Tinbergen remarks on the gull's lack of intelligence in rolling a displaced egg back into its nest laboriously with the underside of its beak, when one sweep of its wing would accomplish the whole desired change in a second,[33]

---

[31] Eibl-Eibesfeldt, in "Angeborenes und Erworbenes im Verhalten einiger Säuger," p. 737, describing the nest building of rats, says: "Man gewann nicht den Eindruck, als handelten die Tiere zielstrebig." A young rat would often bring nesting material, hold it against the wall, drop it, and make all the motions of pressing it into place in empty air. But to squirrels burying nuts (or sometimes trying to do so on a solid floor) he attributes a purpose and constant interest in its achievement, saying: "Die Tätigkeit zielt offenbar darauf hin, die auslösende Reizsituation zu ändern. . . . Der Bewegungserfolg wird in jeder Phase wahrgenommen und wirkt auf das Verhalten zurück." And then, surprisingly: "Ähnlich nimmt die nestbauene Ratte das 'Passen' der Bewegung wahr" (p. 745).

[32] Konrad Lorenz's King Solomon's Ring is, perhaps, too much a piece of whimsy to be seriously adduced as an example; but in the inhibition that stops a wolf from killing a weaker one when the latter cowers and looks up he does see an act of "submission" met by one of "mercy." William Etkin, in his "Social Behavioral Factors in the Emergence of Man" (1964), is certainly in full earnest when he extolls the "social relations" of wolves and claims that pre-human primates had to learn these virtues—monogamy, cooperation, and "instruction of the young"—to attain our moral status (perhaps Mowgli's Brothers are still somewhat ahead!).

Another animal psychologist has even contrived an experiment to test the readiness of a rat to rescue another one, which was being hurt and was squealing, by manipulating a familiar apparatus to release the victim. The experimenter, R. M. Church, reports the results in "Emotional Reactions of a Rat to the Pain of Others" (1959). Unfortunately, the positive results—which were not very spectacular—could bear several interpretations besides the altruistic one.

[33] See p. 50 above.

[118]

he supposes—as a human observer naturally would—that the gull's purpose is to push the egg back into the nest, and that it knows no better than to reach for it in a difficult, inefficient way. If, however, one views the total complex of relations of gulls to their nests, eggs and young, it appears very likely that the bird retrieving an egg has no such purpose at all, no idea that the egg ought to be brought back by one means or another, the easier and quicker the better; it seeks contact with the egg, and makes it at a part of its body that seems to be especially sensitized for contact with the young, the underside of the bill. This is the location of the famous red spot at which the chick afterwards pecks, a sense organ and effector organ in one, an organ of interaction with the new generation.[34] It may be that the parent bird also craves a contact of its breast and belly with the egg; Jacques Benoit suggests that replacement laying is elicited by the change which removal of an egg makes in the feeling of the clutch of eggs in the nest.[35] Herbert Friedmann, speaking of the number of parasitic eggs a small bird will tolerate in the nest in addition to its own, remarked: "What we have here is not a matter of latent counting ability in the hosts, enabling them to sense a 'correct' number of eggs in the nest, but more probably a reaction to the visible proportion of the combined mass of eggs to the available space in the nest, or even the amount of surface stimulation the eggs of a given clutch size produce on the brooding surface of the body of the host birds."[36]

Usually, upon a little introspection and reflection, we can find in ourselves some analogue, at least vestigial, to the feeling that seems to guide a lower mammal or a bird in its adjustments to each momentary situation. The need of contact between a bird's bare, feverish brood patch and the smooth and cooler eggs, perhaps heightened by the sight of the eggs, is sufficiently comparable to the varied feelings in the breast of a nursing woman, with the sudden increase of lactation when her infant cries, to be quite comprehensible in terms of human experience. The notion of such local sensitivity can be carried over to explain the gull's use of the underside of the bill, as well as several phenomena to be discussed in the course of this chapter. But occasionally one meets a response, or absence of response, that is hard to understand by any analogy with our own ways of feeling; and when one reflects on the differences it suggests between animal and human motivation, these

[34] Tinbergen, *The Herring Gull's World*, p. 242.
[35] "États physiologiques et instinct de reproduction chez les oiseaux" (1956), p. 239.
[36] *Host Relations of the Parasitic Cowbirds* (1963), p. 13.

may prove to be far-reaching. Tinbergen's "stupid" gull is a case in point: as soon as one applies animal measures to its inefficient acts, it becomes apparent that labor-saving is not one of its values,[37] that the practical results of acts are not motivating ideas, but that bodily feeling and immediate desire, fear and a medley of other fleeting emotions control instinctive performances, rather than any humanly acceptable "goals" or purposes. That is a basic insight gained by the observation of a relatively small deviation from rational behavior.

Another apparently trivial phenomenon which ultimately draws one of our natural assumptions in question is the behavior of female pigeons which, by all signs, are physiologically ready to lay, but will not do so in solitude, though they will start laying as soon as they can see another pigeon—male or female, or even their own reflection in a mirror. In a gregarious bird like a pigeon the need of companions for the development of normal instinctive behavior is not surprising; solitude may be frightening, and produce an inward tensity which inhibits laying. In that case the presence—even the apparent presence, such as her own image in a mirror provides—of another bird would relax her nerves and in this way implement the deposition of an egg. This is, of course, no more than a guess, yet we can at least make this and other guesses to account for the facts. But what is indeed surprising to a human psychologist is that the very audible cooing of pigeons in adjacent cages hidden from the experimental bird has no influence on her readiness to lay.[38] To us, the sound of other persons talking in an adjacent room would be just as suggestive of their presence as the sight of them.

Because sound is so obviously a social medium in human life, we are prone to assume that utterance is always communicative, that animals, like men, listen to each other and that their sounds are intended to be heard and reacted to by others. This belief is supported by the fact that there is a fairly steady relationship between sound production and sound reception; the frequency range of the voice, stridulation, humming, drumming, etc., of a species ordinarily lies within its own hearing range, so individuals of the same kind are physically equipped to hear

[37] J. M. Holzworth, in The Wild Grizzlies of Alaska (1930), p. 294, comments on the great amount of energy a bear will spend, overturning rocks and logs, for a mouse or even a beetle.

[38] See Benoit, "États physiologiques et instinct de reproduction chez les oiseaux," p. 239: "Matthews observa qu'une femelle vivant dans l'isolement ne pond pas, mais que si elle voit dans une cage voisine un mâle, ou même une femelle, elle pond. Elle pond aussi si elle voit seulement sa propre image se refléter dans un miroir. La vue seule est en cause dans ces expériences. L'audition de Pigeons placés dans une cage voisine, mais invisibles d'elle, ne stimulent pas la Pigeonne. Les sensations olfactives ne paraissent pas agir davantage."

each other. They may hear much more, too; the ear of a deer mouse is sensitive, above all, to rustles,[39] and the hearing of many dogs is said to have a high-frequency range that reaches into the supersonic for man.[40] The reception of sounds uttered by other individuals may be a secondary function in the evolution of hearing, and the noting of such tonal patterns may even, in some cases, be restricted to those made by the young; all degrees of emotional reaction could be exhibited in different animal species which have equally adequate aural mechanisms.

So it is possible that to a primarily visual being like the pigeon the sound of other pigeons has no exciting or reassuring value. We ourselves are not only gregarious, but communicative, and have exploited vocal communication to a degree that is peculiar to our species. We naturally interpret all animal utterance as intended to be heard and automatically interpreted by other beings, i.e., received as warning, lure, advertisement, identification or other sort of "signal." But this obvious, common-sense interpretation may be fallacious. The first important relation between utterance and hearing may be that the animal hears itself. The two functions, expressive and auditory, stem from different phylogenetic sources; audition certainly served originally for information of general ambient conditions, and was preceded by vibratory sensations with which it still merges, for human sensibility, at the lower end of the audible frequency range. Vocalization and its various functional substitutes, wing-rubbing, leg-rubbing, bill-clapping, etc., are originally expressive acts of inward excitation, and it is quite conceivable that their basic motivation is self-expansion, enlargement of the act in its noisy consummation. If that is the primary motivation of utterance it may be that the earliest sounds were not loud, but were felt by their producer rather than heard even by him—the ears being engaged in listening for the sounds of moving things, breathing, scratching, or alarms, even

[39] See D. B. Webster, "A Function of the Enlarged Middle-Ear Cavities of the Kangaroo Rat, Dipodomys" (1960). Webster found, by frequency analysis of the kangaroo rat's utterances, that its chirps are far above its own best hearing range, which consequently does not seem to be adapted primarily to vocal emissions of other individuals. So he writes: "Our data suggest instead that the increased hearing sensitivity may be an important means of detecting predators. It will be recalled that [in previously described experiments] the unoperated kangaroo rat was especially adept at avoiding both owls and snakes, whereas the animals with experimentally reduced middle-ear volumes were not. Furthermore, analyses of the sounds produced by the predators immediately prior to the attack fell within the most acute hearing range of the kangaroo rat" (p. 253).

[40] I. P. Pavlov, *Lectures on Conditioned Reflexes* (1928), p. 127: "in the dog it can be shown ... that his ability to distinguish high pitches is much greater than that of man; he reacts to vibrations of 70 to 80 thousand per second, whereas the limit of the human ear is not higher than 40,000–50,000."

while sexual or hostile excitement was finding expression in posturing that involved some automatic vocalizing. Both erotic and angry excitement evoke the desire to feel large, and lead naturally to any way of expanding the body—by piloerection, wing-spreading, gular inflation or whatever the animal's native repertoire provides—acts known as "display," and universally supposed to be performed to impress a partner or adversary (as the case may be). Vocalization is quite unquestioningly regarded as a sexual lure or aggressive warning; so much so that the mention of it is almost automatically accompanied by the stock phrase, "to warn rivals and attract females." It may well be a part of fighting and mating behavior, but to what extent it impresses either rivals or females may vary according to species, from a powerful influence to none at all. It may, of course, have either or both of those effects; it may even have communal functions, such as the mutual encouragement of frogs in a chorus. There the "song" is certainly heard by others than its producer, since a few chirps or quacks will set the whole company off. But the interpretation that the first utterances mean something like "all clear, go ahead" is misleading; there is no message carried in the sound, but a suggestion which spreads like a chain reaction throughout the frog assembly in the pond. Suggestion and suggestibility are the bases of most exhibits of so-called communication among animals. The trouble with calling sounds and motions "communication" or "signaling" is that these words connote not only an effect on the hearer, but an intention on the part of the performer to produce that effect— to warn, direct or solicit another creature. Even "attracting females" may well be a by-product instead of a motive of courtship utterances and antics. Those overt acts, which normally evoke the responses of a partner, were probably not purposive in their origin, but purely autistic, spontaneous acts of self-enlargement, enhanced by the hearing of the agent's own resounding accompaniment.

For the rest, the animal's ear was attuned to mechanical sounds of movement in his ambient: predators and possibly prey. Insect sounds may have been among the first highly distinctive noises to primitive insectivores. If, then, an animal's own autogenic vocal activity became an effective part of its self-inflation in high excitement, this aural feedback would have a new path to the ear—internal conduction—and a separate feeling tone, more allied to kinesthesis than to peripheral perception. In the pristine stages of its development it might have influenced the locations of the organs of hearing and of sound production in relation to one another. In all animals so far known which utter emotional sounds, these organs are close together; the development of their conjoint functioning may have induced the origin of the sonal apparatus near the auditory, or—if they were of equally ancient origin—encouraged their mutual approach in the course of their evolution.[41]

The important aspect of such a widely based history of hearing would be the peculiar emotive character it was destined to give, at a later stage, to the reception by one animal of sounds produced by another of the same species. Objective and subjective feelings—i.e., the senses of impact and action—are easily mixed in creatures having no conceptual functions to define the subject-object boundary (which can be ruptured even in human experience); in hearing utterances of fellow beings, that boundary, indistinct and unstable as it is in animal feeling, would be quite normally effaced, and the result would be an empathic yet outwardly oriented response intrinsically different from the purely practical impulse pattern guided by ordinary ambient conditions.

At what stage this empathic hearing would become an important bond between animals might vary extremely from species to species. In some it might function only at the high level of sexual excitement, and then be very effective in drawing two individuals together in physical union where subjective feeling seems to perfuse the whole act as if it were that of a single creature. In other cases its effect may be strongest in making a female animal's young seem like a part of herself when they utter their typical sounds, though these are quite different from any she hears in herself at present. Their value is still in her physiological memory. It is, indeed, so forcibly effective there that (as previously remarked) in a mammal it usually causes a sudden increase in lactation. The growth of feeling to embrace the life of the young may be seen in other changes of behavior, too, that suggest an enlargement of self-feeling as well as extended acts of feeding, protection, retrieving, etc.[42]

---

[41] The cricket's ear is in its tibia, close to the mechanism of stridulation (see Louis Guggenheim, *Phylogenesis of the Ear* [1948], p. 78); in most fish, hearing is centered in the lagena and sacculus, and in many species these organs, at the anterior end of the lateral line, are internally connected with the swim bladder, the organ of sound production. See K. von Frisch "Über den Gehörsinn der Fische" (1936), p. 242: "Bei den Ostariophysen (Cypriniden, Siluriden, Characiniden und Gymnotiden) steht die Schwimmblase durch die Weberschen Knöchelchen mit dem Sacculus in Verbindung. Der Sacculus-Otolith ist zum Auffangen der auf diesem Wege zugeleiteten Schallwellen besonders umgestaltet." Another indication of the relationship of vocal organs and hearing organs is given by Van Tyne and Berger in their *Fundamentals of Ornithology*, p. 112, where they say: "The length and configuration of the cochlea vary among birds, and there is some evidence that there is a positive correlation between length of cochlea and complexity of song."

[42] An example came under my own observation: a female rabbit which lived near

Instinctive behavior, whether single, conjoint or communal, is always individually motivated, both as a cyclic whole and from move to move in its enactment. It is neither egoistic nor altruistic; those are moral terms which have meaning only in human society. But it is always egocentric. This is one of the cardinal facts to keep in mind in tracing the motivation and trying to understand the feeling of animal acts. An excellent example of such a non-human approach and the sort of interpretation it gives to instinctive behavior patterns may be seen in Daniel Lehrman's "On the Organization of Maternal Behavior and the Problem of Instinct," wherein he follows, step by step, the progress of an elaborate instinctive act, and construes very plausibly (between the usual polemics against Professor Lorenz) how its development is upheld by immediate enticement and at the same time sets the stage for further subacts of that hereditary pattern. "It may be," he says in reference to his ringdoves, "that the vascularized brood patch is a source of irritation which is reduced by the cool, smooth surface of the eggs, and that this relationship is the basis of the birds' learning to sit on the eggs regularly. . . . After the birds have been sitting for about six days, the crop epithelium begins to proliferate, eventually becoming engorged with crop-milk. . . . The development of the crop epithelium is a reliable indication that prolactin is being secreted by the bird's pituitary gland. The prolactin presumably also completes the defeatherization of the brood patch, and causes it to become edematous, increasing the need for heat dissipation, and consequently strengthening the birds' attachment to the eggs (and nest)" (p. 490).

So the brooding—giving up the uncomfortable heat of the edemic ventral area to the eggs—keeps up the tension that leads to continued contact with the eggs, and in this way maintains the motivation of a long episode in the procreative act. What the bird feels is, in all probability, the comfort of holding the eggs against its naked brood patch, much as we hold a hand to an aching or sensitive spot. This indulgence quickly becomes perseverative, so that even as the brood patch wanes the bird wants to sit, until the hatching of the eggs introduces new situational elements, and the habit is modified in meeting them. But even then the tender area is not quite gone, and the habit of pressing it to the eggs does not vanish at once with their disappearance; the

---

my house used to feed on my lawn at a safe distance from my door, though the finest clover, violets and tender weeds grew around the doorstep. The first time she brought three babies with her, she led them straight to that rich garden, as though her appetite demanded enough for the family she had produced, and her boldness was that of a larger creature than before.

cool, naked young still elicit sitting, which simply changes from incu-bating to brooding.[43] This is an interesting phenomenon, but a common one: that a behavior pattern continues while its motivation shifts.[44]

The nestlings, however, do present a new situation; unlike the eggs,[45] they function, I believe, as an extension of the parents' own being. This, again, is most evident in the species to which Dr. Lehrman gave his special attention, the ringdove, that feeds its young on the "crop milk" produced in its own alimentary system and passed upward from the crop to the mouth cavity instead of downward to be digested. There is probably only the vaguest distinction in bodily feeling between the old dove and the young, especially during the first days after hatch-ing. This is evident from his description of the feeling-guided growth of their conjoined acts from the earliest hours, and especially the stimuli which appear to elicit one move after another:

"After the squabs hatch, the parent continues to sit on the nest. When the squab moves, the parent may be seen to look down, and preen the area against which the squab's head moved. The preening itself often arouses signs of emetic stimulation. Several such episodes may occur without any regurgitation, with the parent bird gradually beginning to peck at the bill of the squab, which is moving against the parent's breast, over the crop. One gets the impression that the parent is preening and gently pecking indiscriminately at its own breast and at the squab's head, which is moved frequently in response to the stimula-tion offered by the preening bill of the parent. The first regurgitation occurs during such an episode, when the squab's head, which is thrust toward any source of tactual stimulation, gets into the throat of the

---

[43] See Van Tyne and Berger, in *Fundamentals of Ornithology*, p. 299: "Birds are essentially 'cold-blooded' (poikilothermic) at hatching, so that marked changes in air temperature result in a much greater fluctuation in body temperature than in the homoiothermic adults." The nestling's chief need, at first, "is not food but warmth"; the parent bird's continues to be local cooling.

[44] Cf. Vol. I, pp. 441–42.

[45] Birds quite generally do not seem to distinguish their own eggs from others. Tinbergen's reference to the inability of gulls in this regard has already been cited (see p. 51 above); the same is true of terns, but the Atlantic murre is an excep-tion, as Beat Tschanz remarks in her excellent article, "Zur Brutbiologie der Trottellumme (*Uria aalge aalge* Pont.)" (1959), p. 24. Among passerine birds this indifference to the appearance and provenance of eggs is often extreme; for instance, Friedmann, in *Host Relations of the Parasitic Cowbirds*, p. 52, reports: "Crude experiments have been made to test the latitude of egg coloration tolerated by the phoebe; the result was that all of the eggs which were tried—from the larger, bluish-green eggs of the robin to the smaller, heavily dotted, cinnamon-reddish eggs of the house wren—were accepted and incubated by the phoebe."

parent, which may still be pecking at its own breast and the squab's head.

"It appears that they must already be sitting on the squab for reasons arising in another behavioral situation (i.e., incubation), in order for the squab to provide stimulation leading to regurgitation-feeding. Once the regurgitation has taken place, however, subsequent feeding episodes are more and more organized as behavior patterns leading up to the act of regurgitation."[46]

In mammals, the process of nursing is a conjoint act in which the two participants, mother and young one, crave each other's activity as implementation of their own pressing impulses. The mother needs relief from her milk pressure and welcomes the act of the nursling, which in turn finds the consummation of its hungry, sometimes blind foraging at the warm, anchoring, milk-yielding nipple. But there is generally more than feeding involved in the postpartum relation of mother and offspring: the close and long bodily contact which bridges the separation of the new lives from the parental matrix. Grooming, licking, in some cases carrying the young, retrieving strays from the nest, covering the litter, adding nest material are all extensions of self-maintaining acts.[47] A cat with a young litter licks any kitten that crawls into a convenient spot to lick, and gives herself a few strokes with the tongue between kittens. Like the preening dove, she seems to groom herself and her young indiscriminately. The small moving bodies, with fine, soft fur like that of her own legs, tugging and shoving at her belly much as she herself massages it in grooming, continue her body feeling and induce mouthing, which invites picking up and moving the peculiarly separate little parts with her teeth and paws. The instinctive hold by the nape in transporting the young is an adaptation of the typical feline killing technique, modified for the moment by her enlarged sense of her own periphery, a quasi-proprioceptive reaction encompassing the kittens.

In protracted instinctive acts such as the complete cycle of procrea-

---

[46] "On the Organization of Maternal Behavior and the Problem of Instinct," p. 491.

[47] Lehrman reports several experiments in which C. P. Richter showed the relationship of hormonally lowered body temperature to increase of nest-building impulses in rats, and remarks: "This suggests that the hormonal effect on nest-building is related to the need to keep up the body temperature. This conclusion is supported by Kinder's observations that the rate of nest-building was inversely proportional to the environmental temperature, and that appropriate temperature conditions could elicit or prevent nest-building in most rats regardless of hormonal state, pregnancy merely lowering the threshold" (ibid., p. 48n).

tion, a sequential order of impulses is guided from one consummated subact to another by a closely similar sequence of waxing and waning sensibilities. The great hereditary behavior patterns have two essential internal mechanisms of control, the nervous system and the endocrine system. Impulses seem to arise in the former by both central and peripheral stimulation, while the highly specific, often temporary feelings that guide their active expression depend mainly on chemical balances and chemical changes in the organism. The process of endocrine influence appears largely as a differential sensitization of perceptual systems —not only receptor organs, but their whole inward extensions—to ambient conditions, i.e., to lures and possibilities for action. Hormonal and some other chemical phases of the vital round impose special values on perceptual objects in harmony with the growth of impulses; not only procreative impulses, but also those to seasonally fluctuating activities, such as food consumption in frogs, which reaches a peak in August and early September, then dwindles steadily until hibernation sets in, and does not fully resume until after spawning in the spring. As the appetite for insects wanes (generally some time before they become unavailable), they lose their act value for the frog. A lure to deep hiding places under woodpiles or curving roots changes the animal's ambient and reduces its movements as much as does the lack of peripheral incentives to forage or hunt.

Changes in responses to sensory stimuli are less often dictated by any physical alterations in the stimulant objects than by an organically motivated shift of cathexis from one sort of thing to another. Such shifts may be gradual, as in the seasonal use of materials which at other times have no value for the agent,[48] or they may be quick and transient, as though the perceived object suddenly seemed different for a moment.[49] In the latter case, of course, one cannot assume a direct hor-

[48] Friedmann, in *The Cowbirds*, p. 178, writes: "On two occasions I have seen female Cowbirds get on old nests, settle in them as though they were going to lay and then fly off without laying. Both of these cases were seen a week before the Cowbirds started laying. It looked as though the birds were just getting interested in nests before their breeding time began."

Derek W. Morley, in *The Ant World* (1953), makes an interesting remark on the behavior of the wingless worker ants in many species, at the time when the winged queens and males emerge from the nest for their nuptial flights and subsequent scattering: "It is a day when little work is done and even the light-hating troglodite workers of the Yellow Lawn Ant (*Acanthomyops mixtus*), never normally seen abroad, swarm in the bright sunlight with their males and queens. Many of the workers themselves behave as if they wished to fly, rushing to the topmost peaks of the surrounding blades of grass, heather, or other vegetation" (p. 20).

[49] Cf. p. 76, n. 75, above on casually evoked impulses of terns.

monal influence, which is always slow and only preparatory in nature. The currently prevailing chemical balance is a general condition underlying the play of perceptions, and as these are essentially emotive perceptions of momentary values the animal's total awareness is governed by the inward pattern of sensitization. Some things are selectively seen in the array of sensory possibilities: tiny bits of food, nesting materials, spots of soft earth that invite digging, obstacles, lookouts, olfactory tracks and excrements. This goes on at all times, and depends on what the animal is doing. Ardent search, for instance, stimulated by the finding of one or two special morsels amid grass or forest leaves, sensitizes the exteroceptors involved in it to respond to the wanted smell or sight and raises the threshold for other perceptions.

We can discover a similar though perhaps somewhat less pronounced phenomenon in ourselves; if we go into woods or pastures to find, say, flat stones to pave a garden walk, we are likely to see such stones by roadsides and in crumbling walls, in quarry rubbish and old cellar holes for days afterwards when we are not looking for them. Our eye is sensitized to those flat gray objects, but generally only within fairly definite limits of size and some standards of shape.[50] The source of that visual selectiveness, in us, is a guiding envisagement of a planned act, which exists concomitantly with many other quite unrelated plans of action, that may be thought about in bewildering succession and alternation and put into effect bit by bit and by turns. As we may think back to the laying of a slab walk long after that plan has been realized, our visual reaction to possible materials persists for a while beyond our need of them. I doubt that non-human creatures find act values in things through remembered needs. They are differently motivated in their gathering and storing food and in their building operations, though these processes may overtly resemble human behavior. But in trying to envisage their mental actions lacking conceptual guidelines, such small contact points as the act-determined sensitization of a receptor organ

[50] An interesting parallel occurs in Mrs. F. T. Parsons' old guidebook, How to Know the Ferns (1961; 1st ed., 1899), pp. 77–78, where she quotes from an article by A. A. Eaton in The Fern Bulletin of several years before (i.e., previous to 1895): "Ophioglossum vulgatum was unknown to me, and was considered very rare, only two localities being known in Essex County, Mass. Early in the year a friend gave me two specimens. From these I got an idea of how the thing looked.... last July, ... in a 'boundout' mowing field, I was delighted to notice a spike of fruit in the grass. A search revealed about sixty.... A few days later, while raking in a similar locality, I found several, within a stone's throw of the house, demonstrating again the well-known fact that a thing once seen is easily discovered again."

to special percepts, which we do seem to share with most animals, point to one of the physio-psychological substructures of all mentality, and also indicate—if only implicitly—the differences of development from that common organic groundwork to the respective mental phenomena of man and beast.

There are other kinds of elementary feeling which we can still find in ourselves and consequently understand subjectively, though they are not of major importance to us, but which enter into animal lives as prime determinants of behavior. Two of these, I think, are controlling functions in the so-called social behavior of animals, which for just that reason is not really social, but communal, however organized and sanctioned it may look. Those two functions are empathy and suggestion.

Empathy is sometimes equated with sympathy, but is really something else; it is a much more direct physical reaction inherent in the perception of other beings, especially of the perceiver's own kind. We experience it when, for instance, the sight of a very sore eye causes our own eyes to water before we have had time to imagine how it must feel, or when the mere sight or sound of vomiting revolts our own stomach, or watching a steeplejack climb to a perilous height makes us dizzy. Empathy is an involuntary breach of individual separateness. Sometimes it does not even involve that breach but, contrariwise, is a stage in the loosening of a closer bond, actual identity, as in parturition, where a new separateness, long prepared, begins. In animals it is probably a fluctuating, gradually fading intimacy of feeling that unites a parent animal and its brood for an indefinite yet transitory period of time. In human life, where conception and imagination pervade the whole fabric of sensory reception and its immediate uses, empathy is largely replaced by sympathy or some other semi-intellectual response; but in animal life it exists unrecognized, unchallenged and operative at all possible levels and to all degrees.

The same is true of suggestion. We know its influence on our own thought and action, but this is probably very weak compared to its motivating power for animals. Although there are many phenomena of "mob psychology" in human behavior, the part played in them by suggestion is hard to isolate from the effective context of publicly held ideas, social attitudes and individual motives which go into each participant's act in the crowd. In animals, however, such mental conditions are not operative, and suggestion has free play. The speed with which it operates where it is unobstructed has made human observers assume that in such suggestible creatures as flocking birds or schooling fish there must be a special signal given by a leader, which reaches all the members of the group at the same moment, like the conductor's signal to an orchestra. But considering that in a flock of blackbirds feeding on a lawn each one is as ready for flight at any moment as all its companions, the suggestion of takeoff and direction given by the first one to rise is enough to steer every other one which reacts at all. Some may not fly, but normally none flies a different way.

Upon close examination, both in laboratory tests and in less formal observation, it is quite generally found that what is loosely called "imitation" in animals is really suggestion. The distinction between these two phenomena is neither trivial nor verbal. Imitation is a progressive act of watching another creature's movements and repeating them, one by one, in the same succession; imitation can stop in the middle of a series of moves, without breaking any unifying tension, consummation or cadence.[51] Suggestion, on the other hand, motivates an impulse similar to that of the individual setting the example, but may eventuate in a very different expression. There is a clear illustration of behavior started by suggestion but not guided by imitation in a report by J. Fisher and R. A. Hinde, "The Opening of Milk Bottles by Birds" (1949); after one bird succeeded—or happened—to pry the cap off a milk bottle left beside a kitchen door, many birds of various species learned the trick, but each species in its own way.[52]

Imitation, *sensu stricto*, is rare in animals, if it occurs at all, which is not certain.[53] Even in apes, which are said to imitate each other's and

[51] There is a children's game, "Follow the Leader," wherein the leader performs all sorts of arbitrary movements which his followers imitate. The interest of the game is in the absurdity of his tricks. There is no goal to be achieved, so the sequence can break off at any point. That is true imitation.

[52] Peter Kunkel, in an excellent study of eleven species of waxbills, "Zum Verhalten einiger Prachtfinken (*Estrildinae*)" (1959), relates a similar observation (p. 308): "Gibt man einer Gruppe von Prachtfinken zum erstenmal Mehlwürmer, so wissen sie nichts damit anzufangen; erst nach geraumer Zeit versucht einer, die relativ zu grosse Beute zu fressen; hat erst einmal einer Erfolg, so fressen binnen kurzer Zeit alle Mehlwürmer."

[53] See, for example, Hall, "Observational Learning in Monkeys and Apes," p. 211: "Crawford and Spence used a new method in which an O [observer] chimpanzee, previously trained in discrimination learning, is given a series of chances to observe another (D) [demonstrator] chimpanzee's differential responses to a pair of stimuli, D's choices being irregularly rewarded with food.... Results on nine animals are said to be inconclusive and variable, and to provide little evidence of imitation over and above effects attributable to the social facilitation." Toward the end of the article the author concludes (p. 223): "As Thorpe has pointed out, there is plenty of evidence for social facilitation and local enhancement in mammalian behaviour, but the evidence for 'true imitation, in the sense of copying a novel or otherwise improbable act' ... is hard to discern."

Bierens de Haan, in *Die tierischen Instinkte*, p. 310, claims to have seen true

their keeper's acts, direct imitation of postures, movements or step-by-step procedures has not been recorded; to "ape" another individual is to follow his suggestion in the use of a situation, but not to watch his behavior closely and copy it as faithfully as possible. Animals are not inclined to watch each other objectively; they see the act a companion is engaged in, and at once have an impulse to do the same thing themselves, but they may do it by a different method. Suggestibility is their forte, and makes some species so sensitive to one another's impulses that the first "intention movement" runs through a whole drove of individuals. This is one of the alleged "mechanisms" holding the members of herds, flocks or swarms—constant or temporary—together. It is not a special mechanism, but a heightened degree of a general feature in animal psychology. In close individual relations, sexual, parental or possibly sibling (e.g., in play), it is likely to be so entwined with empathy and other reactions that it becomes impossible to isolate.

To conceive of animal ambients, organized as they are by act values, is difficult for us not only because we find it hard to eliminate the objects and centers of interest that exist for us, but because we cannot imagine many that do not. So, for instance, we know that smells mean more to most other mammals than to man, but we can conceive of this difference only as an exaggeration of our own olfactory experience; the fact that for a rat there are odors we have never smelled and, especially, epicritical distinctions within such general sensory impressions far below our limen of perception,[54] makes it well-nigh impossible to interpret the

---

imitation performed by a monkey that tried in vain to extract a fruit from a bottle with its finger, and failing to obtain it in that way, threw the bottle away, whereby the fruit rolled out: "Als dann Bierens de Haan auch diesem Tiere langsam die richtige Bewegung vormachte, wurde diese von dem aufmerksam zuschauenden Tier sofort nachgeahmt und an den folgenden Tagen selbständig ausgeführt." To this he adds the interesting suggestion that the monkey's attention to the man's exact movements was due to the fact that it was itself just on the point of trying them: "Hier wurde also fraglos eine Bewegung von dem Experimentator übernommen, wohl eben darum, weil das Tier selbst nahe daran war, sie selbst zu erfinden." Of the great apes he says (p. 312): "Wo bei ihnen Nachahmung des Menschen vorkommt, ist sie meistens spielerischer Art, d. h. es werden im Spiele Handlungen wiederholt, die sie beim Menschen beobachtet haben." This is, of course, a suggested performance, not imitation in the sense of following a pattern of moves. Even Bierens de Haan's monkey, "watching attentively," may have been watching for its own turn to try the stunt rather than for the way to do it.

[54] The exudations of animals' skins seem to vary for their companions with the physiological (especially, emotional) condition of the emitting organism. See, for instance, J. G. Valenta and M. K. Rigby, "Discrimination of the Odor of Stressed Rats" (1968), p. 599 (authors' summary): "Albino rats can reliably distinguish between the odors of stressed and unstressed rats. Five animals learned to interrupt

rat's *Umwelt*. Jakob von Uexküll has made some brave attempts to imagine and picture non-human ambients;[55] but selective simplification, and different degrees of detail in humanly recognized "things," are all the differences between the so-called objective environment and the various animal *Umwelten* that he managed to project graphically. The pictorial effect of his attempt, here shown (Fig. 14–1), to present the difference between the visual percepts of a human being and a fly was made by photographing the same scene first with the usual lens used by amateur photographers and then with a filter which eliminated all but the big light areas and dark volumes. The image imputed to the fly still has the same form, the same binocular perspective from the same level, and roughly the same scope, especially in depth, as a man's. There is no radical allowance for the difference in size or structure between the two organisms. That a fly would see anything more than 5 or 6 feet away except motions and light sources (windows, bright chinks, reflecting surfaces) is unlikely; still more, that it sees houses, vehicles and people as dark masses against a background, and a street as a receding passage with something—object or pale area—at its end. Even most mammalian vision, made by two simple eyes, seems not to be pictorial, but dynamic, directive, like our own peripheral vision—the higher primates with their forward gaze and binocular focus being an exception.

It is often said that animals have fewer percepts than men; it seems safer, however, to say that they have different ones, and lack many which we find important because we have built our world on them. Birds and beasts make use of sensory data that are lost on us because our intellectual habits override them and, when we do notice them, cause us to ignore them as "not significant." Animals live in a fabric of redundancies, and apparently feel the slightest little deviation from this pseudo-statistical steady state in forming their immediate expectancies. David Hume called this kind of perceptual background "unphilosophical probability."[56] Most of the tiny abnormalities which enter into

---

an ongoing response when air from the cages of stressed rats was introduced into the test compartment, and to continue responding when air from unstressed rats was introduced. The discrimination does not seem to depend on recognition of odors of individual rats." Similarly W. K. Whitten, F. H. Bronson and J. A. Greenstein report an experiment with sexual odors, in a brief paper, "Estrus-Inducing Pheromone of Male Mice: Transport by Movement of Air" (1968). Their procedures would be somewhat lengthy to describe, but their concluding comment is: "These findings show that the pheromone from male mice is volatile and further support the concept that it acts through olfactory receptors" (from the summary, p. 584).

[55] See "A Stroll through the Worlds of Animals and Men: A Picture Book of Invisible Worlds" (1957; orig. pub., 1934).

[56] *Treatise on Human Nature* (1740), Book I, part 3.

Uexküll has made some brave attempts to picture non-human ambients; but . . .

the image imputed to the fly still has the same form . . . as a man's

Figure 14–1. (*Upper*) Village Street as Seen by Man; (*Lower*) Same
Village Street as Seen by Fly

(Jakob von Uexküll, "A Stroll through the Worlds of Animals and Men: A Picture Book
of Invisible Worlds," in Claire H. Schiller [ed.], *Instinctive Behavior: The Development of
a Modern Concept* [New York. International Universities Press, 1957].)

[133]

motivating situations for instinctive behavior would be ruled out by intelligent men as statistically non-significant, and discounted in recording "information."[57]

Quite apart from greater reactivity, however, some non-human beings may actually have more complex perceptions than human senses provide. We may see a bird and hear it twitter, but the sound does not modify what we see, namely, the surface form and many of the locomotory changes of the visible body (the movements of wings, erection of feathers, etc., on the side turned away from the observer are not visible to him). As J. J. Gibson has pointed out, surfaces are essentially what the ordinary vertebrate eye most readily sees and wherein it learns to discern textures, lines and contours.[58] Sound may have important meanings for us, especially of location, approach or retreat, speed and direction of the passage of bodies in our environment and, in the case of living bodies, above all, vocal utterances bespeaking excitement and often indicating its more particular character. But sound, to our ears, is diffuse, like smell, or relatively massive, impinging without any precise spatial articulation. Such detail as it may convey is temporal. The crash of dishes sliding off an unbalanced tray, or the rustling of a mouse fleeing through dry leaves, has certainly more audible structure than an explosion, but it is the progress of an event through time that it conveys, not spatial form.

Some animals, however, make a special use of sound by virtue of equally special mechanisms which work on the principle of our radar detectors; echolocation of objects in space. This has already been touched upon in Chapter 13 with reference to bats, which find both their flightways and their prey in open air without light.[59] A close

---

[57] Otto Koenig, in *Kif-Kif*, pp. 211–12, provides an example of such instinctive judgment on behavior that deviates statistically rather than by specific symptoms from normal: "Als echte, hochspezialisierte Jäger erkennen Greifvögel selbst an kleinsten Bewegungsstörungen und Ungeschicklichkeiten das kränkliche Beutetier in der Schar der Gesunden.... Auch Geier verfügen über diese subtile Unterscheidungsfähigkeit, ja sind sogar wahre Meister dieser Kunst und erkennen auf den ersten Blick, wie es um ein Tier bestellt ist."

[58] In *The Perception of the Visual World*, p. 8, he states the fundamental proposition: "The elementary impressions of a visual world are those of surface and edge. These are the fundamental sensations of space, the stimuli for which need to be discovered." The book is an exemplary progressive record of that discovery without any disconcertment by its implications, as of new definitions, e.g., of "stimulus" and "seeing."

[59] Many bats and echolocating birds have a fair degree of eyesight, and when flying by daylight use it in place of echolocation. The supersonic pulses they emit in darkness have not been found where they were demonstrably using vision. See

parallel to this phenomenon, an aquatic version known as "sonar," is found in cetaceans, and has been systematically studied chiefly in dolphins. These extremely mobile animals seem to travel by night as well as by day, and can follow moving bodies in murky waters where vision would be a weak and faltering guide. Both behavioral experiments and anatomical researches have demonstrated quite beyond doubt that dolphins and possibly other marine mammals emit supersonic tonal impulses and have a specialized receptor organ to pick up the returning echoes of these emissions from objects in their vicinity; the proportions and locations of fixed or moving things—rocks, great plants, fish, fellow dolphins—seem to be perceptible to them by a form of hearing which we do not possess. W. N. Kellogg has observed many details of the utterance-and-echo process, especially the way the "sound" (for dolphins, not for us) is broadcast by oscillating head movements so the echoes probably come back as a broad sound texture, in which objects appear as differentiated sonal figures. So he says: "Since the noises which make up the echoes are emitted by the animal itself, the activity as a whole amounts to a kind of scanning, by sound. We suggest, therefore, the term 'auditory scanning' as a good name for both the acoustic and the general behavior comprising [sic] this elaborate pattern of activity."[60]

After describing some experiments he returns, in a later passage, to the detector function of the "sonar" mechanism and its apparent capacity to distinguish different physical substances. "The process by which such a distinction is accomplished," he suggests by way of eluci-

---

Griffin, *Listening in the Dark*, pp. 252–53: "Most of the Megachiroptera are strictly *visual* animals. They rely almost wholly on their eyes...." Yet he observes: "When Möhres studied *Rousettus* [the tomb bat] in Egypt he found that in the dark they emitted clearly audible Ticklaute or clicking sounds.... Novick has found that other species of the genus *Rousettus* behave in much the same manner, orienting themselves visually if there is light but relying on easily audible clicks when vision is hindered.... *Rousettus* can be caused to start clicking whenever the light is switched off, and it falls silent as soon as the lamp is turned on again."

Cf. also "Fisherman Bats of the Caribbean Region" (1945), by E. W. Gudger, who retails some observations made by J. E. Benedict, naturalist on the Albatross in 1883–84, in the waters near Trinidad; Benedict saw bats (probably *Noctilio leporinus*) fishing in company with pelicans, and Gudger points out as a remarkable fact "that the bats fished in bright daylight" (p. 8). See also Suthers, "Optomotor Responses by Echolocating Bats."

[60] *Porpoises and Sonar*, p. 105. It is unfortunate that Dr. Kellogg perpetuates the popular error of calling dolphins "porpoises," instead of joining with other writers to designate *Tursiops truncatus* as "the Bottle-nosed dolphin" and reserving the name "porpoise" for the genus *Phocoena* and other true porpoises.

dation, "can perhaps be understood by comparing it to vision or to optics. Daylight or white light contains all the wave lengths of the visible spectrum. Yet, when white light is used to illuminate a red surface, red light is all that is reflected back. . . . The coefficients of 'reflection' of the various surfaces are not the same. . . .

"A series of porpoise clicks . . . is similar to 'white noise.' Some of the original frequencies transmitted by the animal are absorbed and some are reflected. . . . The echoes from different materials would therefore differ in composition or in quality. They would vary in the pattern of frequencies which they contain.

"Wood, in other words, simply 'sounds different' from metal to a porpoise, in the same way that it looks different to the human eye. It is the sound spectrum of the returning vibrations which gives the clue to the nature of the reflecting surface."[61]

A human being naturally thinks that the echoes coming back from (say) another *Tursiops* should report the same smooth, streamlined, elastic outer surface that our eyes, and perhaps the dolphin's, see when there is light. But light and sound, though both refrangible and differentially reflective, have very different properties of penetration, so light reflections and echoes do not necessarily render comparable aspects of one and the same object even if both impinge on it and come back from it at the same angle. The only recognition and psychological use made of this fact is in John C. Lilly's *The Mind of the Dolphin* (1967). This book is so full of unscientific fancy that it can hardly be called "controversial," since controversy against its articles of faith would be bootless;[62] but Lilly's analysis of the sonar operation and his speculation on the "sonar image" form a really brilliant piece of scientific imagination. After remarking, much as Kellogg had done before, on the possibility of differentiating among the echoes from various substances, he says:

"If we were placed underwater and looked at one another by means of sonar, what would each of us look like to the other?

---

[61] *Ibid.*, pp. 122–23.

[62] See, for instance, p. 83: "We have found that, in dealing with such a large-brained mammal, we must keep the working hypothesis in mind that 'they are highly intelligent and are just as interested in communicating with us as we are with them.' . . . If we use any other hypothesis, we have no success whatsoever in dealing communicatively with them." Like the "signs" clearly seen by mystics, one has to believe in the significance of snorts and whistles before they will sound like conversation. Dr. Lilly's animals, with their desires to tell us their thoughts and experiences, are reminiscent of the fairytales in which human beings, held under a sorcerer's spell, have to live in the forms of frogs, deer, rats—or maybe dolphins.

"Sound waves in water penetrate a body without much external reflections or absorptions. Skin, muscle, and fat are essentially transparent to the sound waves coming through the water. The internal reflections are from air-containing cavities and from bones. Thus we see a fuzzy outline of the whole body plus the bones and teeth fairly clearly delineated; the most sharply delineated objects are any gas-containing cavities. We have a good view of portions of the gut tract, the air sinuses in the head, the mouth cavity, the larynx, the trachea, the bronchi, the bronchioles, the lungs, and any air trapped in or around the body and the clothing." And further: "living dolphin-wise, we would have little need for external facial expression.... The truth. of our stomachs would be immediately available to everyone else. In other words, anyone could tell when we were either sick or angry by the bubbles of air moving in our stomachs. The true state of our emotions would be read with ease."[63]

"Please notice that in the above descriptions of the sonic acoustic underwater world I use primarily visual language 'to see by means of sound.' Since we are more visual than we are acoustic, this is necessary, using our current language. This language requirement is reflected in the construction of our nervous systems. We have ten times their [the dolphins'] speed, their storage capacity, and their computation ability in the visual sphere; the dolphins have something of the same order of speed, storage capacity, and computation ability in the acoustic sphere. This, then, is one of the major differences between the minds of men and the minds of dolphins."[64]

These last comparisons go beyond what most marine scientists would consider to be "known," but the point on which I agree with Dr. Lilly is that animal perception is not simply an impoverished version of human perception. It contains possible sensitivities to impingements that we cannot feel, and where it parallels our sensory modes it is limited or extended by the values that enter into the animal's instinctive life. Not everything that is physically perceptible is necessarily noted and utilized by dolphins, songbirds or monkeys, any more than by men. Ethologists today are so anxious to find the blueprints for ethnological phenomena in their animals that every component of bodily postures or uttered sounds is treated as a signal for "social communication."[65] But I am inclined to believe that signals, and especially

[63] P. 132.
[64] *Ibid.*, p. 134.
[65] B. F. Beebe, in *African Elephants* (1968), pp. 115–16, reports the bizarre fact that a deep rumble, which sounds like a tractor engine starting up, is "the ele-

communicative—intended and interpreted—signals, play a very minor part among even the highest non-human beings, if such devices occur at all; and that directly felt inward and outward acts, springing from impulse and ambient pressions and opportunities, are sufficient for all animal needs. The many claims for concept formation and symbolic thinking in animals all rest on special definitions of "concept" and "symbol" invented to fit rats or ravens, but entirely inadequate to the mental processes of *Homo sapiens*; they do not cover man's uses of speech and logical thought, so the evidence for the similarity of human and animal types of cerebration is specious.[66] Another source of hasty

---

phant's way of expressing contentment little different except in volume from a cat's purring.... Dr. Ivan Buss investigated this phenomenon among elephants at the Basle, Switzerland Zoo. He found that the noises were made by air exhaled from the throat and trunk tip in staccato-like bursts. He believed that this rumbling may also serve as a form of communication between elephants."

In a similar vein G. M. Sutton and P. W. Gilbert, in their article, "The Brown Jay's Furcular Pouch" (1942), having found a special air sac possessed by just one species of bird, the brown jay, and having noted that this organ produced a peculiar, hiccup-like sound, say: "This sound, which usually was heard at the close of a scream, but often quite independent of it, was not unlike the syllable *puck* or *huck*." And following a careful anatomical and physiological description of the sac and its sound production, they report further that "the hiccup was used as part of the bird's vocabulary just as definitely as were the scream and other purely vocal sounds. The hiccup was a signal for quiet, for stealthy approach, for close attention to some not quite solved problem.... So the hiccup is a Brown Jay word" (p. 161). Why the signal for quiet and stealth should be given at the end of a scream while the birds kept up a hubbub of screams and "quiet, please" is a problem for ethologists.

[66] Some of these word-engendered claims have already been adduced in Vol. I, Chapter 2, *passim*; but a typical argument for animal rationality on the basis of terms defined *ad hoc* might illustrate the futility of such intellectual legerdemain. Paul E. Fields, in a serious monograph, *Studies in Concept Formation* (1932), p. 4, declared: "If Hull is justified in using the term 'concept' to denote the observable behavior of a child when it makes a specific language response to a certain stimulating situation, then we should be allowed to use the term 'concept' to denote the observable behavior of a rat when it makes a specific muscular response to a similar stimulating situation.... so far as the present study is concerned, the specific acquired reaction involved in the 'jump to triangle' of the rat will be considered as equivalent to the child's specific language response 'triangle.' " So, by a (further equivalent?) "jump to conclusions," we learn that rats entertain concepts; for "when white rats are given a training period specifically designed to provide a large number of different 'triangle experiences,' the rats are able to perfect a type of behavior which is fully described by the implications in our use of the term 'concept' " (p. 69).

For good measure, let me also add N. R. F. Maier's *Reasoning in White Rats* (1929), in which "reasoning" is defined as forming a new pattern from elements

attribution of conceptual thinking and understanding to non-human brains is that it is extremely difficult for most people to explain a fitting action on any other ground than "insight" into general principles, especially of cause and effect; and the reason for this difficulty, in turn, is the fact that instinctive life has not been systematically studied, except recently under the aegis of the act-center hypothesis of the Lorenz-Tinbergen school with its inhibitors, releasers, sign stimuli, ritualized social signals, etc.; and how this devil's tattoo of stimuli, mechanically activating inborn responses, could ever eventuate in human intelligence and feeling is a problem. Consequently there is a tendency to sweep aside the undeveloped and moot notions of "instinct" and look for signs of rational action and approaches to human ways of thinking wherever an animal performs an act which simulates such processes. In studying the so-called higher animals—primates, cetaceans, Corvidae, elephants, dogs—our whole interest is slanted toward the demonstration of conception and reasoning in them.

During a discussion following the reading of a symposium paper, "The Cetacean Brain," one of the symposiasts remarked: "This paper obviously rests very heavily on the concept of intelligence, which is the thing we hoped we could argue about. This problem is of the utmost interest to the human being. I don't know why. The first question we are asked in our work with forty-five different species is: which is the most intelligent animal? We have been working at it for fifteen years, and we still don't know the answer. . . .

"We feel that when you are looking at neuroanatomy and neurophysiology, and want to find the definitive aspects of what is commonly

---

of older patterns of perception or behavior. Summing up his experimental results, this author concludes (p. 92) "that a new pattern, the solution, which is made up of essentials from two other patterns, has been formed seems to have been indicated.

"As the combination of two patterns in the solution of a problem is at the bottom of theories of reasoning that make reasoning more than 'trial and error,' it must be granted that white rats also reason."

It might, of course, be argued that conception and reasoning could be better demonstrated in higher animals than rats; but such investigations, too, begin with some arbitrary and simplistic definition of the intellectual terms. So R. T. Kelleher, in "Concept Formation in Chimpanzees" (1958), p. 777, says: "Learning to respond to a class of stimuli on the basis of some common physical characteristic is referred to as 'concept formation.'" His chimpanzees were to form the concept "three" by seeing three lighted squares (out of a set of nine) first in a row, which they learned to recognize, and then in other distributions, on which they failed. The experimenter, however, declared, "With a different procedure, the chimpanzees could probably have been trained to respond to the common element of the second concept problem" (p. 778).

called intelligence, if you find a state of affairs in which all the instinctive stuff breaks down, crosses up, and becomes interconnected and mutually available, then you will have it."[67]

This is, I think, a widespread conception;[68] but to make "all the instinctive stuff break down" requires a catalyst, which I believe really entered upon the scene to make the human mind take shape. How the destruction of instinctive life, *per se*, should cause the elements to become "interconnected and mutually available" (for what?) I do not understand.

If, however, one views all animal life, including man's, as a great texture of impulses and enactments, in which special patterns emerge somewhat as the forms prepared in low relief on a background, and perhaps scarcely visible, emerge when pigment passes over them in a rubbing, the wholeness of instinctive life appears much more vital than when it is conceived as a product of interlocking mechanisms or concatenated involuntary reflexes. It is pushing from the matrix of impulsive organic activities all the time. There is no need of looking to animals for the specialized human functions of concept formation and symbolic expression, not even to apes. What does distinguish the "higher" animals is a great increase in emotionality, which entails a corresponding increase of perceptive functions, not necessarily by virtue of better receptor organs, but of increasing values imposed on what anciently developed senses convey. Without a true appreciation of the richness and completeness of life built on instinctive action, and of the heights to which discriminate sensibility and emotional reaction can rise on that foundation, one cannot recognize the critical point where an overcharged system of mental operations breaks over into imagery and symbolic conception, and the great shift from animal mentality to mind begins.

---

[67] K. S. Norris (ed.), *Whales, Dolphins, and Porpoises* (1966), p. 253. The commentator was Keller Breland, the author of the paper Lawrence Kruger.

[68] Cf. Hebb, *The Organization of Behavior*, p. 169: "Instinct is not a separate process from intelligence or insight. It is intelligence, or insight, that is innately limited in variety."

15

Interpretations

T HE conception of instinctive behavior as a product of countless, competitively enacted impulses raises the question of motivation in an acute, ineluctable way; a problem which the hypotheses of hierarchically arranged "act centers" and that of integrated reflexes both sidestep and replace by the alternative assumption of innate mechanisms predisposed to perform typical acts. The basic assumption here proposed is the constant guidance of overt animal action by feeling, both peripheral and central, i.e., perceptual and emotive; the complex and often puzzling observed phenomena of non-human behavior—the part of the ethologists' contribution with which I rarely could or would quarrel—must, therefore, be constantly and consistently interpreted in terms of direct individual impression and equally immediate expression. This bars any explanation in terms of "social" usefulness or prevision of future conditions. All the conditions are "now," and the guidance, from the total impulse to consummation of the fully elaborated act, is by the agent's own feeling. The motivation of a behavioral act has to be conceived as a felt element in the situation from which it arises, that is, as something with a luring or driving value for the performing organism, not only as an inherited reaction established by "natural selection" for the good of the species.

In the ethological literature there are various examples of specialized animal acts interpreted by reference to their survival value, not for the individual agent (usually, the aggressor in a fight), but the stock. So, for instance, I. Eibl-Eibesfeldt explains the fact that many animals fight in one way with the natural enemies of their kind and in another with members of their own species on the evolutionary principle that in the latter case the opponent is not really to be killed or seriously injured; being weak, he is to be excluded from mating at present, but is to remain alive so he may win and procreate in the future.[1] As an illustra-

---

[1] "Angeborenes und Erworbenes im Verhalten einiger Säuger," p. 723: "Der Selektionsdruck, der zur Ausbildung solcher Kommentkämpfe führt, ist leicht zu

tion he cites the fact that oryxes fight their rivals by glancing, sidewise swipes of their straight horns, whereas they gore attacking predators with the sharp points. The explanation of that difference might, however, be much simpler than by reference to an evolutionary specialization for non-fatal methods: two oryxes attacking one another must each avoid the other's horns as well as use his own, and the result is a sparring contest without any direct thrust. Dogs, jackals and leopards have no horns; their fangs can be avoided in an attack with the long, pointed horns of these antelopes.

This is a very simple reinterpretation, but has many parallels: the throat bite of dogs and cats is developed by every puppy or kitten in evading the teeth of its opponent; the lizards and snakes which are said to hold "ritual" contests are caught between tactics of aggression and evasion, so their movements express the special circumstance of having to meet natural weapons exactly like their own, and consequently are often reduced to protracted, ineffectual posturing.

But there are behavioral patterns much harder to explain, involving subtler reflections on animal situations and feeling. One phenomenon that immediately comes to mind is the alleged "magnanimity" of a wolf which has overcome another one in a fight; according to report, the loser, when he gives up, crouches and offers his most vulnerable spot, generally his throat, to the victor, who thereupon stops his attack, apparently satisfied to be acknowledged the stronger.[2] There are two

---

verstehen: Es wirkt arterhaltend, wenn der schwächere Nachbar vertrieben und von der Fortpflanzung zunächst ausgeschlossen wird. Aber er soll leben bleiben, so dass er später einmal siegen kann." The logic of this argument is none too clear. If the loser of a fight may, under subsequent conditions, be the winner, then he is genetically just as fit now as he will be then to continue the stock.

[2] Otto Koenig, in *Kif-Kif. Menschliches und Tierisches zwischen Sahara und Wilhelminenberg*, p. 172, says even more generally: "Angeborene Demutsstellungen zeigen bei allen Tieren immer die gleiche Tendenz, dem gegnerischen Artgenossen einen besonders empfindlichen, dem Gegner ungefährlichen Körperteil zu bieten, wodurch sein Angriff gehemmt wird. Junge Hunde werfen sich auf den Rücken und bieten die Kehle dar, alte Hunde drehen dem Gegner diese im Stehen zu. Sumpfhühner, Tauben und viele andere Vögel präsentieren dem angreifenden Artgenossen den so hackempfindlichen Hinterkopf. Demütige Affen drehen sich um und zeigen dem Feind die harmlose Kehrseite. Der Mensch wirft sich nieder und bietet das empfindliche Genick." The last two instances do not really warrant the ethological interpretation; the monkey's "presenting" is hardly an exposure of his most vulnerable part, and the man's act is primarily to protect his face, not to offer his nape.

Lorenz, in *King Solomon's Ring*, pp. 206–7, tells the same story, applying it explicitly to dogs as well as wolves. As far as I can determine, the interpretation of the loser's cowering and looking up at his conqueror as a "submissive gesture" and deliberate presentation of his own throat was introduced by Lorenz.

versions of the subsequent act; according to one, "after waiting to make certain that the loser is not going to move, the victor urinates on any nearby object. This is an act of dismissal and the loser then departs hurriedly."[3] But in the version given by Lorenz—romantic enough, without carrying the "magnanimity" of the victor beyond his refraining from biting the exposed throat, neck or whatever the loser seems to present in his "gesture of humility"—the moment the cowering wolf changes his attitude, the aggressor resumes his attack. The submissive gesture and noble acceptance of it produce only a momentary suspension of the fight.[4] Finally, however, the winner feels the urge to urinate, and as he backs away to seek a stump, tree, or perhaps hydrant or lamp post to do so, the underdog makes his escape. Lorenz says nothing about an "act of dismissal," i.e., a signal to the loser that he may go; if Evans' story is taken from *King Solomon's Ring*, it has acquired a new elaboration in the retelling. But the older account does treat the act of urinating at that moment as a symbolic performance, not as a signal to the vanquished, but as laying claim to the battlefield[5]—an interpretation for which I can see no other basis than the ethological assumption that urinating is always a claim to something, wherefore it is often referred to as "marking" without any explanation of why the place, object or animal on which it is performed should be "marked."[6]

Robert Ardrey, in *The Territorial Imperative* (1966), declares that "when wolves indulge in final debate, the loser rolls over on his back,

---

[3] W. F. Evans, *Communication in the Animal World* (1968), p. 104.

[4] In Lorenz' book there is a curious ambivalence between his realization that all animal acts are instinctive—which he states explicitly and repeatedly—and his irrepressible tendency to see them as noble or base. So he cannot desist from asking: "Who is a 'wicked' animal, the roe-buck who will slit the bellies even of females and young of his own kind if they are unable to escape him, or the wolf who cannot bite his hated enemy if the latter appeals to his mercy?" (p. 211).

[5] *Ibid.*, pp. 206–7: "It seems as if the victor is only waiting for the moment when the other will relinquish his submissive attitude, thereby enabling him to give vent to his urgent desire to bite. But, luckily for the 'underdog,' the top-dog at the close of the fight is overcome by the pressing need to leave his trade-mark on the battle-field, to designate it as his personal property—in other words, he must lift his leg against the nearest upright object. This right-of-possession ceremony is usually taken advantage of by the under-dog to make himself scarce." Why the victor should lay a territorial claim to the spot in the woods or to the street corner where he had a fight, which he will probably leave in a few minutes if not seconds, is hard to guess.

[6] See, for instance, R. Schloeth, "Zur Biologie der Begegnung zwischen Tieren" (1956), p. 9: "Kot und Harn wurden bei vielen Säugern der verschiedensten Gruppen im Schock der plötzlichen Gegenüberstellung sehr oft unmittelbar— vielfach auch mehrmals hintereinander—abgegeben. . . . *Panthera pardus* markierte bei einer Begegnung mit einem ♀ innert einer Stunde 29 mal."

exposing his belly to the victor; the winner, incapable of attacking him further, walks away. It is a behavioral gesture in no wise different from the human gesture of raising one's hands in surrender" (p. 340). Evidently Professor Lorenz and Mr. Ardrey have observed different wolves (according to Otto Koenig's account, quoted in n. 2 above, the former saw an old wolf and the latter a young wolf) brought low. Neither Lorenz nor Koenig claims to have seen the victor simply walk away. Yet even Ardrey's nonchalant top dog is supposed to understand and honor a formal gesture. It is this statement, explicitly made or subscribed to by all the authors here quoted, that I would challenge.

In animals, movement which may terminate in a posture characteristic of a mood, an intention (the covert part of an act, usually felt both emotionally and somatically before the overt phase is reached, if it ever is) or an expectation is a direct enactment of an impulse motivated by the situational complex of the passing moment. In Mr. Ardrey's wolf combat, the weaker fighter rolled over on his back, but there is no indication that he meant to expose his belly as a formal act of submission. This form of yielding to superior strength is not a gesture, but an actual collapse, in which the loser can still use mouth and feet in purely defensive action but gives up all aggressive tactics, so the casual fight is really over, and the victor gives up the encounter, too. Its original fury is generally not sufficient to carry it to great lengths. An older defeated animal no longer finds the puppy habit of lying on its back and struggling with all fours the most natural defense; it cowers and looks up at the foe to counter his moves, groveling abjectly and, of course, watching. I can see no indication that it means to expose its throat. No matter what posture a shrinking animal takes when fear overcomes it and holds it motionless, it is sure to expose some vulnerable part—throat or nape, belly or skull.[7] To see any intention of registering humility in its attitude is an arbitrary "in-reading" of symbolic human values.

The interesting problem is the action of the superior wolf, which is supposed to be inhibited by the "appeal for mercy." If the ethological principle of interpretation, the treatment of animal movements and postures as formal acts, with communicative intent, is to be dispensed with in judging the cowering pose, the winner's alleged recognition of the "appeal" also has to be treated in a more strictly animalian sense. The empirical fact, attested by many observers, is not to be doubted, namely, that the top wolf's aggression seems to be suddenly inhibited.

[7] In Lorenz' jackdaws the back of the head, in gulls the top, is said to be "presented" (see *King Solomon's Ring*, pp. 211–12).

The only problem is to explain the motivation of that apparently "social" limitation of his fighting spirit. The statement that it has survival value, though probably true, is no explanation; neither is the allegation that "a mechanism" must have evolved which "shuts off" his aggressive behavior at a critical point. The question is what mechanism, if there be a special one, or else what interplay of general psychological operations effects the sudden abstention from further attack.

The answer, I believe, can be found in the principles of animal motivation offered in the previous chapter as alternatives to those of the ethological school: the complete egocentricity of acts, even those usually classed as "social," their guidance from move to move by progressively developing psychical phases just ahead of the next major impulse, and the lability of individual separateness, which facilitates episodes of empathy and raises the normal levels of their intensity and frequency above those of man. It is possible—though I certainly would not assert it categorically as a psychological fact—that the groveling posture of the worsted animal suddenly evokes an empathic sharing of that animal's emotional tensions in the victor, as though he himself were wholly overcome and suffering what is happening to his victim. The fight no longer has two participants; it is no longer going on. There is only this cringing underdog. Quite possibly, such shared and indistinct feeling governs the whole conflict: as long as both antagonists attack each other, empathy might heighten the bellicosity of both, but give no behavioral indication of its existence. Certainly a fight would be a more intimate joint act if the movements of each angry attacker struck into the other's sense with something like the emotive quality of the impulses behind them.

Lorenz (still in *King Solomon's Ring,* p. 213) has written: "Whatever may be the reasons that prevent the dominant individual from injuring the submissive one, whether he is prevented from doing so by a simple and purely mechanical reflex process or by a highly philosophical moral standard, is immaterial to the practical issue. The essential behaviour of the submissive as well as of the dominant partner remains the same. . . ." To the practical issue the motivation may be immaterial, but to our understanding of animal mentality it is not; and Professor Lorenz surely is not indifferent to the psychological issue, nor does he think the alternatives he proposed, one of which is simplistic and the other silly (except, perhaps, to delphinologists), exhaust the possibilities of interpretation. He is, of course, just making room for his neurological theory of the hierarchy of cerebral "centers" and of "inhibitors," "releasers" and other hypothetical mechanisms. But to point out that there must be an "inhibitor" to inhibit the stronger wolf's fighting impulses does not set up any principle of how the inhibition is motivated, why it works where it does, and what other phenomena its incidence or absence explains.

Naturalists and photographers in the wild have given us a wonderful store of factual knowledge,[8] and with it some very jumbled and wavering, largely anthropomorphic commentary, mixed with constant warnings that we must not think of even the higher mammals in anthropomorphic terms. This shows that there is no systematic frame of animal psychology, in terms of which they could easily and freely interpret the behavior they have so closely and conscientiously observed. Such a framework is, indeed, not easy to construct, and to remember that all animal acts fit into it and not into our own conceptual system of mental action takes practice before it becomes easy, just as switching from our traditional measurements in feet and inches to the metric system does at first. But once we have a few major operational concepts I think it can be done, and the sign of its feasibility is that more and more facts are drawn together under the same principles of interpretation, while the latter all lead back to the same basic generalizations. The assumption that animal behavior is guided by feeling, not envisaged purpose, and that this makes it consistently egocentric although it may encompass acts and even needs of other beings seems to me a promising start, although—like all theory that goes beyond *ad hoc* explanation of gross empirical fact—it involves some speculation and indirect evidence where direct verification is impossible. Perhaps the most convincing test of its validity would be to reinterpret, one by one, in these non-human terms the main accepted facts of animal behavior which are currently supposed to rest on symbolic communication, ritual, codes, property claims and other conceptual functions. Such an inductive procedure is, of course, impossible in the confines of a chapter; so I shall select typical phenomena and their usual interpretations and try to reveal the anthropomorphisms implicit in them (which are sometimes plain, but also sometimes subtle), and propose, in each case, a more zoological conception in terms of animal values, impulses and immediate feeling, sensory and emotive.

Let us return to Professor Lorenz' fighting wolves. One of the distinctly non-human aspects of the formal surrender is that it does not

---

[8] Some of these investigators of large wild animals have taken heroic risks, e.g., Jane van Lawick-Goodall in her close proximity to chimpanzees, G. B. Schaller, and, more recently, Dian Fossey among the gorillas and W. J. Schoonmaker photographing grizzly bears at close range with no retreat.

end the hostility, but lasts only as long as the "appeal for mercy" itself is being made. This does suggest strongly that the inhibition springs from momentary feeling and ends with it. The possibility that it is a product of empathy has several supports, in that this hypothetical assumption would explain some attendant facts. For one thing, the winner's "magnanimous" or "merciful" act is bound so closely to the despairing partner's active expression that it seems to spring from the sight and feeling of the latter's yielding body and probably the smell of his terror, as though these all melted into one overweening dread that communicated itself, for the moment (a psychological moment may be long), to the top wolf, and inhibited his attack. That would explain why his "mercy" lasts no longer than the loser's "submissive gesture": if a sudden wave of empathy interfered with the winner's aggression, any change in the beguiling *tableau vivant* would naturally break the induced restraint.

Another fact such an empathic basis would elucidate is that the inhibiting mechanism works only among members of the same species. Again, a graphic example is given by Lorenz, this time from the farmyard. "If a turkey cock has had more than his share of the wild and grotesque wrestling match in which these birds indulge," he states, "he lays himself with outstretched neck upon the ground. Whereupon the victor behaves exactly as a wolf or a dog in the same situation—that is to say, he evidently *wants* to peck and kick at the prostrated enemy, but simply cannot; he would if he could but he can't! So, still in a threatening attitude, he walks round and round his prostrated rival, making tentative passes at him, but leaving him untouched." But if a turkey comes to blows with a peacock, the turkey is disconcerted by the latter's swift attack, and usually ducks under its blows and "freezes" in its characteristic pose, whereupon "a ghastly thing happens; the peacock does not 'understand' this submissive gesture of the turkey—that is to say, it elicits no inhibition of his fighting drives. He pecks and kicks further at the helpless turkey, who ... is doomed, for the more pecks and blows he receives, the more certainly are his escape reactions blocked by the psycho-physiological mechanism of the submissive attitude. It does not and cannot occur to him to jump up and run away."[9]

The peacock simply is not overtaken by any empathic feeling of the turkey's collapse, of which the overt, terror-frozen prostration is an integral part; seen by another turkey this visible element functions as *pars pro toto* in presenting the whole act, and motivates a conflict of feelings in him; but it has no such value for a bird whose bodily responses are

[9] *King Solomon's Ring*, pp. 212–13.

too different in every detail from the turkey's to mediate any contagion of feeling.

In the canine encounters described by Lorenz, Koenig and several other ethologists, the fight ends when the victor withdraws to urinate on some upright object; and each writer, as already mentioned above, gives this act a symbolic function. The most widely accepted of these interpretations is that the victorious beast marks the place of his recent triumph as his own. But in animal memory a finished act probably has no retrievable form which could impress its value on the place of its occurrence. Animals do not celebrate past achievements. Perhaps the successful fight has done a great deal to make its location a "place" for both animals, not necessarily to be sought or avoided, but known as a station on future courses, and urinating close by helps to give it its place character. But one does not need to attribute to animals any intention to leave the mark which the maker of it and many others afterwards sniff, and are seen to "renew," or to "cover" with a different scent, according to whether the observer judges the visitor in question to be the originator of the scent post or a different individual. The first act of micturition was a most natural one after a fight; any excitement causes most animals to urinate.[10] No one seems to have noted when and where the defeated animal next relieves itself, perhaps because no one has invented a symbolic value for the act, which obviously can only be performed at a safe distance, after the underdog has made his escape.

As for the subsequent uses of the post, this involves a further basic principle of motivation which plays a more important and constant role in the life of lower vertebrates than at the specialized human level: the principle of suggestion. The smell of genus-specific urine is enough to evoke micturition especially in male dogs, and, according to the few available accounts, other canines. Even human beings know the suggestive character of the sight or sound of this act, and even of running water. Many animals seem to be similarly affected; dogs going the round of scent posts in their familiar range urinate briefly at each one. The difference between male and female postures for that purpose lets the males develop the use of such stations in much the more visible

[10] Alison Jolly, in her book *Lemur Behavior*, p. 37, says of *Propithecus verreauxi*: "As with other primates, any emotion or fear provokes a barrage of urination and defecation.... They urinate and defecate if mildly alarmed by an observer, after moving overhead to see better or 'sifaka' [vocalize]. The joint effect may be unpleasant for the observer, but there is no reason to think this result premeditated as with some New World monkeys." The reference to the New World monkeys is explicitly to C. R. Carpenter's field study, which will be discussed below.

pattern, and points to a subtle difference in motivation, which illustrates how motivational patterns in general grow up and become articulated by integration of quite separate, opportunely coincident elements. The male dog's ability to lift a hind leg laterally lets the musculature of the groin pull the penis in a similar sidewise direction as the animal stands on three legs, so the urine is sprayed toward a definite point beside instead of beneath the agent. This evidently gives vent to another impulse, namely, to orient toward a goal, which we see especially in aggressive gestures, such as the spontaneous aiming of missiles at another being by apes,[11] usually without practical effect (another revealing fact in animal behavior, to be considered in due order), but enacting the inward focusing of feeling on an external object overtly in a self-expressive gesture. The goal need not be a creature, nor need the emotion which momentarily cathects it be aggressive; a scent post is of intense interest, so it evokes a directed response, an extension of the organism in the form of a shot of urine, which is facilitated by the convenient shape and suggestive smell of the post. The female cannot combine the suggested urination with the emotional expression toward the communal post, so the formalized response of the male does not develop in her,[12] and even the impulse to relieve herself at the site is not as automatically carried out.

[11] G. B. Schaller, watching gorillas, saw no aggressive throwing, but only signs of interest in the path of the missile; in *The Mountain Gorilla—Ecology and Behavior* (1965), p. 224, he writes: "Occasionally gorillas throw with seeming deliberation. First the animal looks around for an herb or branch, detaches it, . . . and flings it away, following the flight of the object with its eyes." (This is apparently a self-expressive act of excitement, for he continues, "One male looked intently to one side, then at a branch above him as if debating whether or not to break it off, but finally rose and beat his chest"). Jane Van Lawick-Goodall, however, who was observing chimpanzees, found that "some adult males throw missiles with definite aim during aggressive encounters. Although the missiles usually travel in the right direction, they often fall short of the target and are frequently too small or ineffective to inflict damage anyway." One ape, throwing at a baboon three feet away, hit him twice. "As weapons," Dr. Van Lawick-Goodall tells us, "he used a handful of leaves, a banana skin, and a small pebble" (*My Friends the Wild Chimpanzees* [1967], p. 35). A six-year-old female developed the trick of collecting a whole handful of pebbles, but again: "Luckily for her victims, Fifi's aim is far from good —the stones descend on her own head as often as they reach their goal" (p. 36).

[12] The male's way appears to be facultative, fitting his anatomy but not necessitated by it; there must be some feeling complex that normally motivates it, but may fail to do so or may operate abnormally, as Daniel Lehrman has recorded in the article already adduced in other connections, "On the Organization of Maternal Behavior and the Problem of Instinct," where he says: "Males castrated in infancy do *not* raise their legs to urinate, but will do so if injected with male hormones.

A similar combination of the same two motivating conditions in the production of directed urination, and—in this case—defecation, too, probably underlies the action of howler monkeys observed by C. R. Carpenter;[13] according to his account, "an animal may break off dead limbs and drop them, or fecal matter may be released with reference to the observer." In the case of throwing branches, "at times, the animals behave as if selecting a limb which may be broken and dropped. The forepaws are used to pull and wrench the piece of wood free, and then it is dropped toward the observer while the animal is watching him. The object is rarely moved away from where it was attached but is merely broken and released at a point nearest the observer." Here the two impulses, aggressive advance toward the intruder and the visceral response to general excitation,[14] are only loosely integrated in that the latter, too, often seems to be directed; and as it is released from above, it requires no such technique as the adult male dog's, but can be practiced by young and old of both sexes. Dr. Carpenter describes the typical behavior, saying: "I would usually be sitting quietly observing the animals as they were in the trees above me. Either seen or unseen, an individual would slowly approach to a place directly above me or as near-by as possible, and then would release excrement, either urine or fecal matter or both. When the act was completed, the individual would usually quickly withdraw. While observing animals from within a blind located under the line of march of a group, I have seen as many as half of the animals release fecal matter on the blind as they crossed over it. The animals would stop, complete the act, and then hurriedly continue. The behavior of stopping and remaining for as long as a minute over a nearby disturbing object is behavior inconsistent with a flight reaction."[15]

In this monograph, Dr. Carpenter is very precise and as literal as possible in his statements and especially his interpretations. It is fairly

---

Female puppies and spayed female dogs also show the male micturition pattern if injected with male hormones" (p. 488). An interesting psycho-sensory phenomenon follows, namely: "Freud and Uyldert ... showed that local anesthetization of the olfactory epithelium causes the disappearance of the male micturition pattern and appearance of the female pattern. When the anesthesia wore off, the male pattern reappeared." Obviously the post is truly a "scent post" even as a lure to the performance.

[13] A *Field Study of the Behavior and Social Relations of Howling Monkeys* (1934), p. 27.

[14] The text continues: "That monkeys defecate and urinate when frightened is a common observation. Captive howlers defecate when greatly excited."

[15] P. 27.

clear that he regards the monkeys' actions here recounted as intentional; in fact, he concludes: "Seemingly, the dropping of branches and excrement are kinds of primitive instrumental acts" (p. 27). His judgment is probably correct. But real forms of attack on the disturbing person or his blind they are not, or they would be performed by the gathered group, like the "mobbing behavior" of some birds, which seems to give super-avian courage to otherwise shy and fugitive little individuals.[16] Each monkey pauses in its course over the human watcher to throw a branch or excrement at him; sometimes, apparently, a single animal ventures to approach him for the purpose and quickly withdraws again. The author, furthermore, remarked previously that this performance was only one of five possible reactions of howlers to man.[17] The motivation of the "attack" is evidently not simply hostile, nor is it entirely unintentional momentary excitement.

An act which does not fit exactly into any of our preconceived categories of animal motivation is a challenge to our theoretical inventiveness and powers to construct further hypotheses. In the quest for alternative interpretations one has to be guided by hints and pointers from other animal acts, mainly in the same species but sometimes in very distant ones, and by such basic principles as underlie one's analysis of animal behavior as a whole. In this case, a suggestion comes from far afield, from an observation made by J. L. Kavanau on deer mice that were given access to a running wheel which could be started and stopped by the experimenter or by the mice, according to various arrangements. "Once male deer mice, *Peromyscus crinitus*," he says, "have learned to turn on a motor which drives a running wheel (for a set time), they repeatedly perform the act and run the motor driven wheel. Given control over both the onset and cessation of rotation, they turn the motor both on and off themselves, running the wheel (for varying periods) on a purely volitional schedule. But they will only run a motor driven wheel when the rotation is self-initiated. As often as the motor is turned on by the experimenter, they doggedly press a lever (within seconds) that turns it off, even though this entails giving up wheel-running entirely.

"... similar behavior results when deer mice control ambient illumi-

---

[16] See, esp., R. A. Hinde, "Factors Governing the Changes in Strength of a Partially Inborn Response, As Shown by the Mobbing Behaviour of the Chaffinch (Fringilla coelebs). I. The Nature of the Response, and an Examination of Its Course. II. The Waning of the Response" (1954).

[17] *A Field Study of the Behavior and Social Relations of Howling Monkeys*, p. 26.

nation. Animals repeatedly press certain levers ... that turn light off in steps, after it is turned on by the experimenter; conversely they press other levers that turn light on in steps, after it is turned off by the experimenter; while if given complete control over illumination, they repeatedly run back and forth between levers, stepping light on and then off."[18]

In the course of learning experiments (light-dark discrimination) on rats, "three groups were used: moderate electric shock for correct responses; moderate electric shock for wrong responses; and no shock. All three groups received food for correct responses. It was surprising that shock-right groups learned faster than no-shock groups, although not as fast as shock-wrong groups."

Reflecting on the significance of his findings, the author remarks: "These experiments led some investigators to question the traditional concept of the effect of punishment in learning.... It would seem, however, that it is the traditional concept of what constitutes punishment that should be questioned. Thus, when dealing with stimuli that are only mildly aversive, the responses of animals may depend less upon the sensations produced than upon whether or not the stimuli are self-initiated." And in conclusion he says: "These 'paradoxical rewarding and aversive effects,' as they are termed by Miller, are only paradoxical if the experiments are interpreted solely in terms of the sensations produced by the stimuli.... It might be more fruitful to regard the sensations as secondary, and simply to interpret the experiments in terms of compulsion and environmental control."[19]

These experiments certainly reveal a long-ignored animal value, namely, opportunity to initiate a perceptible change in the external situation, not necessarily for the better, but simply a change which completes the consummation of a novel kind of act. If the effect can be reversed, the first change of situation offers a new lure to action; the

---

[18] "Compulsory Regime and Control of Environment in Animal Behaviour. 1. Wheel-Running" (1963), pp. 251–52. Toward the end of this article, Dr. Kavanau adds: "If the switches on one side of the enclosure ... turn the lights full on (or step them on) and those on the other side step them off (or turn them full off), deer mice run back and forth all through their active period turning them on and off. In one case, an animal turned the light on and off 119 times in one day ..." (p. 276).

Another observation furnishes a parallel from feline psychology: "Cats learn to run a T-maze to escape stimulation near the posterior thalamic nucleus when the stimulation is applied by the experimenter, but they press levers which deliver exactly the same stimulation themselves" (ibid.).

[19] Pp. 276–77.

alternately encouraged impulses may even become rhythmicized into a continuous activity. Rushing to and fro between widely separated light switches is, of course, a behavioral artifact of captivity; but nothing could illustrate better the principle that an organism always performs all the acts its situation allows. If it does not engage in what looks to a human being like a momentarily possible act, the normal reason is that it is doing something else; not necessarily something overt, let alone as spectacular as pressing levers—it may be completely busy digesting, sleeping, sunning, purring, etc., at a low level of bodily tonus; or at fairly high tonus, perhaps rising toward the limen of active behavior, for a while it may be inwardly playing off incipient phases of more acute acts against each other so none of them develops to the stage of gross muscular movement, and the organism still maintains a motionless posture.

Monkeys are active creatures, and although howlers are less so than many other species, this is only a comparative impression, strengthened by the fact that they become indifferent and withdrawn in captivity.[20] In the wild they appear to be stimulated as much as any sociable beasts by unusual situations. The presence of a human being who does not really frighten them is an enticement to make that being move, without treating it as an antagonist. As Dr. Jolly remarked, a barrage of excrement from above "may be unpleasant for the observer," so he is likely to change his place. Some monkeys singly draw as near as they dare, and when they are close, perhaps directly overhead, the autonomic visceral effect marks the limit of their temerity, whereupon, as Dr. Carpenter states, "the individual would usually quickly withdraw." The howlers may be primarily motivated in the same way as the deer mice controlling the running wheel and the lights in their cages: what they try to turn on and off is Dr. Carpenter. A whole file of them passing over his blind would merely stop, one by one, especially if their mounting excitement evoked its usual enteric expression; the presence of companions changes the action somewhat in that it bolsters each monkey's courage to pause for a longer period, sometimes up to a full minute, to attack the blind as if they expected that the man within it would somehow react. It is in the nature of animal perception that they do not see the change in his situation made by the roof over his head.

The behavior of the howlers is especially interesting in that the

---

[20] Carpenter, in *A Field Study of the Behavior and Social Relations of Howling Monkeys*, says: "Howlers are rarely kept in captivity, presumably because of wildness, and also because they soon die. They are said to be slothful, melancholy, phlegmatic, and peaceful" (p. 20).

directedness and concentration of their impulse is expressed in their throwing twigs and branches toward the intruder. Animals with hand-like paws naturally grasp things and drop them, and chimpanzees have been quite clearly observed to throw in an oriented fashion. The howlers do not do as well; but both species show a complete indifference to the suitability of their missiles to harm or even reach the supposed antagonist.[21] This may bespeak a purely self-expressive function of the directed gesture, prolonged as it is by the departure of the projectile; in that case, the character of the hurled object is really of no account, so our judgment that they do not perceive its physical attributes is misplaced, even if true. But an equally plausible interpretation is that in throwing wood, leaves or bark they do try to hit the human observer; if that is the nature of the act, their lack of feeling for the basic mechanical properties of inanimate objects is indeed astonishing. Yet this would be quite in keeping with many other exhibits of such unawareness in advanced animals, including the great apes. The howlers' imperception of the shielding function of the blind in relation to the man who is their target, mentioned above, fits together with many more striking limitations of the same sort; for instance, lemurs, apes and monkeys, which must have a fine sense of their own bodily equilibrium, weight and strength, have poor judgment of the resistance or resilience of branches and of their relative size and carrying power.[22] They have apparently no ability to project their own body-feeling into inanimate objects visually or tactually perceived, such as human beings develop in fairly early childhood (babies, like the adult primates in question, throw paper, bits of cotton, etc., toward other people in anger). Perhaps their attack on an intruder is as much a gesture as an aggressive instrumental act, wherefore the usual failure to complete the latter does not eliminate the response.

The use of excrement for the same purpose provides an example of entrainment of a basically unrelated act for the implementation of an

[21] Cf. above, p. 149n.

[22] See Jolly, *Lemur Behavior*, p. 72: "*L. catta* do not apparently choose 'safe' branches, but even leap onto dead sticks and loose dead branches lying on live ones. When a branch breaks, the *Lemur* can usually reach or leap to another. I have twice seen animals fall 15 m from a dead branch to the ground. On both occasions the *Lemur* bounced and then ran up the nearest tree without apparent injury. I was told, however, of a mother who fell with her infant; they both were killed."

Also G. B. Schaller, in *The Mountain Gorilla*, says of gorillas, "they appear to be poor judges of what branches can support their weight, and small or dead limbs commonly break beneath them. . . . Although gorillas possess good balance, they occasionally fall" (p. 83).

intentional, directed one. The animal knows from experience the process of approaching a challenging quarry, or perhaps an antagonist, as an exciting act which involves the feeling of visceral evacuation as part of its consummation. The occurrence of that phase at the moment when the monkey has ventured to a place directly over the disturber is probably a purely autonomic release of tension that has reached its height. But in cases where either courage or overhead access will not quite suffice to deliver the barrage from above, the monkey extends his own physique as well as he can toward the goal in aiming his urine and feces, which are still part of himself, toward the being he longs to stir up or possibly drive away.

The intense empathic reactions of animals toward each other contrast sharply with their lack of intuitive judgment of firmness, balance and tensile strength in objects. All their feeling seems to be for action. But acts may involve two or even more agents and still be felt as each one's own, and passive materials transiently—though perhaps repeatedly —enter into acts as enticements and means. While such things are functioning they are embraced by animal consciousness, but what to us is their "objective" character apparently does not exist below the human level of mentality. This is, of course, a hypothetical assumption; but if we hold to it seriously it demands several reinterpretations of reported animal behavior, such as "staking out" territory, warning, display, and the larger acts of cooperation, imitation, leadership, communication and the alleged beginnings (or even complete mastery) of language.

To begin with territorial claims, these are generally said to be established by "marking" with urine, and sometimes feces, the boundaries of the pre-empted ground. The nature of animal space and the making of "places" have been sufficiently discussed in the previous chapter to require no further argument here against the anthropomorphic conception that the marked locations are points on an imaginary boundary line enclosing the territory the resident animal will defend. But since, at least in some cases, they do indicate the more or less permanent whereabouts of their producer, the true function of their frequent renewal has to be explained. One incentive to that renewal has already been considered in connection with the scent posts of dogs, which generally do not indicate the private domains that most domestic dogs possess and know very well as their own. A single animal, especially in the wild, will be stimulated to repeat its micturition at the scene where its own smell suggests it. On animal paths such deposits surely act as a pheremone, but not necessarily with respect to other animals; thus

Eibl-Eibesfeldt, in a study of the common house mouse (*mus musculus*), decided—against his sometimes questionable penchant for endowing animal acts with "social" meanings—that mice, which constantly defecate and urinate as they run about, are "marking" their paths and stations to make them familiar to themselves rather than as a deterrent to other mice.[23] That seems to me a likelier effect of most "marking," intentional or (as surely in this case) unintentional. Some ethologists, however, have thought to see signatory functions in various "marks" deliberately made to convey information to other animals. The first promulgators of this doctrine appear to have been J. von Uexküll and E. G. Sarris, who observed the typical, brief, repetitious urination of domestic dogs and gave it the interpretation which has become a firm tenet of the ethological school.

The really dogmatic formulation of the territorial and possessive theory of visceral responses may be found in H. Hediger's article, "Die Bedeutung von Miktion und Defäkation bei Wildtieren" (1944), where one finds such confident assertions as "the frequent micturition of the dog is obviously not a physiological compulsion, but a biological ceremonial" (p. 176). Hereupon he quotes Von Uexküll and Sarris[24] to the effect "that the male dogs mark with their urine a particular, frequently shifting area in their ambient, and thus create a scent-field of their own, documenting their claims to it in this fashion. Everything within

---

[23] "Beiträge zur Biologie der Haus- und Ährenmaus nebst einigen Beobachtungen an anderen Nagern" (1950), pp. 561–62: "Ihr stark riechender Harn dient weniger als Warnung für revierfremde Eindringlinge, die sich dadurch eher angezogen als abgeschreckt zeigen; vielmehr machen die Harnmarken das Revier dem Tier selbst vertraut und dienen als Orientierungspunkte. Markante Übergänge, Durchschlupfe, aber auch ganze Wege sind mit dem Urin der Tiere bezeichnet und man erkennt diese Pfade, wenn man Mäuse längere Zeit im zimmer hält, als schmale klebrige Spuren. Sooft ich die in meinem Zimmer ansässige Mausbevölkerung gegen eine neue, fremde austauschte, fanden sich die ortsunkundigen Tiere bereits in kürzester Zeit zurecht, ja sie erkletterten sogar noch am Tag der Aussetzung einzelne schwer zugängliche Regale, was ihre Vorgänger erst nach langem Erkunden fertig gebracht hatten."

The reference to that author's not infrequent imputation of "symbolic" and "ceremonial" character to typical movements and postures of animals is based on such writings as "Der Kommentkampf der Meerechse (*Amblyrhynchus crystatus* Bell.) nebst einigen Notizen zur Biologie dieser Art" and his afore-mentioned account of intraspecies fighting in "Angeborenes und Erworbenes im Verhalten einiger Säuger," pp. 720 ff, where he cites Lorenz in support of the belief that such fighting is ritualistic rather than real, intended to establish superiority of the victor without harm to the loser.

[24] "Das Duftfeld des Hundes. (Hund und Eckstein.)" (1931).

this scent-field becomes the property of the dog." To which Hediger adds: "By the setting up of scent-banners the 'territory' is staked out, 'marked off.'" From dogs he passes on to galagos, which urinate on the "palms" of their front paws and smear the soles of their hind paws with them, "indubitably" to "mark" their tracks[25] (since they proceed quadrupedally, the front ones might have been enough); tapir and hippopotamus squirt their excrements backward as far as possible to hit bushes that hold their "scent banners."[26] There are about a dozen more cases, including lizards and birds whose droppings are widely visible when dry, but no better circumstantial proofs of the alleged "marking" motivation, which is simply designated as "obvious" or "indubitable."

The chief danger to animal psychology in such established interpretations is that they tend to impose themselves directly on the data of observation; the observer simply sees the behavioral act as an example of the intentions he has previously imputed to the agent. As all excre-

---

[25] This action has been described many times, e.g., by Stuart Altmann, "Primates" (1968), pp. 477–78. Altmann cites D. R. Ilse, who made firsthand observations on two animals—unfortunately, both males—in his own possession. In an article titled "Olfactory Marking of Territory in Two Young Male Loris, *Loris tardigradus lydekkerianus*, Kept in Captivity in Poona" (1955), Ilse subscribes to the ethological doctrine, and as his animals were both very young but both developed the habit before they were full grown, he says, "we may wonder ... whether the young male loris may, even in the wild state, start at an early age to help with the marking of his parents' territory." He had previously remarked that earlier observers had given it a different interpretation, namely, "making hands and feet smooth for climbing." But climbing would hardly be facilitated by smooth soles. The assumption that the odd "urine-washing" habit must serve some general purpose seems to me a false basis for any interpretation; a tendency for the dry soles to itch would be my first guess, and would lead me to investigate the nature of the loris' skin through specialized studies such as those which William Montagna and several other dermatologists have published during the past decade in the *American Journal of Physical Anthropology*. (See, for instance, "The Skin of Primates XXIX: The Skin of the Pygmy Bushbaby [*Galago demidovii*]" [1966], by H. Machida, E. Perkins and L. Giacometti, which remarks on some differences between the friction surfaces of the paws and the rest of the skin. Such findings might or might not prove to bear on the subject of "urine washing.")

[26] P. 173: "Die Männchen von Zwergflusspferd, Nashorn und Tapir spritzen ihren Harn in weitem Bogen zwischen den Beinen durch nach hinten, *zweifellos* im Dienste der Territoriumsmarkierung" (italics mine). Unfortunately, Bernhard Grzimek, who made more extended field observations at the same site that Hediger had visited, subsequently declared: "Contrary to the reports of Hediger, according to whom each [hippopotamus] bull marks his territory by discharging faeces, several bulls were seen to defaecate, one after the other, in exactly the same place" ("Einige Beobachtungen an Wildtieren in Zentral-Afrika" [1956], p. 150 [from the English summary]).

[157]

tions are self-evident ceremonial marks, all utterances are just as obviously "signals," and every alternation of sound-making between two animals, "communication." If he scares up a ground-nesting bird that runs away from its eggs or chicks dragging one wing, he can see that it is trying to decoy him from the nest. Otto Koenig's complete acceptance of such intention and "technique" has already been cited.[27] A. J. Marshall, in *Bower Birds*, declares that these birds, which are noisy, versatile mimics, use their voices to attract a predator's attention to themselves instead of to the nest, and adds: "Gaukrodger says that if an outburst of noisy mimicry failed to engage his attention, the female would 'suddenly almost fall to the ground and with neck stretched out, feathers ruffled and wings spread, she would creep through the grass, pretending helplessness.' Intermittently the mimicry and 'antics of pretence' continued for as long as the human intruder remained still, but if he moved to touch the nest, the bird abandoned her distraction activities and approached closely to hiss, scold, and 'show fight.' McLennan witnessed an excited display of mimicry by a Spotted Bowerbird immediately after he shot its mate in February. The surviving bird flew to a nearby tree and mimicked 'all the birds in the neighborhood.' "[28]

Certainly the actions here described are not unequivocal evidence of a bird's intention to lure a predator away from its nest or its clutch. Its mimicking other birds is a new element to be adduced as "distraction display"; and the comparison with the behavior of the bird whose mate had been shot (there is no mention, at least by Marshall, of a nearby nest) makes the outburst of all its available calls seem more like a symptom of general excitement or emotive self-augmentation than an intentional display to distract the enemy.[29] This casts some doubts on a different ethological doctrine, namely, the "social" motiva-

---

[27] See p. 107 above.

[28] Pp. 83–84.

[29] Some years ago, I watched a pair of wood thrushes (*Hylocichla mustelina*) build their nest on a branch where this adjoined the trunk of the tree. Every time a cat or dog strolled by on the wood road passing my cabin, the thrushes made a great outcry. One day, when there were young in the nest, the alarm notes lasted so long that I looked from my window for the cause, and saw a falcon on the ground in the road, eating one of the parent thrushes. When I opened my door he flew off, carrying his prey along. The moment he was gone, the remaining thrush, sitting close to the nest on the same branch, burst into full-throated song, and sang with only short pauses for about fifteen minutes. From its voice I judged it to be the male. It then flew away and returned to feed the young, which had another week to stay in the nest (the unaided father raised them).

tion of bird song, and should be remembered in this connection. As an instance of purposive distraction display, however, I think it may be dismissed.

This leaves the other, more familiar part of the supposed intention to lure a dangerous visitor from the nest site, the so-called injury-feigning act. Gaukrodger's account of the bower bird's sudden drop to the ground in a depressed posture—"with neck stretched out, feathers ruffled and wings spread"—is very reminiscent of Lorenz' turkey which assumed the "submissive attitude." If one does not immediately impose a gestic value on spectacular acts, such as signaling surrender or trying to deceive a hunter, one naturally notices a similarity between the two behavior patterns here in question. They contain essentially the same repertoire elements in almost the same order, which suggests that similar emotional tensions are expressed, sometimes repetitiously, by these outwardly ineffectual movements. Many birds "feigning lameness" drag one wing and consequently stagger as they walk away from the nest. The extension of one wing, throwing the body somewhat off-center, is a natural posture to birds in several situations: sunning, preening, stretching and brooding a single chick (Fig. 15–1). Tinbergen observed that gulls always stretch one wing at a time;[30] in the same book he reported the discovery that a gull charging a creature which menaces its nest usually extends one leg to strike the enemy.[31] Such one-sided action seems, in fact, to be a primitive repertoire element (Fig. 15–2). The other major instinctual element in the "injury-feigning act" is the cowering attitude which makes the bird appear to be physically unable to run or fly away. This same posture appears in all the "gestures of submission," but also in many courtship movements of birds and other animals, where it is unlikely to have any such significance in reference to the sex partner. From the standpoint of feeling, however, it may have the same value and be the same subaction in the different behavior patterns that contain it.

The emotional feeling expressed in the cowering posture may be viewed, hypothetically, as desperation, being overwhelmed by circumstances. In human experience this is an ultimate degree of terror, and

[30] See *The Herring Gull's World*, p. 215.

[31] Pp. 195–96: "Towards the end of the incubation period, the tendency of the gulls to defend their nests against predators is increasing, and shortly before the young hatch it reaches a peak.... At this time the birds show the magnificent 'charge.' When a dog, or a human intruder, comes near the nest, the gulls will swoop down on him again and again.... When we made some slow motion films of this attack, we noticed to our astonishment that most of the shots showed the bird extending only one foot...."

[159]

Figure 15–1. Herring Gull Stretching Wing, Foot, and Half the Tail,
All on One Side

*the extension of one wing, throwing the body somewhat off center, is a
natural posture to birds in several situations*

(After Nikolaas Tinbergen, *The Herring Gull's World: A Study of the Social Behavior
of Birds* [London: Collins, 1953].)

Figure 15–2. (*Left*) Pigeon Stretching Right Wing and Leg;
(*Right*) Pigeon Sunning

such one-sided action seems . . . to be a primitive repertoire element

(Drawn by Sibyl A. Hausman after a photograph by Oskar Heinroth in Oskar and Käthe
Heinroth, "Verhaltensweisen der Felsentaube (Haustaube) *Columbia livia livia* L.," *Zeitschrift
für Tierpsychologie*, VI [1948].)

Figure 15–3. Killdeer Pretending Helplessness

the bird chased up from its nest by a huge predator . . . is torn between
two impulses, to cover its brood and to flee

(C. Douglas Deane, "The Broken-Wing Behavior of the Killdeer," *The Auk*, LXI [1944].)

as it is apt to be a direct reaction to immediate conditions in us as in birds and beasts, the assumption that they feel it much as we do is a fairly safe one. Such an emotion is natural when a creature can do nothing at all to counter the danger that is upon it. The bird chased up from its nest by a huge predator, moreover, is torn between two impulses, to cover its brood and to flee (Fig. 15–3); the dragging wing points nestward and bespeaks its reluctance to abandon the young, the flight impulse strains irresistibly away from the deadly foe. In that desperate situation, the bird cowers, staggers and makes little progress; but the moment the nest is out of sight and the young out of earshot, it suddenly regains its coordination and flies away. It may even subsequently pass by, come full circle back to the nest as if nothing had happened; but if the enemy suddenly looms up again, the "distraction display" may be repeated.[32]

[32] Lorenz and Tinbergen, in their joint article, "Taxis and Instinct: Taxis and Instinctive Action in the Egg Retrieving Behavior of the Greylag Goose" (1957; orig. pub., 1938), declare that the act cannot be repeated if the "nervous impulse

The same sense of helplessness at a moment of total defeat may motivate a turkey to fall prone in midst of a fight, or a dog to cringe beneath a conquering antagonist. The intensity of emotion which pervades such a spontaneous gesture of giving up the struggle runs through every quiver, every erecting feather or hair of the loser's skin, and in a mammal through every sweat gland exuding the smell of terror. In this extremity the presumptive destroyer suddenly suffers an empathic pseudo-identification with his victim and, for the instant, cannot strike. If then the victim tries to escape, the emotional contagion is broken, so the conqueror resumes his attack; but if it is the latter that leaves the spot, the fight is ended.[33]

Now, what about the courting bird that periodically ducks and creeps around a coy or unresponsive female? His situation does not look desperate, overwhelming, hopelessly frustrating. Yet so it may be. The human observer looks beyond the female's current act, and expects her to yield in good time, when she becomes sexually ready; but the male bird, with the female in sight, under pressure of his mating impulse frantically seeking enactment to consummation, may be suffering recurrent moments of desperation. He does not know the asynchrony of male and female rhythms, nor that they will ultimately coincide, as the ethologist foresees, to whom the bird's acts are stimulus-"triggered" or "released" antics phylogenetically predesigned to attract the female. The bird is motivated by feeling which engages the entire organism for

---

flow" from the act center for the "instinct" is exhausted. "Many a behavior pattern," they say, "such as feigning lameness to lure enemies from the vicinity of the nest, can be performed only a very few times in succession. The action is not repeated, even though the releasing situation continues to exist. Instead, the bird, in the presence of a human being who but a little while ago elicited a reaction, turns to some indifferent pursuit: it begins to search for food, to groom, etc." (p. 202). Perhaps, however, the psychological situation of the bird is not the same, even though the physical one, perceptible to an ethologist who sees the bird as a physiological automaton containing hundreds of hierarchical series of act centers, may be unchanged. An emotional crisis is necessarily single and transient. The bird's emotion continues at a lower level after one or two episodes of desperate terror. (Note that these two authors, while offering a mechanical theory, still use the phrase "feigning lameness to lure enemies." No wonder the anthropomorphism sticks.)

[33] Nothing, probably, could be more wrong than R. Ardrey's confident statement that the submissive attitude is a formal gesture "in no wise different from the human gesture of raising one's hands in surrender" (see p. 144 above). If the interpretation here proposed can be accepted, we need not postulate any accepted "social code" which (unlike a human surrender) does not govern action beyond the moment of "signaling" the admission of defeat.

its expression. In watching the sexual excitement of a small bird, e.g., a wren, it is interesting to see practically all of his repertoire elements emerging in kaleidoscopic sequence during such ardent courtship. This random outpouring is suggestive of the bower bird's confused perform- ance when it saw its mate killed and responded by exhibiting its whole stock of native and acquired calls.

The purpose of these reinterpretations is to offer a psychological approach to zoological phenomena which so far have been treated with- out any consideration of animal mentality as we know it from other angles. The assumptions implicit in the notion of "distraction display" and ruses to decoy an enemy from an animal's nest, den[34] or horde[35] are assumptions of characteristically human mental acts: imagining one's own appearance to other creatures and speculating on the way such creatures would react to their own impressions of the deceiver. Short of such conceptual powers, intentional deception is impossible; consequently, I hold that no animal can deliberately feign, deceive, dis- tort evidence, or invent any ruse to trick an antagonist.

If we consistently maintain this principle, we have to interpret some other activities, too, without recourse to communicative or recording intentions on the part of the agents. The widely acclaimed "social" functions of leaving and even applying excrement as a spoor have already been discussed; but beyond such alleged practices, woodsmen, hunters, country folk generally and many ethologists believe that bears and beavers, for instance, put up their personal signatures in prominent places, as many human tourists carve their initials on walls and statues wherever they go. Those sympathetic observers regard the piles of mud which beavers are wont to leave along the shore, and on which cas- toreum is often deposited, as "sign heaps" erected with some communi- cative purpose, though addressee and message are unknown.[36] For the

[34] S. Young and E. Goldman, in *The Wolves of North America*, relate how the male wolf watches from a high lookout point over his den and gives warning of any approaching enemy: "The male wolf in such instances has been observed to scamper away from his lookout and the immediate vicinity of the den, and by voicing a succession of howls to attempt to distract the attention of the intruder, especially if a human, so that the den will not be discovered" (p. 103).

[35] W. Hoesch, in a highly interesting paper, "Über ziegenhütende Bärenpaviane (*Papio ursinus raucana* Shortridge)" (1961), claims that the male guardians of the baboon horde try to "distract" potential enemies with their noisy clamor, but only after the clan has retired to a safe distance: "Erst wenn eine bestimmte Flucht- distanz erreicht ist beginnen die alten Männchen ihre Schimpf-Kanonade, wodurch sie den Verfolger von der Herde ablenken und vielleicht auch potentielle Feinde des in ihr Revier Eingedrungenen alarmieren" (p. 297).

[36] See E. R. Warren, *The Beaver* (1927), a little book in which fact and hearsay

"bear tree," however, a message has been invented (not by bears); it is: "I'm so big, I can reach up to here!" According to one confident endorser of this and other legends, "bears mark trees by sticking some of their body hairs to the tree with mud. First the mud is smeared on the tree; then the bear scrapes his back several times against the muddy spot, applying enough pressure so that the rough tree bark pulls out a few hairs. This mark ... probably conveys a good deal of information about its size and sex to another passing bear. ...

"In another kind of sign language, a bear standing on his hind legs reaches up on a tree and makes deep scratches with his teeth and claws in the bark. The next bear to come by sniffs the tree, looks at the marks, and tries to scratch higher up. Failing in this effort, the bear may move on to find a territory where he can make the highest tree mark. By the same token, any bear already residing in this area may leave if he discovers higher marks than his, made by the newcomer."[37]

No one so far claims to have seen that second bear read the message and act on it. People who really observe animals in the wild all too often report that they saw no evidence of the social motives imputed to the species they studied in its native habitat. Bears do rub their backs on trees and scratch off the bark with their claws. But the story of the tree that tells the size of the biggest bear and makes him the acknowledged owner of the territory is a typical piece of folklore, and its entry into the ethological literature is, I am afraid, a blot on the new "science." In tracing that story back through the references from one work to another, one finds that the first serious scientists to credit the bear's communicative intent include no less a person that Jacob von

---

are generally carefully distinguished, and the last chapter of which bears the title, "Things That a Beaver Does Not Do." Yet Warren himself writes on "sign heaps" (p. 146): "A means of communication used by the beaver, more especially if it is traveling about the country and wishes to leave some indication of its presence, is what we may call for want of a better name, the 'sign heap.' Seton calls these things mud pies.

"Sign heaps are little cakes or piles of mud near a stream or pond on which the castoreum is deposited. One which it was my good fortune to find ... was merely a round cake of mud, but so placed that it ... was really quite conspicuous and easily seen. I could detect no odor about it.

"Morgan gives an account of something similar: 'After selecting a suitable place upon dry ground near the pond or stream, they void their castoreum here and there upon the grass, and, in the musky atmosphere thus created, spend some hours at play or basking in the sun. The trappers call these playgrounds "musk bogs." ' " This sounds more as though the animals established a place with their musk than as if they "wished to leave some indication" of having passed the site in their travels.

[37] Evans, *Communication in the Animal World*, p. 97.

Uexküll. And where did he get it? From Ernest Thompson Seton, who presents it in a book of "nature fiction," the imaginary biography of a bear, composed of actual observation, Indian and white hunters' lore, and poetic fabrication. It is a storybook for children of ten to fifteen years.[38]

Other direct observers of bears in the wild have flatly denied the relation of rubbing trees to possession of territory. Mr. and Mrs. Peter Krott, who spent several years in a wild sector of the Italian Alps with the sole purpose of following the fortunes of two brown bears (*Ursus arctos*) which they had raised only through infancy and liberated as soon as possible, not permitting them in the house even as cubs nor feeding them out of hand once they could feed themselves and could shift their range with seasonal conditions, etc., declare with well-founded conviction that bears have no territory, wherefore they cannot mark any as their own,[39] and that "bear trees" serve solely as firm rubbing trees to scrub an itching skin especially at times of changing pellage; and to this they add the interesting observation that such a reaction also occurs in conflict situations.[40]

[38] It was Hediger who ran the story back to its beginnings, but was not shaken in his ethological faith by finding so specious a source. In the paper cited before, "Die Bedeutung von Miktion und Defäkation bei Wildtieren," he says: "Der Bär richtet sich nach Uexküll und Kriszat [*Streifzüge durch die Umwelten von Tieren und Menschen*, (1934), p. 73] zur Markierung seines Heimes zu seiner vollen Grösse auf und reibt 'mit Rücken und Schnauze die Rinde einer einzeln stehenden, weithin sichtbaren Kiefer ab. Dies wirkt als Signal für andere Bären, die Kiefer in weitem Bogen zu umgehen und das ganze Gebiet zu meiden, wo ein Bär von solchen Ausmassen seine Heimat verteidigt.' Diese ursprünglich übrigens auf Ernest Thompson Seton (1922, s. 77) zurück gehende Beobachtung konnte im Basler Zoologischen Garten für den Braunbären noch ergänzt werden: gleichzeitig mit diesem Baumschaben lässt nämlich der aufgerichtete Bär Harn und kennzeichnet auf diese Weise die Umgebung der optischen Signalstelle auch noch mit Geruchsmarken."

[39] Peter and Gertraud Krott, "Zum Verhalten des Braunbären (*Ursus arctos* L. 1758) in den Alpen" (1963), p. 192–93: "Wie sich durchweg ergab, spricht nichts dafür, dass die Alpenbären an bestimmte Territorien gebunden wären und sie gegen Artgenossen verteidigen.... So sahen und hörten wir weder von Kämpfen um ein Territorium noch Markierverhalten.

"Da der Bär ... kein Territorium hat, kann er auch keines markieren. 'Bärenbäume' als Markierungspfähle gibt es nicht, auch wenn Lindemann sie 'Warntafeln für Artgenossen' nennt."

[40] P. 197: "Allein zur Zeit des Haarwechsels scheuert der Bär häufig und gründlich alle Körperteile systematisch ab.... Besonders in Triebkonflikten reiben sich Bären gern an Felsen, Stubben und Bäumen.... Um sich daran zu scheuern, muss der Bär eine feste, nicht nachgebende Reibfläche haben, die guten Überblick zum Sichern gibt.... Das ist alles, was ein 'Bärenbaum' leisten muss, und er dient zu eben nichts anderem."

The "signboard" needs no further elucidation, but the Krotts's passing remark, quoted above, that rubbing is also performed in conflict situations does require some explanation. A practical value of such an act as a means of resolving any sort of conflict is hard to imagine; there remains the supposition that the arrest of smooth instinctive action, produced by a collision of two or more acts in progress or incompatible impulses motivated at the same time, is emotionally felt somewhat as fright and anger are, and tends similarly to raise the hair on the bear's back and cause a creepy feeling to run up along his spine. In a heavily furred animal like a bear such a somatic expression of emotion should last longer than the first shock, the hairs remaining erected until the skin itches. The frustrated animal has to do something immediate to fill the moments of halted action, so it rubs itself to allay the itch.[41]

Another large animal capable of rearing upon its hind feet showed a similar reaction. Jane Van Lawick-Goodall described a chimpanzee's behavior in a conflict situation as follows: "In captivity a young chimpanzee when unable to attain a desired object may start rocking its body from side to side. This behavior was seen on many occasions [in the wild] when William [one of the apes] was prevented from getting bananas by his reluctance to approach me. Glaring at me, he rocked while

---

[41] Tinbergen would probably call such scraping a "displacement activity." To give a phenomenon a name and assume that "there must be a mechanism" serves only to shelve the further investigation of its nature. But Hans Lind, in a thoughtful article on such "displacements," proposes a connecting phase between the frustrated act and its apparently unrelated proxy, namely, a common instinctual element which can express itself when the major part of the large impulse comprising it is frustrated, and which then initiates a different behavioral response. Such a turn may take place even without any obvious conflict, as when a bathing duck suddenly starts to grub for weeds—a competing instinctive act abruptly induced by the feeling of the water as the bird submerges in its bath. In his paper, "The Activation of an Instinct Caused by a Transitional Action" (1959), p. 128, Lind cites as a typical conflict situation that of a female duck courted by several males, which is torn between flying away and diving away, and suddenly dives for food. "The new activity," he says, "is a typical displacement: It is of short duration and incomplete, it is irrelevant, it belongs to another instinct than those activated before, and it arises in a conflict situation. However, ... the displacement is in this case a normal autochthonous activity. No 'spark-over' of impulses from one hierarchy to another [the reference here is, of course, to the Lorenz-Tinbergen neurology] takes place.... This supports the supposition that all displacement activities are autochthonous, since owing to the thwarting ... of the dominating drives they get a chance to be performed." This certainly fits the case of the bear; in any conflict of impulses, e.g., to brave an ominous encounter or to retreat, both major responses probably include piloerection as a scarcely noticeable autochthonous element which can motivate an apparently "displaced" consummation.

sitting or standing upright. . . . Erections were observed of the hair on his back, shoulders and arms, and of his penis. After rocking vigorously for a few minutes he sat and scratched his side or arm with slow downward movements of one hand while almost imperceptibly moving his head from side to side."[42]

Skin sensations seem, indeed, to be more intensely felt by many animals than by man; this is certainly suggested by the prevalence and evident importance of interindividual grooming among mammals, birds and insects. But the roles they play in animal lives are but little understood, and perhaps too simply and superficially conceived. Closer observations on the practices sometimes called "allo-grooming"[43] (that is, grooming another creature's skin or feathers, without further relational concepts such as are implicit in the terms "mutual" or "social" grooming) raise questions of animal feeling, both cutaneous and emotional, that merit more than a reference to beneficial effects like "group cohesion," or "social" practices such as rank-holding, submissive gestures and leader-recognition. These terms may all fit the acts of grooming, licking or scratching other individuals, but it is highly dubitable that the animal agents themselves know anything about rank, dominance orders, leadership, their own submission (which they are supposed to declare symbolically), or even the fact that they belong to a group which their interaction with its other members holds together.[44] Their acts are not motivated by social aims, but by their own felt emotional tensions and constantly emerging perceptions.

If, then, we can muster the patience to suspend the advanced ethological approach to animal behavior and analyze some elementary aspects of interindividual bodily contact, we may come to the problems

[42] "Chimpanzees of the Gombe Stream Reserve" (1965), p. 468.

[43] The term was introduced by J. H. Sparks. See his "Allogrooming in Primates: A Review" (1967).

[44] There is a remarkable observation, recorded by L. Pardi, of wasps which immediately recognize the rank of any wasp in a strict dominance order without, necessarily, any individual recognition; the wasp in question may be a total stranger. It seems that the dominance relation is established in spring by the relative degrees of ovarian development, before females join to make a nest. Through the practice of trophallactic feeding—the subordinate insects regurgitating to the high-ranking ones—the latter advance faster than the former, which suffer an atrophy of their ovaries. Whether some exudation indicates their status or whether the signs are behavioral, or both, Pardi did not claim to know. See his "Beobachtungen über das interindividuelle Verhalten bei *Polistes gallicus*" (1947).

See also C. R. Ribbands, "The Defence of the Honey-Bee Community" (1954), p. 524: "The queen is recognized *as a queen* in addition to any possible recognition as a member of the community."

of "allo-grooming" and related actions with a somewhat deeper insight into the potentialities of such contact *per se*, and their expressions in cutaneous sensibility, from mere touch, tickle, prick, scratch, etc., to emotionally significant impingements, caresses and abuses, and the reinforcement of intense interactions as between mothers and young.

Allo-grooming has been so commonly observed in many kinds of creatures that the oldest interpretation of it as a service rendered by one animal to another for cleaning the latter's skin, especially in inaccessible places, is generally accepted as the obvious, sufficient explanation. Mothers groom their young; similarly, adults help each other out in awkward passages of self-grooming.

But the cleanliness of a comrade's skin is ordinarily not a value to an animal whose own skin feels comfortable. The great eagerness of some animals, especially lemurs, monkeys and chimpanzees, but above all the baboons, to groom their companions, which often appears—upon behavioral evidence—to exceed the beneficiaries' desire for the treatment, indicates that what induces and guides the act of examining and handling another animal's skin is primarily an impulse on the part of the groomer, not the recipient of the service.[45] Sometimes it is initiated by the latter, which presents its itching surface in a suggestive fashion;[46] but where grooming is one of the most prevalent interactions among members of a company the usual motivation is something else, and can only be guessed at by observation of the normally attendant circum-

[45] A fairly strong proof of this proposition is furnished by an aftermath to Mrs. Van Lawick-Goodall's story, recounted below (pp. 187–88), of a chimpanzee's killing a baboon, and the action of his comrade Mike, who finally possessed the victim's severed head. The story ends: "In the coolness of the evening we saw perhaps the most grewsome sight of the day. Mike stopped feeding for a few moments, lay on his back in the last of the sunlight and, holding the baboon head above him with one foot, groomed the fur of his trophy—not once but time and time again" (*My Friends the Wild Chimpanzees*, pp. 68–69).

[46] Starting the process in this way, i.e., as a joint act from the beginning, makes it a practical fulfillment for the recipient, but probably a routine response to the groomer. Cows often invite each other to mutual scratching, and in the absence of a willing partner rub their own throats, pates and other inaccessible spots on posts and fence rails. Schaller, in *The Mountain Gorilla*, p. 245, says, "Mutual grooming was not a prominent activity among gorillas, and the behavior was never reciprocal." Also, "Adult gorillas . . . rarely groom other adults, and the grooming that does occur is concentrated on those parts of the body which the animal cannot itself reach with ease. . . . Mutual grooming in adults appears to be primarily utilitarian, with the animals usually grooming their own bodies" (pp. 247–48). "Utilitarian," however, need not refer to cleansing the skin; it is doubtful that apes have standards of cleanliness; the groomed animal exploits the other one's impulse to groom, in order to get relief from itch, and presents the spots it cannot scratch itself.

stances and the typical relations between the two creatures involved in each case. Most firsthand reports on primates in their natural habitats provide some data on allo-grooming in the species under observation, and the behavior patterns, especially those of pairing for the purpose, show great differences from kind to kind. Most accounts are too brief to support any study of motivations, except Hans Kummer's two books of similar titles but unredundant contents: *Soziales Verhalten einer Mantelpavian Gruppe* (1958), and *The Social Organization of Hamadryas Baboons* (1968). To appreciate the role of grooming in the life of these highly gregarious monkeys, to which Dr. Kummer has given his special attention for many years, one has to know something of their communal life and main reactions to each other. There appears to be a fairly stable "dominance order," based on the simple principle of fear inspired in the weaker members by the stronger, which naturally creates a hierarchy of relative domination. The most feared animal of the entire troupe the author designates as "the alpha animal," or "α," normally an adult male. But within this basic hierarchy in which, of course, many members hold closely similar rank, falling into sex categories and within these into age classes, many other relations than dominance develop: that between mothers and their young, which goes through several phases, from ventral transportation—the young clinging to the hair of the mother's breast and belly, sometimes helped by her clasping paw as she proceeds on three legs, dog-fashion—to riding on her back, finally following after her, but fleeing into her embrace at the slightest scare; then the relation to playmates, from infants to two- or three-year-old juveniles; then the more settled relations of the subadult males and females to the clan as a whole, where the dominance hierarchy is apparent, and finally the adult interaction pattern which is the main structure of the baboons' life.

The commonest actions aimed by one baboon at another (leaving aside sexual behavior) are: (1) agonistic—usually short, superficial fights in which one contestant is put to flight; (2) threat, most commonly no more than a stare and a frown directed at a particular comrade, but with growing intensity, pounding the earth; (3) a bite that elicits no retaliation; and (4) approach of one animal to another with anxious desire to groom the latter's pelage, and sometimes with a pseudosexual "presenting" gesture (by female or male) inviting the dominant member to mount. It is this act of approach that raises baffling psychological problems, for its typical motivating condition is any sort of fear, even a threat or abuse stemming from the dominant male himself. Dr. Kummer has collected some interesting episodes in point (numbers with lower-case letters refer to individually known monkeys. As the observations in the early part of his first book are all on acts directed by one monkey at only one other, he speaks of these animals as "the actor" and "the receptor," respectively).

"The nearest behavior to the ventral carrying of young by their mothers is the mutual ventral carrying of juveniles elicited by a fear reaction of the receptor. . . .

"[scene 1740] 4a in play-fight with 2z. At a sharp bite the latter suddenly screams, whereupon 4a embraces him and carries him to α.

". . . This ventral carrying is initiated by the actor. The releasing stimulus is the screaming of a small infant. The fact that in scene 1740 the carrier himself had caused the screaming did not change his reaction to it in any way.

"Besides mothers, only subadult males briefly carried little ones ventrally, when the latter—left alone—screamed or 'geckered.'[47]

"The final dispenser of all threatening actions is the α-male. Every quarrel that produces more than a slight geckering is brought before him" (p. 29). This is true even if he is the source of the alarm; and the frightened animals running to him usually seek at once to groom him, or present to him though he often does not react to the invitation.

Another odd circumstance is that if a large subadult monkey has caused a small one to cry out, it is the little one that receives α's frown and stare, not the one which has made it cry. In cases where the threat is directed to the older animal, it clearly does not express disapproval of his maltreatment of the younger, but is elicited by the visible fear which the scream has aroused in him that caused it. "This case," says Dr. Kummer, "is often to be observed, and is an example of how little sense most threatening actions make" (p. 30).[48]

The whole discussion cannot be retailed here, but the notable points are that any fright causes a baboon to run to a higher-ranking animal, if possible the α-male, and that this superior animal directs a menacing grimace at any comrade showing fear; that the receptor of the threat, instead of running away, seeks to groom the actor and in every way to initiate close contact with him. It makes one wonder whether the frowning face and drawn-up, challenging posture characteristic of readi-

[47] *Soziales Verhalten einer Mantelpaviangruppe*, pp. 14–15. The English translation of *"geckern"* (or, sometimes, *"keckern"*) as "geckering" is found in Thelma Rowell's "Some Observations on a Hand-Reared Baboon" (1965), p. 79.

[48] "Nicht das Quälen des kleinern Jungen wird 'bestraft'; vielmehr ist es die durch dessen Kreischen ausgelöste Angst des Verursachers selbst, die sich in ganz spezifischen Elementen äussert und zur Bedrohung führt" (p. 30).

ness to fight always signify an intention to fight or bite the "threat-ened" one. Perhaps the perception of any sign of weakness, such as fear, makes the superior male express his strength, as a human warrior feeling courageous brandishes his weapons and perhaps utters a war whoop without preparing to attack anyone.[49] That would point to a peculiar play of interindividual exchanges of empathic feelings. It would also explain why the frightened animal seeks the highest-ranking one he can find: that fearless one, precisely by his menacing appearance, gives the weak one confidence. The effort to groom and invitation to copulate spring from a desire to make the closest possible contact with that source of strength—penetrating his fur to touch the skin,[50] or try-ing to initiate the closest of all unions, coitus. To the scared baboon, the frown and stare which the ethologist sees as a threat may not be a threat, but part of a luring and assuring display.

The purpose of this rather extensive presentation of Kummer's baboon studies has been to show what unexpected conditions may come to light when observation goes beyond the superficial stage of finding the most evident facts of animal life and giving them sociological labels—"staking out territory," "submission" and "recognition of status," "problem solving," "training the young," "cooperation" and "communication." Every one of these categories imposes the image of human society on the activities of animals, and not even only on gregarious ones. But a single odd fact such as the passion of many primates for grooming others of their kind immediately raises questions about the motivating situation, and paradoxical findings like the ba-

---

[49] *Ibid.*, p. 41: "Drohwirkung hat jede plötzliche, ruckartig knappe Bewegung des Oberkörpers. Solche Bewegungen sind immer von Brauenziehen begleitet und werden alle im charakteristischen Zeitabstand von 1 bis 2 Sekunden wiederholt. Diese Bewegungsform ist geradezu ein Drohprinzip, gleichzustellen etwa der Ver-grösserung des Körperumfanges oder dem Darbieten der Waffen bei vielen Arten."

[50] In *The Social Organization of Hamadryas Baboons* (1968), p. 36, Dr. Kummer writes: "The bite on the nape of the neck or on the back is the sharpest reaction a unit leader makes to a straying female. It immediately causes the female to follow him closely." And subsequently, after several detailed descriptions: "females will groom their males after having received neck bites or after aggressive encounters with other females. At such times grooming movements are much more rapid than usual, and the normal removing and eating of particles from the skin is left out" (p. 45).

In a separate article on a special relationship which he calls *"gesicherte Drohung"* and in English "the tripartate relation," Dr. Kummer offers a very interesting hy-pothesis of the motivations, in terms of individual feeling, of the whole grouping behavior of the hamadryas baboons; but that material belongs to the next chapter and will be considered there.

boons' tendency to approach a threatening individual rather than flee from it may require far-reaching systematic interpretation. Such interpretation can rest on various principles. Thus, behaviorally judged, Kummer's "α-animal" shows intention to attack; ethologically, he asserts his dominance and command; psychologically, he seems to feel his competence as self-enlargement, so the signs of fear in another monkey promptly make him expand and display his own strength. Because my interest is to trace human intellect and society back to its beginnings in animal feeling, I am following the psychological method, i.e., seeking the most probable mental acts to explain overt behavior in each animal species on which sufficient observations have been made by reliable persons, professional or self-trained.

Two further imputations of human psychical capacities to animals require an alternative treatment in non-human terms of instinctive action directly felt from move to move: the relatively simple case of cooperation, and the moot and difficult question of communication. The reason why an explanation of cooperative behavior is easier to give no matter on what theory is that we know what empirical events we mean by the word,[51] which is not true of "communication." Let us consider one or two typical instances of animals' cooperative acts and try to account for them in terms of impulse and immediate feeling.

William Etkin, in his ambitiously titled little paper "Social Behavioral Factors in the Emergence of Man," p. 83, writes: "Wolf packs are probably family organizations. A breeding pair and their litter are supplemented by a number of other adults who are presumed to be older offspring.... Hunting is a cooperative enterprise, often involving not only concerted action in isolating and bringing down the quarry but cooperation in such stratagems as driving the prey toward a waiting partner." This allegation of a deliberate division of roles is a naïve trans-

---

[51] Even this is no longer true; the peculiar ambition of ethologists to use maximally extended and diluted concepts so as to let one word cover as many phenomena as possible has made even "cooperation" an ambiguous term. So M. P. Crawford, in *The Cooperative Solving of Problems by Young Chimpanzees* (1937), said: "The term has been used to describe a great variety of behavior patterns, some of which are only remotely related, so that definitions of cooperation range between wide extremes." He notes that one writer calls all cumulative action of plants, protozoa or primates, even such as reducing a food supply or wearing a path, "cooperation"; whereas to another, "cooperation means sympathy, identification of one person with another, and teamwork, the coordination and integration of action ..." (p. 2). But at least there is still a prevalent "working concept" by which we may measure and judge whether a joint act of two or more agents is really cooperation or only simulates it.

fer of the English hunting meet, with beaters to stir up the game, dogs to keep it running and men stationed to bring it to bay, to the pursuit of a quarry by a pack of wolves or wild dogs. The division of roles according to a generally accepted plan is often attributed to packs and droves of animals, but no one, to my knowledge, has ever described how the plan is made and the roles are assigned in advance. The fact is that every pursuer tries to reach the quarry, but since most running animals tend to take a circling course, the predators on the inside of the curve (however slight) have a more open track to dash around the rest of the pack and intercept the victim's course. The act requires no plan, but springs from momentary opportunity and individual perception of a special chance.[52]

In W. J. Hamilton's *American Mammals* there are several explicit statements to the effect that animals cooperate with one another in hunting and defense, with examples drawn from general observation or from the anecdotal literature. So, for instance: "That some species may aid their kind at critical moments in escaping a common enemy is evident from the following. A young pika was observed to be closely pursued by a weasel which followed the pika with amazing accuracy through the rock slides and crevices. As the weasel was about to capture the fast-tiring pika, another pika cut into the race, keeping ahead of the weasel and just behind the exhausted pika, which dodged out of the death race at the first opportunity. Soon a third pika joined the race, but was unsuccessful in diverting the weasel's attention from the second pika, which was showing signs of weariness. Shortly a fourth pika joined in the exciting relay, which by this time had resulted in a very fatigued weasel. The weasel shortly gave up the unequal contest. The pikas apparently aid each other in such crucial moments in escaping a common enemy by forcing it to run a relay race against an overwhelming number of opponents."[53]

Pikas do not live in bands, but like other lagomorphs space themselves out over a suitable area for their solitary lives and seasonal family affairs. That a weasel chasing a pika would scare up others in the course of its pursuit at fairly regular intervals, and that sometimes, especially

---

[52] Wolfdietrich Kühme, whose camper was parked for four months close to the dens of a pack of African hunting dogs on the Serengeti grasslands, where he often watched the pack pursuing gazelles and other prey, observed no strategy or seemingly premeditated behavior. See his "Freilandstudien zur Soziologie des Hyänenhundes (Lycaon pictus lupinus Thomas 1902)" (1965).

[53] *American Mammals: Their Lives, Habits, and Economic Relations*, (1939), p. 289. As the source of the anecdote he names Joseph Dixon in the *Journal of Mammalogy* (1931).

on the first such occasion, the livelier motion of the suddenly disturbed new animal would distract the predator long enough to let its original quarry duck into a shelter, requires no explanation in terms of purposive cooperation. It is certainly more plausible that each animal is running for its own life, and the faster motion of a fresh quarry is a stronger lure to the weasel than the one it has been following, though it would, of course, be more reasonable to track the tired one down. But weasels don't reason, they just run. Nonetheless they must catch their prey often enough so they live to run another day.

There are, however, acts of genuine cooperation among animals, and these are the ones that put the principle of interpretation in terms of immediate feeling to the test. C. R. Carpenter observed some unmistakable cases as he watched troupes of howling monkeys move along arboreal paths, which required some crossings from tree to tree where the closest branches were several feet apart. In at least two such cases he saw a female, followed by a young one, suspend herself by a tailhold on the last branch of one tree and a handhold on a branch of the next tree, gained by jumping, so her body made a bridge over which the young one—after long hesitation—finally crossed.[54] That certainly was a cooperative negotiation of the gap, although the mother did the greater part of it; but the infant had to make its own onward move while she remained still.

The principal elements in this rather elaborate joint act are ordinary enough: carrying the young, waiting when it does not follow. The little one had outgrown the riding stage, so it went forward as soon as it could jump to the second tree, but its mother's back was still the needed and natural vehicle (Fig. 15–4). Each move of each animal emerged from the motivating situation; the two agents needed no plan or direc-

---

[54] In A *Field Study of the Behavior and Social Relations of Howling Monkeys*, pp. 73–74, he quotes some of his own protocol notes bearing on such maternal behavior. The young are classified according to stages of development; "infant 3," mentioned in the legend to the accompanying illustration, refers to the last stage of infancy, when the young one usually follows its mother instead of riding on her back, but still may be helped over difficult crossings from tree to tree. For his classification of young from "infant 1" (first month) to "juvenile 3" (about three years old), see the table on p. 60. Unfortunately, in the protocols the designations "infant" and "juvenile" are not strictly distinguished; in one, for instance, one reads that "a juvenile 3 came to a wide crossing," and after its mother had carried it over the gap, "the infant then dismounted and resumed independent locomotion." It is hard to believe that a juvenile 3—characterized in the table as "entirely independent"—would or even could be carried on its mother's back while she takes a leap it is afraid to negotiate. Yet there are several allegations of such services to a "juvenile 3."

Figure 15–4. An Infant Howling Monkey Completing a Critical
Crossing

its mother's back was still the needed and natural vehicle

(C. R. Carpenter, A *Field Study of the Behavior and Social Relations of Howling Monkeys*
[Baltimore: Johns Hopkins Press, 1934].)

[175]

tive communication. Animals that carry their babies as constantly as monkeys do must feel them as part of themselves so intimately that, even when they no longer ride, the awareness of the young one's reach, strength and jumping span is empathically felt by the mother; she stops and waits between trees, especially where her following offspring falls back, afraid of the leap.

There are few situations in which cooperation between animals has been observed without involvement of the mother-child relationship. The famous St. Bernard dogs, which were kept especially as trackers of lost persons in the Alps, and in other environments have been known to save many a human being from drowning, work best alone; in a quandary, another dog would be no help. The only genuine cases of collaboration I know, carried out as if by one organism, are among colonial insects, which are semi-individuated beings. Vertebrates may cooperate by chance, the action of one animal giving opportunity for successful acts by another, but each one is trying to realize an impulse of its own all by itself. Dogs have been trained to help human beings— the work of our "seeing-eye" dogs is a spectacular example[55]—but that is not entering into an act with a joint aim; the human partner conceives the purposes and the dog has been taught to play its role on command. Other working dogs, even closely associated in a team (as in the arctic) or in a hunting pack, never watch each other's moves to cooperate in the attainment of a common aim.

In the laboratory, experiments have been arranged to test the capacity

[55] The training for the canine role is given preferably to females, exploiting their maternal instincts to care and wait for other beings, and the selection of animals for such training favors various breeds of shepherd dogs, which have a tendency to watch and guide members of other than their own species. It has been asserted that this tendency is uniquely canine; Bastian Schmid, for instance, in "Zur Psychologie des Treibens und Hütens" (1937), said explicitly: "Niemals ... vermöchten wir einen *Schimpansen* oder einen anderen Anthropoiden zum Betreuen *einer Schafherde* ... zu erziehen wie den Hund.—Der Affe kann nicht allein deshalb nicht hüten, weil seinem Triebleben jene dem Hund zukommenden Bedingungen fehlen, sondern auch weil ihm die characterlichen und speziell für dieses Geschäft die in Richtung der Intelligenz liegenden Anlagen fehlen" (p. 255). But Hoesch, in "Über ziegenhütende Bärenpaviane (*Papio ursinus raucana* Shortridge)," tells of a South African farm where the herd of goats, numbering about eighty animals, was tended solely by a female chacma baboon which had never been trained, but was simply kept in the compound with the herd. She spontaneously first accompanied the goats to pasture, then assumed the role of the leader, running ahead and luring them with her "ho-ho-ho" call instead of driving them as dogs do. She had had two predecessors, one of which had served for six years. The author remarked in passing: "Diese Betätigung des Muttertriebes an Artfremden erscheint mir besonders beachtlich" (p. 300).

of chimpanzees to join forces in the accomplishment of an act which promised the same "reward" for them both; M. P. Crawford taught two young apes to pull simultaneously at two respective ropes fastened to a box outside the cage, and either lying too far apart for one animal to pick up together, or else leading from a box too heavy for a single one of the pair to move. The results were "positive" to some extent, in the sense of meeting the experimenter's wishes, but anomalous in that they did not demonstrate any spontaneous cooperation. In the first place, the conditions, task and learning processes were so highly artificial that the records of the experiment tell more about chimpanzees' trainability than about their interest in the "problem," let alone any spontaneous insight into the way to solve it by cooperating. Each move was learned separately by each animal; at last the pair was caged together and trained for teamwork.[56] After that, of course, the trick was often practiced by the animals even without reward; captive apes use every possible act of their fully developed repertoire in play, and incite each other to join in the game.[57]

All the genuine instances of cooperation which I have been able to study seemed to rest on direct or extended parental impulses, sometimes modified or enhanced by other characteristics of animal action and feeling, such as empathy, physical communion (as by trophallaxis and mutual licking), self-enlargement, etc. Today, the most spectacular instances and the most enthusiastically discussed in the current literature refer not to primates, but to a distant order, Cetacea. The intensive study of marine mammals, especially dolphins of the species *Tursiops truncatus*, began only a few decades ago with the discovery that they were eminently trainable to perform elaborate stunts for the entertainment of spectators at big seaside aquariums.[58] This led, of course, to

[56] *The Cooperative Solving of Problems by Young Chimpanzees.*

[57] Paul Schiller, in "Innate Motor Action as a Basis of Learning. Manipulative Patterns in the Chimpanzee" (1957), argues throughout his article that play, not "problem solving," is the basis of learning skills. See esp. pp. 268–69: "Once a complex pattern is mastered, the chimpanzees develop a liking for it. They perform the trick even in situations in which the complex pattern is not necessary for adaptive behavior.... With no incentive the chimpanzees have displayed a higher variety of handling objects than under the pressure of a lure which they attempted to obtain.... the problem situation impeded the play." And finally (p. 272, with reference to the famous "problem solving" act of joining two bamboos to make one long stick to reach a banana outside the cage): "Those who used the stick connection for work took much more time to develop this habit than to join the sticks in play.... The problem of joining sticks was never solved, of course, by animals who had not performed the connection previously in play."

[58] For an account of this discovery and its original exploitation see Stenuit, *The Dolphin, Cousin to Man*, pp. 124 ff.

speculations on the cause or causes of such trainability; and the speculations in turn initiated psychological, physiological and highly interesting
anatomical studies of these truly amazing animals.[59]

It is in the dolphins that mutual aid among adults, which is rarely
recorded in other animals and then uncertain, can be clearly observed,
sometimes by several watchers together. That such aid is really given
to sick or injured *Tursiops* is, I think, beyond dispute; the attentions of
strong and healthy individuals to incapacitated ones is claimed to be so
reliable that trainers and keepers of dolphins in captivity have learned
to leave the tendance of the sick—which requires help to rise for breath
every one-half to five minutes, around the clock—to one or two other
dolphins in the same tank. Even a single animal can perform this service, which would be impossible for a human being, because of our basic
rhythm of sleeping and waking. In such an indefinitely protracted activity we would have to pause for variable but finally ineluctable periods
of rest and inattention. That the dolphin apparently needs no respite
from its task is certainly as remarkable as the fact that it voluntarily
assumes it; but because the latter phenomenon can be regarded as a
"social act," and ethologists at present are avid for social relations, social life and social organization of animals, the strange physiological
aspect has been generally ignored. Yet when it is earnestly investigated
the findings bear heavily, though in a roundabout way, on the intellec-
tualist school's theoretical foundation.

Dr. Lilly's "delphinology," as it has been seriously called, rests on a
single fundamental belief, namely, that the level of mentality of a species is wholly determined by the size of the brain. In *The Mind of the
Dolphin,* he has declared his doctrine quite explicitly, saying: "As I
theorized in *Man and Dolphin,* we speak and communicate complex
matters partly because our brains are large enough (in terms of numbers
of active elements) to do it. Therefore, any similar brain of similar size
and complexity can do a comparable job though possibly in ways very
strange to man" (p. 35).[60] Later in the book our intellectual abilities

[59] Some good reports of investigations on the dolphin's brain with implanted
electrodes and also post-mortem examinations, up to ca. 1960, may be found in
Lilly's otherwise very controversial *Man and Dolphin* (1961), chap. v. More general
anatomical and physiological findings are recorded in Appendix I of the same book.
Since then there have been a considerable number of special studies, as, for instance,
those collected by H. Andersen in *The Biology of Marine Mammals* (1969).

[60] Within the next dozen pages Dr. Lilly works up to the enthusiastic statement:
"The United Nations does not recognize race, color, or creed as a means of differentiation between human beings. Let us add 'species' and use this approach as a good
example of the kind of thinking which we should be applying to the dolphins and

are no longer "partly" determined by brain size, but the author sums up his argument in the statements: "The size of the mind is a direct and eventually specifiable function of the size of the brain. The size of the brain is a direct and eventually specifiable function of the number of active elements contained therein, i.e., present theory says the number of neurons and possibly the number of glia cells contained within the total brain itself determine functional size. The size of the brain in terms of numbers of active elements is close to a linear function of the total weight of the mammalian brain. Thus, we can say that the total weight of the living mammalian brain is a gross measure of the size of the contained mind, and hence, a gross measure of complexity and apparent variability of the information which can be transmitted."[61]

It is dangerous to base a whole "-ology" on what "present theory says," especially where there are several theories at present; and as for the "information which can be transmitted," that is a highly ambiguous phrase with reference to a brain, since in the jargon of today's psychology "information" means any influence of anything on anything. So this impressive brain might be doing quite other things than perceiving, thinking, making general and communicable judgments and memorizing legends to tell the young (all of which Dr. Lilly has explicitly attributed to it). There seem, in fact, to be some peculiarities of the dolphin's brain which make it functionally less similar to man's than many a lower animal's in which the general mammalian brain structures (cortical layers, thalamic nuclei, pyramidal tract, etc.) are less developed than in cetaceans. There is as yet no way of knowing how much cerebral activity in any being is redundant; and one peculiarity in the dolphin's behavior suggests that redundancy in his brain may be very high—namely, his ability to stay awake indefinitely and carry out a voluntary activity for twenty-four hours a day. Dr. Karl E. Schaefer noted this possible reason for the size and apparent complexity of the central nervous organ. In a symposium paper on physiological adaptation of marine mammals, he remarked:

---

whales. In addition to race, color, creed, and religious beliefs [besides creed?] the new criteria should read: 'No matter differences between species, no matter differences of anatomy, no matter differences between media in which they live, creatures with a brain above a certain size will be considered 'equal' with man" (p. 48).

[61] P. 99. Unfortunately, neurologists have long investigated the relation of intelligence to brain size in human beings, with negative results. See J. A. Hamilton, "Intelligence and the Human Brain" (1936): "In 1885 Topinard ... was able to report that 10,182 brains had been weighed by 35 investigators. ... each of these men took pains to mention that, in his own series, there was no evidence of an association between size of brain and intellectual endowment" (p. 311).

"The cetaceans have an astonishing cerebral development. These air-breathing diving animals have a much greater brain weight than water-breathing animals of comparable size. . . . The relation of brain weight and body weight in the dolphins is about the same as in man.

"The dolphins have a unique sleeping and waking rhythm. They are awake at every breath and always sleep with one eye open. It seems that they are constantly surveying their surroundings with at least one eye, which means maintaining afference to half the brain. That may explain the great weight of their brains, which is required if one part is to be in a waking state while the other is recovering in sleep."[62]

John Lilly himself, in his sober scientific observations, unwittingly has brought some support to Schaefer's hypothesis by discovering the multiple, functionally equivalent mechanisms in the delphinic brain, sometimes reflected even in the immediately connected effector organs. Lilly, of course, thinks of these reduplications of brain potentialities simply as sources of added mental powers, and extrapolates from known animalian actions to hypothetical higher processes such as symbolically constructed speech and abstract thought.[63] But such may not be the true effect of the equivalent yet easily uncoupled mechanisms which he has noted in the two large cetacean hemispheres. It is possible that these may sometimes work in conjunction, but their separability is their unique feature, and this seems to stem from the fact that they were developed with the evolution of air breathing in a watery ambient. So, for example, he refers to a previous study which described the whistles produced by dolphins in each other's company, and says: "In addition, we showed that they exchanged not only whistles, but also exchanged trains of clicking sounds. We also showed that the two kinds of sonic exchanges do not correspond in time, i.e., they can be talking with whistles and talking with click trains, the whistles and the clicks completely out of phase with one another. . . .

"These observations led to further studies in which we demonstrated unequivocally that each dolphin has at least two communication emitters, both in the nose, i.e., below the blowhole, one on each side. . . . Thus a given dolphin can carry on a whistle conversation with his right side and a clicking conversation with his left side and do the two quite independently with the two halves of his brain."[64]

[62] "Physiologische Anpassung bei Meeressäugetieren" (1968), p. 188.

[63] M. C. Caldwell and D. K. Caldwell, in an all too brief article, "Vocalization of Naive Captive Dolphins in Small Groups" (1968), say in their own summary (p. 1121): "We found no evidence of a dolphin 'language,' but we present evidence of social response to acoustic signals."

[64] The Mind of the Dolphin, pp. 75–76.

Whatever the capacities and motivations of dolphins may really be, there certainly is great scope for hypothetical explanations. No matter what premises one adopts as a framework, there always could be some alternative hypothesis; only, some interpretations fit better than others into the general system of zoological concepts. This seems to me to hold for the notion of animal values as permanent or transitory cathexes, imposed on objects by their immediate entrance into what William James called "live options" in the active progress of life. So, instead of judging dolphin behavior in terms of "intelligence," "problem solving" and "learning,"[65] it may be wiser to approach it first in terms of animal feeling, as an expression of impulse, steered by the perception of opportunities and the felt fluctuations of ambient conditions, and developing from within by a constant generation of reinforcing or competing impulses.

Having, then, at least an idea of how a dolphin could be capable of tending a sick comrade unintermittently day and night, we may return to that rare exhibit of cooperation among adults to question what instinctive proclivities could initiate it and what feeling could support it. An extraordinary response in a species bespeaks a coming together of several behavioral potentialities through the development of an integrated emotive pattern; in this case, apparently, an extension of the parental relation to any individual, young or old, male or female, that relapses into the helplessness of the newborn in immediate need of air. One reason for the dolphin's readiness to respond in this motherly way may lie in the fact that its mode of life reduces early physical contact with the young to a minimum, compared to the constant hugging, grooming, carrying and cuddling of little monkeys and apes by their mothers. The maternal responses which cannot develop maximally in marine mammals upon giving birth, but are restricted to nursing and vital first-aid care, still lie partly in abeyance—perhaps from the beginning of life to the end, with or without any actual motherhood. Be-

[65] All such phenomena are selected from animals' displays of repertory items to fit into categories taken from human psychology. Alison Jolly has aptly remarked this fallacy in "Lemur Social Behavior and Primate Intelligence" (1966), saying: "What does one mean by monkey-level intelligence? One usually means an ability to solve problems with objects, under controlled laboratory conditions. . . . whenever a psychologist tests learning, it is of inanimate objects: symbols on the alleys of a maze, plaques covering food-wells, hardware toys or sticks or boxes. Whether the aim is 'learning' or 'insight,' whether the reward is food, sight of another monkey, or just the chance to play, intelligence is measured in relation to gadgetry.

"This use of intelligence is our own forte, but not the monkey's" (p. 504). Perhaps a better measure of animal mentality would be versatility in play. Certainly, by this criterion, the dolphin would rank high; so would many primates.

cause there is so little physical contact to support and sustain parental feeling, it must be intrinsically strong; and perhaps the dolphin's great neural and muscular versatility is reflected in the wide scope of its centrally engendered feelings and its ambient emotive lures. The proclivity of an occasional dolphin to play with human beings on beaches, which has been demonstrated repeatedly and beyond doubt, points to the same readiness to transfer companionship from one sort of individual to another, even creatures of remote species.

Another cardinal reason, though I can adduce it only hypothetically, may be a very strong tie of empathy between dolphins. Since the surfacing for breath in these animals is irregular, which suggests that their moments of oxygen requirement are variable, a dolphin playing nurse to a sick comrade evidently feels, somehow, when its charge is in need of breath. There may be a two-way adjustment, the invalid falling in, after a fashion, with the respiratory periods of its nurse; but there surely must be some fusing of felt somatic tensions to implement the cooperative activity. That points to a close empathic relationship. Now, empathy is a typically animalian form of communion; so it is a supreme development of non-human capacities, rather than an approach to human intellect, that is strongly indicated in the dolphin's care for its sick.

There are, moreover, some fantastic-sounding yet well-authenticated stories of *Tursiops'* pushing wounded creatures—not only their own kind, but large fish and even human beings—into shallows and up on beaches. This practice has always been regarded as a further elaboration of the "care-giving" behavior toward the sick. On this natural assumption, however, it presents some very puzzling aspects, both as a whole and in special cases. As a whole, it has been extolled as a rescue operation because its most spectacular and publicized instances have been those in which a human being has been steered ashore by one or sometimes two dolphins, and thus saved from drowning.[66] But to be

---

[66] According to W. N. Kellogg, *Porpoises and Sonar*, p. 13, "An example was published not long ago in the journal *Natural History* [LVIII (November, 1949), 385–86]. A mature, well-educated woman, who was walking waist deep in 2-foot waves about 10 feet from an ocean beach, was pulled down because of the undertow and was swept beneath the surface. She floundered, swallowed a great deal of water, and was unable to regain her footing." He quotes from her own account: "As I gradually lost consciousness . . . someone gave me a terrific shove, and I landed on the beach, face down, too exhausted to turn over. . . .

"When I got enough energy to get back up the steps, a man who had been standing on the other side of the fence on the public beach came running over. . . .

beached, especially on shores where the tide periodically goes out, would be no blessing to a disabled dolphin, as the breathing aid in water is; also, the "succorant" acts of carrying and pushing are often administered to dead creatures, sometimes for days, both in the wild and in captivity.[67] Whether the free dolphins intended to bring their burdens ashore is unknowable; in a tank, of course, there are neither shores nor shallows. Fishermen on the California coast maintain that dead dolphins are brought ashore and pushed up on the beach by their comrades.

Some of the animals which have been seen carrying carcasses were transporting dead infant dolphins. In at least two cases under natural conditions these young ones were apparently bitten in two, the observers guessed by a shark or barracuda, so the heads were all that was left for their elders to carry about. The motivation of such behavior is easy enough to interpret as a persistent attachment of a female to her offspring, an impulse to keep and tend it, protracted by the baby's failure to show independent action. What may seem strange to a human being is the long duration of that relationship; yet the same phenomenon, lasting even longer, was observed by R. M. Yerkes in a rhesus monkey, which held, licked and fondled a stillborn male baby till all its flesh was worn away by handling and decomposition.[68] There is little doubt, I think, that such "epimelectic behavior" toward a dead young one springs from the unnaturally ruptured bond of mother and neonate, which has traumatic psychological effects.

But what of the dolphin's strange reactions to dead creatures, sometimes observed where no frustrated maternal functions seem to be involved? The most bizarre exhibit of this kind was seen in July, 1956,

---

He said that when he had arrived, I looked like a dead body and that the porpoise shoved me ashore."

This report is followed (p. 14) by a longer one which Dr. Kellogg received from Mrs. Y. M. Stuart, who fell overboard in the Bahamas, and was guided, in darkness and shark-infested seas, to shallow water in reach of a shore, by a dolphin.

[67] J. C. Moore, "Bottle-Nosed Dolphin Supports Remains of Young" (1955), cites three cases from open range observations, one of them his own. In captivity the phenomenon is frequently seen.

[68] *The Mental Life of Monkeys and Apes* (1916), p. 120: "Thus it appears that during a period of five weeks the instinct to protect her offspring impelled this monkey to carry its gradually vanishing remains about with her and to watch over them so assiduously that it was utterly impossible to take them from her except by force.

"... Dr. Hamilton informed me that Gertie had behaved toward her first stillbirth as toward her second. And, further, that Grace, a baboon, also had carried a still-birth about for weeks."

by K. S. Norris at Marineland of the Pacific; it is described in an article by the observer and J. H. Prescott, "Observations on Pacific Cetaceans of Californian and Mexican Waters" (1961), p. 293, as follows: "A large adult female of the species *Tursiops truncatus* was discovered pushing a 5-foot adult leopard shark (*Triakis semifasciata*) around the 80-foot diameter circular display tank. The animal, named Myrtle, repeatedly forced the shark to the surface by pushing it upward with her rostrum. The shark died after a day of this treatment. For the next 8 days Myrtle carried the dead shark on her rostrum, supporting it under its lower jaw. During this period Myrtle regularly brought the shark to the surface, released it, and then dived about 10 feet downward and retrieved the sinking carcass. The staff divers attempted to take the shark from her because its rough shagreen was rubbing the skin from her rostrum, but these attempts failed until the eighth day. Myrtle, who had fed very little during the time she carried the shark, at once resumed her normal feeding habits."

This peculiar behavior, indulged in by one *Tursiops* in the tank, might be brought under the usual heading of maternal activity, in that the shark was about the proper size and shape to seem like a pup to Myrtle, and in that it failed to rise up for air when a young dolphin should have done so. Consequently it might have been "helped" by its elder (especially a female, but not necessarily its mother). She may have killed it with purely succorant intention, and subsequently carried the carcass in typical dolphin fashion. There was, however, one anomaly in her behavior, namely, her treatment of the dead animal, her constant releasing it at the surface and retrieving it from a considerable depth. That is not the usual pattern of baby-carrying; and small abnormalities of behavior may point to major differences in motivation.

After "her" shark was finally removed, two other living sharks were put into the aquarium, and were promptly attacked and killed—this time quite certainly not with kindness—by the two male dolphins which shared the tank with her. According to the observers, "Myrtle picked up one of these dead sharks and carried it through part of the night of July 25. The shark was found on the floor of the tank next morning. Myrtle fed nearly normally during this final episode, in contrast to her behavior in the first instance. In both cases, when she fed she dropped her burden, took her food, and then retrieved the shark, usually before it had drifted to the bottom."

Eight days of handling the previous shark in a fixed, repetitious pattern may have set up enough of a habit so that when a second dead specimen was provided it enticed the dolphin to continue her peculiar reaction to a carcass in the tank. Animals in captivity very readily establish compulsive repetitious behavior.[69] The fact that she showed less attachment to the second shark, however, makes it seem as though she were using it to finish an act which the aquarium divers who took the decomposed first fish away had interrupted near its natural end. But what was the likeliest motivation and nature of the whole performance?

The most obvious explanation to occur to anyone in this case is probably that which I first proposed: a female dolphin's maternal reaction to an animal having some resemblance to a pup that did not rise to take air. Her action really presented a familiar behavior pattern; only her pushing the shark round and round the tank instead of lifting it repeatedly in one place, and, after it died, her peculiar manner of dropping it to retrieve it by a deep dive, cast some slight doubt on its status as misplaced maternal behavior. Add to this the fact that the two

[69] Koenig, in *Kif-Kif*, pp. 199–200, makes a general statement on this point: "Wer aber laufen kann, der muss auch laufen. Springmäuse produzieren enorm viel Bewegungsenergie, die sie wieder loswerden und irgendwie abreagieren müssen. Hält man sie in einem kleinen Raum, rennen sie genausoviel wie draussen in der endlosen Wüste. . . . Was aber in unbegrenztem Gelände wie freies umherstreifen aussieht, wird auf engem Raum zur trostlosen Bewegungsstereotypie. Im kleinen Terrarium springt die Maus dann nächtelang unablässig in derselben Ecke hin und her und hin und her. . . . Der dauernd in Achterschleifen laufende Elefant, der nur noch rythmisch mit dem Oberkörper pendelnde Bär, der auf seiner Stange ein um das andere Mal dieselbe Welle drehende Papagei, alle leiden an der typischen Raummangelkrankheit—an Bewegungsstereotypien, die allmählig infolge der absoluten Ereignislosigkeit zur völligen Abstumpfung der Tiere führen.

"Solche eingefahrenen Bewegungsfolgen lassen sich nicht einfach durch Vergrösserung des Lebensraumes beseitigen."

Kellogg, in *Porpoises and Sonar*, pp. 28–29, gives a striking example of this effect of close confinement. A dolphin named Betty at the Florida State University marine laboratories was put into a small cage for experimental purposes. "While in the cage, she tolerated petting and handling by persons who went into the water beside her, and at first she took food readily from the hand.

"The space was quite confining, however, and Betty soon developed a kind of up-and-down motion without going anywhere. This was presently characterized by observers as 'the rocking-horse movement.'. . . Moreover, she went up and down at a faster rate than was necessary for breathing. . . . she usually took a breath only on every fourth or fifth rise of the rocking-horse movement.

". . . Eventually, she refused to accept any food at all, and so we transferred her back to the larger pool.

". . . but the rocking-horse movement remained a regular part of her repertoire even after she had been released from the cage." When attempts were made to lure her with fish, "She would swim to within 5 or 10 feet of the feeder and remain there, eyeing him as she rocked rhythmically up and down. On more than one occasion she came close, *then turned her back on the attendant*, and began her rocking routine." Several other witnesses have told the same story.

males in the enclosure did not touch "her" shark in life or death, though they promptly finished off two others which were put into the tank, which is a peculiar circumstance. Perhaps the accepted "epimeletic" motive masks the true psychological source of Myrtle's protracted act, from the pushing and lifting that killed the fish through the long manipulation of the putrefying body, pursued so intensively that she scarcely took food, and finally the half-hearted aftermath with a shark she had not killed, and soon abandoned.

The possibility of a different impulse altogether as the origin of a superficially familiar behavior pattern is likely to occur to one only in the light of other, apparently unrelated phenomena. In this case, the parallels lie very far afield, but what aligns them with the dolphin's corpse transport is that they are all aftermaths of large and often exciting acts. In such acts, it seems, the consummation may be achieved before the impulse is spent; then the act has to have a long cadence, which a human being, to whom the physical change effected by its consummation always seems the "aim" and rational end of action, can only regard as useless motion. Yet the extension of an overt act to give expression to every subact implicit in its total impulse may be a necessity to an animal, and sometimes even to man. We try to counteract, displace or sublimate an internal pression which has overshot its goal; for instance, if we are working passionately to achieve a particular political change, woman suffrage, abolition of slavery, or the like, and the change suddenly, fortuitously, takes place through events quite apart from our efforts, we have to reorganize our emotions and conations, and switch our actions to another "cause." Animals do not attempt such rational control of their impulses, but seek the most complete actualization of them even if their central drive was quickly consummated. Their performances are not always finished when we think they are; some subsequent acts may still be parts of the supposedly completed ones. So, for instance, Paul Schiller remarked that when a chimpanzee, unable to either pull in or push away[70] a piece of food outside its cage with a stick, finally throws the stick away, that throwing is part of the reaching act, and marks its real end.[71] A more familiar example

[70] "These two alternatives [pulling in and pushing away] are originally equally frequent" ("Innate Motor Action as a Basis of Learning," p. 274). Evidently it is the doing, not the getting, that intrigues the ape.

[71] Pp. 274–75: "He is giving up and turns his back on the scene of frustration. Later, he turns back and then he suddenly picks up the stick again and points or shakes it toward the 'goal.' If there is no effect on the goal, the stick is scooted or thrown away. Comparing this sequence to the free play with sticks, it is clear that the throwing is an end-member of a series of activities which seem to induce one another."

is the behavior of a cat which has caught a mouse and proceeds—as is popularly supposed—to "play" with it. The belief that the cat follows the act of catching the mouse (which may include subacts of watching, stalking, muscular preparations, building up tensions for the crucial leap) with a playful act in which the mouse becomes a toy is universally accepted. Yet in terms of impulse and feeling it is really a questionable interpretation; more likely, the cat is protracting the hunt which is too quickly successful, by repeating the final phase in a telescoped fashion, letting the mouse just start to run away and retrieving without killing it until the impulse with all its contributaries is spent. Young cats often kill their prey inadvertently, and then throw the carcass around for an hour or more. Gradually, in kittens, a play impulse may supervene; but I have seen a typical course of action which makes me doubt that.

Two six-month-old cats, a male and a female of the same litter, ordinarily shared every toy in joint play. One day the female caught a mouse. She released it to catch it again, tossed it, rose on her hind legs, rolled over while clutching it, and in a few minutes had killed it, but continued her so-called play with the carcass. Her brother did not touch the mouse, alive or dead. He held absolutely aloof, watching passively and distantly, until the mouse became too unpleasant for the human cohabitants, so the hunter, still clutching her mouse, was ejected via the front door. I do not think she ever ate the mouse, as the cats had just been fed.

A comparable observation, under more exciting and spectacular circumstances, is recorded in Jane van Lawick-Goodall's *My Friends the Wild Chimpanzees*. One of these usually harmless animals, a large male she had named Rodolf, killed a young baboon with such fierceness that the other apes were terrified. "Three other chimpanzees with him," she writes, "screamed loudly and threw their arms around one another, so intensely agitated that they seemed no more than a black, hairy tangle of bodies, arms and legs" (p. 65). Though the killer was of relatively low rank among the adult males, none of the others dared to take his booty away from him. The baboon was much more than a generally herbivorous animal could eat, but Rodolf carried the carcass around with him all day. When his first hunger for the meat was assuaged, he allowed his peers to take little pieces of it, though he jealously guarded the body itself. Mrs. Van Lawick-Goodall interprets the restraint of his fellows as a recognition of his property, saying: "Nothing could demonstrate more clearly a human-like acknowledgement of the rights of ownership than their behavior that day. Mike, J. B., and Goliath all held a higher social rank than Rodolf; yet as they gathered around the hunter they simply gazed longingly at the red meat, making no attempt to wrest it away.

"Tentatively, Mike [the top male] reached toward the kill. Rodolf, who normally goes into a frenzy of submission if Mike merely approaches, pulled the prize away. Goliath held his hand to Rodolf's mouth, begging for the flesh he was chewing. Rodolf pushed his hand away roughly."[72]

Yet the "right of ownership" lasted only as long as the rightful owner kept his hold on the dead baboon. In human society possession may be nine points of the law, but in the chimpanzee horde it is all ten points, and functions, indeed, in place of any law or recognized right. No matter how clear the demonstration of "human-like" behavior may have been, it did not follow the human pattern quite to the end of the episode. After eating his fill and drinking, the hunter lay down, still holding the dwindling baboon. "Fifteen minutes later Rodolf sat up.... Suddenly he abandoned the carcass, moved about ten feet away and sat down.... For a few moments the other chimps stared without moving.... Then all together they converged on the meat, grabbing and pulling and screaming....

"They pulled and tore and screamed until after a few minutes each emerged from the fray with a share. Not very even shares though— Mike had the head and shoulders, David the tender rump, and the other three got only small pieces."[73]

If respect for the hunter's right to his kill is not what made the apes refrain from depriving Rodolf, a subordinate individual, of the baboon or at least fighting for a share of it, what did inhibit them? Very probably the magnitude and ferocity of his abnormal act, which threw them all into a panic at its violent beginning; the monkey was part of this act which no other animal would dare to interrupt. During its progress Rodolf was not submissive, low-ranking or subordinate; he was the agent in a fearful display. As long as he held his prey it belonged, not to him, but to what he was doing, and his companions knew the intensity of his impulse and everything his instinctive expression of it involved: his temporary fearlessness and imperiousness, the day-long carrying of his victim (he killed the baboon at 8:40 A.M. and left it just before sundown), his renewed attacks on it as he bit and ate it at intervals. They also sensed when the act was finished and he was through with his prey. There was no problem of a formal right to its future possession, such as a man might have claimed.

[72] P. 66.
[73] P. 68.

If, now, we look back at the act of the dolphin at Marineland of the Pacific, and consider the way she pushed the shark around the tank until it died, this may be viewed as lifting it up to breathe, but also as more nearly akin to another cetacean trick, namely, stranding dead, dying or floundering animals. There are no shallows or tidal sandbars in a tank, as there are in wild marine environments; nothing to permit an animal to push another up a beach or a rocky shelf. And here one may even raise a question of the real emotional feeling expressed in such "rescuing" acts: is it "epimeletic," derived from the maternal instinctive repertoire, or is it adverse, if not hostile, a desire to remove the weak, disabled or dead body? Was Myrtle's first, daylong, vigorous pushing and prodding of the shark a fight to shove it up the wall, carried on for a week with its unresistant dead body? That might account for the fact that no other dolphin attacked the shark or offered any interference with her long procedure. Her act was almost over when she allowed the divers to remove the carcass and finished the abreaction of her agonistic feeling with another fish.

This does not mean, of course, that all the behavior generally viewed as succorant should be regarded as aggressive. Far from it. The help given to the newborn, not only by their mothers but sometimes also by other adults, is certainly maternal, and seems to be carried over from instinctive patterns of motherhood to wider and looser forms of motherliness.[74] The important point is that actions which a behaviorist would find identical may be the overt aspects of very different total acts. The aim of animal psychology is to understand whole acts as the elements of behavior and the indicators of feeling, whereby the evolution of perception, emotion and ultimately more and more specialized cerebral functions, the characteristically human ones, may be traced to their evolutionary sources. Prevision of changes in the outer world, i.e., envisagement of the results of acts (including very complicated acts), is probably a late achievement; perhaps—as I strongly suspect—a mark of humanity.

Motivation is the ever-recurrent key problem; and where our interpretation of a behavioral episode meets with some disturbing anomaly the chances are that our assumptions of the motivating situation in which the animal is acting are wrong—over-simplified, anthropomorphic or hastily carried over from some other case which they fitted. What closer study shows is that very different impulses may underlie similar overt acts, or to put it conversely, a given mode of behavior may arise from any of several emotional tension patterns. Such patterns may even

[74] See above, pp. 176 on dogs and monkeys and 181–82 on cetaceans.

lapse for intervals which are filled by other impulses upholding the performance, especially if it is repetitious and has become rhythmic. Myrtle's act of releasing and retrieving her dead shark may have entrained some play impulse which filled the lapses of her dominant feeling. The whole act apparently was sustained by the tendency to perseveration that characterizes the movements of captive animals. The repertoire elements in it include so many which occur in maternal and "epimeletic" behavior and in pup transport that to identify the basic motivation of the whole strange phenomenon is not easy, for often the appearance of an instinctual unit in a new context casts doubts on its most accepted meanings.

So it is with many of the cetacean interactions which are generally interpreted as social services. The propensity of dolphins to help disabled ones breathe is, perhaps, the clearest case, known only in captivity, and possibly elicited solely in that condition. An equally well-attested phenomenon, observed mainly in the wild, is the support given to stricken whales by their companions, two of which immediately rush to the shot or harpooned beast's sides, closing in to hold it upright and sometimes swimming away with it.[75] Naturally, the accepted interpretation of that astounding response is that the uninjured whales come to save the disabled member of their group, but where they take the victim, which is usually dying if not instantly dead, is unknown; the ocean keeps the secret.

These remarkable joint and even communal actions of sea mammals, hard to observe because of the unsurveyable vastness of the ocean theater, are said to have their parallels in the behavior of the largest land-dwelling animals, the elephants. There are several accounts in the writings of ivory hunters, photographers, rangers and a few ethologists of apparent attempts by elephants to rescue wounded comrades. W. Buckley, a noted sportsman who had followed close behind many a

---

[75] Norris and Prescott, in "Observations on Pacific Cetaceans of Californian and Mexican Waters," attest the fact that "many species of cetaceans will offer assistance when a 'schoolmate' becomes injured or otherwise unable to maintain normal locomotion. Usually this assistance consists of a normal animal or animals swimming with the incapacitated member, helping it stay at the surface, or actually taking it away from the apparent source of danger. The first recorded observation of this sort is found in the writings of Aristotle. . . . Even very recently the existence of such behavior has been denied, but evidence has begun to accumulate which shows that, in this particular, Aristotle was correct" (p. 292). An interesting item occurs on the next page, in support of the various stories of aid to human beings: "Interspecific cooperative behavior was noted when a striken adult male of *Lagenorhynchus obliquidens* was assisted by an adult female of the species *Tursiops truncatus*."

herd, described the following scene: "I had singled a bull from the herd and given him the shoulder shot, which had the effect of crumpling him up. As he subsided, three cows ran to his assistance, and two of them, one getting each side of him, with the aid of their tusks levered him up; the other making a demonstration at me. . . . In the meantime, the others had picked up the male and, one on each side of him, were hauling him off as fast as possible. After the cow had made her demonstration she ran after the others, I following on their tracks. We had not proceeded for more than a mile when I saw the bull drop again, upon which the cows started trumpeting and dashed off. On going up to the bull I found he was quite dead."[76]

This story, as Buckley tells it, sounds like a sober report of what he observed, yet the wording describes what he saw in terms of what he made of it: as the bull fell, three cows "ran to his assistance," they "picked up" (not only lifted) his body, they were "hauling him off" by pressing against him from both sides. We are not told how the rest of the herd behaved; usually an elephant group stays together in action, but the account sounds as though the three cows were alone and the herd non-existent.

Other hunters have told very similar stories; the phenomenon apparently is not rare. Marius Maxwell, more bent on recording the ways of his quarry in photographs than on bringing home trophies, though he occasionally did shoot for ivory, tells of routing a herd by dropping the largest bull, whereupon "the leaders of the panic-stricken herd managed to form up their terrified charges into an irregular column, roughly three abreast. . . . They had among them the fatally wounded bull, which a few of the slowly moving titans succeeded in carrying away by pressing, with their heavy bodies in concerted action, against the flanks of their stricken brother. We found, on visiting the spot the next day, that they must have carried him a few hundred paces with them, and carefully deposited the lifeless body among the scrub of a clump of bush."[77]

The intention of the animals to transport the bull is even less beyond doubt here than in Buckley's account, since Maxwell described the herd as crowding together in panic, and there is, consequently, more than a possibility that the dead body was held upright automatically by the ensuing pressure, as human beings have been known to be lifted and held off the ground in a close-packed crowd, which moves slowly because of mutual impedence. That the leaders "managed to form up

[76] *Big Game Hunting in Central Africa* (1930), p. 45.
[77] *Stalking Big Game with a Camera in Equatorial Africa* (1924), pp. 72–73.

their charges" in some sort of marching order is a typical literary addition. As for the careful deposition of the body, no one witnessed it; but if the stampeded herd finally veered into a thicket the dead or half-dead bull would surely have dropped there.

Had the hunter followed slowly to observe the whole act instead of hastening to procure his elephant, he might have seen in less than a mile where they meant to deposit their burden—if, indeed, they meant to deposit it anywhere. They may not have intended even to lift it, but have done so as they butted their companion to make him get up. There are other records of such attempts made not only by elephants.[78] It seems that even the highest non-human animals dealing with carcasses have no realization of death. The creature they are nudging or carrying makes no response, but they seem to see no other difference between a living body and a dead one. A hunting animal immobilizes its victim so it can eat it; if the quarry can be laid low without being killed, it may be eaten before it is dead, as Kühme witnessed in the case of a wart hog brought down by wild dogs and still trying to escape while its entrails were already being devoured some distance away. As long as it moved the dogs avoided its tusks.[79] A surprising fact to most people, however, is that the animals carrying or guarding dead ones seemed undisturbed by the stench of putrefaction. The smell of the passive body changed, but did not appear to revolt the living partner; this was what the young one, the uneaten quarry or the antagonist, now smelled like. Here again we may be dealing with a naïve anthropo-

[78] Maxwell tells of mistakenly killing a cow rhinoceros that had a calf, concealed by her body and the tangled bushes. Almost immediately, "the male rhinoceros appeared on the scene at a fast gallop.... Standing still for a moment beside the carcase of his mate he lowered his head and prodded at her with a resounding thud. This was repeated several times with increasing vigour until frenzy seemed to overcome the desperate beast and retreating a pace or two he charged the carcase wildly again and again in rapid succession and finally rolled the heavy body over, stepping over it through the surprising momentum of his rush" (pp. 160–61).

Hans Klingel, in an article already cited, "Soziale Organisation und Verhalten freilebender Steppenzebras," p. 60, writes that a zebra stallion, one of whose mares fell dead as the family group was walking, turned back and tried to rouse her with his nose and make her follow him to the waiting group.

Even the allegedly human-minded dolphins do not seem to understand death. A. F. McBride and H. Kritzler, in "Observations on Pregnancy, Parturition, and Postnatal Behavior in the Bottlenose Dolphin" (1951), p. 254, say: "In several of the stillbirths, the parents actually attempted to raise their dead young to the surface. When one stillborn infant sank to the bottom, the mother endeavored to raise it by grasping a pectoral fin with her jaws."

[79] Freilandstudien zur Soziologie des Hyänenhundes," p. 508: "Als die Hunde einmal einen Warzenschweinkeiler erlegten, wagten sich die Jungen nicht daran, *und die Jäger nicht an den Kopf.* Sie frassen ihn von hinten allmälig auf."

morphism: we find the smell of decaying flesh unbearable, and, knowing that most other mammals have a keener olfactory sense than we, imagine that they must be even more offended by it. But trappers often smear traps for carnivores—wolves, foxes, weasels—with a concoction of rotten fish in water left long in the sun (known as "smell charm"), which attracts those animals, while herbivores just show no particular reaction to foul but non-significant smells. Charnel odors apparently do not have the *"memento mori"* association for them that they are often claimed to have. Death is a concept, entailing the knowledge that in future the dead creature will never respond to anything again. The inability of even the most intelligent beasts to recognize the state of death, though they are quick to perceive needs and dangers, bespeaks their non-conceptual mentality.

As for the elephants which saw their leader fall and "rushed to his assistance," all we know is that they rushed to gather around him, press close to him, and perhaps prod him to get up. Running to the biggest and boldest male and getting as near to him as possible is a frequently observed reaction of herd and horde animals in emergencies;[80] so is their impulse to crowd against each other.[81] The transport may have been a product of panic, and its anticlimactic end the only natural one

[80] On the nature of this response in baboons, see Kummer's observations, cited above, pp. 169–70. Wolfgang Köhler reported very much the same behavior in his chimpanzees, in *The Mentality of Apes* (1931; 1st ed., 1925). Köhler regards this approach, often directed to the author of their fear, as a plea for forgiveness, as the Kelloggs also interpreted it in their infant chimpanzee, Gua (see W. N. Kellogg and L. A. Kellogg, *The Ape and the Child* [1933], p. 172); but being forgiven for a transgression is a highly abstract concept, and Gua's first reaction was to run with open arms to her chastiser to be picked up. Köhler wrote: "I noticed, whilst feeding the squatting animals, . . . that a little female, at other times quite well-behaved, was snatching the food out of the hand of a weaker animal, and as she persisted in this, I gave her a little rap. . . . The next moment she had flung her arms around my neck, quite beside herself, and was only comforted by degrees, when I stroked her. This need, here expressed, for forgiveness, is a phenomenon frequently to be observed in the emotional life of young chimpanzees" (p. 293). A few pages later he makes quite clear that the apes' fear of punishment contains no consciousness of guilt, but only of consequences; seeking safe harbor is not the same as seeking forgiveness.

[81] Every sheep rancher knows how sheep huddle together at the alarm of a thunderstorm, usually around a large tree, so that if the tree or just one sheep is struck by lightning the whole flock as a single body is apt to succumb. Again, Köhler (*The Mentality of Apes*, p. 321) adds a simian parallel: he describes how he came into the apes' enclosure carrying some stuffed toy animals of which his brightest subject, Sultan, when tested alone had shown visible terror, and how "in a moment a black cluster, consisting of the whole group of chimpanzees, hung suspended from the farthest corner of the wire-roofing, each individual trying to thrust the others aside and bury his head deep among them."

when the central dead body in the stampeding group slipped to the ground.

There are sporadic reports of elephants' team work and social work throughout the unscientific literature of hunting exploits and wilderness adventure. They differ chiefly in the degree of anthropomorphism with which they are presented. Mrs. B. F. Beebe has collected some half a dozen of them in *African Elephants*,[82] and Frank Melland in his *Elephants of Africa* (1938) gave several detailed descriptions.[83] Some of these, from both authors, do make the interpretation of the transport as accidental sound somewhat forced, and the facts—even allowing for their romantically humanized rendering—seem to involve some real intention to pick up and carry the disabled or dead creature. But that does not justify the assumption that the "rescuers" meant to aid the stricken beasts. Lifting and carrying and pushing are actions in the elephant's instinctual repertoire, and when in a moment of crisis the leader of the herd (which is usually the specimen a hunter selects as his victim) is suddenly defunct, the first desperate effort of the routed herd might well be to keep him with them. With abatement of the panic he is then abandoned. The pressing crowd falls apart, especially in making its way through the bush; it may even gather around the carcass for a breathing spell before the herd forms again for its future peregrinations. Such behavior would not necessarily contain either a rational aim to do anything with the carcass or any charitable element. It could be

[82] P. 10. In a later passage (pp. 42–43), the author tells of further cases in which the fallen animals were conducted or carried into the obscurity of the jungle, and remarks that their comrades seemed to be trying to make the dead one follow.

[83] The brief third chapter of the latter book bears the heading, "Rescuing Wounded Elephants." Unfortunately, this writer's convictions about the mind of the elephant match John Lilly's concerning the mind of the dolphin; so he tells how sometimes an elephant wishing to fell a tree which is too big for his own powers "quite naturally gets his team together and directs operations, displaying that human characteristic of being born to command ..." (p. 20). In making rescues, he claims, "the action of the herd resembles that of a well-trained crew taking up boat stations. . . . it is team work and has every appearance of well-drilled team work" (p. 23). (No one, so far, claims to have seen the drill in progress.) On trek, "when danger arises the calves are called by their mother with a particular note or call. . . . At the call the calf runs to the mother and then the mother talks to it. Her trunk goes around the youngster and she conveys her message" (p. 76). And so on, throughout the book. Altogether, as he states in another place (p. 39), he is convinced that "the elephant is a thinking animal who makes plans."

The United Nations did not exist when this book was written, but I am sure that today its author would put up elephants for membership on a par with Dr. Lilly's dolphins.

purely, even characteristically, animalian, yet produce a beguiling appearance of human rescue operations.

One fairly well-attested phenomenon that might speak for a genuine care-giving impulse is the carrying or defending of dead young by their elders, usually presumed, with good reason, to be their mothers.[84] That, of course, is not peculiar to elephants; the carrying, at least, has often been seen in monkeys and dolphins and perhaps other animals too. But maternal care is something quite different from "social" interest in other creatures. As for the defense of a dead infant, it is again Mrs. Beebe who provides the following instance:

"In the Queen Elizabeth National Park game rangers watched a cow elephant rushing back and forth toward two crouching lions. The next day they saw the same scene and eventually discovered that she was guarding her dead calf which she had covered with limbs. The lions left on the third day but the mother guarded three more days before leaving."[85] This is the only statement I have found to the effect that a mother elephant covered a dead calf with branches, and neither the claim of her having done so nor of her being the calf's mother rests on direct evidence, though the latter is certainly highly probable.

The scene itself, however, to which the rangers testified brings up another subject on which most elephant hunters and other persons with experience of the African jungle agree—the fact that elephants do "bury" dead creatures with boughs, sticks and even earth. Melland describes the practice in his own euphemistic phrase, saying: "They have been known to 'bury' the victim, covering him decently with leafy branches, and there are even cases on record of people simulating death being thus covered."[86] But decent burial is an unlikely purpose, especially as all the "burials" which followed actually witnessed deaths seem to have been conducted by very angry undertakers. Bernhard Grzimek, who was a careful student of ethology, described the practice as purely aggressive. In the five cases which he quoted, three of the covered corpses had been killed by an angered elephant, and were very probably "buried" by the same creature, though none of the horrified people who saw the slaying stayed to watch the rest of the animal's act. The other

[84] See, for example, B. F. Beebe, *African Elephants*: "In a Uganda national park a cow elephant was observed carrying her dead calf, holding it between her jaw and shoulder in the position a violin player rests his instrument. When she stopped to eat she laid it carefully on the ground and when she was ready to travel she picked it up again with trunk and one tusk. After two more days of this she put it down and left it" (p. 10).

[85] Pp. 10–11.

[86] *Elephants of Africa*, pp. 49–53.

two cases were not fatal, so the victims could tell their story; one of them was quite sure that the elephant which had tossed him into a thicket, where he lay stunned as if dead, had also piled the heavy branches on him.[87]

The only eyewitness testimony I know of certainly makes no impression of proper burial for a dead antagonist. It is retailed by Mr. Melland, and is the story of one Mickey Norton, a well-known figure in the bush: Norton tried to evade a herd of elephants on one side of a river by crossing the wide shallow bed to the opposite bank, when a large male elephant loomed up there, obviously ready to take on the intruder. The bank was some 20 feet high, ascendable where rhinoceros and hippopotamus had broken paths. Norton, leaving his intended path to the bull and going downstream to another ascent, found himself suddenly faced by the angry animal at close range. He ducked under the bank; the elephant threw branches, saplings, logs and roots at him until the bank gave way under its charges and the man was effectively bogged, but the furious bull brought more branches to throw on him. Finally Norton's bearers came up, shooting from the other side, and rescued him. "Norton's adventure," says Mr. Melland, "presents no picture of a reverential covering of a body presumed to be dead, but, to put the kindest possible construction on it, was a deliberate attempt by an elephant to immobilize an enemy."[88]

Perhaps it was not deliberate, and intended only to "immobilize" the enemy (indeed, the kindest construction!), but was simply an act of rage. The avalanche of earth that in effect did immobilize the intruder certainly slipped under the elephant's weight after he had torn and twisted the trees, with their soil-holding roots, out of the steep, water-cut bank. The earth slide had suddenly accomplished the work of felling and engulfing the man, but the elephant's act was not finished; it overshot the practical goal, and no one knows how long it would have continued if its course had not been interrupted.

Therewithal, we have very little knowledge of how many different motivating situations might engender such dramatic scenes. The effects have been found repeatedly, but Norton's direct observation of the bull's behavior and the several very plausible surmises mentioned by Grzimek and Beebe may not exhaust the psychological possibilities; for instance, they do not seem, offhand, to fit the case of the elephant cow that defended the carcass of a calf covered with boughs. No one knows how the calf died, whether she had covered it before the lions ap-

[87] "Ein merkwürdiges Verhalten von afrikanischen Elefanten" (1956).
[88] *Elephants of Africa*, pp. 50–53.

proached it, or had subsequently put that slight barrier between it and the predators, or—as I would immediately suspect—another elephant had killed and covered it before the lions smelled and stalked the carcass. Her defense of the "buried" calf makes it seem improbable that she killed it herself in a rage, yet it is not altogether out of the question; and the question brings us back to the dolphin literature, where a similar problem may be found.

There is something eerie about the number of cetaceans that have been seen in aquaria or sighted offshore transporting mutilated baby bodies, in three known cases only the head ends. Two dolphins observed in captivity carried and tended their own dead babies, though in life they had treated them in most unmotherly fashion, repeatedly pulling them to the bottom of the tank and holding them there.[89] Anoxia in dolphins leads to irreparable brain damage, and was undoubtedly a cause, if not the whole cause, of these infant deaths. What the motivation of the mother's behavior was is hard to guess; captive animals do develop abnormal reactions which cannot be attributed to the species as typical, but even insane impulses originate from the same matrix as normal ones, and must have their instinctual sources in its deep reservoir of potentialities. Margaret Tavolga, in a short, sketchy survey of dolphin life in captivity, makes it sound as if taking the baby down to the bottom of the tank were a punishment for straying from its mother's side;[90] but the whole phenomenon of punishment involves concepts of

[89] See M. C. Caldwell and D. K. Caldwell, "Epimeletic (Care-Giving) Behavior in Cetacea" (1966), p. 765.

[90] "Behavior of the Bottlenosed Dolphin (*Tursiops truncatus*): Social Interactions in a Captive Colony" (1966), p. 721: "At times during the first months of its life a young dolphin may leave its mother's side to swim with another animal, or may approach a new object in the tank. . . . Under ordinary circumstances, the mother of such a calf will swim to it and herd it away from the other animal or foreign object. When a calf repeatedly swims away from the mother, her action becomes more aggressive.

"In one instance, after such a series of flights by the young one, the mother swam over the young animal and pinned him to the floor for some thirty seconds, effectively immobilizing him. She released him only when she rose to take a breath of air."

In the much more precise report by M. C. Tavolga and F. S. Essapian, "The Behavior of the Bottle-Nosed Dolphin (*Tursiops truncatus*): Mating, Pregnancy, Parturition, and Mother-Infant Behavior" (1957), their detailed account of a highly interesting case makes no mention of the baby's "disobedience"; the three eyewitnesses to the abuse of the infant, which was held to the bottom of the tank by its mother and her mother, all came upon the scene when the act was already in progress. Since the young one in this case was a female, it is presumably not the same animal referred to above, which had made several excursions and was caught

[197]

dictation, transgression, disobedience and coercion, which have never been unequivocally established for any non-human species. Though Dr. Tavolga observed that after harsh treatment the baby stayed close to its mother, this fits as well with the fact that any fright or hurt makes a young animal seek an elder, even if that elder caused its distress, as with the claim that the little dolphin had been "disciplined" and now realized its transgression. The mother's apparently agonistic impulse may well have been a product of confinement; in the ocean she would swim with a school and her young one with her or temporarily with another female going in the same direction, so there would be no occasion for it to stray and be constantly retrieved. In captivity the little dolphin learns a place, inviting exploration, instead of a stream of animals going forward and taking it along at top speed.

Another form of maternal brutality was observed in several mothers, one of which, a somewhat abnormal creature named Spray, Tavolga and Essapian describe as follows: "On March 14, the baby [then ten days old] persistently left Spray and swam among the other animals. If she strayed more than about twenty feet away, Spray brought her back, but if she stayed within this distance, no attempt was made to restrict her movements. Twice, however, when she strayed to the other side of the tank Spray went to her. Then Spray turned on her back, positioned the baby on her chest between her flippers and rose to the surface, pushing the young one out of water. Other dolphin mothers have been seen to do this when their young infants swim evasively away. The effect is to temporarily immobilize the young one."[91]

This act, which a human being would naturally see as a deliberate punishment to teach the youngster a lesson, may have no such purpose, but be consummated simply by its physical effect. The normal mother-infant bond is restored. An interesting aspect of this procedure is that lifting and holding the young one out of the water in the tank is reminiscent of the dolphin's tendency in the wild to push dead or floundering bodies—cetacean, elasmobranch, human—out of the water and maneuver them up the beach. Perhaps if we understood the impulse that prompts one of these phenomena we could make a guess at the other. It is imaginable (and nothing more) that in the confines of a somewhat crowded aquarium the baby, removed from the mother beyond a distance of (say) half of the tank, or maybe less, suddenly ceases to

---

and nearly drowned by its mother alone, and to which Dr. Tavolga referred as "he." In the case of the female infant, the authors say: "There was no apparent reason for this action, and its significance is not clear" (p. 23).

[91] *Ibid.*, p. 23.

seem to her like an extension of herself, and becomes a new, alien thing that awakens an impulse to strand it. The length of time she can swim on her back, i.e., hold her own breath, may be sufficient to exhaust the changeling phase of the infant for her; when she lets it drop back into the water it is close to her and part of her again. So the shifting pattern of impulses, sometimes absurd in themselves, might unintentionally restore broken bonds and hold some balance of communal relationships.

There are two principles of animal psychology involved in this interpretation of dolphin behavior as instinctive: the first is the constant development of new motivating situations from minute to minute in the course of a life, which has been sufficiently discussed. The second is the rise and decline of values, the slow or sudden change of cathexis which an object may undergo as it enters or leaves an agent's transient "world." If a mother dolphin, losing familial contact with her infant, suddenly sees it as something alien in the swimways, why does it not always appear that way to the other inmates of the aquarium? Because animals, having no relational concepts, can only feel relationships in moments of their acute changes, i.e., abrupt emergence of a new relation or sudden break of an old one.[92] When the baby was born, and

[92] This principle, too, can be traced through biological act forms to much deeper levels than mental processes in such high animals as cetaceans. It operates in the perceptual mechanisms themselves, which respond with vigorous action to the beginning or sudden cessation of a stimulus, but drop to low levels between, even if the stimulus continues unabated. So A. M. Monnier said, in "Élaboration du message sensorielle au niveau de la rétine" (1957), p. 17: "le rythme des influx est très rapide au début de l'éclairement et se ralentit distinctement, même si l'éclairement est prolongé. Ce ralentissement de la cadence des influx rend compte de ce que nous pouvons observer ... quand, sortant d'une pièce obscure, nous allons vers la lumière. Nous avons alors une sensation ... lumineuse violente, qui cesse au bout de quelques secondes." The same effect of a break in a stream of generally redundant stimulation has been found to underlie the perception of lines and contours in vision and acute tonal changes or accents in hearing. See Gibson, *The Perception of the Visual World, passim*, but esp. pp. 151 ff; Fred Attneave, "Some Informational Aspects of Visual Perception" (1954); for the neurological basis of the fast-fading response, W. H. Marshall and S. A. Talbot, "Recent Evidence for Neural Mechanisms in Vision Leading to a General Theory of Sensory Acuity." These authors specifically remark that "the *suddenness* of photic change, as well as its amount, determines the neural output of a receptor.... The fluctuating gaze sweeps the long dividing edge over the receptors, whose subliminal effects add ... to evoke a differential sensation. But similar summation must be assumed for the hair-line observation.... If this were not impressed suddenly (by the fast moving image), and to many receptor 'rows,' the line might well be subliminal. A similar picture applies to tactile acuity" (p. 138). It applies even to non-visual functions of the retina, as R. N. Danielson discovered in studying the effect of light, received through the eye, on the color of the skin in fish. In "The Melanophore Responses of Fishes in

was a sudden novelty in the tank, the other dolphins did take note of it, and some tried to push or manipulate it, but its mother and perhaps another female defended it.[93] Soon it lost all value for the rest of the adult population; the normal changes presented by growing young creatures are gradual and unlikely to beget any conscious relationships.

The literature of ethology, though not yet old, is already large, and has established a language of its own embodying highly anthropomorphic concepts which go unchallenged because they are brought in as part of the jargon rather than as explicit assumptions with recognized and accepted implications. The reinterpretations of a few phenomena proposed above are only random samples, meant to show that animal ways may be viewed as acts based on self-centered impulses and courses of immediate feeling. So far, so good; but here, finally, we come to the Asses' Bridge of animal psychology, the problem of communication.

This entire subject, as already remarked, is confused and obfuscated by the stretching of its definition to cover everything from speech, writing and "the media" to the chemical transmission of a fear reaction among fish in an aquarium,[94] and even the eating of one animal by another. William Evans and Jarvis Bastian, for instance, define animal "communication" as any sort of interaction among animals, and then spend paragraphs demonstrating by "deduction" that in animals interaction and communication are identical.[95] A definition that permits no distinction between phenomena which analytic thinkers are trying to bring into systematic relation is pragmatically a bad definition. Note, also, that if we accept the widest sense of "cooperation," cited above (p. 172 and n), then, since communication = any interaction and cooperation = any interaction, communication = cooperation. With such broad definitions one cannot make precise or even significant statements. In order to fuse animal and human "communication," our authors have to play down the conceptual content of language, i.e., the information

---

Relation to Contrast in the Visual Field" (1941), p. 101, he states the conclusion: "Although all parts of the eye are not equivalent, the state of the melanophores appears to be determined not by the stimulation of particular regions of the retina but by the degree of contrast in the visual field as a whole."

[93] Tavolga and Essapian, "The Behavior of the Bottle-Nosed Dolphin," p. 80.

[94] Schultz, in The Life of Primates, classes the color changes in the female sex skin of some monkeys and blushing as "communication" (p. 226).

[95] William Evans and Jarvis Bastian, "Marine Mammal Communication: Social and Ecological Factors" (1969), p. 427: "Everyone agrees that communication is a matter of social behavior but it is also clear [by their definition] that there can be no social behavior without communication. As the two notions mutually imply one another, there is no basis for distinguishing them." Unfortunately, implication can hold only between propositions, not between "notions."

intended to be conveyed by means of words,[96] and dwell on "the non-linguistic forms of human communication, which are no less significant in the conduct of human social life ..." (pp. 427–28). If facial expression, tone of voice, winks and shrugs are really "no less significant" than the verbal statements of our discourse, then typewritten proposals, printed books and newspapers must present very poor fragments of what a writer wishes to assert. The aim of this exaggeration is to support the standpoint they thereupon take explicitly, as they point out that in the many current books and symposia on human language "the overall direction of these recent discussions is to show linguistic interactions as an exceedingly specialized form of animal communication" (p. 427).

Messrs. Evans and Bastian may be right about the direction taken by most of these discussions; perhaps that is why no better understanding of the nature of language has come out of them. They chide Dr. Lilly, not for his claim that dolphins talk to each other, but for letting "communication" mean specifically such intentional transmission of information. "In Lilly's recent book [*The Mind of the Dolphin*]," they remark, "communication is pointedly defined as 'the exchange of information between two or more minds' " (p. 428). I am inclined to follow Lilly's lead, and even go beyond it to say, "communication is the intentional transmission of ideas from one individual to one or more others." If the intention miscarries, i.e., no idea "goes across," the individuals fail to communicate, though they may interact closely, elaborately, even violently. Unlike Dr. Lilly, however, I would not first declare that dolphins "communicate" in some sense, and then establish the sense by definition and let that authenticate their possession of language, but in consequence of accepting his definition as the strict sense of "communication" I would make bold to say that dolphins do not communicate, any more than other animals—crows, elephants, chimpanzees. It is better to start systematic thinking with precise though narrow concepts and proceed to widen them by stepwise generalization than to start with highly general notions which, being carried from one context to another, change their meanings.[97]

[96] The crucial difference between animal "communication" and human language lies in the conceptual messages conveyed in the latter and absent from even the most beguiling semblance of human speech produced by trained animals. J. Bronowski and Ursula Bellugi, in "Language, Name and Concept" (1970), epitomized the essentially conceptual nature and basic function of language. Since I am in close agreement with them, the linguistic theory they hold will receive more detailed discussion below, in Chapter 18.

[97] I am quite aware that throughout this essay, starting with an explicit statement in Chapter 1, I have used the word "feeling" in its broadest possible sense, to sub-

If, then, animals make no communication, what is the nature of their mutual bond apart from sexual union and fighting? I would call it communion. It is practiced and felt without highly cerebral responses, and differs from communication in having no propositional contents— nothing that could be paraphrased in words, such as "that looks dangerous," "this is mine," "column right," or "I mean no harm." Communion is a mutual awareness, a sense of safety in nearness and, amongst gregarious animals, sometimes in numbers. It is not established and upheld by signals, gestures of submission or dominance, but primarily by physical contacts, extended by smell and, in some species, sounds and movements which pass on bodily feelings, large or small alarms, expectations, impulses. A school of fish or a swarm of locusts move as one body. Many animals are so suggestible that the first "intention movement" toward an act, made by another individual, evokes their own impulse to perform the whole act themselves. If we analyze an animal's behavior, noting its incidental postures and vocalization, grimaces and tail switches, we may decide that this or that item in the characteristic pattern is a "social signal" noted and understood by others as a demand or proposal, i.e., as a vocal or gestic communication. Then we see a leader making his followers form their ranks according to a preconceived marching order, or a dominant animal expressing his dominance while another signals submission, mothers giving instruction to the young, experienced elders teaching cubs to hunt. These are all naïve anthropomorphisms. G. B. Schaller speaks more correctly when he says, "A dominant male who stands motionless, facing in a certain direction, indicates that he is ready to leave and the other members of the group crowd around him."[98] There is no reason to believe that he gives an order or intends to indicate anything. Though Schaller, like other present researchers on animal ways, uses "communication" to include what I would distinguish as "communion," his accounts are

---

sume "anything that can be felt." But that is a different practice altogether from using a word in different senses, as "communication" in the human sense and in that of animals' interactions or even just figuring in each other's ambients. Under the general heading of "feeling" there are immediately divisions into major categories such as sensibility and emotivity, and within these, various sorts of feeling with distinctive patterns, e.g., starting peripherally or centrally, acutely or with gathering intensity, etc.; but no "logical proofs" to such effects as that all feeling is really sensation, that sensation is peripheral emotion and hence all feeling is emotional, and altogether, as in Anaxagoras' conception of the world before the coming of νους, that "all things are in all things."

[98] "The Behavior of the Mountain Gorilla" (1965), p. 344. Note "that *he* is ready to leave"—not that they must do so.

generally empirical and restricted enough to make apparent which kind of psychological interaction he means. The dominant male—in the particular group he was observing, also the leader—was a center of attraction for the others. Indeed, all the members sought each other's company, but each apparently on its own initiative, and on the same basis set up its more particular contacts.[99] Especially interesting is a description of the relation of the group to the leader, which seems to exist and continue without any code of explicitly recognized signals. "Every independent animal in the group," says the author, "appeared to be aware of the activity of the leader either directly or through the behavior of animals in his vicinity. Cues reflecting a changed pattern of activity were patterned after the leader. Thus, the entire daily routine—the distance of travel, the location of rest stops, and the time and place of nesting—was largely determined by the leader."[100]

In animal communion signs do not refer to acts or situations, but are always genuine parts of acts; and where they function as cues, they are genuine parts of situations in which the recipients of the cues initiate or change their acts.[101] Consequently an act that arises in a situation prepared by other creatures (conspecific or not) embodies the subact

[99] P. 346: "Though the members of a group spent most of the day very close to one another and were highly tolerant of each other, persistent aggregations of specific individuals were rare. Once two females in group VII consorted closely for several days. One juvenile tagged behind the sole black-backed male of group IV for more than one month. Various members of the group sometimes sought the vicinity of the dominant male for brief periods.... Females now and then approached the dominant male to lie by his side, and on nine occasions rested their heads on his saddle or leaned against his body. Juveniles and infants were also attracted to the silver-backed male. At times as many as four youngsters climbed over the reclining male, slid down his rump, and pulled his hair without eliciting a response." Such familiarity with the powerful dominant gorilla is in sharp contrast to the cringing approach of baboons to the "α-animal" of a troop.

More detailed reports of the observations on which this article is based may be found in the same author's *The Mountain Gorilla*, but no such succinct account.

[100] P. 347.

[101] In this connection, C. R. Carpenter has written: "Specific movements and vocalizations occur in howler groups when the animals are immersed in an environmental matrix, and the behavior corresponds to the stimulus flux.... After the primary response has been made, by one or a few individuals, their responses become parts of the situation to which other animals of the clan react.... It is unnecessary to assume that the animal or animals producing the primary responses 'intends' to 'communicate' with associates. It is unnecessary to infer that the animal making the primary response has 'foresight' of the impending responses of associated animals, although an individual may *learn* that a particular vocalization, at first given spontaneously, is a means of provoking a certain response in other animals" (*A Field Study of the Behavior and Social Relations of Howling Monkeys*, pp. 105–6).

or subacts which entered into its motivation, and is to that extent already a conjoint act. Furthermore, what animals perceive seems to be not so much expressions, positions and movements of others as whole acts, sometimes to be countered (so we think the antagonist has anticipated the next move as "most probable") or completed, like the egg deposition of a female fish followed by the male's fertilization of the eggs. What looks to human eyes like cooperation to get something done[102] is perception of an act in progress which functions as a lure to pursue its development, literally to "get into the act" and carry it to completion. The practical result need not be preconceived or foreseen at all; but if it entails relief from empathic stress (as in the case of freeing or aiding a fellow or a young one), it is "reinforced," i.e., its repetition in other situations is encouraged.

The most striking instances of communal instinctive action are found among insects, where it looks most deceptively like planned human labor with different tasks assigned to different classes of workers or even to individuals. Yet it is in insects that the purely animalian nature of conjoint acts is easiest to see, upon analysis unencumbered by metaphors such as "state," "queen," "dancing" and "instructions" of honeybees, and, with reference to ants, expressions like "slave making" or "tool using" (the latter for joint acts of adults and larvae). Insects have simple responses, but not simplified human ones; their own principles of behavior are masked by figures of speech borrowed from man's political, educational and social institutions. A hive is not a state, because it is not governed; its individual members have no rights and obligations, and there is no reason except the influence of an anthropomorphic model to think of it as an ideal republic. Also, there is no other reason to believe that a "dancing" bee sends out other foragers with factual information and instructions where to go and what to look for. The nature of her abreactive oscillations[103] and the smell and taste of the

[102] Evans and Bastian, in "Marine Mammal Communication: Social and Ecological Factors," pp. 430–31, provide a ready example of common-sense presuppositions borrowed from human psychology, in their comment on cetacean "succorant behavior": "There are many reports of a behavior pattern in several delphinid genera that appears to be akin to artificial respiration efforts by humans.... Now, if we supposed that such actions involved the animals' intentions to help the injured animal to breathe we would also be required to suppose that the animals performing these actions had an understanding of the consequences of their actions for the injured." In men, they would; in dolphins, the act may be quite differently guided by empathic distress and impulse to reach for air.

[103] A. D. Blest, studying the peculiar rocking motion of moths of the genus *Automeris* as they settle after flight, was struck by the features it shares with the supposedly symbolic and indicative "waggle dance" of bees. In a brief but substantial article, "Interaction between Consecutive Responses in a Hemileucid Moth,

nectar she carries motivate the next cycle in the foraging act, which is performed by bees that have been in physical contact with her, joined her movements and tasted what she brought in. The similarity of their excursions to that which she just completed rests on the cyclic nature of the total act that is handed over from one highly sensitive semi-individual to others. The "queen" bee, likewise, is not a queen. She gives no orders, no verdicts, neither does she lead a swarm that gathers around her as it leaves the hive to start a new colony.[104] The only thing that has caused her to be popularly called the "queen" is that she does no work and receives constant feeding, licking and tending from the pseudo-females, the ordinary bees—a truly popular concept of royalty: "The queen was in the parlor, eating bread and honey." The derivation of a name for the one large fertile bee from such a source would be just one of many philological accidents, theoretically of no significance, save for the fact that it has long and insidiously shifted the emphasis of functional analysis from organic to organizational patterns, and masked what is probably the motivation of the "royal" treatment this all-important female receives. She is the womb of the colony; as such, she embodies all feminine sexuality, and in so intersensitive a group as the denizens of a hive she represents every sterile worker's sex organ. Their tendance rests on their desire for contact with her, and emotively is

---

and the Evolution of Insect Communication" (1958), pp. 1077–78, he writes: "The strength of the rocking response [which the moths, *Automeris* ssp., show when settling after flight] increases with increase in preceding duration of flight, to which it bears a simple linear relationship which shifts as the moths age. . . . it is stable, certainly for periods of 30 min., and probably for at least 90 min., and would seem not to be affected by intercalated activities unrelated to flight. . . . Results of this kind have been obtained in studies of the behaviour of other arthropods. . . ." Speaking of the "waggle dance" of the honey bee, he says: "The relationship between distance flown and the number of oscillations in each repetition of the straight run of the dance is simple and nearly linear over much of its range; it is not affected by the sugar concentration of the food source." The sugar content, he holds, has been shown to be conveyed "in terms of the known mechanisms governing the central regulation of taste thresholds," but the indication of distance flown must have some other evolutionary precursor. "Such a system would appear to be involved in the interaction between flight and settling behaviour in *Automeris*, which already possesses two of the most salient features of the 'waggle' dance, namely, the linear relationship described above, and a considerable measure of quantitative stability. It is not, however, used in communication."

From this he draws the scientific moral for which I adduce his study here: "The presence of a teleologically perfect relationship of this kind in a non-communicating insect implies that it is dangerous to assume that the mere presence of an isolable factor in the bee dance necessarily means that it is used in communication."

[104] Cf. Roger A. Morse, "Swarm Orientation in Honeybees" (1963).

more like masturbation than like rendering a social service.[105] This is one possible spontaneous source of behavior which so far has required the assumption of a special "instinct" in the workers to take their turn at a necessary task. Bees are emotional, their moods are affected by temperature and light, but above all by acts going on around them, which may elicit feeding in the presence of larvae and—perhaps for a dozen situational reasons—also of adults (a returned forager, circling and waggling, gives the bees that make contact with her little tastes of the nectar she has), and the queen bee is an excellent big mouth to feed. All kinds of cathexis may attach to her, and a constant mild tension somewhat like a sexual excitation seems to surround her wherever she is. When a swarm moves, she is usually deep inside it.

As for the ants, they show even more clearly the principles of holistic act perception, suggestibility, rhythmic perseveration even in overt behavior, empathy, and communion by constant touching, licking, sharing food by trophallaxis. One expert myrmicologist, Derek W. Morley, says of the ant colony, "it is a system of fluxion. The emotive forces flow outwards from each individual to his neighbors and in the opposite direction at varying *tempi*. . . . This flow of the nervous energy of ants throughout the community is a definite and little understood phenomenon. Nervous tension can be produced by the physical conditions of a thunderstorm, or rather of the tension prior to the actual storm." (One is reminded of the "electric" feeling of which some human beings complain, and which others who are immune to it cannot imagine; evidently to ants it is a major emotive pression, perhaps a sensation.) And further: "This rising and ebbing nervous tension in the ant community is something distinct from such general effects as those of hot and cold temperature on their metabolism. Once the activity of the colony is established [for the day or the season] . . . there is always a light tension throughout the colony. . . . this tension varies throughout the area. There are localities of concentration where jobs are being undertaken, and localities of low tension where the current may be said to flow weakly."[106]

In the first chapter of his book, Dr. Morley described the work of some exceptionally responsive and energetic ants in each colony, among

[105] See M. D. Allen, "Observations on Honeybees Attending Their Queen" (1955), p. 67: "Most of the attendants busily examine the queen with their antennae, a few lick her body, while an occasional individual provides food." Bees not in the mood for following her, however, were not excited when she passed among them; especially, "no undue excitement was caused by the passage of the queen through a group of bees not recently in contact with her . . ." (p. 69).

[106] *The Ant World*, pp. 170–73.

the average, relatively passive members; these moving spirits, always first to find what needs to be done, stir up the other ants to conjoint action. He called them the "excitement centres" of the community,[107] and in his final discussion, from which I have quoted above, he says: "The excitement centre mechanism operates through this nervous tension which early in this book was called 'empathy,' or 'sensitivity,' or 'interaction.'... The excitement centre ants, the job-getters, have in fact to be retranslated at this stage of the formulation of the problem into units of high potential in the general field of nervous tension, which is spread out through the whole ant colony. It may prove, in the light of future experimental work, more advisable to call them units of higher metabolic rate." Speaking behaviorally rather than physiologically, he concludes: "They have no language in the sense we understand it, but they copy one another's actions and responses to situations. Certain individuals ... tend to be the ones to start off all the many activities of the division of labour in their complex societies. Yet they have no leaders who say 'come here and do this.'... The mystery of the ants is in their empathy, the bond of nervous tension which builds so quick a response one to another that it seems more akin to a response to a nerve-carried impulse within a single individual than one involving two quite separate and recognizable characters separated by space."[108]

Disregard of the suggestibility and empathic relations which let two or more animals participate in one obviously holistic act has led many excellent naturalists to apply anthropomorphic concepts to their behavior, like the use of tools commonly imputed to the so-called weaving ants, especially the green tree ant, *Oecophilla viriscens*. These insects build their nests out of leaves joined together with sticky silk threads produced by the larvae of their species; and since adult ants manipulate the larvae, those manipulators are considered the agents and their method generally classed as "tool using," the grub being employed as a shuttle.[109] The process has been described many times, but usually in words which impose the image of the human weaver on it, with the

---

[107] P. 10: "They are called 'excitement centres' because, although they determine what activities are carried out and when, they do not do so by sitting down and thinking about it and then giving directions to the other ants; but they excite the other ants into doing the different jobs by starting to do them themselves."

[108] Pp. 173–75.

[109] See, for instance, J. A. Bierens de Haan, *Die tierischen Instinkte*, p. 395: "Das klassische Beispiel eines solchen instinktiven Werkzeuggebrauches findet man bei den Weberameisen (*Oecophylla smaragdina* und verwandten Arten)." The rest of this passage belongs into a later context, where it will be continued.

Morley, too, accepts the purely instrumental function of the grub, saying: "The silk weaving ants use tools to make their nests. It is true that these tools are living

threaded shuttle in his hands. By way of exception, one writer of a popular but sound little book, John H. Sudd,[110] has given a purely behavioral description of the actual procedure. According to that account, the leaves are drawn close to each other until their edges are made to touch, and then, while ranks of ants are holding them together, they are fastened with the larval silk. The method of bringing the leaves into contact is itself a wonder of group action, but I shall not discuss it here because it is only the first phase of the total act; the second—the use of the silk—is the one which I think is generally misconstrued. Here is Dr. Sudd's factual description:

"At about the time that the leaves touch a few large workers appear each with a half-grown larva in its jaws. The larvae are held about one third of the way back from their head end with their backs towards the worker's body.... The worker walks about the leaf edge with its larva until it finds a stretch free of ants. Then it touches the larva with its antennae. The larva thrusts out its head segments until it touches a leaf with them. As soon as it has touched one of the leaves the worker moves it across to the other leaf and so on, backwards and forwards from leaf to leaf, so that a zigzag of silk is laid between the leaves. The zigzag is so close set that adjacent threads of silk stick together to form a continuous sheet between the leaves."[111]

Following the "ethological" principle of interpretation, which is to treat any resemblance of animal and human overt behavior as an identity of the respective acts as a whole, the superficial appearance of worker ants holding and placing the larvae as a human workman might hold and move a tool has been quickly accepted as an astounding instrumental act of the adult ant carrying a purely passive, helpless thing, the grub. But a grub is a young ant, with the ability to produce the sticky material that is drawn out as a thread if the producer can move from place to place. Since it cannot move far or fast, it needs the help of an adult to perform its webbing function. At the touch of the worker's antennae it protrudes its anterior segments and spins its thread. The nest-building process at this stage is a joint act of two ants, one a larva and one an imago, supported by a dozen other builders that hold the leaves together during the work (Fig. 15–5).

---

and ready fashioned but the behaviour of the weaving ants is none the less remarkable for that" (*The Ant World*, p. 157). Perhaps no less remarkable (as if its value lay in making observers gasp), but more plausible as animal action, and not "tool using."

[110] *An Introduction to the Behavior of Ants* (1967).

[111] P. 75.

Figure 15–5. Weaving Ant Using a Larva To Fasten Two Leaves
Together

*the nest-building process at this stage is a joint act of two ants, one a larva
and one an imago, supported by a dozen other builders that hold
the leaves together during the work*

(William Saville-Kent, *The Naturalist in Australia* [London: Chapman & Hall Ltd., 1893].)

Another misapplied phrase borrowed from human sociology is "slave making" for the practice, found in several species, of raiding colonies of other kinds and carrying off some of the pupae, which then hatch and grow up in the home of their captors. If, as Morley says, ants have no language and can give no orders, then "slave making" is another misleading anthropomorphic term like "state," "queen" and other traditional misnomers. The kidnapped grubs, carried away to augment the population of the raiders' colony, have no relation to their captors resembling that of slaves to masters. They are not constrained to work for others instead of themselves, nor to hold any inferior status. The only excuse for the metaphor is that they were captured; but in their new home they are adopted, not enslaved.

Animals never order each other around, because without language they cannot communicate a demand or any idea of something they wish to have done or not done. This holds as much for mammals as for insects. The frequent statements found in popular writings (and all too often in learned ones) that birds and beasts send others on missions, assign tasks to them, or forbid their taking or doing something without physically preventing them[112] are all fabled.

A team of psychologists staged an interesting experiment with rhesus monkeys to find out whether a dominant animal, put into a position in which it could not obtain food except by coercing its subordinate cage-mate to operate the apparatus that yielded the usual pellets, would learn to use its dominance to that end. At first, pellets were released only when the subordinate monkey turned the handle, so the other one could obtain food only by snatching it before its cage-mate had a

---

[112] At the highest popular level, we find such statements as "soon the lion dispatched his consort to procure some fresh meat for him . . ." (J. C. Lamy, "The Beauty and the Beasts of East Africa," in *Réalités* [1967], p. 42). In the *National Geographic*, a photograph accompanying Dian Fossey's "Making Friends with Mountain Gorillas," pp. 52–53, which shows the author and a gorilla "signaling submission" to each other in perfect ethological style while some younger (black-backed) apes are visible in the vicinity, bears the caption, "subordinate males, called blackbacks, . . . serve as sentries." Buckley, a famous hunter though not a great naturalist, tells of coming upon twelve elephant cows resting in a ravine, and remarks, "an old cow evidently had been told off to mount guard . . ." (*Big Game Hunting in Central Africa*, p. 47). Who "told her off," and how, he does not say.

So much for laymen's fare; but even Tinbergen, in *The Herring Gull's World*, pp. 121–22, says of a colony of jackdaws observed by Lorenz: "The situation is much like that of a school form or a boys' soccer team. There is a recognized 'leader,' . . . who is obeyed whenever he asserts his power." The only "obedience" he receives is that others withdraw when he threatens them. He can give no orders to be "obeyed."

chance; when it had learned to do so, its partner was fed, and returned to the cage without any hunger incentive to operate the machine. The experimenters say, as the essential part of their findings: "The dominant monkeys failed to demonstrate, during three successive presentations, that their prior training taught them anything concerning the function of their partners. This suggests a similar interpretation of the processes involved in primate observation learning and communication. . . . Thus we think the monkeys learned a chain, not a concept, when coercive actions were obtained, and that the effectiveness of shaping [teaching the dominant monkey, one step at a time, to simulate the hypothesized response], when required, is in keeping with this view."[113]

One obvious explanation of the failure of animals to give any commands is, of course, that they have no words to convey instructions or proposals. But this may be too simple a solution. There are, today, several chimpanzees which have acquired a considerable vocabulary in the standard American Sign Language (ASL) used by the deaf.[114] The two psychologists who trained the first of these animals, Washoe, to use words in that language knew from earlier records that vocal expression in apes is limited and ejaculatory, and auditory stimuli not readily noticed, let alone distinguished, while arm and hand movements are quickly made and elaborated. They had the excellent judgment to exploit the native talents of their subject, by teaching her speech in a mode that was natural to her.[115] Despite her extreme youth (she was still an infant, wild caught, not more than fourteen months old and perhaps a good deal younger when brought to the laboratory) she learned easily to imitate gestures. To associate them with objects was a harder task, but was gradually mastered, so that today she has command of about a hundred and fifty linguistic items.

Her training was one of the greatest experiments ever made on the psychology of language. It has revealed unexpected aspects of language

[113] J. A. Horel, F. R. Treichler and D. R. Meyer, "Coercive Behavior in the Rhesus Monkey" (1963), p. 210.

[114] R. A. Gardner and B. T. Gardner, "Teaching Sign Language to a Chimpanzee" (1969).

[115] In this connection they remark (pp. 664–65): "Psychologists who work extensively with the instrumental conditioning of animals become sensitive to the need to use responses that are suited to the species they wish to study. Lever-pressing in rats is not an arbitrary response invented by Skinner to confound the mentalists; it is a type of response commonly made by rats when they are first placed in a Skinner box. . . . We chose a language based on gestures because we reasoned that gestures for the chimpanzee should be analogous to bar-pressing for rats, key-pecking for pigeons, and babbling for humans."

which will come under discussion in a later chapter of this book. For our present purpose, however, it has shown above all where the true line between animal interaction—both emotional and pragmatic—and genuine communication lies. In their report, the Gardners wrote: "We wanted Washoe not only to ask for objects but to answer questions about them and also to ask us questions. We wanted to develop behavior that could be described as conversation."[116] This, however, seems to lie beyond the frontiers of animal mentality, and from this outermost edge one can look back and see that all her acts, even those that look most like human acts of conception, may be understood in non-human terms. The most intriguing of these is her spontaneous naming of objects she saw but apparently did not want. "One day, in the 10th month of the project," her observers noted, "Washoe was visiting the Gardner home and found her way into the bathroom. She climbed up on the counter, looked at our mug full of toothbrushes, and signed 'toothbrush.'. . . She had no reason to ask for the toothbrushes, because they were well within her reach, and it was most unlikely that she was asking to have her teeth brushed. This was our first observation . . . of behavior in which Washoe seemed to name an object or an event for no obvious motive other than communication."[117]

One is immediately reminded, of course, of the famous passage in the autobiography of Helen Keller, in which one rare human being who could recall her first recognition of a word as a symbol, not a means to get something or a move in a game, described that sudden, world-opening experience. But here is just where we stumble brusquely on the difference between Washoe and the speechless human child. The world of speech and conceptual thought did not open for the chimpanzee. She subsequently used other words in the same spontaneous way, but I cannot see any convincing evidence that there was "no obvious motive other than communication"; no indication that she would not have made the gesture at sight of the toothbrushes if she had been alone. Object and gesture were closely associated for her in a non-symbolic learned response, chiefly to the sight of a toothbrush and the stimulus ASL words: "What is this?" The sight alone could elicit the spontaneous completion of her part in a game she usually played with human companions.[118] It would be wonderful to know whether

116 P. 665.
117 P. 667.
118 The tendency to complete an act, whether the agent's own or started by another animal, is found even at high evolutionary levels (in low degree, even in man), but is certainly most apparent in lower forms. A really exaggerated case has

Washoe, if housed with a naïve simian companion of appropriate age, would try it on that playfellow, and whether any part of her repertoire would be passed on.

In all her contact with people who speak to her in sign language, this ape (so far as I know) has never asked a question or made a comment, i.e., a remark about anything.[119] Besides immediate demands and protest, all her verbal behavior is naming directly perceived things, or sometimes—rarely—missing counterparts of them. Conversation has no sources in her word-stocked brain; as Goethe said, "Wörter machen nicht Worte."

To take up every kind of ethological misconception and propose a

---

been found by R. D. Alexander in some meadow grasshoppers, which have a two-phase song consisting of ticks followed by a buzz. "In a quart jar containing two males of *Orchelimum agile* (De Beer) it was noticed ... that while the sound being produced was much like that of a single male singing alone, one male did all the buzzing while the other produced all the preliminary ticks. Two such groups of males were taperecorded and observed on several different days, and each time this peculiar chorusing was maintained for long periods of time." In another experiment in which the author took part, using *Magicicada cassinii*, "a tape recording of the calling song of this species was played to males in nearby trees, which were not normally singing because of unfavorable weather conditions. When the first half of a phrase was played and then the sound was abruptly cut off, the males finished the phrase, but then dwindled off without chorusing through another phrase. When the second half of the song phrase was played, and the sound was abruptly stopped afterward, the insects chorused the first half of their normal song phrase and then dwindled off without finishing the phrase in chorus" ("Sound Communication in Orthoptera and Cicadidae" [1960], pp. 78–79).

[119] In a recent popular article, "Chimpanzees and Language" (1971), Emily Hahn, who had just visited several places where apes were undergoing speech training, claims that one young chimpanzee, using the ASL language, did ask a question. The performance, however, leaves a large opening for doubt as to the animal's real interrogative intention. The author says of this little ape, Lucy, whose teacher had just been called to the telephone in midst of a tutoring session: "Suddenly, she asked me a question. It was the first time I had seen any of the chimpanzees do this, and I was not expecting it. 'What is that?' she signed, pointing to my heavy bead necklace and forming a question mark." Not knowing the word for "necklace," the visitor used one she did know, "string." "I made this sign," she writes, "and Lucy seemed satisfied." To the animal, a heavy bead necklace can hardly have looked like string. One may wonder whether Lucy would not have been just as satisfied with any answer, wanting only to reverse the usual game of "What is it?" and a word in reply from the other partner. That the question mark meant anything but the familiar formal addition to the challenger's sign seems very unlikely. Her own correct replies were always rewarded, usually with a little tidbit that had nothing to do with the meaning of the word she had produced; so, as in the training of animals for circus acts, they may have served only to reinforce her proper plays on demand, even to the point of simulating conversation.

more instinctual and zoological interpretation of the behavioral acts to which it is believed to apply would make this chapter a book. The purpose of the samples I have offered here is to show how very high the development of instinctive life can be, how far and how variously it can expand before the pressure of felt impulse and the impact of perception becomes too great to let the most advanced organisms advance any further without breaking the framework of their mental functions. So far, all treatments of instinct have aimed chiefly at deprecating its functions and proving that "clever" animals have concepts, see causal relations, and make plans of purposive action. Without a more solid theory of instinct than that, one cannot appreciate what must have happened at that critical line which the human stock has crossed, and the highest other animals have not. Also, without a real appreciation of animal mentality we cannot discover and understand the functioning of instinct in human life, confused and masked as it is by conception and the communicative power and peril of language.

16

The Specialization of Man

THE phenomenon of mind, arising in just one primate stock, is such a tremendous novelty in animal evolution that it could not have occurred without a peculiar prehistory of coincidences, leading up to special developments in the organism that produced it. The shift from animal to human mentality is so radical that any serious philosopher, analyzing those two types of cerebral activity in their respective highest forms, i.e., animal intelligence and human understanding, is apt to balk intuitively at theories deriving the latter by simple steps from the mental activities of other primates which show analogous behavior in some respects. The growth and elaboration of feeling in man which culminated in the making of mind must have been a story with many beginnings and long, obscure preparations; a story one cannot hope to tell in a brief fashion, because it involves too many facets of evolution. No single principle, however great (for instance, differential survival, adaptation), is likely to explain the rise of language and thought in one primate line, the Hominidae, which involves the whole nature of that line itself, before and above the pressions and opportunities it encountered to form its destiny.

There is an interesting theory regarding the unique character of the human genus, according to which man owes his versatility and adaptability to the fact that he has undergone no specialization. This thesis, which seems to have been original with Louis Bolk,[1] was independently proposed at almost the same time by Otto H. Schindewolf,[2] and subsequently developed by Arnold Gehlen in *Der Mensch: Seine Natur und seine Stellung in der Welt* (1940). Gehlen's book has enjoyed a wide popularity with the general intellectual public in Europe, although —if not because—its author often goes beyond the careful anatomist Bolk and the paleontologist Schindewolf to build up his picture of man

[1] *Das Problem der Menschwerdung* (1926).
[2] "Das Problem der Menschwerdung, ein paläontologischer Lösungsversuch" (1928).

as a helpless *"Mängelwesen,"* an unadapted creature without hair, pigmentation (his early man evidently was white-skinned and blue-eyed), without claws or fangs or any natural defenses, who had to develop his brain power in order to survive. This he was able to do precisely because he was unspecialized; all his potentialities were still at his disposal.[3] The very lack of specialization had an obverse side, namely, that the *"Mängelwesen,"* so lacking in physical adaptation, still had all the potentialities which other animals lost when they realized one set of them to the exclusion of others. His inadequate physique expresses his supreme advantage as well as his disadvantages, for in his adulthood he still has the receptive, malleable character of a child, open to environmental and social influences; Gehlen calls it *'Weltoffenheit."*[4] His form is permanently pedomorphic; he has the round calvarium which in other primates characterizes only the fetal and early infant stages, his open fontanelle closes long after birth and then not solidly, since the sutures always remain visible and, in life, somewhat capable of yielding to expansion of the brain, his face is shortened and placed vertically below the brain case, his arms are short and pliable, like the forelegs of a fetal ape but not an adult one. In man, they are not fit to support the body either in standing, as with most fur-bearers, or in brachiation, as they do in gibbons. Most strikingly, his teeth show no specialization for food tearing and fighting like the canines of carnivores and the great apes, or for rooting and digging like the tusks of pigs, or like lemurs' horizontal lower front teeth, said to be specialized for grooming.[5] As a permanent fetal trait, he keeps the central position of his *foramen magnum,* and as a protracted one the fact that his brain continues to grow for four or five years after birth, and to develop beyond puberty.

There are several important ideas in that book to which I can give unqualified acceptance, and we shall come back to them in due time.

---

[3] P. 109: "Alle diese Eigenschaften sind Primitivismen in einem sehr besonderen Sinn: *sie sind permanent gewordene fötale Zustände oder Verhältnisse,* mit anderen Worten 'Formeigenschaften odor Formverhältnisse, welche beim Fetus der übrigen Primaten vorübergehend sind, sind beim Menschen stabilisiert.' " Idea and quotation are taken with complete approval from Bolk.

[4] See *ibid., passim,* esp. pp. 208 ff, on this "world-receptiveness."

[5] They are undoubtedly convenient for that activity, but baboons groom much more than lemurs and seem to do it just as well with their more upright incisors; and there is one extinct animal somewhat resembling a dugong, quite unlike any primate and unlikely to have had a fur to groom, which had the same dentition, and can hardly have developed it for use as a comb. Grazing and browsing animals often approach it. But cf. J. Buettner-Janusch and R. J. Andrew, "The Use of the Incisors by Primates in Grooming" (1962), to the contrary.

But many other statements and basic notions in it are downright impossible, especially the conception of man as unadapted to the natural world, physically inadequate, defenseless, a *"Mängelwesen,"* i.e., originally a creature of wants and deficits. No organism can be unadapted *ab initio* to its surroundings, or it could not have evolved there; and had one been wafted from some other sphere into this unfriendly world, no pressure of need could have caused it to develop a saving brain in time to meet the crisis. Like millions of animals it would have been summarily extinguished. But Gehlen rejects the evolutionary derivation of man from any animalian primate stock; and as he also rejects Scheler's attribution of *"Geist"* to him as a metaphysically distinct spiritual endowment, the phylogeny of his hero remains mysterious.[6] All the supposed processes of self-help are vague to the point of inscrutability, because they are phylogenetic assets, not individual resources; they may work in a million years but not a lifetime. Childish traits which never develop further, but are fixed as such, are no aids for survival in the lives of higher animals, but require the sheltered environment of childhood which beasts and men have to be able to abandon before they can provide it for their own offspring.

Yet extended pedomorphy may sometimes have been an evolutionary factor, if the immature form had some advantage for the individual which was destined to lose that asset at maturity. Animals which go through larval stages usually have various ambients and various abilities in the course of their successive forms. If maturity did not have to be reached before they procreated they might keep the larval benefits, as Gehlen holds that adult human beings keep the round and roomy skull which marks a transient phase in the ontogenesis of other primates. But that is not the same as keeping the infantile state of great potentiality, which he considers man's highest advantage; for permanently unrealized potentialities are not assets to an individual. Pedomorphy can only be maintained if the creature in its youthful phase can already cope with all the vicissitudes of its environment and, moreover, can support the great physiological disharmony known as "neoteny," the growth of its sex organs to maturity while the rest of the body remains juvenile.[7] If

[6] *Der Mensch*, p. 22.

[7] The most familiar examples of neotenic procreation are found in Amphibia: the axolotl, which is a permanently larval *Ambystoma tigrinum*, and the mud puppy, *Necturus*. The axolotl's further development is held in abeyance, so that under some environmental conditions it can still grow up into an adult salamander; *Necturus* has never been known to do so. These larval creatures are not arrested in a particularly favorable state, nor have they made significant new adaptations, but simply remained "backward" in a zoological class which is not given to engendering prodigies at its best.

such conditions occurred, the species could settle for life in its most favorable state and ambient, and in the course of millennia prove ancestral to a higher species, genus or even family, i.e., to organisms which can negotiate a greater ambient by virtue of more complex bodily mechanisms and behavioral acts.

The theory of neoteny as a possible condition for evolutionary advance was originally propounded by Walter Garstang, who wrote so little[8] that our best sources for his ideas are secondary ones, the most succinct of which are two essays by C. A. Hardy. Garstang was not only a scientist, but also a humorist, who wrote jocular verses on his own biological ideas; Hardy, who recognized their serious import, gathered these zoological levities into a little book,[9] to which he contributed an Introduction (one of the essays just referred to) presenting the main lines of the underlying theory.

The crux of Garstang's thought is that adaptation is not solely an adult process, but that every stage from the egg onward has to be adapted to its ambient to perform its essential functions. In many low marine animals, which are sessile like plants, there is a need to disperse their progeny, as there is in plants. Many such permanently anchored adult animals and also benthonic, bottom-creeping ones, in their youthful, larval phases were free-swimming, drifting as plankton, sometimes also self-propelled by cilia or flagella. They were adapted to a different environment from that of their elders and their own presumptive maturity, in which they would creep, dig or sit rooted and procreate; their larval business was to disperse their species as widely as possible, while their structure gave them freedom and mobility, until its advancing change of phase would pull them down to the safer, restrictive life of the sea bottom. But it may happen in organic development, which depends upon hormones controlled by vast, shifting complexes of genes, that general somatic development and sexual development do not keep step with one another in the normal fashion, so procreation may occur before the organism has realized its standard adult shape. By neotenic sexual functioning in the free-swimming state the bottom-living phase would come after the procreative, and ultimately be eliminated altogether. In this way some stocks, closely adapted in their adult life to

---

[8] His theory is formulated chiefly in three technical papers, "The Theory of Recapitulation: A Critical Restatement of the Biogenetic Law" (1922), "The Origin and Evolution of Larval Forms" (1928), and especially "The Morphology of the Tunicata, and Its Bearings on the Phylogeny of the Chordata" (1928). There are a few corroborative articles on special subjects, which I have not seen.

[9] *Larval Forms, with Other Zoological Verses* (1962).

restricted environments, and hence, according to the theory held by Gehlen and shared by Huxley and others in England, doomed to stagnation or extinction, might evolve into free and active creatures which only inquisitive scientists would ever think of tracing to their humble benthonic forms.[10]

Gavin de Beer, like Hardy, saw the cogency and scope of Garstang's ideas, and carried them into some interesting researches of his own. In a little book, *Embryos and Ancestors*, he speculated that the Insecta might have derived from primitive Myriapoda, assuming that the latter —like the modern millipede—hatched from the egg with only three pairs of legs, and developed other pairs successively during the larval phase; if such an organism were arrested in the six-legged stage long enough to achieve neotenic sex life, its basic form would be that of a primitive (wingless) insect. The further evolution of such sexually precocious beings would tend to be along quite different paths from those of their ancient, wholly maturing ancestors.[11]

As for Garstang himself, he followed the wide implications of his theory in the direction of the rise of the Chordata from such primitive organisms as ascidians; and again, Hardy has given a succinct summary of Garstang's work, saying: "He imagined a sessile invertebrate animal

[10] In another article, "Escape from Specialization" (1954) (the explanation of the title is given in a reference to Huxley's "widely accepted view that specialization must lead to a dead-end from which there is no escape"), Hardy says: "Garstang has shown us the key with which such animals may sometimes escape from the maze; it is to be found in his conception of paedomorphosis linked with that of neoteny. . . . In making a survey of the larvae of many different groups he pointed out how in each there is a compromise and adjustment between two rival needs—or, in other words, two selective advantages: on the one hand to grow up into the adult so as to reproduce the species as quickly as possible, and on the other to remain floating as long as practicable so as to distribute the species over the widest possible range. . . . The young stages, varying as much as the older ones, may be modified in quite a different direction from that in which the adult structure is adapted, especially if larva and adult inhabit two very different zones of life; the greater the contrast, of course, the greater will be the metamorphosis involved" (pp. 123–24).

[11] *Embryos and Ancestors* (1940), pp. 54–56. On grounds of exactly the same similarities, the rise of Myriapoda from Insecta has been proposed. So F. G. Sinclair, who wrote the section on Myriapoda in *The Cambridge Natural History* (1922), said: "Their structure shows resemblances to several widely different classes of animals. One cannot help being impressed with their likeness to the Worms, at the same time they have affinities with the Crustaceans and still more with the Insects. In the latter class the likeness of the Thysanuridae to *Scolopendrella* and *Pauropus* have induced a celebrated Italian anatomist, Professor Grassi, to claim the former as the ancestors of the Myriapoda" (Vol. V, p. 47).

living like an Ascidian (a sea-squirt) and sending up planktonic larvae. He then imagined the dual forces of selection acting upon this larval form to such an extent that (a) its powers of remaining afloat were prolonged by the production of more and more motile forms having a tadpole-like tail and (b) the development of its gonads was greatly accelerated by neoteny. Finally he imagined this prolonged larval stage becoming actually sexually mature while still in the plankton: just as the axolotl may become sexually mature while still in the aquatic phase. Now the more dramatic step is easily taken—the former sessile bottom-living adult stage can be eliminated, as indeed the once lung-breathing former adult Necturus was surely eliminated.

"The ascidians, or tunicates, actually do send up little tadpole-like larval forms which keep themselves up in the water by the development of muscular undulating tails.... Now there is one group of the Tunicata, the Larvacea, which has every appearance of having done just what Garstang supposed the ancestors of the vertebrates to have done; they are pelagic adult forms and there can be ... little doubt that they are in fact permanently neotenous one time larval forms now specialized for their particular mode of life. Garstang did not imagine that the main chordate stock was actually derived direct from an ancestor like a modern ascidian—but ... he suggested that the chordate stock had arisen from some sedentary ascidian-like invertebrate of the distant past having a common origin with the echinoderms."[12]

The significance of the hypothetical prolonged pedomorphy of the parent type lies not in its continued potentiality without specialization, but in the chance that neotenic development may give rise to a new and different specialization. In the cases of grand mutation speculatively adduced by Garstang, the advantage of the larval forms was simply that they were motile and consequently had a much wider, more varied ambient than their sedentary, bottom-dwelling elders. Making that motility lifelong might have been the liberating shift in the history of the tunicates. In the case of De Beer's primitive insects, however, their further evolution would require two steps to their new specialty: (1) the concentration on the anterior part of the body, which encouraged the elaboration of the thorax, and (2) the development of wings. The possession of wings is what gives the higher insects their immense territorial expansion and lets them speciate to meet new conditions, often local, of temperature and vegetation and animal rivals or hosts; but wings, and the peculiar flight mechanisms of alate insects,[13] would not

[12] Introduction to *Larval Forms*, pp. 9–10.
[13] See Graham Hoyle, *Comparative Physiology of the Nervous Control of Muscu-*

have been possible without the shortened body and specialized thorax. It is interesting to see how a single advantageous condition, such as dispersion over wider living-space, may be attained in many different ways, by entirely different opportunities.

The striking pedomorphic features of man which Gehlen interprets as signs of a neotenic organism may have had other origins than arrest at an infantile stage of primate ontogeny, and be a deceptive appearance produced by very different means. But, although his concept of the helpless creature which had to develop a supreme brain in order to survive may be biologically impossible, the supreme brain is certainly real, and is both anatomically and functionally as genuine a specialized organ as the elephant's trunk or the bee's honeysack. Its extraordinary development, moreover, has been implemented by other specializations.

Every animal makes use of its bodily assets, such as the structure or placement of its eyes that may make them particularly fit for distance vision, as in hawks, night vision, as in nocturnal hunters, water-surface vision,[14] panoramic vision[15] or whatever other kind. Its life habits are determined by its developed talents, chosen by phylogenetic chance and coincidence from its potentialities; and in the struggle for development many possible advantages also go by the board.

The potentialities, however, include behavioral acts as well as trophic and physiological ones; and in the advance of evolution, facultative behavior becomes more and more important in the lives of animals. Where physical endowment is really rather poor, it is often made to

---

lar Contraction (1957), p. 106. In insects with fast, vibratory wing movements, the elastic exoskeleton bearing the attachments of the flight muscles apparently responds to each activating nerve impulse by a reverberation, somewhat as a stretched rubber band reverberates when plucked, so the number of wing movements is greater than that of nervous impulses.

[14] There are some fish, *Anableps* spp., which have a bifocal lens, enabling them to see above and under the water surface at the same time. J. Z. Young, in *The Life of Vertebrates* (1962; 1st ed., 1950), pp. 214 f, says: "The upper part of the cornea is thickened, the iris provides two pupils, the lens is pear-shaped, and there are two retinas in each eye." A similar eye is found in the common whirligig beetle, *Gyrinus*, and its larger relative, *Dineutes*. See Klots and Klots, *Living Insects of the World*, p. 110.

[15] Eyes seem to be among the earliest specialized organs, and even in their advanced forms to retain great adaptability. So N. B. Marshall, in *The Life of Fishes* (1970; 1st ed., 1966), p. 132, remarks the specialized structure of fishes' eyes, to wit: "If each eye of a fish is to have a wide visual field, the lens must not only protrude through the pupil, taking the place, so to speak, of the absent cornea, but also stand out from the surface of the head itself. In this way all-round vision can be obtained by fishes, most of which have eyes on the sides of the head."

suffice, or even put to new uses beyond the obvious old ones, by specialized yet unpremeditated and even unconscious instinctive responses. One of the behavioral devices to which some animals of widely separate classes resort to attain greater accuracy of vision than their laterally placed eyes can negotiate by looking directly at an object is to scan the presented scene by moving their heads as much as the structure of the neck permits, in that way gathering a complex impression in which the forms that interest them are passed across the retina or even from one eye to the other; something like an image of a static object may be made in that process. The physiological condition which invites this substitute for binocular focusing is that immediately successive visual impressions fuse subjectively, as we all know from the moving picture illusion.[16] Perhaps that is why lizards of various sorts,[17] some short-necked sea birds, as, for instance, the Atlantic murre,[18] and at least one large mammal with small, widely spaced eyes, the rhinoceros, all share the habit of standing still and nodding their heads when confronted with another being, as if they sought to improve their sight of it.[19] In most birds, the ability to rotate the head is highly developed, and sev-

[16] See J. J. Gibson, "Visually Controlled Locomotion and Visual Orientation in Animals" (1958), p. 184: "The total array [of light rays] can then be registered only by rotating the eyes and head. The registration process is successive, not simultaneous, since different angular sectors of the array are picked up at successive moments of time. Nevertheless, by a mechanism as yet not well understood, successive registration seems to be equivalent to simultaneous registration."

[17] Noble and Bradley, in "The Mating Behavior of Lizards; Its Bearing on the Theory of Sexual Selection," p. 55, say: "The function of the head nod is not definitely known. It very probably aids vision by permitting several views of the same object from slightly different angles. Since these views are obtained in rapid succession, the images would tend to super-impose and make objects stand out from the background."

[18] A very similar habit of nodding is reported by an excellent observer, Beat Tschanz, in a long article, "Zur Brutbiologie der Trottellumme (*Uria aalge aalge* Pont.)." Tschanz does not suggest that the head nod is motivated by visual needs, but says only that at the slightest disturbance one bird standing in the territory starts to nod, and others promptly follow suit. The only interpretive comment is, "Das Nicken ist ein Zeichen geringer Erregung" (p. 6).

[19] See Maxwell, *Stalking Big Game with a Camera in Equatorial Africa*, p. 161: "An indication of the difficulty which these animals have in gaining a clear sight of objects may be found in the action of the head, which they repeatedly raise and dip ... when they are approached in the bush, as they stand peering in the direction from which the intruder is coming towards them. Their uneasy cogitation often expresses itself in the way they sway their head and the forepart of the body from side to side, while standing on one forefoot and then the other alternately. At such a moment a sudden decision may be expected, the tail goes up, the animal either rushes forward at the intruder or—turns and trots off."

eral species have been observed to turn their heads from side to side so they fixate a target alternately with one eye and then the other before they react to the object by approach or flight.[20]

The most interesting aspect of this perceptual device, however, is that the capacity to use it seems to be in the instinctual repertoire of human beings, and may promptly appear if their focal vision is frustrated, as, for instance, by a central scotoma. What makes its use seem instinctive even in man is that its employer is ordinarily quite unaware of his own new way of seeing shapes which ought to be broken up or largely obscured by the scotoma. Hans-Lukas Teuber discusses several cases, chiefly of war-injured men, which illustrate the unconscious change of method from focusing on an object to scanning the visual field, making the object visible where a fixed eye would find only a blind area. He cites two cases, in one of which the whole field of vision was lost except for a very small central part, while in the other this central fovea was destroyed, with preservation of peripheral vision. Both men were unaware of the nature of their impairments, which perimetric examination showed up clearly. In the first case, Teuber says, "the man's experience of his own defect is limited to some vague awareness of necessity for moving his head in order to gain a full view of peripheral details in his field. Besides that, he performs surprisingly well with his central remnant of vision; earning his living as a mail sorter, he pulls each letter carefully and laboriously across a small area of preserved vision, and then flings it with excellent aim into the appropriate compartment on a shelf provided for this sorting task. He thus has no difficulty in spatial orientation nor any difficulty with the recognition of things seen in the residual field, even though this remnant is surrounded by a ring of complete blindness." As for the other soldier, who had only peripheral vision, Teuber again remarks that "this scotoma does not seem to enter in any direct fashion into this man's conscious experience.... He is merely aware of some vague reduction of his visual acuity."[21] By slight

[20] In an ornithological journal there is a brief note by I. K. Dunbar: "Observations of Visual Activity in Birds" (1961), describing the action of an osprey that had its habitual fishing post on a dead limb some 35 feet above a creek: "He sits there and scans the pools for trout. When he spots a fish he takes aim by weaving his head back and forth, ... possibly getting a momentary binocular view as the image is passed from side to side. When the Osprey has secured a satisfactory orientation he plunges and gets his fish." A second notation in the same report was on a great blue heron, which was similarly observed to look at an intruder always with one eye and then the other before taking flight; and another observation of the same phenomenon was made on a hairy woodpecker (personal communication).

[21] "Alterations of Perception after Brain Injury" (1966), p. 189.

movements, with reference to "a vicarious fovea," he compensates for his lost central vision, so that "straight lines, plain-colored surfaces, grid patterns, or herringbone patterns are all 'completed' across the area of his scotoma."[22]

Specialization, far from always limiting a creature to one possible way of life, may invite further developments by realizing more complex impulses as a basis for such advance. De Beer's hypothetical insects derived from neotenic larvae of sessile animals may be unreal, but there are more convincing cases, as for instance the odd position of the eyes in the woodcock, *Philohela minor*, so far toward the back of the head that forward vision is limited and undoubtedly requires some scanning movements.[23] But the woodcock's way of feeding, employing his long, straight, powerful bill as a probe which it drives deep into the ground vertically to find its food under leaves, moss and soft earth,[24] has created a new need; in that process the bird practically stands on its face, and its head is immobilized at the time. As long as the constant watch that birds always have to keep depended on scanning its surroundings, the use of its bill to exploit a food source unshared by other birds could not have fully developed, since it must have constantly divided its action

[22] *Ibid.*, pp. 186–87. These two illustrative cases were chosen from about four hundred recorded in U.S. Navy hospitals after World War II, which yielded the material of Dr. Teuber's study. After the previous war, Kurt Goldstein had made similar observations, and in an essay, "Über die Plastizität des Organismus auf Grund von Erfahrungen am nervenkranken Menschen" (1930), declared: "Der Ersatz bildet sich unbewusst aus" (p. 1164). He found, furthermore, that in more serious nervous impairments, i.e., not sensory but mental losses, where no substitute methods could meet the demands of the environment, the unconscious adjustment went so far as to shut the excessive challenges out of the patient's world altogether. Of such cases he says: "Hier bleiben so eklatante Defekte bestehen, dass noch andere Momente dafür verantwortlich sein müssen, dass die Kranken so wenig behindert erscheinen.... Der durch die Störung in quantitativer und qualitativer Hinsicht veränderte Organismus muss jetzt wieder *ein seinem jetzigen zustand entsprechendes* Milieu haben, und das ist tatsächlich der Fall. Die genaue Beobachtung lehrt: eine ganze Reihe von Aussenweltvorgängen, die zur normalen Umwelt des geschädigten Menschen gehörten, existieren für ihn gar nicht mehr" (p. 1167).

[23] Cf. Van Tyne and Berger, *Fundamentals of Ornithology*, p. 111: "The Woodcock's eyes are set so far back on the head that 'the posterior binocular field probably is much wider than the anterior" (quoting from G. L. Walls, *The Vertebrate Eye*).

[24] Personal observation. C. J. O. Harrison, in "Open-Billed Probing by the Princess Stephanie Bird of Paradise" (1964), pp. 162–63, reports that this bird used essentially the same movements as the woodcock to retrieve mealworms which had dug in, and "to break open pieces of soft fruit before eating fragments of them." Most acts highly developed by one kind of animal have less pronounced analogues in other species.

between probing and looking around. But that chronic situation favored and ultimately seems to have induced another specialization: the woodcock's eyes have migrated further and further back so that now, when its bill points straight down, its field of vision includes most of the area above its bent neck and to both sides, and a little rotation of the bill in its hole should be enough to give it a full panoramic view of its immediate vicinity. A further specialization has occurred, without disturbing the use of its mobile neck for head rotation when the woodcock is walking and scanning the environment like other gallinaceous birds.[25]

An evolutionary course, being a long-term tendency growing with successive generations, requires some constant ambient conditions to let it proceed; and conversely, just about every possible age-long repetitious situation has been exploited by animals which could specialize in its opportunities, so it is reflected in biological shape, physiology or behavior somewhere. That is the explanation not only of the oddities which occur in nature, the variety of forms and activities, but also of the amazing convergences in organisms of entirely different sorts (Fig. 16–1). It brings home forcibly the vastness of the pool of unexpressed genes in every stock,[26] ready to take advantage of any new opportunity given by changes in external conditions and in physiological patterns which reach a new integration or, just as often, a new separate elaboration. Learning in animals, states of being "conditioned" or trained, as well as discovering foods or techniques of living in the natural course of maturation, are all expressions of inherited potentiality finding usual or unusual opportunities for enactment. The unrealized potentialities of an organism are existent biochemical structures which, however, are

---

[25] Scanning instead of fixating seems to be a common alternative to focal vision; and it is an interesting fact that it is not restricted to the optical mode of perception. Kellogg has stated that dolphins using echo location scan the sonar field by moving their heads to and fro through an arc (*Porpoises and Sonar*, pp. 104–5). Donald Griffin, illustrating a lecture held at Connecticut College (New London, Conn., 1958), showed moving pictures of a bat about to take off in flight from his hand; the bat, with open mouth, moved its head as if broadcasting its ultra-sound to scan the surroundings. Snakes which find their prey by following temperature gradients registered in their facial pits weave their heads to pick up the comparative impingements from different quarters. The method of localization is the same in all these creatures, though the sensory means may vary.

[26] P. B. Weisz, in "Morphogenesis in Protozoa" (1954), p. 212, speaks of "implicit capacity" becoming "explicit process"; and E. W. Sinnott, in *The Problem of Organic Form* (1963), p. 189, observes that "an organism possesses potentialities, both formative and otherwise, that are far greater than it is usually called upon to demonstrate. Its genetic repertoire is very wide, but only when a particular environmental factor is introduced ... does a given response occur. An organism's genotype is vastly more extensive than is ever shown in its ordinary developmental phenotype."

Figure 16–1. Shark, a Primitive Fish, Ichthyosaur, a Reptile,
and Dolphin, a Mammal

the amazing convergences in organisms of entirely different sorts

(R. S. Lull, *The Ways of Life* [New York: Harper Brothers, 1925].)

currently or permanently quiescent. Most of these structures, though perhaps not all, lie in the chromosomes, i.e., they are genes; and as any action of a gene requires a distinctive chemical situation to elicit it, organisms always contain vast numbers of inactive genes, many of which may never encounter the conditions that would activate them.[27] The

[27] Cf. Marko Zalokar, "Ribonucleic Acid and the Control of Cellular Processes" (1961), p. 129: "It is the rate of RNA synthesis which is the main determining factor for the amount of enzyme or protein to be produced in the cell. This rate depends on gene activity—all genes are not active at all times."

Cf. also C. C. Lindegren, "The Role of the Gene in Evolution" (1957), p. 350: "It is clear that the genes that control the splitting of carbohydrates in *Saccharomyces* confer advantages that depend upon competitive conditions, and that the cell could do as well without them if competition were negligible. These capacities have been localized and sequestered in the nucleus where they lie in wait for the specific conditions in which they will be useful. They are maintained in a prepared condition over countless generations."

odd results one may get from putting animals, and even excised parts of animals, into abnormal conditions shows the enormous range of potential responses which normally do not occur.

Very different organisms may make similar adaptation to an ambient requiring specialized modes of living; that is spectacularly evident in the convergent forms of fast-swimming fish, reptiles and marine mammals, shown in the accompanying picture. Sessile animals of unrelated sorts, too, show similar environmental influences by similarities of their gross shapes; the two colonial organisms here photographed together are even of different phyla, one a coral and the other a sponge. The same water action is reflected in their respective forms (Fig. 16–2). More complex approximations to a general pattern often result, too, from influences having nothing to do with each other, because the vital impulses of organisms tend to come to the same expression. Radial symmetry, axial symmetry, spiral and annular structure, fibrous and tubular and fan-shaped growth, division, lamination, etc., are basic principles of organic form which operate under so many kinds of stimulation and

Figure 16–2. (*Left*) Coral; (*Right*) Sponge
the same water action is reflected in their respective forms
(Photo by Philip A. Biscuti.)

restriction that they may appear in the most distantly related organisms developing in the most diverse situations. Wherever an opening for trophic activity is given there seems to be a living stock to capitalize on it. Prehensile tails have developed in many kinds of monkey, but not in all kinds; in the common opossum, *Didelphis marsupialis*, and several related species, but not all; in the true chameleons, *Chamaeleo* spp. and three or four lesser genera (not the misnamed "American chameleon," which is an iguana, *Anolis*); in a fish, *Hippocampus*, the sea horse. Any animal having such an appendage naturally puts it to use— Carpenter's example, cited and pictured in Chapter 15 above, is only one of several in his monograph—but species which can grasp and hold with that added member have not displaced related ones that are caudally underprivileged. There are so many alternative ways of living that no asset seems to be indispensable until it has become so by being exploited. Only then, mainly within the species, differential survival sets in and promotes phylogenetic development of the trait.

Every species, however, must have some assets, and where an ordinary sense organ, effector system or internal mechanism is absent the stock can continue only if another potential structure able to serve the same purposes utilizes the opening for its own advance. The distribution of unsuspected genic capacities brought to light in this way is often surprising; countless unknown genes, or perhaps unknown multiple capacities of known genes, seem to lie in wait for ambient conditions which have not occurred in millions of years of waiting, until some odd coincidence produces them. Consequently, convergent forms of organization and behavior arise in widely differing creatures. W. H. Hildemann tells of fishes which, as young fry, feed entirely on a mucuous substance secreted by the skin of both parents, and remarks that this habit seems to be unique among fishes;[28] Thomas Barbour, in *Reptiles and Amphibians* (1926), describes a generally similar method as one of the many ways of larval feeding among frogs.[29] One of the most improbable structural convergences, unexplained as yet for either member, is

[28] "A Cichlid Fish, *Symphysidon discus*, with Unique Nurture Habits" (1959), p. 34.

[29] See p. 85, where he tells, in connection with accounts of mouth-brooding, froth nests on land for the eggs, brooding in the male's singing pouch or in a specially developed dorsal pouch, and other specialties, how "in the moist mountains of the Seychelles Islands a tiny species, *Arthroleptis seychellensis*, carries its little brood of tadpoles on its back to which they are attached by specially developed ventral suckers. In the rain forest of Central and South America several species of both Phyllobates and Dendrobates may be observed to carry their tadpoles stuck fast to the dorsal skin by their suckerlike mouths."

mentioned by E. Walker and his associates in their excellent *Mammals of the World*, Vol. II, p. 1465, in the description of the saiga antelope, *Saiga tartarica*: "A remarkable feature of this genus is the inflated and proboscis-like nose . . . ; in each nostril there is a sac lined with mucous membrane which appears in no other mammals but the whale." Also, there is one bird, the rosy finch, *Leucosticte tephrocotis*, which has food-carrying buccal pouches resembling those of rodents, instead of the crop or distended throat in which some other birds carry more food for their nestlings than they can hold in their bills.[30] The extreme of bodily adaptation is a phenomenon known as "phragmosis" (from *phragmos*, a partition), which consists in the use of the animal's own body to form a door or screen between its hiding place and its natural enemies. Phragmosis is found in insects, spiders, amphibians, reptiles and mammals,[31] indicating that in many diverse classes and even phyla some

[30] H. A. Miller dissected a rosy finch in the nesting season and reported his findings in a brief paper, "The Buccal Food-Carrying Pouches of the Rosy Finch" (1941), p. 72, as follows: "The two sacs are well-formed chambers, with definite openings connecting to the buccal cavity, and are not merely fissures or open pockets in the mouth lining. There is an opening on either side of the tongue and glottis in about the region of the median mandibular gland. . . . These lead downward, each to its own sac which is lined with moist buccal epithelium. The two sacs are loosely joined anteriorly by connective tissue in the median plane. . . . Each sac extends backward and laterally between the external integument and the floor of the mouth. . . . The sacs resembled the cheek pouches of kangaroo rats when they were first encountered in skinning over the bird's neck and head." These rodent-like pouches are certainly as extraordinary in a bird as the occurrence of the nasal sacs in whales and antelopes described by Walker et al.; in the latter case the convergence is between two mammals of different orders, but in the former it is between representatives of different classes.

[31] See Barbour, *Reptiles and Amphibians*, pp. 75 ff. Barbour attributes the term "phragmosis" to W. M. Wheeler, and lists the following examples: "in many frogs the skin of the head becomes involved in the cranial ossification and becomes adherent, indurated, and rugose. This makes a hard bony head, and should the frog back into a burrow it has but to tip this head down to close the entrance effectively. . . . There are other . . . toads and some tree frogs in which the head is curiously and elaborately expanded, beyond doubt for the same purpose. . . . There is also a group of phragmotic snakes, the Uropeltidae, where the head is sharp and the tail knobbed and shielded or even sometimes roughened on the phragmotic surface. Perhaps the most marvelous example of all is to be seen among mammals, in the two species of Pichiciegos of Bolivia and northwestern Argentina. These little armadillos of the genus Chlamydophorous burrow and live underground. Their body is nearly cylindrical, the head sharp and pointed . . . , but the posterior end of the body is as if sharply chopped and is covered with a bony shield. This closes the burrow perfectly and no prying snake following its underground path could possibly get its jaws about it. This is the most perfect example of phragmosis which can be found."

quite advanced creatures have evolved together with their ecological settings and in continuous adjustment to their surroundings. Perhaps the most spectacular phragmotic development is the caudal plate of a trap-door spider, *Cyclocosmia truncata*, a horny shield bearing a face-like design, used by the spider like a cork to close the bottleneck of its burrow (Fig. 16-3).

The intimate connections between animal forms and the conditions under which they develop are further shown by the way many traits arise again and again within a phylogeny, apparently independently, after the divergence of species, genera, families or even classes, though with a common path of preparation which may be devious and obscure.[32] Some potentialities find repeated opportunities to come to expression in the life of a stock, with long terms of reduction or total repression between. An instance of such reappearance may be seen in the history of those birds which today are swift runners with wings unfit for flight, like ostriches and emus; while they seem to "recapitulate" the primitive condition of birds just departing from the ancestral reptilian form, ornithologists are fairly well convinced that they have

---

For an instance from entomology, see Morley, *The Ant World*, p. 85, where the author describes the action of *Colobopsis*, the janitor ants: "Always they live in twigs, or within the branches of trees, gall nuts, or bamboo. Each nest has but a single entrance, which is cut out of the outer bark and is small and of a circular shape. These entrances are very difficult to find ..., for the only sign of them will be the sudden appearance of a dark round hole just near a scurrying worker, through which it will dive, only for the hole to disappear immediately. The opening and closing of the hole is due to the retreat of the janitor to let the scurrying workers in and her sudden reappearance. For it is her head which, well armoured, specially rounded, and matching in colour the surface of the twig or branch, has blocked the hole and forms the door."

[32] Tumarkin, in his article "On the Evolution of the Auditory Conducting Apparatus: A New Theory Based on Functional Considerations," p. 239, commenting on the fact that all mechanisms of hearing known from the most ancient records are still found, often in a single order, says: "It is indeed implicit in evolutionary theory that some species will develop a feature ... more rapidly than others. Nevertheless, ... there is something revolutionary in the suggestion that within such a restricted group as the Lacertilia there can have been such a marked diversity of development as to produce on the one hand the perfect air-sensitive ear of *Gecko* and on the other hand the V.Q. [vestibular-quadrate, conduction via lower jaw] mechanism of *Chameleon*—little different from the ancestral ear of the Jurassic.... parallel evolution of the middle ear is taking place *within* the Lacertilia under our very eyes. They are all evolving air-sensitive ears—at different rates—quite independently. This conception of parallel evolution is becoming more widely accepted nowadays.... it would follow that the middle ear mechanism also developed independently in the different mammalian groups."

Figure 16–3. (*Upper*) Trap-Door Spider, *Cyclocosmia truncata*;
(*Lower*) Spider at the Very End of Its Retreat, Rear View

a horny shield bearing a face-like design, used by the spider
like a cork to close the bottleneck of its burrow

(Photos by Andreas Feininger.)

[231]

evolved to and through the flying stage and secondarily lost that form of locomotion when ambient conditions encouraged a re-development of powerful running legs.[33] The ancient genes that developed the bipedal stance and running power of pre-avian reptiles may be actively engaged again, but in a total organism so transformed that they function in another context and with another history than they did millions of years ago. Produced under such different circumstances, the old and the new phenotypes are really convergent rather than identical. The normal flight of present-day birds and that of the extinct feathered, gliding reptiles in their heyday is certainly a convergence, perhaps with very remote, common hereditary pathways reaching back far beyond the appearance of birds or possibly even saurians on earth.

Another, less familiar example of convergent evolution in very anciently divergent classes, both carrying the same, even more ancient potentiality, is the appearance of a temperature organ in the faces of two families of snakes, the pit vipers and boids, and one family of birds, the mound-builders. In the snakes this organ is the pit, so heat-sensitive that they follow their warm-blooded prey—birds, mice or other small mammals—and discover clutches of eggs by means of it;[34] in mound-

[33] See W. J. Leach, *Functional Anatomy, Mammalian and Comparative* (1961), p. 75: "The long-extinct flying reptiles appear not to have been ancestral to the class Aves. Evidences rather clearly show that primitive birds and their reptilian ancestors were bipedal in locomotion with relatively weak thoracic limb (wing) development, a condition somewhat similar to that of ostriches and emus. The ancestral forms of birds apparently were swift runners that first utilized the wings as stabilizers in gliding rather than as features designed for active flying.

"Present-day running birds, such as the ostriches, are regarded as having undergone degenerate specialization in their flight apparatus rather than exhibiting the primitive ancestral conditions of these parts."

The opposite view, however, may also be defended; see, for instance, Percy R. Lowe, "Some Additional Anatomical Factors Bearing on the Phylogeny of the Struthiones" (1942), for arguments to the effect that ostriches and their kin are primitively non-flying birds.

[34] See G. K. Noble and A. Schmidt, "The Structure and Function of the Facial and Labial Pits of Snakes" (1937), p. 263: "The New World vipers, Crotalidae, are distinguished from all other snakes by a sensory pit on each side of the face. Some Boidae have a series of sensory pits on the scales of their upper and lower jaws. Experiments have shown that both types of pit serve to detect the body temperature of the snakes' prey...." The snakes can invariably distinguish between covered electric light bulbs, one warm and one cold, when ... the temperature gradient produced by the warm bulb is only two tenths of a degree Centigrade or less above that of the environment...."

"In the absence of vision, the labial and facial pits are the most important sensory mechanism for directing the strike towards warm blooded prey."

building birds there appears to be a similar sensory organ, probably of recent development though surely not recent as a hereditary anlage, in the bill.[35] Whether these biological thermometers are homologous or have developed along different phylogenetic routes has not, to my knowledge, been investigated. The interesting fact is that the two evolutionary products have arisen so long after the phylogenetic division of reptiles and birds that now they appear as convergent forms, high and late specializations in both classes.

A specialization that may be put to a particular use requires several conditions for its development: an initial tendency from which it can arise, an inductive influence, or a succession of such influences, during its ontogeny, and an ambient into which it automatically fits as an asset to its possessor. The first of these requirements has its chance of fulfillment in the enormous potential hidden in every hereditary gene pool. The second, the presence of an inductive embryonic milieu, constantly though perhaps variously operative, is the most fortuitous condition, and the fact that it is ever met at all rests on two general aspects of acts *per se*, which have already been mentioned: that every articulated structure in an organism tends to take on any function which it can perform,[36] however transiently, and that this activity gives it what looks like a protected path of development in the competitive struggle of cell aggregates for continued existence. The first of these two characteristics is a corollary to the principle that an organism, or even a living part of one, always does everything it can; the second, to a less certain, but more and more generally apparent physiological fact, that the regular performance of an organic function has a trophic influence on the performing structure. This encouragement may also spring from heightened action of associated tissues, so that any unit that is drawn into a larger functional assembly tends to hold its own in the ontological competition and also to develop the complex of activities around it.[37] It protects itself, and needs no preferential treatment because of future teleological value.

To understand such a unique specialty as the human brain requires a more serious treatment of the phenomenon of specialization than to condemn it *in toto* as a fatal limitation to the evolution of every heredi-

[35] See above, Chapter 13, p. 69.

[36] See Vol. I, Chapter 10 passim, esp. pp. 395–96.

[37] Cf., for example, V. C. Twitty, "Influence of the Eye on the Growth of Associated Structures, Studied by Means of Heteroplastic Transplantation" (1932), of which a brief abstract in *Archives of Neurology and Psychiatry* says: "The eye exerts an important influence on the growth of its related extrinsic structures.... The results are regarded as instances of true correlative growth...."

tary line. It is itself one of the cardinal principles of evolution; its expressions are immensely various, for it really governs the whole process of adaptation. Organisms which tend to evolve with the changes of environmental conditions and widen their ambients as they do so are adaptable, specializing rapidly in many small ways to meet and exploit new opportunities, sometimes putting their old specialties to new uses by behavioral tricks for thousands of generations until encouraged mutation and differential survival motivate long-dormant potentialities to develop.

There are different types of specialization; some of them do, indeed, fit the animal particularly for one sort of life and preclude all others. Moles can live only in fairly soft, rich earth, where earthworms and cutworms occur, and a mole's feet can dig tunnels. Their underground life, already close to extinguishing their powers of vision, offers little scope for behavioral advance or a widening ambient; exaggeration of digging and nosing, and perhaps some specialization of food-seizing organs, seem to be the main evolutionary records of the species. Yet by the measure of survival and continuance, moles are a successful kind, because the conditions they can meet are simple, and common the world over. The same is true of a much more interesting and versatile animal, the beaver, almost as specialized as the mole for one particular way of life; in the beaver it is not only paws, tail and other fairly plastic parts that are modified to fit his ambient, but that most honored badge of zoological order, the dentition.

The beaver's jaws and teeth are amazingly specialized to fit into the sort of environment in which and with which he surely has evolved, and wherein he has developed speed of movement, diving and swimming skills and an elaborate repertoire of building with wood and mud, which involves cutting trees with his peculiarly shaped mouth parts (Fig. 16–4). Since his food is obtained in this same process (being mainly the cambium of live trees), his molars are adapted to that curious fare as his front teeth are to his curious operations. Yet beavers not only have held their own, but taken possession of large tracts of land by flooding them, and invaded most of the northern hemisphere, because woods and water are widespread conditions, streams and ponds often connected, and even short overland paths between them no insuperable barriers to these animals.

Specializations, in short, may be extreme, yet not lead to any foreseeable extinction or, as in the oyster, stagnation, a dead end of evolution. Very fine specializations may be subtle; Paul Leyhausen has remarked the adaptation of many felines' canine teeth to the killing

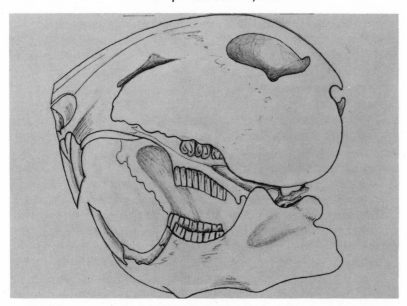

Figure 16-4. A Beaver's Skull, Showing the Huge Cheek Bones
and Teeth

the beaver's jaws and teeth are amazingly specialized

(Drawn by Sibyl A. Hausman from a specimen in the Connecticut College collection; the
upper part has been somewhat tilted to show the molars, which are actually hidden by the
bony cheeks in profile.)

strike exactly between a victim's cervical vertebrae (Fig. 16-5). The
teeth are so perfectly fitted to the anatomy of smaller vertebrates and
for working together that if only one of them strikes bone or even
sinew, all four of them are guided to slip between the segments of the
spinal column behind the skull.[38]

[38] See "Über die Funktion der relativen Stimmungshierarchie," p. 454: "Die
Feliden treffen . . . in einem *sehr* hohen Prozentsatz der Fälle das Halsmark mit
nur einem Zubiss, obwohl die Zähne selbst bei 'guten' Nackenbissen doch aus sehr
verschiedenen Richtungen in den Beutehals eindringen können. Dies ist aus der
Orientierung des Tötungsbisses nicht zu erklären. Meiner Vermutung nach sind die
Eckzähne der Feliden . . . so an den Verlauf der Muskeln, Sehnen und Bänder wie
die Richtung der Halswirbelflächen angepasst, dass diese von den vier eindringenden
Eckzähnen mit hoher Wahrscheinlichkeit wenigstens einen nahezu automatisch an
einen Zwischenwirbelraum heranleiten. . . . Die letzte 'Feineinstellung' dürfte pro-
priozeptorisch sein: Wenn eine Zahnspitze auf Hartes, also Knochen, stösst, könnte
die Katze etwas herumtasten, bis die Zahnspitze in einen Spalt gleitet, und dann
erst fester zubeissen. Die oben vermutete 'Automatik' brauchte dann nur bis auf

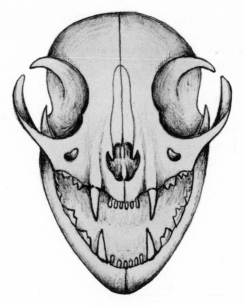

Figure 16–5. A Cat's Skull, Showing the Perfect Shape of the Canines
To Guide Each Other in Finding the Intervertebral Spaces
in a Quarry's Neck

very fine specializations may be subtle

(Drawn by Sibyl A. Hausman from a specimen in the Connecticut College collection.)

There is, in fact, a little-known animal whose talents have all progressed to the point of visibility, but none to that of true specialization
such as it shows in animals which have really developed it; that creature
is the sewellel or "mountain beaver," *Aplodontia rufa*, which has
gathered up a rare assortment of traits generally considered distinctive
of other animals, so it has, I daresay, the most mixed bag of tricks ever
combined in one repertoire. Like many rodents, it hoards food, and in
captivity stores it in protective corners; in the wild it stocks dugout
chambers with provisions, like a muskrat, although it does not hiber-
nate, and in its very restricted habitat without severe winter[39] some
food plants such as spatterdock roots are probably available at all times.

---

den Wirbelknochen und nicht so unwahrscheinlich genau zwischen zwei Wirbelknochen zu leiten."

[39] Its occurrence is limited to the western slopes of the North American coastal
range from southern British Columbia to northern California. There are other relatively primitive mammals, all restricted to small localities; Robert Stenuit, in the
most objective part of *The Dolphin, Cousin to Man*, which is the taxonomic survey

It digs canals, often filled with water led off from a brook, in which it moves like a beaver; its dens, said to be used only by females with young, are high and dry above these artificial waterways. It carries nesting materials and builds like a laboratory rat, but less elaborately. It gnaws branches and small tree trunks, again like a beaver, and—most spectacular likeness—in captivity it built a rampart of big branches about its home. It was observed to carry green fodder such as lettuce to its water dish and "wash" or rather soak it like a raccoon. Its mode of defecation is to some extent all its own, as it takes each fecal pellet directly from the anus between its teeth and tosses it on a pile of earth selected (and in captivity, supplied) for that purpose. What is "all its own," however, is only the second part, the tossing of its excrement, for other animals have developed the first part in a physiological connection, reingesting the pellets,[40] while *Aplodontia* throws them on a heap and then covers the deposit with earth like a cat, but (again) rather imperfectly. It also uses tongue and paws like a cat or a rabbit in washing its face and ears. In great fright it exhibits cataplexy, like a rabbit, and will retain its stark pose for a while if carefully picked up and held in hand.[41]

---

of genera and their distribution, describes some of these animals (p. 37): "The fresh-water dolphins are the quiet ones, those who have never looked for adventure out in the wide wild seas. They get along, although they have evolved very slightly.... In some ways, they are a bit like living fossils....

"The Susu or Platanista (Platanista gangetica), who lives in the tributaries of the Brahmaputra, the Indus and the Ganges, still has a caecum in its intestinal system; it is black; and it is blind for lack of a crystalline lens. It gets its food by foraging with its beak in the river mud...." Although so much has been written on the probable and improbable mental acts imputed to highly evolved cetaceans, primitive forms have commanded no interest. This holds for animal psychology generally, and indicates its lack of systematic theoretical structure.

[40] Cf. Young, *The Life of Vertebrates*, p. 663: "the lagomorphs share with rodents the habit of passing food twice through the alimentary canal (caecotrophy). Dried faecal pellets are produced only during the day. At night soft pellets covered with mucus are formed in the caecum and are immediately taken from the anus by the lips. They are stored in the stomach and later mixed with further food taken. The double passage of the food is necessary for the life of mice and guineapigs as well as rabbits. The animals die in two or three weeks if prevented from reaching the anus. The moist pellets probably contain the metabolites that have been produced by breakdown of cellulose by the bacteria of the caecum, which cannot be absorbed by the organ itself."

[41] The study from which most of these facts are taken is an article by Irene Wandeler and Georg Pilleri, "Weitere Beobachtungen zum Verhalten von *Aplodontia rufa* Rafinesque (Rodentia, Aplodontoidea) in Gefangenschaft" (1964). (The word "weitere" in the title refers to a single, brief observation by Pilleri on an animal that died after a week.) It contains many other points of interest.

Now, what is the significance of these behavioral traits, most of which have been highly developed in distantly related species—not only rodents, i.e., rat and beaver, but raccoons, cats, lagomorphs—but appear somewhat casually in *Aplodontia*? The sewellel is the most primitive rodent, and its limited range suggests that despite its many talents it is not a very successful one. Something in its evolution has been missed. It is a Jack-of-all-trades, showing the early stages of all sorts of repertoire elements, none carried to great perfection as in more specialized animals.[42]

What has been missed is specialization; its potentialities are astounding, but none of them has been realized. The notion that all specialization must lead to fixation in a narrow ambient or to over-growth of special features—horns, tusks, scales—finally making the species unviable seems to me to rest on an overly simple concept of biological adaptation. There are several kinds of specialization, notably adaptation to special conditions, which may lead to the evolutionary stagnation of many marine organisms, the same today as in the Cretaceous; and, by contrast, specialization by progressive refinement of an organ, appendage or talent. This latter kind is seen in the cat's mouth, where the conjoint aim of the canines is coupled with nervous developments that lead to great sensitivity in "mouthing"—using teeth and tongue, without mutual interference, for carrying, grooming, selecting and manipulating quite apart from grabbing or fighting, as Leyhausen's example of proprioceptive guidance suggests. This sort of specialization, far from limiting the agent's individual powers of adjustment, increases them, and may even lead to a point where new functions are induced and new physical developments encouraged, as in man. The elephant's trunk is surely a specialty derived from the trophic possibilities of the elongated and somewhat movable nose that is found today in the tapir, the hyrax and the anteaters; but far from condemning the animal to a small ecological "niche," it has allowed his great increase in numbers, in size and in animal intelligence, i.e., capacity to realize his instinctive impulses. The happy condition that supported these advances was that the specialization took place in a highly important sense organ, the nose,

---

[42] See, for example, the statement (*ibid.*, p. 571): "Obwohl das Tier keine morphologischen Wasseranpassungen aufweist, hat es für Wasser grosse Vorliebe und kann im Versuchsfalle gut schwimmen." Also, p. 574, telling of the woodcutting operation of their animal (referred to as "M"): "In beiden Haupträumen lagen für M viele Äste ... am Boden ausgebreitet. Von Buchenästen hatte M meist nur die Rinde angenagt, seltener auch ins Kernholz hinein. *Ein einziger Kirschbaumast trug einen Kegelschnitt, wie ihn der Biber macht*" (italics mine).

which implements two primary senses in most animals, smell and touch; by making this organ a prehensile effector as well as a double receptor, the development of the elephant's nose into a trunk has given him an asset surpassed only by the human hand.

Behavioral acts are, of course, more variable than acts of growth and form, and can change more radically in a short time. So, because of their freedom to take advantage of any constellation in ambient events, there are more convergences in hereditary behavior, sometimes so odd that they seem utterly accidental, as when Leyhausen observes that a wildcat's technique of manipulating its prey is perfected in the maned wolf, *Chrysocyon brachyurus*;[43] or when E. A. Armstrong, in his monograph *The Wren*, compares in detail the courtship antics of that bird to those of the three-spined stickleback.[44] Norris and Prescott report that the Pacific dolphin, *Tursiops gilli*, slaps his flukes on the surface of the water as a beaver slaps its tail (which, of course, has been interpreted in both cases as a warning of danger, but does not bear the interpretation very well),[45] and D. K. Caldwell tells the same story of *Stenella plagiodon*, the spotted dolphin.[46] The flat appendage and the ability to leap out of the water seem to be all it takes to provide a noise-making talent which is duly exploited wherever it exists.

[43] Leyhausen, "Über die Funktion der relativen Stimmungshierarchie," p. 419: "Mit dem ersten Zubiss schnappen auch die Zibethkatzen nach dem *nächsterreichbaren* Körperteil der Beute. . . . Mit dem Nachschnappen befördern sie dann oft in einem Zuge den Kopf der Beute in einen Mundwinkel und beginnen, diesen abzukauen. Kleine Ratten fressen sie so ohne abzusetzen auf, wobei sie diese nach wenigen Kaubewegungen mit einem *Kopfschlenkern* in den jeweils anderen Mundwinkel befördern (eine Fresstechnik, welche Mähnenwölfe vollendet beherrschen . . .)."

[44] See his p. 128 for parallel tables comparing the courtship sequences of bird and fish, respectively.

[45] Norris and Prescott, "Observations on Pacific Cetaceans of Californian and Mexican Waters," p. 322: "Lobtailing is a very common behavior pattern in this species. Many times when we were pursuing a particular group of animals they would sound immediately after one or more members had slapped their flukes on the surface. The pattern was sometimes used when no pursuit was involved, such as when animals were quietly feeding in the still waters of a bay. Usually before each deep extended dive one or more adult members would lightly slap its tail flukes upon the surface, and then sound." This fits exactly with my own observations of beavers, except that I have never watched a group together.

[46] "Notes on the Spotted Dolphin, *Stenella plagiodon*, and the First Record of the Common Dolphin, *Delphinus delphis*, in the Gulf of Mexico" (1955), p. 469: "Occasionally one would vigorously slap the water several times with its flukes, and one jumped completely clear of the water in a low arc nearly parallel with the surface." These animals were sexually excited, several seen to mate.

[239]

Some special traits, behavioral or anatomic, found in very distantly related animals are, however, probably not convergent developments, but similar potentialities at different stages of realization. Any highly specialized form or function characterizing a species or a larger taxon is likely to have rudimentary analogues in other creatures, which may represent quite remote hereditary lines. It is surprising, to say the least, that physiologists have found a striking similarity between the digestive systems of many ungulates specialized for rumination and those of langur monkeys, which, oddly enough, show no behavioral adaptation, such as regurgitating and rechewing, to that peculiar organ.[47] The same sort of analogy between highly developed forms in one or a few species and rudimentary forms of the same traits in others holds for behavior as it does for bodily shapes and mechanisms. The incubators built by the mallee fowl of Australia are the result of a fantastically elaborated behavior pattern; but a similar impulse seems to be in the repertoire of the Egyptian plover, which makes some moves to utilize the heat of the sun in similar fashion, though it has developed nothing like the techniques of *Megapodius*.[48] Thomas Barbour, meanwhile, found the same practice incipient in reptiles, which in the main depend entirely on the sun to hatch their eggs, but present one family—Crocodilidae, comprising crocodiles and alligators—that "pile up a heap of vegetable trash which warms as decay progresses and so helps incubation. . . ."[49]

Examples could be almost endlessly multiplied, demonstrating the wide range of potentialities which come to fruition only under peculiar circumstances in a few animal stocks. The point of the whole discus-

---

[47] See T. Bauchop and R. W. Martucci, "Ruminant-Like Digestion of the Langur Monkey" (1968), p. 698: "A superficial resemblance of the stomach to the rumen of herbivorous animals has been noted, but a number of authors have stated that rumination does not occur. Although rumination is an obvious characteristic of ruminants, recent work has placed greater emphasis on the fermentative processes occurring in the rumen. . . . Drawert *et al.* analyzed samples of gastric contents obtained from colobus monkeys in Africa and found high concentrations of short-chain volatile fatty acids, similar in concentration and character to the fermentation end products found in rumen contents." In the silvered leaf monkey, *Presbytis cristatus*, "the greatly distended and sacculated portion (saccus gastricus), corresponding to the fundus, is followed by a tubular portion (tubus gastricus), which leads to a third or pyloric segment."

[48] See Kendeigh, *Parental Care and Its Evolution in Birds*, p. 290: "The Egyptian plover, *Plivianus aegypticus*, is supposed to bury its eggs in the sand and depend largely on the sun's heat to hatch them. However, only in the Megapodidae is artificial incubation generally developed to such a high degree as to constitute the sole means of reproduction."

[49] *Reptiles and Amphibians*, p. 63.

sion is that vast possibilities are handed down from unimaginable antiquity, to be brought to light by coincidences of organic and ambient conditions. Almost anything can happen in the course of time, on no other basis than the inherent growth of acts in competition with each other, and the opportunities created by the flow of ever-changing situations—even the emergence of mind in animal evolution. Man seems to carry no more genes than countless other beings on earth, even plants, but the particular turn his development has taken has shifted his mental functions into a new dimension, which makes it hard to believe that in his advance he carries some rudimentary abilities which have more admirable parallels in lower animals. There is probably no reason for regarding them as "vestiges"; they may have had a greater day, but are more likely to be unrealized potentialities. By way of example, consider a completely unsuspected human response to a rare situation, which came to light when a record-making breathhold diver, Robert Croft, made his deepest dive—240 feet—in the presence of three underwater photographers, who watched and recorded the performance. They noted "a pronounced caving in of the thorax and of the abdomen at depth," and especially "skinfolds flapping around the chest" as he moved through the water.[50] This last phenomenon is a seldom-realized potentiality in human skin, but has a high development in a creature specialized for diving, the bottle-nosed dolphin. Winthrop Kellogg, in *Porpoises and Sonar* ("porpoises" here referring to *Tursiops truncatus*), has described it in some detail, saying: "Essapian has shown that the skin of the trunk is loose and pliable. It may hang in folds or wrinkles if an animal is picked up and carried. The external layers of the skin also contain a multitude of tiny ducts which are filled with a spongy material. As a result, the entire surface undulates in waves according to the turbulence or waviness of the water. The external shape of the animal, being somewhat flexible, assumes the natural contour of the flow of water which is rushing past it. . . . The configuration of the skin matches the wave-form of the water, instead of opposing it. The result is known as 'laminar flow.' It has the effect of reducing friction drag by as much as 90 per cent over the friction of an unyielding surface" (p. 7).

Man is probably as full of unrealized potentialities as the lower creatures. And just as we carry rudimentary organs and functions which

---

[50] Croft's remarkable powers and achievements are reported by K. E. Schaefer *et al.* in a brief paper, "Pulmonary and Circulatory Adjustments Determining the Limits of Depth in Breathhold Diving" (1968), p. 1020.

other stocks have exploited, our own assets have analogues—sometimes well-developed ones—in other forms of life, not always obviously related, i.e., not necessarily primates. The grasping reflex in the toes of human infants is found in the feet of fledgling cuckoos,[51] as well as in those of monkeys; but it is only in the latter that the analogy has been noted, because there it supports an established view of our evolution, the quite unshakable assumption that man was once as arboreal as most monkeys and apes are today, and owes his chest expansion to a period of gibbon-like brachiation.[52] But some recent paleological finds call the doctrine of a long, wholly arboreal phase of his prehistory in question.

So far, the outstanding feature of man to which anthropologists had always attributed his ascendency over all other animals was his highly developed brain in the wide, vaulted cranium; this was supposed to have led the process of his *"Menschwerdung,"* his departure from ancestral apes, abandonment of his arboreal life and his recent, though presumably gradual, assumption of an upright posture, on his hind feet alone. That this stance and the bipedal walk it induced were modern and met needs created by his mental advance was generally agreed. During the past three decades, however, at several points in southeast Africa, the discovery of hominid remains that antedate the oldest Asiatic fossil records by millions of years has brought to light a prehistoric being with a small, ape-like cranium and the upright carriage of a man. The pelvis of this "man-ape" is entirely human and so is the leg, to judge especially by one femur that has been found. S. L. Washburn has described the condition of the australopiths and its

[51] Van Tyne and Berger, *Fundamentals of Ornithology*, p. 299.

[52] For a statement of this standard assumption, see A. L. Kroeber, *Anthropology* (1948; 1st ed., 1923), p. 72: "if our ancestors had not once lived for a long time in the trees, along with the rest of the primates, we should probably never have had any kind of hand. The clever or lucky thing we 'did' was to come down out of the trees after we had hands, and early enough to re-evolve a pretty fair true foot—that is, a limb extremity built for general terrestrial locomotion."

The same history is tacitly assumed by so excellent an evolutionary thinker as A. H. Schultz, who writes, in "The Specializations of Man and His Place among the Catarrhine Primates" (1950), p. 43: "In man the foot has lost its grasping ability much more completely than even in adult gorillas and has become highly adapted to its specialized functions for bipedal, terrestrial support and locomotion" —for bipedal locomotion, yes; but terrestrial use is not so certainly a recently specialized function.

Franz Weidenreich, in "The Trend of Human Evolution" (1947), p. 225, wrote similarly: "The precise evolutionary phase in which man lost the grasping (climbing) character of his foot is a matter of speculation. Probably it happened at a very early period."

evolutionary significance succinctly, saying: "These forms have brains which are in the range of the living apes, and their teeth show both human and ape characters, but the ilia are practically modern-human. Men were bipeds first, and later large-brained, small-faced bipeds. Just as the differences between monkey and ape are in the upper extremity and trunk, so those between ape and man are in the pelvis and foot.... The bone-muscle functional complex of the leg distinguishes man from the apes as sharply as the comparable complex of the arms shows their similarity and distinguishes both from the monkeys."[53] The impact on evolution theory, of course, has been profound. There is fairly wide agreement among paleontologists today "that the first hominids were small-brained, newly bipedal, proto-australopith hominoids, and that what we have always meant by 'man' represents later forms of this group with secondary adaptations in the direction of large brains and modified skeletons of the same form."[54]

The discovery of *Australopithecus*, which Washburn aptly described as "an animal with a human ilium and an ape's head," led to a renewed study, both speculative and empirically demonstrative and in both respects exciting, of the gradual evolution of the human skull. Between the snouted heads of apes and the domed crania and rounded, reduced jaws of modern man, the skulls of extinct hominids show almost every transitional stage. But we have no fossil evidence for the supposed back-mutation of the pongid hind foot to the human, plantar extremity; we have no prehensile proto-human foot.[55] The nearest simian foot is the

[53] "The Analysis of Primate Evolution with Particular Reference to the Origin of Man" (1950), pp. 68–69.

[54] W. W. Howells, "Origin of the Human Stock" (1950), p. 84. Howells was summing up the results of a symposium, *Origin and Evolution of Man*, which included Washburn's paper cited above.

A few years earlier, Franz Weidenreich had written: "It follows from all the recorded facts that the adoption of the upright position and the correlated adaptation of all skeletal parts is the fundamental specialization of man" ("The Trend of Human Evolution," p. 230).

[55] See John Napier, "The Antiquity of Human Walking" (1967), p. 125: "In 1960 L. S. B. Leakey and his wife Mary unearthed most of the bones of this [a previously mentioned] foot in the lower strata at Olduvai Gorge known collectively as Bed I, which are about 1.75 million years old. The bones formed part of a fossil assemblage that has been designated ... as possibly the earliest-known species of man: *Homo habilis*.... On the basis of functional analysis the resemblance to the foot of modern man is close.... The stout basal bone of the big toe lies alongside the other toes.... in apes and monkeys the big toe is not exceptionally robust and diverges widely from the other toes. The foot bones, therefore, give evidence that this early hominid species was habitually bipedal."

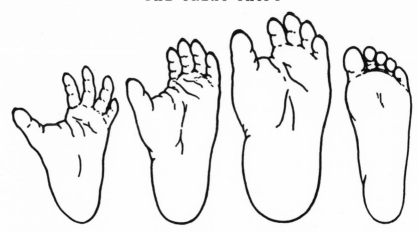

Figure 16–6. Foot of (*Left to Right*) Chimpanzee, Forest Gorilla, Mountain Gorilla, and *Homo sapiens*

the nearest simian foot is the gorilla's . . . but that is chiefly a basic, phyletic likeness, for . . . the weight of its body is not borne . . . from heel to big toe, but along a more central line

(Reprinted by permission of Edinburgh University Press and Quadrangle Books from *The Antecedents of Man* by W. E. LeGros Clark, copyright © 1959, 1962, 1971 by W. E. LeGros Clark.)

gorilla's, which Gregory and Hellman considered so similar to man's that the difference did not preclude common ancestry;[56] but that is chiefly a basic, phyletic likeness, not a physiological one, for despite the large hallux and sole of the gorilla, the weight of its body is not borne near the inner edge of the foot from heel to big toe, but along a more central line terminating in the gap between the opposable hallux and the other toes (Fig. 16–6).[57] The ball of the foot consequently gives no leverage to throw the weight forward, but the animal's balance shifts mainly sideways from foot to foot and allows only a flat-footed, waddling advance (Fig. 16–7).

Naturally the question has often enough been raised how the hominids came by their upright stance and especially their stride, with

[56] W. K. Gregory and M. Hellman, "The Dentition of *Dryopithecus* and the Origin of Man" (1926), p. 109.

[57] According to W. E. LeGros Clark, the human foot shows somewhat the same torsion of the metatarsals, orienting the hallux toward the rest of the toes and vice versa, which would permit prehension, save that the tendons and the whole musculature hold the five digits in parallel. See *The Antecedents of Man* (1963; 1st ed., 1959), pp. 222–23.

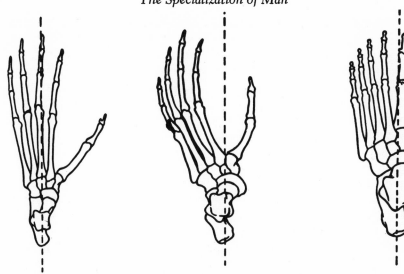

Figure 16–7. Foot Skeleton of (*Left to Right*) *Macaca*, Chimpanzee, and *Homo sapiens*, Showing the Functional Axis in Each Case

the ball of the foot . . . gives no leverage to throw the weight forward

(Reprinted by permission of Edinburgh University Press and Quadrangle Books from *The Antecedents of Man* by W. E. LeGros Clark, copyright © 1959, 1962, 1971 by W. E. LeGros Clark.)

straight legs, on the soles of their hind feet. Various theories have been offered, but they all seem too casual and trivial as explanations of such a momentous characteristic. The latest of these proposals, known as the "food-carrying" hypothesis, is inspired by the acts of Japanese monkeys which have learned (supposedly without suggestion from men) how to walk on two feet while carrying trays, even entering the water to wash the sand out of the scattered grain they have scooped up.[58] But there is no evidence that this new use of legs and hands (for their paws are really four prehensile hands) has affected their mode of walking apart from the grain-washing act. It seems highly plausible that the main reason why upright walking does not become the common habit of locomotion in these animals which are capable of it is that their feet are not preadapted for it; they are walking on hands, which is not an easy mode of progression even when the hands are in the right anatomical place for footing it.[59]

[58] See Hewes, "Hominid Bipedalism: Independent Evidence for the Food-Carrying Theory."

[59] It should be remembered that the Japanese monkeys which seem to walk on

The fact that, so far, we have found no evolutionary halfway station between the simian and the human foot nor, for that matter, between their respective associated leg and hip structures indicates that this anatomical specialization of the Hominidae goes farther back in pre-history than our fossil record; and as the upright posture may have played a large part in the spectacular brain development which followed its achievement, and certainly in the human use of the hand, it has very probably been the decisive change that precipitated the divergence of our ancestral stock from the rest of the incipient Hominidae, as several Evolutionists hold today.[60] A mammal walking habitually on straight hind legs is certainly an anomaly; so much so that to reason from its obvious relatedness with the pongids to its own derivation from typical early pongids, already specialized for locomotion through the treetops, may be reasoning from shaky premises.

If the human foot has really undergone a reversion from the prehen-sile simian foot back to the older, common cursorial form, that change must have taken place with extraordinary speed, between the develop-ment of the manus-like hind paw of the apes and the time of the bipedal man-apes with their human extremities. We are so convinced of an arboreal phase in prehuman life that it is regarded as axiomatic. Yet to take such a former way of life in our phylogenetic past simply for granted on the basis of our anatomically obvious relation to the apes may not be a perfectly safe backward extrapolation. Despite all skeletal similarities, mankind may have had its own behavioral specialties from an early stage of the primate radiation; for instance, the hominids might never have been entirely arboreal, yet excellent climbers, that lived in dense coverts under the trees but fed largely above, in the branches (they might even have been driven or held to that way of life by the ancestors of today's pongids, if those animals had taken to the treetops even as branching trees developed, and had made a faster and fuller adaptation to the uplifted feeding grounds in which they finally lived). Much climbing, but still sleeping and freely moving on the forest floor would have induced the slightly deviant development of man's foot, the flexible toes and flattened nails, not by back-mutation from prehensile monkey feet, but by ordinary progressive evolution

---

their hind legs with ease and carry food trays with their hands are walking on beach sand; I have seen people walk on their hands on the damp sand of a beach, where the ground shapes itself to their palms as their curved fingers and outspread thumbs dig in for support, in a way they could not possibly walk on hard soil.

[60] Washburn, Weidenreich and Napier, who have already been cited to that effect, are not by any means alone in their opinion.

from an older still cursorial type[61] in which the metatarsal of the hallux lay parallel, as yet, to the other four. Our primate foot might simply ₄ never have gone as far in its modification as the ape's.

The human hand and arm, however, show the typical anthropoid form, specialized for climbing and reaching, clinging and swinging, catching, holding, perhaps even brachiating, so there apparently has been some arboreal adaptation in our pre-history. Why, then, should our single primate line have remained terrestrial, and become bipedal instead of four-handed?

One important condition favoring this odd development may have been the wide range of the early hominids' diet. Monkeys and apes are mainly herbivorous and fructivorous, living on leaves, fruits and young shoots (though many will occasionally kill and eat other warm-blooded animals, and possibly all eat some insects). With the spread of forest trees they would seek their food more and more aloft, if their stock derived from an archaic progenitor capable of climbing. The Hominidae, on the other hand, may always have been partly carnivorous, and have hunted as well as harvested from day to day. Certainly those man-apes that made the East African bone desposits at Taungs, Matapansgat, Starkfontein and the Limeworks Cave seem to have lived largely on meat.[62] If the still earlier man-apes, that must have been good

---

[61] A serious discussion of this possibility is given by William L. Straus, Jr., in his article, "The Riddle of Man's Ancestry" (1949), p. 217. Straus envisages the earliest hominids as "capable of both terrestrial and arboreal life," and sets up the hypothesis that "in their evolution they avoided brachiating specializations and early became terrestrial bipeds, capitalizing upon the tendency toward part-time erectness of the trunk that is characteristic of all primates. Thus they never passed through an actual anthropoid-ape stage. . . . It is quite probable that they indulged in some swinging by the arms and in that sense might be regarded as primitive brachiators, for many catarrhine monkeys indulge in occasional brachiation. . . ." But, he declares: "That outright, habitual brachiation was a necessary prelude to the terrestrial bipedalism of man, as Keith once believed and as others still imagine, appears to be an illusion." Incidentally, this author describes his hypothetical earliest man as an unspecialized primate, and makes reference to Bolk.

There is a suggestion of a similar theory in Howells' "Origin of the Human Stock," p. 83, casually given in commenting on LeGros Clark's symposium paper: "Notice that LeGros Clark includes all our forms under hominoid—i.e. non-cercopithecid—while leaving open the question of whether the hominids might have arisen from a brachiator or from a Proconsul-like creature not yet adapted to brachiation."

[62] Raymond Dart, in "Cultural Status of the South African Man-Apes" (1955), p. 329, gives an inventory of the animal remains found with the hominid bones at Matapansgat: "at least 39 large bucks of udu and roan antelope size, 126 medium of wildebeeste proportions, 100 small ones of the gazelle order, and 28 of the tiny

climbers to have developed the pongid physique from the waist upward, lived on the forest floor to which the foot remained adapted, the constant shift from their terrestrial domain to the branches and down again would have placed a premium on the straightening of hips, loins and legs, for straining upward to reach the lowest branch in starting their ascent and stretching down to touch their baseline, the solid ground, in descending. Those animals which had effectually abandoned the terrestrial milieu and lived aloft went on evolving prehensile feet, for there was no fixed ground to negotiate. So it may be that the greater evolutionary change took place in the apes and monkeys, paradoxically leaving the hominids, which actually underwent less of a mutation, as the more specialized in posture and locomotion.

The next question that arises is, then, whether the upright posture has played a crucial part in the evolution of the "large-brained, small-faced bipeds" of today from some ape-headed bipeds like those of the African early Pleistocene (if not those very ones), and if it did, what was its role. The answers are not simple and, being speculative, not really scientifically confirmable. But some which have been offered are convincingly reasonable. The thinning of the cranial bones and their tendency to expand upward into a domed calvarium, which Gehlen considered a retention of fetal conditions, may have had other sources than "fetalization." It occurs for obvious mechanical reasons in the gibbon, which is usually hanging by its front paws. The gibbon has a very small face and rounded skull,[63] but the muscular development in its arms and shoulders, which is required and enhanced by its brachiating form of locomotion, exerts great pressure on the cranium at the areas of muscle insertion and militates against the enlargement or changes of form of the brain cavity. This ape is usually vertical but not standing up. When he walks he generally holds his arms in their normal position above his head so that even when he is erect the head is still sunk between his shoulders. His usual walk is along a branch, where his prehensile toes come into play. When he is suspended his hind legs hang loose, the knees are somewhat flexed and the feet used mainly as hands, i.e., for reaching, holding and gathering things. In sharp contrast, the upright posture of man is a stretch against gravity, from his

---

duiker type. . . . In that bone breccia are also remnants of 4 fossil horses, 6 chaligotheres (an extinct type of tree-browsing creature), 6 fossil giraffes, 5 rhinoceroses, a hippopotamus, no less than 20 wart hogs, and 45 baboons."

[63] See Schultz, "The Specializations of Man and His Place among the Catarrhine Primates," p. 47: "In gibbons . . . the face is proportionately no larger than in man and this in spite of the fact that the gibbon orbits are exceptionally large."

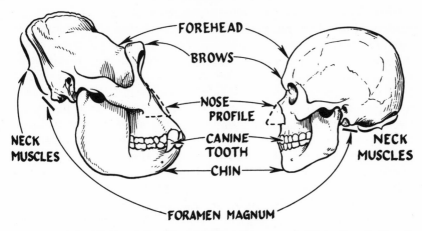

Figure 16–8. Skulls of Gorilla and Man Compared. Note the Angle of Entrance of the Spinal Cord into the Skull.

the balance of man's head on the supporting (not only anchoring) vertical spine ... made the powerful neck and jaw muscles of animals with front-heavy, snouted skulls unnecessary

(William Howells, *Mankind in the Making* [New York: Doubleday, 1967].)

feet—especially the halluces and their metatarsals, bound to those of the other toes—through the straight knees and hips and continuing in the same direction up the spine to the atlas, on which the head is balanced.

This balance of man's head on the supporting (not only anchoring) vertical spine is probably the main source of its human modification; for it made the powerful neck and jaw muscles of animals with front-heavy, snouted skulls unnecessary, as it also obviated the thickness of the simian calvarium, the adult gorilla's bony crest, the heavy brow ridges of all apes and early men (Fig. 16–8).

The domed human cranium, which Schindewolf, Bolk, Gehlen and some intellectually related writers treat as the chief exhibit to support their theory of fetalization, may have had a different phyletic history; there is an alternative theory (even based on some scientific findings), which derives this seeming pedomorphism, too, from man's basic structural specialty, the upright posture. Its proponents, E. L. Du Brul and D. M. Laskin, in a theoretical and experimental study,[64] demonstrated quite convincingly how a skull borne on a vertical spine would be influenced by evolutionary forces, and even mechanical ones operating dur-

[64] "Preadaptive Potentialities of the Mammalian Skull: an Experiment in Growth and Form" (1961).

ing each normal life, to be "rolled in" upon its axis, and to expand at the top and converge round its support so the *foramen magnum* would tend to shift toward the fulcral point between the chin and the occiput. Dr. Du Brul had noted even in his doctoral dissertation, submitted in 1955, how all the ancient structures, the limbic lobes and sensory relays, in the human head are crowded into the bottom of the skull around the rearing brain stem, instead of being deployed freely on its horizontal dorsal surface.[65] He and his co-author of the afore-mentioned article also showed, by experimental interference with the cartilaginous base from which the embryonic skull starts, what effects were achieved in animals by ablation of one of the two synchondroses, the spheno-occipital and spheno-presphenoid, which form the crux of that base.[66] The more anterior synchondrosis, i.e., the spheno-presphenoid, was the target of their operations, and the results varied, presumably, with the relative completeness of its removal in their many rats. They summarize their results as follows:

"In lateral view the changes are: (1) a general shortness and round-ness of the total skull, (2) a curvature of the cranial roof, (3) a ventral migration of the nuchal crest, (4) a ventral and rostral swing of the nuchal plane around a center of rotation at inion, and (5) a marked forward displacement of the occipital condyles. In basal view the changes are: (1) a ventral and forward rotation of the plane of the foramen magnum so that one can see directly into the cranial cavity, (2) a ventral and forward rotation of the occipital condyles in addition to the forward displacement noted above, (3) a marked shortening of the cranial base, (4) a crowding forward of the auditory bullae onto

---

[65] "Phylogenesis of the Speech Apparatus," followed in 1958 by a small book under the same title but of much abbreviated content, with emphasis mainly on cultural evolution. In the larger work he wrote that the human head "is the drastic expression of all the adaptive contortions concomitant with the new persistent verti-cal posture in the gravitational field. All the skull floor is crowded, all of the roof is expanded. The oral space is extremely shortened. It seems, in compensation, to be wide and deep."

[66] Du Brul and Laskin, "Preadaptive Potentialities of the Mammalian Skull," p. 117: "The cranium of mammals first takes form from the development of a cartilaginous base ... but ... the base does not continue into a cartilaginous cranial roof in the embryos of higher mammals. The roof is made of membrane bone. This complex finally fuses into a rigid working unit when the cartilage is invaded and replaced by bone. But the cartilaginous base is not merely a memento of phylogenesis. We believe that it has always had potent preadaptive value. It is a firm, temporary but necessary, scaffold for the organs of the head which will permit growth in different rates and directions in differently adapted species. It acts as a template for the final definitive bony form of the skull."

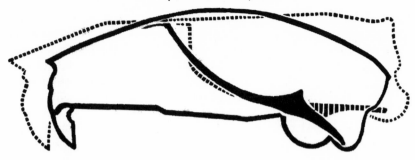

Figure 16–9. Outline of the Experimental Mammalian Skull (*Solid Line*) Superimposed on That of the Normal Skull (*Dashed Line*)

the "fetalization" of the skull of a long-headed animal may thus be produced by artificial means

(From E. L. Du Brul and D. M. Laskin, "Preadaptive Potentialities of the Mammalian Skull: An Experiment in Growth and Form," *American Journal of Anatomy*, CIX [1961], 130.)

the posterior margins of the temperomandibular joint, (5) a shortening of the medial pterygoid plate and (6) a notable increase in the angle formed by the long axes of the auditory bullae."[67]

One of the notable features in the distortion made by removal of the spheno-presphenoid synchondrosis (which, in the rat, involves a series of cartilage plates) is its effect on the base of the skull, which becomes extremely short and concave, and forms a deep hollow ending in a raised rim at the spheno-occipital fusion. "The back of this hollow," the authors observe, "houses the hypophysis (reminiscent of the hypophyseal hollow in primates). The plane of the basiocciput then bends sharply down to simulate a clivus as in man." The loss of basal cartilage, then, hampers the normal expansion of the skull. "However, as the brain still grows a bit, it must bulge out at the cranial roof."[68]

The "fetalization" of the skull of a long-headed animal may thus be produced by artificial means (Fig. 16–9); and what a relatively simple ablation of a controlling factor such as a basal synchondrosis may effect could also be the work of a gene. Indeed, two other experimenters, J. A. Dye and F. S. Kinder, working more than a quarter of a century earlier on endocrine influences on development, had produced almost exactly the same modification of skull shape in young puppies by ablation of the thyroid gland.[69] Thyroid formation and action are under

[67] *Ibid.*, p. 120.
[68] P. 121.
[69] "A Prepotent Factor in the Determination of Skull Shape" (1934).

gene control. Thyroidectomy in dogs three weeks old effected a shortening and incurvature of the base of the skull, essentially like the distortion more recently achieved by Du Brul and Laskin through excision of the anterior synchondrosis in infant rats. Dye and Kinder had, in fact, already proposed, on the strength of other observations on their animals, that the changes induced by thyroidectomy were due to "a disturbed development of the basal cartilage bones."[70]

Since the thyroidectomized pups observed by Dye and Kinder show the effect somewhat more drastically than the rats growing without the anterior synchondrosis, the dog skulls are pictured here (Fig. 16–10). Note the kinking of the basisphenoid, the downward shift of the inion, and especially the bulging of the skull roof and shortening of the face.

Du Brul and Laskin remarked that a similar shortening and bulging of the cranium occurs in calves deformed by the expression of the "short-spine" gene carried by some cattle, which is lethal to the phenotypical offspring after a brief postnatal existence.[71]

To a calf, that grotesque genic deviation is fatal, but in another animal a very similar influence may be perfectly tolerable; some comparable gene, though perhaps quite different in its other actions, evidently proved viable in the phylogeny of the ocean sunfish, *Mola mola*, for it is normal in its heredity today. The entire growth in that species is in harmony with the short spine and huge, shortened head, and the fish occurs in no other form (Fig. 16–11). Perhaps a gradual increase of this trophic expression was possible because the deep body form was already

---

[70] *Ibid.*, pp. 343–44: "Brachycephaly is characteristic for young animals and as age advances the skulls become more and more dolicocephalic.... The picture presented by these basal bones of cretin skulls is then in the direction of retarded growth. This is probably the primary factor, but that it is not the only one is shown by the fact that when cretin and normal animals of approximately the same size are compared, the basal bones of the former are not only as broad relatively, but may actually be broader.

"A second fact which seems to indicate a disproportionate growth following thyroidectomy is found in the forward shift of the foramen magnum, or the backward shift of the nasion and posterior parts of the cranium. Since this is absent in the skulls of younger normal animals, and comparable in age, it is not an indication of an infantile skull or of retarded growth. It would seem that this shift in the relations is determined wholly by normal growth tendencies being distorted by a disturbed development. Restricted growth in these bones, together with a similar disturbed growth in the ethmoid bones which form a rather inflexible base, cramp cranial and brain growth in the anterio-posterior direction.... This cramping results in both lateral and posterior expansion of the cranium, the direction of least resistance, to accommodate the relatively more rapidly developing brain."

[71] "Preadaptive Potentialities of the Mammalian Skull," p. 124.

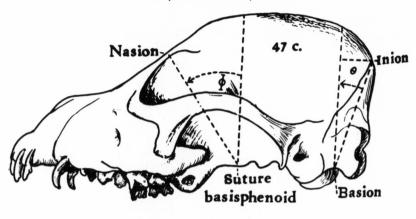

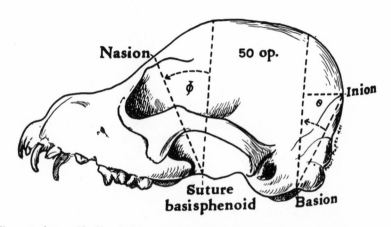

Figure 16–10. Skulls of Pups Thirty-Nine Weeks Old: (*Upper*)
Normal; (*Lower*) Thirty-Six Weeks after Thyroidectomy

the thyroidectomized pups ... show the effect ... drastically

(J. A. Dye and F. S. Kinder, "A Prepotent Factor in the Determination of Skull Shape,"
American Journal of Anatomy, LIV [1934], 342.)

present, as it is in the boxfishes and trunkfishes to which *Mola* is related, so the exaggeration could be accommodated by the rest of the
genome. As a rare occurrence in a generally elongated animal such a
disharmonious gene produces a monster.

The bipedal bearing of man must have met with many fortunate conditions to permit and uphold the ever-increasing difference between his
progeny and that of any other hominoid, instead of initiating a heredi-

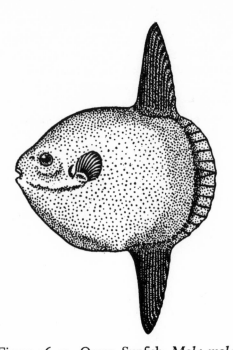

Figure 16–11. Ocean Sunfish, *Mola mola*

*the entire growth in that species is in harmony with the short spine
and huge, shortened head*

(Reprinted by permission of Hill and Wang, a division of Farrar, Straus & Giroux, from A
History of Fishes by J. R. Norman, © M. Norman and P. H. Greenwood, 1963.)

tary line of apes with an anomalous bodily form which shortly would
make them unviable. Every further development that was induced by
the extraordinary posture apparently was at least tolerable by the organism, and, in fact, tended to promote the most important result of
the adaptive change in the skull, which was only just launched in the
australopithecene man-apes: the specialization of the brain. That specialization is often regarded as primarily an increase in the weight of the
brain; such increase it surely entailed,[72] but actually, I think, the crucial
next adaptation was a more subtle, yet more radical one—the gradual
reorganization of its many substructures, and some consequent changes

[72] Cf. Washburn, "The Analysis of Primate Evolution," p. 75: "The lemurs have
bigger brains than the tree shrews, the monkeys than the lemurs, the apes than the
monkeys. With each major advance in primate evolution the brain doubled or even
tripled its size. If the human brain is viewed from this point of view, the remarkable thing about man is that his ancestors went through three major different
locomotor adaptations during the age of mammals and one major reorganization of
the special senses. After each of these the brain at least doubled its size."

[254]

in the relative rates of advance and elaboration of their respective functions. With the crowding of the limbic parts into the lower spaces around the brain stem their trophic potentialities became rather severely restricted; and as every organic structure is in competition with its neighbors, the repression of their growth gave proportionately great opportunity to the unobstructed neopallium to expand and differentiate. Elaborations of the neuropile in the opercular lobes appear to have spread outward during phylogeny and occupied the cortex as they developed; for, in reptiles and perhaps some higher classes, the cortex is still essentially a protective, mainly lipoid covering,[73] but just such a tissue as reaching and expanding axons could easily invade. That is undoubtedly the way the cortex in typical placental mammals has become an integral part of the highest cerebral areas.

In man, where the operculum is particularly favored by anatomical conditions, its cortex seems to have taken the lead in the evolution of his entire central nervous system. The latest-developed mechanisms in a living being are, as Titchener observed, the most active, and in the nervous tissues where electrical and chemical processes are normally of highest intensity they are most ready to attain psychical levels. This leads to a great refinement and quickening of every sort of feeling, peripheral and central, i.e., receptive, somatic, emotive, or of nameless other kinds; and it is in this advance that further changes, facilitated or even motivated by the erect carriage, have fallen in with the paramount change, to support it on its evolutionary course. The most obvious of those auxiliary assets was the freeing of the hands from any involvement with locomotion or bodily support, such as walking on knuckles like the great apes, or clinging to branches while moving or at rest in the trees. The manipulative ability of the human hand has usually been attributed to its long and fully opposable thumb; in fact, that superior, flexible thumb has often been praised as a direct cause of man's ascendancy over all other animals, but Barbour stated that there is a frog, *Pseudis*, which has a fully opposable pollex and is thought to make use of it, too, grasping stems, without becoming an intellectual superfrog.[74] The gene complex which produces the hand-like front foot

[73] Cf. F. Goldby and H. J. Gamble, "The Reptilian Cerebral Hemispheres" (1957).

[74] R. T. Beatty, in *Hearing in Man and Animals* (1932), p. vi, cites Eliot Smith and also Frank Tilney, without exact references, to the effect that the opposable thumb was the real lever of man's evolutionary advances; and Barbour, in *Reptiles and Amphibians*, p. 77, writes: "Professor Shaler [N. S. Shaler] used to say that the development of the opposable thumb by some anthropoid ancestor was probably the most important single step toward the ultimate appearance of man." The idea is old; there are many other expressions of it.

of *Pseudis* does not coincide with an otherwise ready genome to incorporate the manual talent for further ends. Even in much higher animals, the monkeys and apes that have true thumbs, it has not met with all the conditions that would make it a major asset for humanization, although the manipulative skill of some simians is close to that of an untrained human being,[75] and would probably improve if the animal found more uses for it. If an ape could envisage a shelter, a garment or a receptacle it could probably make one; but even under pressure of discomfort, chimpanzees—generally deemed the most "educable" of the pongids—never think of thickening the protective foliage over their heads to make a roof.[76]

What will be an auxiliary advantage to a particular development depends on many coincidences as well as on the fundamental anlagen of an animal stock. The foremost condition for making an animal's paw become a hand was, of course, the fact that it was a primate paw, with a tendency to lengthening phalanges and supple joints (the same suppleness is found in cats' paws, where it does not meet with extraordinary phalangeal growth or any incipient independence of the pollex to make them prehensile; feline forefeet are dominated by their claws, not their phalanges, although cats, like men, may have been good climbers as soon as there were woody trees in their hunting grounds. The slender, parallel metatarsals occur in many insectivores). In an arboreal primate the locomotory work falls largely to the forelimbs, and as these are mainly engaged in it, the animals are apt to reach, hold and carry things with a hind paw rather than a fore paw; and concomitantly, it is the great toe, more than the thumb, that is specialized for such purposes.[77] The hind paw with its hallux may be as prehensile as any front

[75] Schaller, in *The Mountain Gorilla—Ecology and Behavior*, p. 162, writes: "An observation made on a female is typical of the way in which gorillas eat leaves and tender stems: 'She sits, and carefully bends a Rubus runssorensis *branch toward her, holding it between thumb and index finger only; she then bites off and eats the tip of a branch including the young leaves. Next she breaks off another branch tip, using only thumb and index finger.'"*

[76] See Van Lawick-Goodall, *My Friends the Wild Chimpanzees*, pp. 74–75: "To all outward appearances the chimpanzees dislike the rain. At the beginning of a heavy storm they often seek shelter beneath a thick tangle of vegetation or a leaning tree trunk. But once the water drips through their 'roof,' they usually move into the open and sit looking cold and miserable."

[77] Carpenter, in *A Field Study of the Behavior and Social Relations of Howling Monkeys*, p. 28, describes the "hands" of various monkeys: "Spider monkeys have only four fingers (about 5 percent have a rudimentary thumb . . .) which are used as a very adaptable hook, especially effective in the brachiating form of locomotion. The capuchin monkeys use their hands in a human-like way, the thumb being

paw with its pollex, yet it presents an instance of development which does not meet with coincident conditions to further its evolution as an organ of manipulation, because it is not directly exposed to the animal's sight as the front paw is. Bringing objects to the mouth is not as easy with posterior "hands" as with anterior ones; the mouth, under such anatomical conditions, is more likely to be brought to the objects *in situ*. But the Hominidae, predominantly using only their feet for locomotion, had free hands, and came to use them in many other ways than to put food into their mouths.

Whatever the conditions were that promoted human manual dexterity, the greatest role of the hand in our evolution is probably due not so much to its manipulative power as to its gradual specialization as a sense organ. The sensibility of the hand is not only high, but epicritical beyond any animal's tactual sense, except possibly that of the elephant's trunk, which has never, to my knowledge, been really tested, but only estimated and praised.[78] The responsiveness of many creatures' vibrissae is quick, but apparently not epicritical; it seems to indicate contact without further perceptual details. But the human hand is a complex organ in which the distribution of sensory nerves and the extremely refined musculature coincide, as they do in our eyes and ears, to implement perception of form, location, size, weight, penetrability, mobility and many consequent values. Its measured movements and the coordinate orientation of its parts, which permit fingering of objects, make it capable of judging the qualities of surfaces—rough, smooth, varied, patterned—and their characteristic ways of absorbing or reflecting heat,

---

opposable and objects are held in the hand with apparent ease; whereas the hand of the howler monkey functions differently from that of any other primate which I have observed." Yet all these monkeys are about on a par in respect to the things they do.

[78] Maxwell, *Stalking Big Game with a Camera in Equatorial Africa*, pp. 77–78, calls the elephant's trunk "a delicate and sensitive organ, rarely used for rough work," and says that it "serves to warn the animal of danger by its sense of smell and its extremely sensitive power of perception by touch. . . . Doubtless the lower part of the trunk, and particularly the tip of the muzzle, is the most important part of their superficial anatomy with regard to the guiding sense of touch. . . ."

Maxwell's opinion is corroborated by the higher scientific authority of F. Wood Jones, who said, in *The Principles of Anatomy, As Seen in the Hand* (1942; 1st ed., 1920), pp. 327–38: "The great fifth nerve [trigeminal] area of the snout is the tactile field upon which the lower mammal relies for its information. . . .

". . . When a mammal becomes protected by the thickness of its skin, the skin of its muzzle still remains sensitive. The snout of the tapir is that animal's great tactile organ, and the trunk of the elephant might almost be regarded as an extreme specialization of the same thing."

which give us information of temperature contrasts and gradients. The two hands working together can negotiate a single complex impression, as J. J. Gibson has remarked.[79] Also, all the sensory reactions of the skin and underlying structures are engaged together in the tactual perception of substances: feelings of pressure and release of pressure, of warm and cold impingements, pin-pointed encounters with resistance, oiliness, wetness, and mixtures like sliminess, hairiness, stickiness. The result is that we have not only a report of surfaces and edges, but of volume imbued with multimodal, often nameless qualities.

There have been few studies of the tactual sense (or better, senses), and Gibson, in the article mentioned above, suggests as the likeliest reason that it was difficult to range this mode of sensibility with the other distinct modes which have their circumscribed special organs.[80] The two earlier psychologists who did give it due attention, David Katz[81] and Géza Révész,[82] were led to it largely through their studies of perception by blind persons, in whom the tactual mode is, of course, most highly developed. Katz, in consequence, centered his interest largely on the detection of form for purposes of practical judgment, identification and comparison of objects, and such general information as seeing persons usually gather by vision. Révész, writing some fifteen years later and having Katz's work to draw upon, came to the interesting realization that the world built up by tactual means, which Katz conceived as a world of tactual forms, was not filled with completely given or imagined forms, analogous to visual shapes, at all. Distances and directions, terrain and the location of things are its framework, but "things" are not simple sensuous presentations in any mode.[83] They are

---

[79] In "Observations on Active Touch" (1962), p. 481: "When feeling a single object with two fingers, only one object is perceived although two separated cutaneous pressures occur. The separate 'local signs' are not noticed. . . . The unitary perception occurs when all five fingers are applied to an object, and even when two separate hands are applied to the object. In fact, 10 different digital pressures all at the same time yield a wholly unified experience."

[80] Ibid., pp. 477–78.

[81] "Der Aufbau der Tastwelt" (1925).

[82] Die Menschliche Hand (1944; Dutch orig., 1941).

[83] See ibid., pp. 30–31: "Für die Hand ist die individuelle Beschaffenheit eines Gegenstandes meistens gleichgültig, und zwar aus pragmatischen Gründen: dem Tastsinn bereitet es nämlich grosse Schwierigkeiten, Einzelheiten zu einer Individualität, zu einem einheitlichen Formeindruck zusammenzuschliessen. Der haptische Sinn besitzt nicht die Fähigkeit zur anschaulichen Vereinheitlichung des Mannigfaltigen. . . .

"Unsere Tastfunktion wird nicht von dem Antrieb beherrscht, Formgebilde als solche zu betrachten, ein eindeutiges Bild von den räumlichen Formen zu gewinnen, geschweige denn Formen autonom zu schaffen. . . .

functionally known and identified, often by a cursory touch, as by a glance; and although they are bearers of aesthetic qualities, they do not immediately present artistic values. Perhaps this lack of artistic significance made both Katz and Révész overlook the cultural importance of the aesthetic perceptiveness of the hand, and pass over it rather lightly,[84] though it certainly has had its own unnoticed evolution: the reception of aesthetic qualities, purely tactual pleasure as of cool or warm waters, living grass, leaves and petals, fur or human hair, and, contrariwise, repellent impingements of crude, grimy or decayed matter, unhealthy skin, contacts which may invoke disgust and even downright horror. That seems to be a human response; apes will pick up the filthiest items.[85] Aesthetic tactual values have importance for man because his experiences of them readily take on metaphorical significance; expressions for "hard," "soft," "liquid," "rough," etc., seem to have entered into his most peculiar achievement, speech, from their earliest uses to designate more than tactual qualities.[86] Like all his aesthetic perceptions they meet and merge with emotional elements which are not current sexual, maternal or hostile feelings toward other beings, but modes of consciousness, felt attitudes, which motivate the earliest artistic expressions, dance and vocalization. But that is anticipating a theme of a later chapter.

Animals, meanwhile, derive direct emotional stimulation from touch, almost entirely from the touch of other creatures, which is a part of their actual involvement with each other. Such physical contact is found in the social insects, for instance, bees, which cling to a "dancing" returned forager and seem to pick up the impetus of her act, that presently sends the recipients out to perform its next cycle;[87] or the

---

"Die geringe Bedeutung der Form im Haptischen zeigt sich nirgends so deutlich wie bei Blinden ... Wer Blindeninstitute öfters besucht, dem kann nicht entgehen, wie wenig Interesse Blinde für die Form der Dinge ihrer Umgebung an den Tag legen. Keinem Blinden wird es z. B. einfallen, Gegenstände seiner Umgebung zu betasten. Er wird sich mit einer allgemeinen Orientierung über die ihn umgebenden Objekte zufrieden geben."

[84] Katz makes just one mention of "comfortable" warmth (*Der Aufbau der Tastwelt*, p. 163).

[85] E. W. Menzel, Jr., personal communication.

[86] The intimate connection of the hand with the brain is illustrated by a peculiar correlation which William Montagna pointed out in his detailed and comprehensive book, *The Structure and Function of Skin* (1962), pp. 10–11: "Mentally deficient, epileptic, and insane persons often show marked deviations from normal trends in the patterns of dermatoglyphics.... Perhaps dermatoglyphics are affected by the same agencies which impair the nervous system...."

[87] The behavior of *Apis mellifera* in receiving a returned bee has been observed hundreds of times since Karl von Frisch discovered the "dance" and its effect on

bodily touch may be effected by the mouth, as ants apply saliva to their queen and to their co-workers.[88] Maternal licking of the young is seen in most terrestrial mammals, and in gregarious ones such as wild dogs is carried over to mutual approach of adults in meeting.[89] Where contact involves the use of front paws, as in the grooming activities of monkeys, apes and to some extent lemurs, it does not appear to further cutaneous aesthesis so much as manipulative control, largely implemented by vision. Physical intimacy is sought with many parts of the body; and though apes may reach out a hand to touch each other, it is the palm or the back of the hand, not the fingertips, that makes the contact.[90]

The increase of perceptiveness in the hand of *Homo* is only a part and an instance of his high development in sensibility, especially in articulated, usable sensibility. What makes his peripheral receptions so usable is that most of his heightened nervous functions involve some centers in his forebrain, instead of going more simply through the lower centers of the spinal cord to issue in muscular responses. The cord, in man, is small compared to the brain, and many of its functions seem to have been crowded upward into the brain, just as some work of the human limbic lobes has been gradually taken over by the operculum and its hyperactive cortex.[91] This crowding in the vertebral canal, too,

---

other worker bees. The best factual descriptions are probably his, in *The Dancing Bees: An Account of the Life and Senses of the Honey Bee* (1955; German orig., 1927) and the somewhat less popular, more scientific, *Bees: Their Vision, Chemical Senses, and Language.* His interpretations of the "dance," however, have sometimes been challenged, especially by Adrian M. Wenner, who repeated many of Von Frisch's experiments. See his "Honey Bees: Do They Use the Distance Information Contained in Their Dance Maneuver?" (1967); also A. M. Wenner, P. H. Wells and F. J. Rohif, "An Analysis of the Waggle Dance and Recruitment in Honey Bees" (1967). Cf. D. L. Johnson, "Honey Bees: Do They Use the Direction Information Contained in Their Dance Maneuver?" (1967).

[88] See N. A. Weber, in "Fungus-Growing Ants" (1966), p. 601: "The ants, in grooming, apply saliva copiously enough to keep the queen glistening, and much of the time the workers are grooming one another." Cf. Allen, "Observations on Honeybees Attending Their Queen," Chapter 15 above, p. 206, n. 105.

[89] Wolfdietrich Kühme describes their posture and wagging as they meet for the daily hunt, and says in conclusion: "Der solcherart Begrüsste nahm eine ähnliche Haltung an, und dann leckte man sich gegenseitig die Schnauzen, besonders die Mundwinkel" ("Freilandstudien zur Soziologie des Hyänenhundes," p. 513).

[90] Van Lawick-Goodall, in "Chimpanzees of the Gombe Stream Reserve," p. 471, says: "The most common greeting occurs when one chimpanzee goes up to another and reaches out to touch it with the flat of the hand or with the back of the slightly flexed fingers."

[91] See Weidenreich, "The Trend of Human Evolution," p. 232: "Man has the

looks like an effect of the upright posture, via the exaggeration of the double curvature which is incipient in most primates,[92] but very conspicuous in man. Furthermore, the fact that in all the higher primates—monkeys, apes and men—the eyes are forward-directed is another chance asset for the enhancement of sensibility, for such eyes can be focused together on an object, and for near vision binocular focus certainly yields greater precision than any other method of fixating objects. Apes make full use of this talent; if they can't read, the trouble is not with their eyes. We share most of our blessings with many animals, but with none of them the whole complex that has led to humanization.

This most remarkable product of evolutionary coincidence, the human brain, is, however, not without its dangers. The cerebral activity threatens to overgrow the basic functional patterns of animal life and cause the species to break up on the insuperable heights of its own specialization. This brings us back to Gehlen's *Der Mensch*, as promised earlier in the present chapter (p. 216). For the most notable theme of that book is not the most controversial one, the theory of "fetalization" which its author took over from Schindewolf and Bolk, but the difference between man's mentality and that of any beast, however highly developed along animalian lines: the production and use of symbols and their paramount value in all our further mental functions, their distinction from the alleged "signals" of animal communication and from symptoms or other indicators, and the subjective-objective dialectic pattern that builds up "experience" of the human sort (that topic has not been touched upon yet, but will be treated in a later chapter of this part). Gehlen appreciates the uniqueness of man's mentality far better than the psychologists and ethologists who strain to

---

smallest spinal cord in proportion to the size of the brain. In the course of evolution the human brain has 'swallowed' the spinal cord, that is, it took over the functions of the latter more and more, bringing the reflex actions under the control of consciousness and will."

[92] See Schultz, "The Specializations of Man and His Place among the Catarrhine Primates," p. 51: "The first and decisive specialization of man—erect, bipedal locomotion—would never have been possible, had it not been prepared for by his remote progenitor, who had endowed the apes as well with at least the potentiality of the erect position. This preparedness appears in all higher primates during growth and in varying degrees in form of the forward shift of the spine toward the center of the chest, the backward shift of the shoulders, the bending of the spine at its juncture with the hip bones, and other initial, anatomical and mechanical requirements for holding the trunk erect. It seems not at all unlikely that some of these preparations for the upright posture had become more pronounced in a few fossil anthropoids than in any of the surviving forms of apes."

reduce its activities to instinctive reactions of the same type as those of non-human creatures. And he proposed that this unique character (which he would not admit to be a specialization) arose from the extreme receptiveness of the human brain, which consequently is overwhelmed with stimuli and overloaded with perceptions,[93] so its possessor has had to lighten his burden by finishing many impulses not physically as direct responses, but in the brain, in mental acts. This is a defense against unbearable overstimulation; "*Entlastung*," Gehlen calls it.[94] The eschewed behavioral consummation of a started impulse is replaced by the formation of an image in the visual system, especially in the cortical part, or by some comparable, purely sensory event; or perhaps by a momentary tensing of muscles and a fleeting fantasy of aggressive response, which stands in for the unperformed act.

But the "*Entlastung*," having introduced a new activity, goes further in its effects than to take up the surplus of impressions; the new activity in its turn encourages the agent to observe things that play no direct part in his current business, just to make images of them, probably without knowing that he is doing so. This practice widens his ambient inestimably far beyond any other creature's.

Several psychologists and neurologists have arrived at the same hypothesis, apparently by independent approaches. The investigation of physiological processes underlying the covert acts of dreaming—producing entirely subjective, intraorganic perceptions, hallucinating situations and events—has led to the problem of what might motivate such deceptive experiences occurring in sleep, and suggested the theory that dreaming is a cerebral completion of acts which could not be overtly consummated. Ian Oswald has remarked that image formation is apt to occur spontaneously in moments of hesitation or frustration while facing a new task, and also that it bears some resemblance to the "displacement activities" frequently seen in hard-pressed animals;[95] a "displace-

[93] S. J. Bartley, T. M. Nelson and J. E. Ranney, in "The Sensory Parallel of the Reorganization Period in the Cortical Response in Intermittent Retinal Stimulation" (1961), report on experimental evidence that human and animal brains may receive more stimuli than they can transfer to the effectors to finish in responses. On p. 145 they write: "The fact that the optic pathway can resolve certain differences between the timing of elements in an extended (repetitive) photic presentation while these are not resolved in full detail in sensory end results is to be taken [to mean] that the peripheral apparatus of an organism may provide the central mechanism with material which it cannot fully 'handle' " (pp. 145–46).

[94] *Der Mensch*, p. 20 and *passim*.

[95] *Sleeping and Waking. Physiology and Psychology* (1962), p. 84: "A waking person faced with a new task or problem will attend to information passed to the brain from his sense organs in order to utilize potentially valuable information. . . .

ment activity" is a makeshift completion of a frustrated act which has got under way—however slightly—and vainly presses for normal consummation. It certainly is but a step from this concept of image production to the interpretation of our vivid, multitudinous dream images and fantasies as cerebral endings of started but blocked responses to excessive outer and inner stimuli. Another investigator took that step, and has written (in the currently fashionable computer jargon): "the data-processing capacity of the central nervous system is insufficient to allow complete on line processing of input data with respect to its more remote implications, while at the same time carrying out the activity and decision making required by waking activity. In the absence of sleep, recorded unprocessed data would thus accumulate in sufficient amounts to interfere with the normal activity and decision making of the waking state, and this interference would be experienced as a need to sleep."[96]

In weighing this theory of vicarious completion of impulses which are constantly elicited by excessive sensory and central stimulation, one may wonder how so great a novelty as a fictitious image could emerge, even in the most specialized brain, without more broadly based functional preparation. The fact is, however, that the imaginative act is not unprepared, but that most if not all its elements are presented at lower levels of nervous activity. Other than human brains seem to be affected by stimuli of which only some terminate in efferent organs, while many serve to sensitize or, on the contrary, to lower the receptiveness of the brain, and change the "set" or "mood" of the responding organism rather than to elicit overt reactions.[97] We cannot know what experi-

---

Suppose, when faced with a difficult task, his sense organs did not pass useful information to him. . . . This is the situation . . . in which, when there is difficulty and a need for sensory data, imagery appears." And further, p 85: "We may note, in passing, that vivid, irrelevant images have the character of 'displacement activity' according to the definition of Armstrong (1950). These activities are said to appear in animals when, as a 'consequence of tension,' there is 'deflexion of energy' into some irrelevant activity."

Werner Wolf, "Der archaische Sprachorganismus" (1929), p. 120, quotes Paul Schilder ("Über die Gedankenentwicklung") as saying, "Bilder treten vielfach erst dann auf, wenn der Denkprozess stockt und wenn die Gedankenentwicklung gehemmt ist."

[96] Arthur Shapiro, "Dreaming and the Physiology of Sleep. A Critical Review of Some Empirical Data and a Proposal for a Theoretical Model of Sleep and Dreaming" (1967), p. 74.

[97] In an interesting symposium paper, "Quantitative Messung von Stimmungen im Verhalten der Fische" (1950), p. 143, Erich von Holst reports: "die Koordinationsforschung, die Elektrophysiologie des Zentralnervensystems und vor allem die

mental animals perceive or otherwise feel, but in ourselves we can test many indirect effects of stimulations, sensuous yet centrally produced, as, for instance, a red after-image where no red stimulus object is given, but a green one was presented some seconds ago; a fully shaped negative image and its positive counterpart usually alternate on a white or grayish surface actually confronted, until both fade away. This alternation is a perceptible phase of a retinal activity. So far, the phenomenon still bespeaks a peripheral influence within a relatively short and easily measurable time span. But some persons tend to produce purely fictive original percepts, either involuntarily (as in dream) or by volition, which are followed by after-images, just as externally induced object visions are.[98] This fact points to a cerebrally started neural activity involving the visual system and actually producing a retinal image, a real percept, though not of an external thing or scene. Such evidence certainly indicates a neural mechanism of visual imagination, and suggests its derivation from the common optic structures of primate brains.

The underlying unity of the central nervous organ, the brain, could be expected to carry the function of imagination into other sensory systems, too, and finally establish it apart from any special sense as a cortical faculty in its own right. Here it becomes the groundwork of symbolization, conception, and all other peculiarly human forms of cerebration; the evolution of mind is on its way.

---

neuere Verhaltensforschung selbst haben gezeigt, dass nur ein Teil der Abläufe im Zentrum als motorische Impulse wieder nach aussen gelangt, während andere Vorgänge das Organ nur irgendwie umstimmen, d. h. die *Reaktsionsnorm* des Nervensystems ändern." Some of the central acts Von Holst elicited by putting his fish into various controlled situations were shared by all the animals of his seven tested species, but he managed to devise some experiments in which the fish performed higher functions than balance and photic orientation, and there they exhibited considerable individuality (see p. 160).

[98] See Ian Oswald, "After-Images from Retina and Brain" (1957): "One source of evidence relating to AIs [after-images] of purely central origin derives from the occurrence of AIs from hallucinated stimuli. This is a possibility that seems often to have been regarded as not quite respectable.

"Gruithuisen (1812) described how, on awakening from sleep, he experienced AIs from the visual phenomena of dreams. He experienced negative AIs ('umgekehrte Täuschungen') over a hundred times. He once had a positive AI. Dreaming of a lightning flash, he awoke, and observed an AI of 'feeble light' which gradually faded to become darker than the surroundings. . . .

"Alexander (1904) was to describe similar AIs of dreams." Oswald reports, further, several cases from his own investigations.

17

Symbols and the Evolution of Mind

Der Gang des Geistes geht nicht gerade aus.
—W. Harburger

THE Hominidae, whatever their beginnings may have been, have certainly undergone a tremendous specialization of the central nervous system which culminates in the forebrain, and above all the cortices of the cerebral hemispheres. To effect such a high, steady, ever-accelerating development requires constant activation, which may come from one major source or from a play of many influences that mount up to a round of stimulations. Both types of energizing support may be expected in such a reception center as the brain, which has its outposts in the special sense organs, open to chance excitations, and its own rhythmic processes furnishing periodic, if microscopic, stimuli.

The impingement of any act on another—most obviously, the impingement of peripheral acts, sensory receptions, on intraorganic acts, but also that of centrally motivated somatic or cerebral acts on each other and on peripheral ones—effects a change in the situation of the act impinged upon; and a change of situation is what motivates a new impulse. This may reinforce the original impulse to the affected act, facilitating and enhancing its expression, or it may alter, complicate or even block its development. Conversely, every change, such as an increase or acceleration of an activity, requires a change in some circumstantial condition. Several investigators have, in fact, discovered that processes which were deemed continuous are actually upheld by long series of separate stimulations. In order that separate, successive impulses may be similar enough to be repetitive and cumulative, there have to be other acts interspersed throughout the succession, or else a cadential phase of each response must occur to make space for each subsequent impulse in a series of renewals. A good example of the former alternative is the pattern of attentiveness which, according to

D. O. Hebb, underlies the apparently steady perception of a simple shape, such as a solid-colored triangle on a contrasting homogeneous

background. In such a perceptual act, vision centers successively on the three differently oriented angles, a, b, and c. The gaze may go to and fro among them in varying order, so the dynamic pattern is something like a–b–a–c–b–c–a–c. "This 'ideational' series with its motor elements," says Dr. Hebb, "I propose to call a 'phase sequence.' "[1] After a more detailed analysis of supposedly steady gazing, he concludes that "perception of a simple pattern is not a single lasting state, terminated by an external event, but a sequence of states or processes," and subsequently: "The stability of perception is not in a single persistent pattern but in the tendency of the phases of an irregular cycle to recur at short intervals. . . . the train of thought is also a 'phase sequence' of the same kind, but more extended, consisting of a series of phase cycles."[2]

All sorts of quick, ignored impressions—including the well-known momentary alternations of foreground and background—intervene in constantly rebuilding the fixated shape, which emerges from their association. Hebb has designated that integral total shape by "t," the complex that is reiterated in recurrent acts of form perception spaced out by arbitrarily varied, intervening sensory events, so that his final representation of the phase sequence is something like "a–b–t–a–c–t–c–t–b."[3] Such internal reactivation of long, complex processes by the influence of their own minute elements on each other is a basic bodily procedure which probably occurs in all vertebrates, and in our own experience is unfelt, either as a continuous act or a complex sequential one.

This is one of the above-mentioned alternative ways of sustaining a so-called steady state, which is really not a changeless state but a slowly advancing act: by frequent, though irregular, recurrence of an effective stimulus in a phase sequence of related acts. The other possible pattern of renewing the impulse to a protracted activity is given by the tendency of directly repeated acts to set up a rhythm by their own characteristic rise and fall; there is some evidence that brain processes which are not reactivated by sensory impingements may be supported by

[1] *The Organization of Behavior*, pp. 97–98.
[2] Pp. 99–100.
[3] P. 98.

virtue of this inherent, essentially formal property of elementary acts. Hebb, in a passage quoted above, states that trains of thought have the same structure as sustained perception; but an incidental finding made during a differently oriented study, by a different neurologist, suggests a simpler organic mechanism for such covert acts of (perhaps peculiarly human) cerebration. Several decades ago, A. G. Bills found what he considered primarily as a principle of mental fatigue and error, a fairly (though not wholly) regular pattern of lapses in neural response, which makes the phenomenon of sustained thought appear more like a series of acts than like one continuous process. He himself remarked that other investigators had seen in this finding an explanation of the greater endurance in mental work than in muscular work, because "the subject gets frequent short rests which give sufficient opportunity for recovery from accumulated fatigue, and thus cover up or stave off decrement."[4] His principle of fatigue seems, indeed, to be an internal source of mental sustainment. Having failed in attempts to correlate it with larger bodily rhythms, he considered it related to refractoriness, an inherent characteristic of neural processes.[5] One would naturally expect to relate it directly to the familiar attention rhythms, as Hebb did, but its wave form is different;[6] this may reflect the fact that while the attention rhythms depend on peripheral stimuli and vary with the sensory modalities involved, the rhythms of thought seem to be determined by central action.[7]

Evidently the brain has its own central patterns of activity as well as those stemming from its peripheral contacts with the extraorganic world. As for the latter, the experimental use of "sensory deprivation" has shown with considerable detail and certainty that a constant welter

[4] "Blocking: A New Principle of Mental Fatigue" (1931), p. 230.

[5] P. 244: "as to the interpretation of the neural mechanism involved, it appears to be related to the neurological phenomenon of refractory phase. However, since the refractory period does not follow every response but rather occurs after every group of twenty or so responses, it seems necessary to associate it with cumulative rather than simple refraction."

[6] *Ibid.*, p. 243: "The responses between the blocks tend to bunch toward the center, so that a regular effect of rarefaction and condensation, alternating, is produced; the wave is scalloped in formation, rather than sinusoidal."

[7] *Ibid.*, p. 245: "the relation of the present phenomenon to the historical attention wave is doubtful. In the first place, the time relations are quite different. In the second place, the traditional attention wave turned out to be a fluctuation in the clearness of minimal stimuli, and differed in terms of the sense modality investigated and the stimulus, and had a very doubtful relation to any central factor. In fact, it seemed to be conditioned by factors peculiar to the peripheral nature of the sense organ."

of changing, adventitious perceptual acts supports the unity and flow of waking consciousness.[8] But what of the sleeping brain's activity? The sensory barrage of stimuli does not reach it; its current stimulation must come from intraorganic sources. These are not easy to observe, even with electroencephalography and implanted electrodes. But in recent years more direct behavioral studies of sleep, carried out essentially on human subjects but also on animals, have furnished observations at least on the highest levels of brain activity in sleep, which in man is dreaming.

The most notable phenomenon discovered early in the systematic study of sleep was the occurrence of rapid eye movements (so commonly referred to as "REMs" that this abbreviation is really necessary to remember) for more or less protracted periods during sleep, which generally but not exactly coincide with periods of dreaming.[9] The first interpretation of this activity was, of course, that the dreamer was scanning the scene of his illusions; but the nature of the saccadic movements is not that of waking eyes watching any kind of event and, moreover, the movements are normally preceded by a slow, rhythmic rolling of the eyeballs. Several interesting coordinations of REM periods ("REMPs") with subjective experiences of dream have, however, been experimentally established, making the existence of some direct or indirect relation unquestionable.

Yet the proposed direct relation of the spectacular eye movements as following the hallucinatory events in the dream[10] meets with many

---

[8] The newest compendium of research work in this field is *Sensory Deprivation: Fifteen Years of Research* (1969), edited by John P. Zubek.

[9] W. C. Dement's long and detailed "An Essay on Dreams: The Role of Physiology in Understanding Their Nature" (1955) is one of the most exhaustive and sober reports on these studies. See esp. pp. 152–53: "Many aspects of human physiology have been examined during sleep, but often with the sole objective of making a simple comparison with the waking state. . . . The limited scope of such endeavors tended to reinforce the characterization of sleep as a single, uniform state. In recent years, however, research interest has shifted to focus upon variability *within* the sleep period. The most dramatic result of this shift of interest has been the elucidation of the contrast between the physiology of the rapid eye movement period and the remainder of sleep."

[10] In his "An Essay on Dreams" Dement proposes this hypothesis, and supports it with some EEG records, from which he concludes that "the sleeping human moves his eyes to watch or scan the hallucinatory dream images more or less as he would if he were really seeing them in the waking state" (p. 173). And somewhat later (p. 180): "The conclusion that rapid eye movements are meaningfully related to the hallucinatory dream events as opposed to being a random motor discharge is inescapable." I do not find it so, since the two alternatives by no means exhaust the

theoretical difficulties. In the first place, highly visual dreaming does occur to some extent without REMs, and non-visual dreams of situation —fears of things not present, expectancies, messages, etc.—may occur with REM accompaniment;[11] and second, only a few actual visual experiences, such as watching a tennis game, could evoke such oscillations of the eyeballs. Finally, also there is the slow rolling of the eyes which usually precedes the more rapid phase and sometimes underlies it,[12] and corresponds to no acts of watching movements or scanning a scene in waking life.[13]

---

possible explanations. He had previously declared this theory in a brief report, "The Effect of Dream Deprivation" (1960), and, in collaboration with E. A. Wolpert, in "The Relation of Eye Movements, Body Motility, and External Stimuli to Dream Content" (1958).

Several investigators have rejected this view, not only because the alleged parallel of the eye movement record and the dream events is unconvincing, but because an oculomotor pursuit of motions seems unlikely. Ian Oswald, in *Sleeping and Waking*, p. 131, wrote: "An image constructed to cover a large part of the visual field covers that *field* and *not real space*, so that if the eyes turn to the left, the left-hand side of an image is still on the left-hand side of the visual field and is still not 'fixated' by the fovea. So why should the eyes move if there is no external frame of reference? . . . movement of the eyeballs would be irrelevant, for they could not alter the position of something within the visual field of the fantasy world." There have been other critics and criticisms.

[11] Arthur Shapiro ("Dreaming and the Physiology of Sleep. A Critical Review of Some Empirical Data and a Proposal for a Theoretical Model of Sleep and Dreaming," p. 58), speaking of the early (1953) studies by Sanctis and Neyroz on relative depth of sleep, says that "even after REM period awakenings, many of these reports failed to show much of the vividness, bizarreness, and absence of control by the subject usually considered to be characteristic of dreaming. On the other hand, these dream-like characteristics were occasionally present in reports obtained after NREM awakenings."

[12] Dement, "An Essay on Dreams," p. 152: "At frequent intervals throughout the night, slow swings of the eyeballs that are mainly horizontal and often asynchronous may be observed. They are most prominent at the sleep onset, at which time their pendular quality results in a recording that resembles a sine wave with a period of 2 to 4 seconds." See also Oswald, *Sleeping and Waking*, pp. 128–29.

[13] Shapiro, "Dreaming and the Physiology of Sleep," p. 62, makes the cogent remark that "it is difficult to imagine what kind of visual activity would require rapid, darting eye-movements superimposed on slow rolling ones." Oswald, too (*Sleeping and Waking*, p. 134), says: "One may obtain records of the eyeballs twisting violently hither and thither without a break for more than a minute. . . . it is difficult to conceive of any life experiences which would call for such furious activity other than on very rare occasions whereas such experiences would have to be fairly common in dreams."

See also W. Malgaud, *De l'action à la pensée* (1935), pp. 79–80, on non-visual dreams: "Nous voudrions signaler en particulier un type de rêve logique, fréquent

A more fateful stumbling block to acceptance of the picture-scanning interpretation of the eye movements peculiar to sleep is that they are found in newborn infants, both human and animal, including kittens before their eyes have opened,[14] and even fetuses still *in utero*.[15] Such young beings could hardly be looking at visual images. Naturally, serious investigators have sought other explanations of the phenomenon, and of the fact that it is more prevalent in neonates than in older infants, and, indeed, diminishes with advancing age throughout life. H. P. Roffwarg, J. N. Muzio and W. C. Dement, in a valuable article, "Ontogenetic Development of the Human Sleep-Dream Cycle" (1966), have made several suggestions, one of which is that the high REM activity functions as a preparation for behavioral acts which are to develop later.[16] But that is incidental; first of all, it has effects within the sleeping brain, not primarily (if at all) in the visual system. The fact that the abrogation or prevention of REMs seems to cause no disturbance of vision or eye mobility but great changes in behavior and especially emotional response suggests that their influence is primarily on brain activities other than visual use of the eyes. Dement, in "An Essay on Dreams," gives a succinct account of M. Jouvet's experiments on cats, in which "the destruction of a circumscribed area in the pons

---

chez nous personellement qui ecrivons ces lignes. Notre rêve prend souvent la forme d'une conversation et d'une discussion. Or, les arguments originaux nous sont fournis par notre interlocuteur. Alors que dans la vie, ... nous prévoyons le plus souvent la réponse, notre rêve nous prête à nous-mêmes le rôle du personnage à quia. Cette fois, plus de doute, le rêve se meut dans notre moi rationnel."

[14] Dement, in "An Essay on Dreams" p. 152, states that "REMPs and associated EEG changes are present at all age levels in the human from birth to senescence." Also Shapiro, "Dreaming and the Physiology of Sleep," p. 70: "Roffwarg *et al.* called attention to the paradoxical finding that newborn full term and premature infants spend their maximum percentage of sleep time in REM sleep at a time of their lives when they have not yet been able to fixate or follow an external moving object. Fishbein *et al.* have also demonstrated that newborn kittens experience REM sleep before their eyes have even been open."

[15] See L. Astic and D. Jouvet-Mounier, "Mise en evidence du sommeil paradoxal *in utero* chez le cobaye" (1969). The experimenters conclude that in the guinea pig, which has a gestation period of sixty-eight days, periods of REM and "paradoxical sleep" are detectable from the fifty-first intrauterine day.

[16] This idea has been enthusiastically taken up by Shapiro ("Dreaming and the Physiology of Sleep," pp. 70–71), who treats it as their main explanation: the fetal eye movements serve as oculomotor practice. But future usefulness cannot motivate an activity; it is present functional value that encourages growth and development; and once the eyes are in use and functioning smoothly, why should purely preparatory REMs continue at all?

(brain-stem nucleus pontis caudalis) led to a complete elimination of the REM phase of sleep in an otherwise normal animal. However, after the operation, a series of remarkable changes in behavior took place. On about the fourth post-operative day, occurring periodically 2 or 3 times an hour, the cats would suddenly stare fixedly in front of them with their heads raised and their pupils dilated. Then they would begin to hit at an imaginary object with their paws. By the sixth to eighth post-operative day, the animals had become perpetually agitated and restless with their heads always held up. They moved their feet continually as if standing on a hot surface. There was a progressive increase in heart rate from 100 beats per minute on the first post-operative day to . . . 210 on the 12th day. Finally, some of the animals showed a great increase in eating and drinking behavior.

"In some cats, there was a reappearance of the REM phase of sleep after a varying number of days, probably because the lesion was incomplete. If this occurred, all the aforementioned changes in behavior rapidly disappeared. However, Jouvet reports that the cats in which REM recovery did not take place died in a state that seemed to resemble acute manic delirium."[17]

Inability to scan a dream image would hardly have the horrible and fatal effects shown in Jouvet's cats. The most important advance made by Roffwarg *et al.* in their paper is their quite definite treatment of rapid eye movements not as an index to perceptual acts, but as an independent process with its own dynamic pattern, probably an elementary cerebral function. The influence of REMs on dreaming may be general rather than specific; they may be periodically—not always, nor always concomitantly—necessary for the occurrence of dreaming and perhaps other brain activities. They may constitute a homeostatic mechanism that has allowed animal development to take a course which would not have been possible without such activation: the steady increase and concentration of acts in the nervous organ leading to a high articulation of feeling.

The occurrence of a psychical phase seems to require an advanced development of the act which culminates in that phase, but what is an "advanced" act may be relative to the rate of evolutionary progress of the species. Many years ago, when psychologists were still speculating on the nature of consciousness, E. B. Titchener proposed the theory that any phylogenetically "young" action, behavioral or even somatic,

---

[17] Pp. 241–42. Cf. M. Jouvet, "Étude de la dualité des états du sommeil et des mécanismes de la phase paradoxale" (1965).

is felt by the performing organism.[18] The notion of "consciousness" as something added to mechanical acts which makes them conscious was a metaphysical assumption implicit in the language of psychology at the time Titchener wrote; but allowing for that outdated vocabulary, his proposal fits the conception of life as a vast system of events whose fundamental units are not atomic, ultimate constituents, but are themselves highly structured forms of organic action, so what is primitive in terms of acts is not so at all in terms of the physical sciences; the boundary between organic chemistry and life is fluctuant and imprecise.[19] Yet once we are certainly in the biological realm, the idea that in the course of phylogeny the line of behavioral advance is the line where activities are differentiated and intensified to the point of having psychical aspects (perhaps faint and momentary in simple lives) sets up a possible structure for the evolution of feeling.

We do not know where feeling begins; let us assume, then, as a hypothesis, that it begins with behavior. But where behavior begins is another moot question. Titchener held that unconscious acts such as digestion, changes of pupil size, or galvanic skin responses had originated in behavioral acts which were felt and, he thought, voluntary.[20]

[18] A *Textbook of Psychology* (1911), pp. 451–52: "What, then, was the character of the earliest organic movements? There are two answers in current psychology and biology. The first is that consciousness is as old as animal life, and that the first movements of the first organisms were conscious movements. This is the answer which the author accepts. The other is that consciousness appeared later in life, and that the earliest movements were accordingly unconscious movements, of the nature of the physiological reflex.

"It is very important that the issues here involved be correctly understood. The alternatives are: movement with consciousness, movement without consciousness. They are not ... conscious action, mechanical reflex. All actions, biologically regarded, are 'mechanical'; all, that is, may by hypothesis be explained (and probably will, some day, be explained) in physico-chemical terms. The antithesis of the conscious is not the mechanical, but the unconscious action. . . .

"The author, then, believes, with Wundt and Ward and Cope, that the earliest movements were conscious movements, and that all the unconscious movements of the human organism, even the automatic movements of heart and intestines, are descendants of past conscious movements."

[19] Cf. above, Vol. I, pp. 316 ff.

[20] Pp. 451–52: "we can all arrest our breathing, but some of us can do much more,—modify heartbeat, expand or contract the pupil, quicken or slow the peristaltic movements. This state of things is intelligible if we interpret it as a return to a previous state, akin to the conscious direction of a bicycle, or the conscious control of movement in swimming; it is not easy to explain, if we regard the reflexes as prior to consciousness." And below: "the primary resemble the secondary reflexes in their character as movements; they are definite, cleancut, precise. But if this character comes in the one case with lapse of consciousness, it may have come by the same road in the other."

Whether they were voluntary may be questioned, but that somatic acts we normally do not feel were felt in early epochs of our ancestry is certainly possible; at some time they probably were the highest activities of the archaic creatures. Even today, watching lower animals such as frogs, turtles or crayfish, which sit still for hours after a feeding, one may wonder whether they are not sensuously engaged in digestion.

When the species progresses to more elaborate functions, particularly by the evolution of special sense organs, those new functions arise in the context of the older ones which have settled into such perfectly habitual patterns that they are no longer felt, and largely no longer amenable to feeling by any concentration of attention. The total activity of the matrix has been raised to a higher level, so that the variable acts of seeking and meeting food, seizing, eating, maybe rejecting things, as well as many responses to other changes in external conditions, are now the typical felt events of the animal. Inwardly, the fluctuating rhythms of hunger, sexuality, sleep and waking (where these occur), etc., may rise to psychical phases and sink back into the unfelt round of vital being. Even the most intensely felt moment of existence has its unfelt elements, and certainly its preparation in the non-psychical substructure of all higher processes.

The point of this retrospect on an old-fashioned speculation is that the rapid eye movements of mammalian sleep may be an observable passage in a variable yet constantly present cerebral activity, which may change in intensity to exhibit or not exhibit that spectacular phase, dream, but which reaches some or all the higher systems in the brain and keeps them at a normal level of activation. There are several phenomena connected with REM that point toward the presence of such a physiological mechanism. In the first place, the very early appearance of REMs in neonate and even premature babies (human and animal), and their frequent and long periods in early life, may be aiding the brain in meeting the sudden demands of the extrauterine surroundings, and be stimulated by those needs to work at high tension (the same sort of explanation might fit their decline with advancing age, when most of the cerebral functions have become routine and require only minimal reinforcement). In the second place, the fact that they do not seem to originate in the oculomotor apparatus suggests that they are part and parcel of a larger, general stimulative process; the eye movements proper may be present only during intense activity of the mechanism, for they seem to be easily abolished as soon as the eyelids are opened and the oculomotor muscles are pre-empted for visual purposes. If the REM phenomenon is part of a general restimulating activity, its function would be performed during waking hours by the watchful

[273]

eye's constant saccadic movements, which make irregular but continual changes to restimulate the visual apparatus and probably the whole participating brain. The winking of human eyelids, usually unnoticed though easily accessible to attention, supplements the oculomotor changes with tiny lapses. But in sleep these influences are lacking, and it is likely that REMs take over their non-visual task.

Now, what have the eye movements to do with dream? Probably, nothing and everything. Nothing direct, such as recording dreamed events or starting the hallucinatory process; but everything, in that the periodic reinforcement of forebrain activity is essential for hallucinations to occur. These are superimposed on the high-tension passages of that activity, wherefore they may occur whenever the tension is high enough, but are apt to be most vivid, continuous and memorable while —or just after—stimulation is received.

We do not know whether animals have dreams, or whether their REMs serve other cerebral functions;[21] in newborn individuals, human or other, they almost certainly do, unless dream material is derived from intrauterine sensations.[22] The confident statements one often reads to the effect that animals have dreams are generally based on the fact that many household pets, especially dogs, whine, grunt, utter short barks, twitch their limbs or even make running motions in sleep.[23] But

[21] In a discussion following the reading of a paper by Jouvet et al., doubts about animals' dreaming were expressed especially by H. Fischgold and B. A. Schwartz, both investigators of neurological sleep functions. See M. Jouvet, F. Michel and D. Mounier, "Analyse electroencephalographique comparée du sommeil physiologique chez le chat et chez l'homme" (1960), pp. 204–5.

[22] Roffwarg et al., in "Ontogenetic Development of the Human Sleep-Dream Cycle," p. 612, have remarked this possibility.

[23] H. Hediger, in an article "Vom Traum der Tiere" (1945–47), cites several authors in support of his own conviction that such motions and utterances are symptoms of concomitant dreaming, and—invoking the authority of Karl Bühler— that the behavior of sleeping infants indicates dreaming or at least dream-like states. Having once found that support, he goes on to say: "Wer das Gebärdespiel eines schlafenden Jagdhundes beobachtet, sagt Bühler, gewinnt manchmal die Überzeugung, dass das Tier von der Jagd träumt. ... Wir haben keinen Grund—führt Bühler wörtlich aus—solche Beobachtungen am schlafenden Tier wesentlich anders zu deuten als beim schlafenden Menschen. Auch der Hund träumt, d.h. es spielen sich Ereignisse von wahrnehmungsartiger (halluzinatorischer) Beschaffenheit und Lebhaftigkeit in ihm ab, Wiederholungen von dem, was er vor kürzerer oder längerer Zeit wachend erlebt hat." He further quotes Rudolf Bilz, Karl Gustav Carus, Rudolf Menzel and other psychologists to the same effect; only one, the zoologist Friedrich Zschokke, in his book Der Schlaf der Tiere (1916), is admitted to have expressed a doubt of animal dream as a hallucinatory experience, saying: " 'Vielleicht bleibt das Tier auf einer niederen Stufe der wunderbaren seelischen Erscheinung, in der Vorhalle des märchenhaften Traumreiches stehen.' "

this supposed evidence is seriously called in question by the results of many systematic observations. In man, sleep-walking and sleep-talking do not seem to occur in association with vivid dreams, if, indeed, with any dreams at all; they are most commonly observed in "slow-wave," non-REM sleep.[24] In animals, twitches and shifts of limbs often do coincide with rapid eye motions;[25] but the encephalograms accompanying the latter in sleeping cats are sufficiently different from man's to make a simple carry-over of supposed meaning from one species to the other a dubitable practice.[26] One is led to suspect, in fact, that what takes place in the animal's nervous system is an alternative rather than a parallel to the human phenomenon, dream.

Dream, then, may be conceived as a further development of the mammalian sleep pattern through stages of progressive intensification and elaboration to the hallucinatory phase, marked especially by the occurrence of cerebrally produced images and illusory experiences. We

[24] A. Jacobson, A. Kales, D. Lehmann and J. R. Zweizig, in a report on a special investigation, "Somnambulism: All-Night Encephalographic Studies" (1965), sum up their findings as follows: "Using special techniques allowing for subject mobility, we obtained continuous encephalographic recordings of known sleepwalkers. Somnambulistic incidents occurred during periods of slow-wave sleep. The incidents were not related temporally to dream periods, nor did they affect the total time nor the percentage of time spent dreaming during the nights on which the subjects were studied."

W. C. Dement ("An Essay on Dreams" p. 231) suggests that sleep-talking might occur in all phases of sleep. "Audible vocalizations during sleep," he says, "do not seem to be particularly related to dreaming. Kamiya noted 98 instances of spontaneous vocalization in his laboratory subjects. . . . Only 8 percent occurred during REMPs, but when the data were corrected for unequal subject distribution the figures rose to 14 percent, which is not far from what might be expected in terms of the REM fraction of the total sleep time if talking occurs at random throughout the entire sleep period." After discussing some further case materials, he concludes (p. 232): "In view of these results, it is likely that most vocalizations heard in a home setting, for example, the groaning or occasional calling out of sleeping children, also have nothing to do with dreams." There are other corroborative statements in the recent literature.

[25] Dement, "An Essay on Dreams," pp. 160–61: "Luckhardt described the inhibition of gastric motility during periods of sleep in the dog that were characterized by twitching movement of the limbs. These twitching movements are now known to occur during REMPs." Luckhardt took this concurrence to indicate dreaming, but human cases, where dreaming can be known by protocol statements, make it appear unlikely.

[26] See Oswald, *Sleeping and Waking*, p. 134: "An immediately apparent species difference would be discernible in the EEG, for while in the feline 'paradoxical phase' there is fast activity similar to the waking state, the human EEG in the comparable phase of sleep has quite definitely the appearances of light sleep with prominence of low voltage 3-6 c/s waves."

do not know where this phase begins, i.e., whether any animals have imagery in sleep, but it is not impossible. Curt Richter made the interesting observation on sloths, which he studied for several years, partly in their native jungle:

"If I have understood ... Professor Pieron's theses correctly, he has postulated a close correlation between an animal's curiosity, the extent of contact with its environment, and its place in the evolutionary scale. . . .

"The evidence at hand indicates to me that the Sloth has survived not because of curiosity, the seeking of more contact with its environment, but rather the opposite. It seems to have no curiosity and its contact with the environment, and with other animals is minimal: I have never seen it show an interest in anything except food: It appears to want to be strictly alone.

"The Sloth has become ideally adapted to this type of negative existence. In its natural habitat it lives near the tops of trees, or near the ends of branches. . . . Owing to its slow movements and to its camouflaging—it moves through the jungle almost unnoticed. The camouflage depends on the presence of algae on the fluted hairs. In the wet season when the jungle is green, the sloth is green; in the dry season when everything is brown it too is brown. . . .

"In contrast with its general unresponsiveness, the Sloth has a highly developed tactile sense, responding to even the slightest stimulation of a single hair. Furthermore, surprisingly it has a quite highly developed brain, comparable with that of a cat or dog. In other words, the selection of this type of life—offering as it does, so much opportunity for uninterrupted contemplation—may be a sign of superior brain power or more highly developed brain rather than the opposite."[27]

Karl von Frisch made fun of Richter's "contemplative" sloths, saying, "Perhaps they are great philosophers." "Contemplation" does do them a good deal of honor, and may not be the right word; but there is a real problem of what such a stationary, motionless animal is doing. Its fairly advanced brain suggests that it may be dreaming, letting casual, uncontrolled images take shape and melt away again—records of visual impressions of its leafy surroundings all seen against the sky. Impulses do have to be finished—even mere peripheral stimulations like sensory impressions—and these animals give no signs of overt response. If, indeed, they are able to undergo a half-waking dream, this indulgence might become obsessive, and encourage their physically passive life.

[27] From the discussion following the reading of Henri Pieron's paper, "L'Evolution du comportement dans ses rapports avec l'instinct" (1956). See pp. 699–700.

This is, of course, a piece of pure speculation, not even a hypothesis, since there is no way of testing its truth value. If it were true, it would be an instance of extreme specialization, a spurt of evolutionary advance for which the animal finding its peculiar conditions—safety, ease, freedom from wants—all together, was not ready. But in a more normal state of affairs, amid the usual needs and dangers of life, we know that sensory impressions can terminate in this fashion, that is, be consummated in the brain rather than the musculature: that is in man. The expansion of his cerebrum has apparently not been without influence on his sense organs, especially the distance receptors, which his elevated posture calls constantly into play, so his acts of perception chase and crowd each other and start a veritable flood of incipient responses which cannot possibly be all overtly carried out. But (in all likelihood, I venture to say) they are held in abeyance, in waiting, until further external stimuli are abrogated by sleep and the accumulated sensory impressions can be finished in the partially relieved brain. Their consummation is, first of all, the dreamed image.

Since in waking life we are so active in taking up constantly new impressions, these covert enactments of cerebral impulses which have not been otherwise assimilated and indirectly spent must happen in sleep. It is interesting that cortical sleep patterns (EEG patterns) differ much more from waking ones in man than in the animals which have been as carefully studied (mainly cats).[28] One reason, and probably the paramount one, is that we make a still further use of the images that emerge, without volition and apparently without effort, in our brains. For we are overburdened—*"belastet,"* as Gehlen says—not only with excessive sensibility, but also too many emotive impulses, certainly more than can be freely, overtly spent, especially in the social context of human life. So, while animal hallucinations (if there be any) probably pass in kaleidoscopic fashion without any interest except change (emergence, fading, succession), ours tend to pick up emotional values; and their doing so is not a simple process. It is, in fact, the greater part of what Freud, in his early book, *The Interpretation of Dreams,*[29] called the "dream work." Emotional reactions are always to our own impulses in situations which do not immediately let them pass into action, that is, obstructions, long or briefly unmet needs, and especially conflicting motivations, which may be large or almost imperceptibly small. The small ones are the neglected ones, of which we may take no notice at all. They just belong to the fabric of the ever-moving situation in which

[28] See n. 26 above.
[29] *Die Traumdeutung,* 1900; trans. A. A. Brill, 1913. See esp. chap. iv.

one lives. Yet they may summate to impart a general feeling tone to the passage of life in its situational context.

No one knows just where and by what mechanisms dreams are generated, but their elements have been traced with some certainty and detail to remembered, unremembered and often jumbled past situations in the life history of the dreamer. The images which punctuate the dreamed acts and situations may have sources quite apart from the biographical fragments underlying the intracerebrally produced events. These visual images, which are commoner and probably more primitive than auditory ones, show one of the most important functions of the human brain—composition. A dream vision is one presentation, no matter how it may subsequently change; it may embody many old sensory impressions, but they enter into one momentary apparition. What they all contribute to achieve is a quality made visible—sometimes an innocent enough object, a bag, a fishing pole, a restaurant counter—but with a feeling of unknown significance; or a creature, human or animal, with physiognomic character above all other traits. This expressiveness is what dominates the "dream work" of composition.

One of the notable characteristics of dreams is their ephemeral character; a few minutes after waking up with a vivid awareness of having just had a dream we cannot recapture what we dreamt,[30] though we may remember that it was exciting, we were troubled, perhaps driven, perhaps embarrassed in some strange quandary, or—less often—delighted. The object of our joy, dismay or fear may have been something which in waking life would not seem worthy of such emotional reception: a mouse, a watch, an apple floating in a pool. But in dreams there is no causal order, and if there is any ground for valuing things or events it is as specious as dreamed causality. Although dreams do seem to have a story-like structure,[31] one situation succeeding another, often with some carry-over of things or people from one scene to the next, what we remember of the action is usually fragmentary and often vague; and as we try to hold it in memory upon awakening we can feel

[30] See Dement, "An Essay on Dreams," p. 213: "The apparent universality of dreams . . . serves to emphasize one of their most perplexing properties: the extreme difficulty we ordinarily have in remembering them. In spite of the fact that each of us dreams 1 to 2 hours every night of our lives, it is the rare person who is able to recapture even a small fraction of his nocturnal experience."

[31] Ibid., p. 142 (speaking of awakenings at the height of REM periods): "Occasionally, the narration of a single dream 'adventure' runs to several closely spaced typewritten pages when transcribed, and is replete with a variety of imagery and detail almost as if it had happened in real life. Is it possible that the true dream experience is always like this, and that the wide variation in the complexity of our reports only represents a greater or lesser degree of decimation by faulty recall?"

the sequence of events breaking and pieces of it slipping away before we can even verbalize them in our minds enough to hold them in immediate memory.

But although the events in dreams are generally too ephemeral to be more than vaguely and haphazardly retrieved after waking, some images seem to separate themselves from their context, when the context has dissolved to a great or small extent; images tend to remain, like illustrations of a story that has become illegible. We know they were more than images; they somehow concentrate the significance of the vanished story in themselves. What they really have taken on, however, is the whole cargo of emotional acts which have been finished in the course of the dream. The awakened dreamer cannot recollect the events of the dream, but they color the remembered image and make it exciting on every recall, for they belong to its nature as intimately as its form and literal meaning.

Dream images, are, in fact, symbolic forms; they have no practical value, for they were only figments, of purely organic origin, and their emotional charge is not appropriate to the dreamer's known experience and behavior. But it is highly appropriate to primitive impulses, wishes and fantasies which cannot be allowed to enter into waking life and consequently are relegated to the covert activity of dreaming. One of Sigmund Freud's most revolutionary ideas was that forgetting, rather than remembering, is a purposive cerebral act, a process of repression, which allows nothing to remain in memory except symbolic images that disguise their meanings as they convey them.[32] Dreams have no regard

---

[32] The theory of active, though unconscious and automatic, repression of ideas as the cerebral process of forgetting is put forward in *Die Traumdeutung*, but in a reserved fashion, claiming repression only as one of the sources of dream amnesia. A fuller use of the idea is made throughout his next book, *Zur Psychopathologie des Alltagslebens* (1901); but the explicit and generalized statement occurs only in a long footnote near the end of that book, added in 1907: "Über den Mechanismus des eigentlichen Vergessens kann ich etwa folgende Andeutungen geben: Das Erinnerungsmaterial unterliegt im allgemeinen zwei Einflüssen, der Verdichtung und der Entstellung. Die Entstellung ist das Werk der im Seelenleben herrschenden Tendenzen und wendet sich vor allem gegen die affektwirksam gebliebenen Erinnerungsspuren, die sich gegen die Verdichtung resistenter verhalten. Die indifferent gewordenen Spuren verfallen dem Verdichtungsvorgang ohne Gegenwehr, doch kann man beobachten, dass überdies Entstellungstendenzen sich an dem indifferenten Material sättigen, welche dort, wo sie sich äussern wollten, unbefriedigt geblieben sind. Da diese Prozesse der Verdichtung und Entstellung sich über lange Zeiten hinziehen, während welcher alle frischen Erlebnisse auf die Umgestaltung des Gedächtnisinhaltes einwirken, meinen wir, es sei die Zeit, welche die Erinnerungen unsicher und undeutlich macht. Sehr wahrscheinlich ist beim Vergessen von einer direkten Funktion der Zeit überhaupt nicht die Rede. . . ."

for morals or decencies; a mechanism which wipes them out as we return to waking life saves us from conflict and shame. In Freud's day, what little was known about dream as a neurological process permitted his hypothetical staggered "systems" of perception, memory traces and association of different systems of traces by the several traditional associative principles—contiguity, similarity, relations through a *tertium quid*, etc.[33] Today, though we still know very little, these neurological hypotheses look somewhat unpromising; brain action at the level of dream production, thought ("the dream thought") and moral conflict, no matter how primitive, appears so involved that no simple schema of traces and actually known neural links holds out much hope of a model for those cerebral performances. We do not know how images are formed, but only that they are; how they become imbued with emotion, but only that they do carry charges of such feeling, sometimes great, sometimes low-keyed, yet always present; that the distortions, contractions and substitutions which Freud recorded in his early works have proved to be characteristic of dreams; and also, that dream materials are apt to be derived from unnoticed or unimportant details in previously perceived situations, events, pictures and communications.

But though we are not able even to speculate in any reasonable way on the physiological mechanisms which produce and uphold the phenomenon of mind in man, we may nevertheless note such empirical facts as these. Especially the last mentioned, the usual triviality of dream sources, was remarked by many of Freud's predecessors (whose contributions he discussed at some length), and has been carefully investigated and corroborated since then, first of all by Otto Pötzl, in experimental and clinical studies.[34] Pötzl found that no matter what is the reason why a perceptual datum is not properly taken in—too little time, too little light, too great a distance, distraction or some unavowed motive for not wanting to see, hear, or recognize the presentation—the result is the same: the datum is what he calls "indirectly perceived," never at the focus of the percipient's attention, so it is not remarked, and in reflection not recalled. Pötzl was originally led to his observations by his clinical experience with cerebral lesions causing scotomata in the patients' visual fields, obliging some of these persons to use peripheral vision in place of focal fixation. He then experimented on normal subjects with very brief tachistoscopic exposures (one-hundredth of a second) of fairly complicated pictures, and noted the items which were

[33] *Die Traumdeutung*, pp. 542 ff.
[34] See esp. his early article, "Experimentell erregte Traumbilder in ihren Beziehungen zum indirekten Sehen" (1917).

overlooked. In drawings from memory these items appeared in distorted form. Finally he found that they also were favored dream material, perhaps just because they were full of incompletely seen forms. Such forms lend themselves most readily to fantastic distortion and interpretation; the images constructed at their suggestion are the readiest to take on symbolic value, which seems, indeed, to influence the process of their formulation.

Later psychologists have recorded the same pre-eminence of trivial or even entirely unconsciously received visual impressions in the perceptual sources of dream imagery. Most of them have explicitly repeated or continued Pötzl's researches,[35] so that the authenticity of those findings is fairly well assured. The crucial fact in the present connection is that many aspects of a perceptual act may motivate the failure to note a detail,[36] and sometimes even a whole, sizable portion of a picture. The

[35] For instance, Hans Hoff, whose monograph "Die zentrale Abstimmung der Sehsphäre" (1930) was concerned with some striking similarities of structures and materials to be found in dreams and in epileptic auras, says of both phenomena: "Der Vordergrund schwindet, Hintergrundsbilder nehmen den Sehraum ein. Dies ist ja, nach *Pötzl*, einer der Mechanismen des Traumes" (p. 4). And again: "Aus dem Hintergrundsmaterial der optischen Eindrücke des Tages setzen sich innere Traumbilder zusammen" (p. 5).

Shortly thereafter, William Malamud and F. E. Linder repeated Pötzl's experiments with some changes of method, claiming to put his ideas to a test for their theoretical validity rather than their heuristic value; and in the conclusion of their report, "Dreams and Their Relationship to Recent Impressions" (1931), they remark that, working with mentally ill subjects, they met more resistance than Pötzl with his normal subjects, and that the long time they allowed for looking at the picture was so much nearer to the exposure time of ordinary percepts during the day that these gave it some competition as sources of the subsequent night's dreams. But the mental hospital had the necessary records of emotionally disturbing childhood experiences which their hypothesis required, so they decided to accept the adverse conditions which invalidated some of their results, saying: "When we consider the fact that Poetzl in his experiment with normal persons and tachistoscopic exposition obtained the same results in all of his cases, we feel justified in assuming that most, if not all, of our unsuccessful attempts were due to the difference in material used and the procedure that was followed" (p. 1099).

Much more recently, Charles Fisher, in "A Study of the Preliminary Stages of the Construction of Dreams and Images" (1957), says in introduction to his work: "These experiments involve the exposure of pictures to subjects by means of a tachistoscope. I was able to confirm Poetzl's essential finding that those parts of the tachistoscopically exposed picture that are not consciously perceived appear extensively in the manifest content of subsequent dreams" (p. 5). The report following this statement is in entire agreement with Pötzl and hence with the thought of his inspirer, Freud.

[36] See, e.g., Pötzl, "Experimentell erregte Traumbilder in ihren Beziehungen zum indirekten Sehen," p. 346: "Die Bilder des indirekten Sehens, die Fehler gesunder

latter circumstance seems to stem from our normal way of looking at things, "from head to foot" rather than vice versa, so that a very brief exposure may give us only the upper part, or not all of the lower part, of a picture.[37] Many existing forms are lost because the areas which compose them figure as "spaces" in the picture, under the domination of the obvious represented objects; they are the elements used in puzzle pictures, "Vexierbilder."[38] In our ordinary picture perception they go unnoticed, but in the formation of dreams they sometimes give rise to the most important images. Yet all these "peripheral" impressions, no matter what caused them to be peripheral, once they do appear in conscious perception as visions tend to undergo the same fragmentation and recombination, inversions, substitutions and often bizarre distortions as those which Freud found to be originally suppressed by fear or disapproval; and just like the emotionally rejected material, the most casually obscured, unrecognized forms—obliterated by retinal defects or bad presentation—lend themselves to such elaboration and interpretation and are ready vehicles for symbolic values. So it may be doubted that the cause of their indirect perception is what primarily motivates their function in dream, hallucination and fantasy. What, then, inspires the use we make of these trivial, subconscious or unconscious, indirectly seen forms?

I think the answer embraces the findings of Freud, without belittling the far-reaching principle of "psychopathology of everyday life," and also extends to the deliverances of "indirect perception" due to lesions in the visual apparatus and to partially subthreshold exposure; above all, it relates the phenomenon to the general nature of acts. All neglected, unrecognized though physically received impressions are unfinished business. The impulses they touched off were nipped in the bud and not used up in conjunction with other responses, as thousands of starting and pooled impulses are automatically completed (often by entrainment) from moment to moment of actual life. Pictures, speeches, well-formed sound patterns like bird calls or bell tones are somewhat

---

Personen beim tachistoskopischen Sehen, die visuellen Traumbilder und die optischen Fehler der Agnostiker stimmen in vielen wesentlichen Eigenschaften nach Form und Inhalt ihres psychisch Gegebenen miteinander überein."

[37] *Ibid.*, p. 303: "Die Erfassung der Gestalt war bei 1/100 Sek. Exposition nachgewiesenermassen ... auf die obere Hälfte des Bildes gerichtet; die unteren Anteile des Bildes waren also mindestens für die Aufmerksamkeit peripher."

[38] Since they are not intended as puzzles in Pötzl's experiments, "Vexierbilder" has been rendered by his translators and paraphrasers as "embedded pictures." But "puzzle pictures" is the more exact translation.

special elements, impinging on our sensibilities as holistic forms amid the flow of the "specious present." That is why their impressions, however poorly retained in conscious memory, are filled with fragmentary as well as completed forms. The normal course of a sensory impulse engendered by such a presentation is an act of clear perception, though it probably always has some uncompleted aspects. Pictures, distinctive sounds and rhythmic motions are natural sources of spontaneous images, which occur especially when current stimuli are reduced—in sleep, in drowsiness, or hypnotic gazing at hearth-fire, moving water or the like.

Imagination, I think, begins in this fashion; its lowest form is this organic process of finishing frustrated perceptions as dream figments. In primitive stages of hominid specialization dream may not have occurred exclusively or even mainly in sleep. For eons of human (or proto-human) existence imagination probably was entirely involuntary, as dreaming generally is today,[39] only somewhat controllable by active or passive behavior, in the one case staving it off, in the other inviting it. But what finally emerged was the power of image-making. This, too, must have had its evolutionary course, starting with that of dream. At first dreaming may have been limited to the optic apparatus, which took up the first great excess of stimuli. We cannot know; but in visually oriented animals, birds and primates, the "optic thalamus" has largely replaced the rhinencephalic stations which the thalamic nuclei constitute in macrosmatic brains; the shift seems to be demonstrable in all degrees. Likewise, the cortical activating work known only through rapid eye motion and its experimental manipulation, though it probably originated in the vestibular system,[40] in man has struck intimate relations with visual functions, especially in the completion of unfinished perceptions by the production of subjective imagery.[41]

[39] I know just one person who claims to be able to stop a dream if it gets too nightmarish, and start over again. But I am not sure that the experience this dreamer describes is really deep dream and not an enjoyed, long and elaborate hypnagogic fantasy.

[40] O. Pompeiano and A. R. Morrison, "Vestibular Origin of the Rapid Eye Movement during Desynchronized Sleep" (1966), say in conclusion (p. 61): "The present experiments show that the medial and descending vestibular nuclei are of critical importance for the appearance of rapid eye movements during desynchronized sleep."

[41] See, for example, D. Foulkes, "Dream Reports from Different Stages of Sleep" (1962), p. 20: "The greater incidence of involvement of the visual system . . . strikingly differentiates the reports obtained in and outside REMPs. A further index of visual involvement shows that visual imagery is not only more often present in REMP reports, but also, when present, it is more often 'strong' in quality."

At present, however—and there is no knowing since when—dream experiences are not only visual, but involve hearing, touch, and indeed all modes of sense which we know in real life, and above all many non-sensuous forms of awareness whereby we appreciate situations. A dream is a series of events in which causes seem to operate, facts are known though a source of knowledge is seldom presented, future events are fearfully or confidently expected. Yet dreamed reasons and causes are apt to be specious, situations may be quite impossible just as often as they may be possible, and their developments are often completely *non sequitur* shifts of scene or action.

It is the passage of dream events that is so elusive and ephemeral that often we cannot hold even the barest plot of the hallucinated story in memory. As a rule we have to hurry to verbalize what happened in the dream before the action shrinks to a vague surmise of what it may have been—if even that. What permits that modicum of recall is a peculiar paradox in the constitution of dreams: for, while the memory of events dissolves like smoke in air, many images are not only retained without effort, but may be actually haunting for days and weeks, sometimes for years or for life. We pin down the happenings by the images of things, places, people; once in a while—though less often—we have a vision of a being or object in motion, but the motion, in that case, belongs to the object as one of its peculiar qualities. The vision is still an image, self-contained and essentially pictorial. Herein lies, I think, the source of the paradox in our dream recall. A visual percept is given as a single, closed form, because all its parts are simultaneously presented, so it needs nothing to make them cohere; but events can only occur successively, and to have any structure they require causal connections from moment to moment, in a complete, fixed framework of space and continuous time. Otherwise their very nature falls apart, and one cannot even say, in the usual past tense of history, what happened, because there are at best fragments of sequences, but no coherent passage from one situation to another. There is no real "when" and "where," let alone "because." Such experience has no conceivable form, except for the bits the dreamer sometimes does remember, in which acts of his own usually constitute the recollected episode (or episodes).

One aspect, however, the two major elements of dream, imagery and virtual history, have in common: the intensity of emotive feeling which imbues them both. The visual phantasms, whether they be clear or vague, have always a predominantly "physiognomic" character; the most commonplace object, a slipper or a teacup, may have a mysterious quality, or an inviting or forbidding look, or some other air of non-pragmatic value. Its appearance is expressive, though nothing in the dream accounts for that attribute or even for the occurrence of some of the odd things hallucinated in sleep. Only since Freud proposed, and went far to prove, that such irrelevant items are standing in for entirely different ones belonging to another story, namely, the complex of memories, wishes, fears and expectancies not consciously entertained but emotionally effective in the nervous system, has the study of dreams made any headway toward psychological insight. One thing that has become fairly well established is that the driving force of dreams is emotional, and another, that their material is drawn from two sources: very recent perceptions ("*Tagesreste*," "vestiges of the day") and old memories, often very old, from early childhood. The revival of forms seen during the day is not necessarily an emotional experience; it often occurs before sleep has begun, with closed eyes or, in darkness, open, especially if one has looked long at repetitious forms such as fence pickets, coins, or less monotonous but basically uniform objects, daisies in a field, berries, cockle shells, reeds. The resulting visions may be individually eidetic, yet formalized in their deployment; they tend to cover the visual field more regularly than they did in actual perception, somewhat like a wallpaper pattern, not overlapping; sometimes they may be more formalized, all assimilated to one simplified, repeated shape. Some people find that they come and go,[42] others see them in fixed relations, and can even turn attention from one item to another and back again. Such hypnagogic envisagements are not after-images, yet like those familiar photisms they seem to be essentially retinal. They appear quite autonomous, involuntary and what is commonly called "physical." They have been compared to mescaline visions for extraordinary vividness,[43] but in my own experience they are not so much vivid as steady and detailed. They are not completions of fugitive "indirect seeing," but revivals of fully formed percepts, as after-images sometimes are; though an afterimage may show formal properties which its recipient had not noticed in the original impression, but which the retinal pattern reflects.[44] The

[42] J. A. Ardis and Peter McKellar, in "Hypnagogic Imagery and Mescaline" (1956), p. 23, say: "We have been able, on a number of occasions, to time several hypnagogic images. Some came and went in an instant, others remained a few minutes, but the majority ... lasted a matter of one or two seconds."

[43] *Ibid., passim*; on p. 24 the authors note "the unusual vividness which both mescaline and hypnagogic images show."

[44] J. J. Gibson, in his original and challenging book already cited at some length, *The Perception of the Visual World*, p. 63, holds that the stimulus to perception is not the external object of vision, but the pattern of activities produced in the retina by the impinging light rays. The stimulus to seeing is made at the retina. But the stimulus to that stimulus formation comes from without, as he remarked elsewhere: "Unfocussed light is a stimulus to focus."

images here in question differ from after-images in that they do not alternate positive with negative phases; and from dream-like hypnagogic visions in having no metaphorical function and consequently, in themselves, no emotional value.

What makes them interesting is that, without being true products of imagination, they nevertheless show formalizing influences which certainly are not exerted by the eye, but by deeper nervous structures, though these may quite possibly all belong to the visual system. The repetition of forms derived from recent sights (like the grasses and daisies mentioned above) or geometric forms of windows, spots of sunlight, etc., is not haphazard, but evenly spaced out in a design covering part or all of the field of vision. Herbert Silberer relates such an experience which he had while riding in a European railroad coach: "With my eyes closed, I am leaning against the corner of the compartment. Time and again the setting sun shines into my face. It disturbs me but I am too tired to get up and draw the shade. So I let it shine on me and watch the visual impressions that come as the sunshine hits my eyelids. Remarkably enough, the figures are different each time, but each time uniform. This is apparently a specific apperception phenomenon. I see first a mosaic of triangles, then one of squares, and so on."[45] This is the phenomenon of revived but spatially modified visual impression; the modification, consisting of the repetition and the orderly deployment of the repeated forms, is obviously a centrally furnished ingredient in the subjective event. I have had it many times without being sleepy, though probably beset by eye strain, once after identifying delicate feather mosses around a rock, whereupon after dark my whole field of vision was spread with a tapestry of such varied forms—not as repetitious as the simple geometric forms seen on other occasions, not even equally dense everywhere, but all of the same general character and harmonious spacing (Fig. 17-1). The interesting aspect of this retinal reactivation is that it shows the source of some basic principles of design and primitive pictorial representation, namely, the separation and completion of forms and their spacing out on a ground, to lie in the operation of our visual system itself.[46] Certainly in the woods the

[45] "Bericht über eine Methode, gewisse symbolische Halluzinations-Erscheinungen hervorzurufen und zu beobachten" (1910). The translation here quoted is from David Rapaport (ed.), *Organization and Pathology of Thought* (1951), pp. 206–7.

[46] Rudolf Arnheim, in *Art and Visual Perception* (1954), p. 203, remarks that in copying from memory designs in which units overlap, people often separate them; "the tendency of objects to steer clear of each other has its way when the direct control of the stimulus is absent." Similarly the painter Alphonso Best-Maugard, in

Figure 17–1. Feather Mosses, Drawn from Memory
Twenty Years Later

*a tapestry of such varied forms . . . all of the same general character
and harmonious spacing*

little plumes had been standing somewhat crowded, tangled, full of
pine needles and, of course, often leaning against or across others.

But Silberer in his coupé was sleepy, and it is interesting to see how
his retinal visions were quickly overtaken by dream experiences. After
recounting the appearance of squares, triangles and mosaics of other
repetitious forms, he goes on: "Then I have the impression that I myself am putting together the mosaic figures in rhythmical movements.
Soon I find that the rhythm is that of the axles of the train. . . ." That
is the first dream element—an act of his own—though he is only half
asleep. But then: "All of a sudden the following autosymbolic phenomenon occurs: I see an old lady, to the right, setting a table with a
checkered table-cloth, each square of which encloses a figure resembling
one of the sun-mosaics previously mentioned; the figures are all different."[47] Now he is dreaming; and he subsequently analyzes the dreamed
image in terms of its immediate translation of a thought into pictures
and its elements of recent events. But the photisms wrought by the

---

A Method for Creative Design (1926), a little book on principles of decorative
design intended primarily for children, pointed out that in folk art the individual
figures of such design normally do not overlap or even touch each other, but all—
lines, basic forms (e.g., diamonds, circles, hearts or what not), or flowers, birds and
beasts—complete their paths or achieve their unbroken outlines without mutual
interference.

[47] Rapaport (ed.), *Organization and Pathology of Thought*, pp. 206–7.

sunshine striking his face are still there, assimilated to his dream and elaborated to fit it.

The reason for dwelling on the purely ophthalmic reactivations of perceived forms is that, as Silberer remarked, they offer a rare chance to see a relatively bare, physiological process of formalization operating below the generally recognized level of imaginal composition, and remind the speculative theorist that so great a cerebral function as imagination is not likely to be the work of any single neural structure or even subsystem in the brain, but probably draws on many parts, many specializations with different evolutionary paths and origins, so that like most complex living forms it is polygenetic.

The great formative process, however, is a higher development, the relegation of blocked, curtailed, started but uncompleted impulses to perceptual and conceptual mechanisms in which transformations, typified in a lowly way by the patterning distortions of purely optic revived impressions, are more elaborately made, and produce the normal, nocturnal phantasmagoria of dream. In man this process has certainly reached astounding heights, reflecting almost all aspects of his life; and if it does have the source and significance here imputed to it, it shows the range and depth of human awareness and especially the plethora of impressions besetting us. It is in dream that the imaginative powers are born and exercised without effort or intention, unfold, and finally possess all departments of sense, and activate another great class of largely uncomprehended phenomena, the products of memory. Remembered sights and sounds, often unrecorded in conscious experience, sometimes whole situations especially of early life, tactile and olfactory and muscular impressions come together to form the profuse, unsolicited imagery our brains create in sleep.

But the most extravagant imagination, if it occurs only as dream, involuntary and unamenable to conscious control, is no direct asset in waking life, however great its physiological use in the cerebral system as a whole may be. What we ordinarily think of as "imagination" is a directed process, an entertainment of images and often verbalized concepts whereby we organize our practical knowledge and, especially, orient our emotional reactions to the ever-emergent situations which form the scaffold of life. The transition from the automatic completion of started acts which were curtailed in the melee of impulses seeking expression to the deliberate envisagement of things not present and situations not actually given is another major move in the shift from animal mentality to mind; and it springs from the further function of dream figments, after the finishing of sensory acts, the completion of autogenic, emotive impulses, which involves the genesis of the decisive humanizing process, symbolization.

There have been many attempts to prove that animals use symbols in thinking and in communication, but they all involve either a redefinition of "symbol" in terms that do not cover the human case,[48] or simply impute to an animal, such as a chimpanzee or a clever carnivore, the processes whereby a human being would guide his very similar behavior in similar circumstances.[49] A genuine symbol is, above all, an instrument of conception, and cannot be said to exist short of meeting that requirement; that means that an ape thinking symbolically could think of an act he had no intention or occasion to perform, and envisage things entirely remote from his real situation—a termite hill while he was in a laboratory cage far from natural surroundings, etc. Picking up a stem and carrying it even quite far to such a hill in the wild bespeaks an extended act with a preparatory phase in a large, really given situation, but not by any necessity a concept symbolically entertained. Symbolism is the mark of humanity, and its evolution was probably slow and cumulative, until the characteristic mental function, semantic intuition—the perception of meaning—emerged from the unconscious process Freud called the dream work into conscious experience. In the deep, unfelt operations of the brain the generation of symbolic forms may have had a long history, making images that departed from their sensory originals to draw in older, forgotten experiences and gather up their emotional values, until the cathexes they carried were out of all proportion to whatever manifest object-character they had. Only this

[48] Some of these writings have been discussed in Vol. I, Chapter 2, and none of them, perhaps, needs any more than mention by title here (the list could be extended *ad lib.*): Ruth B. Hunter, "Symbolic Performance of Rats in a Delayed Alternation Problem"; L. Petrinovich and R. Bolles, "Delayed Alternation: Evidence for Symbolic Processes in the Rat"; J. P. Seward, "The Sign of a Symbol: A Reply [to G. W. Allport]" (1948); R. J. Herrnstein and D. H. Loveland, "Complex Visual Concept in the Pigeon"; A. L. Kroeber, "Sign and Symbol in Bee Communication"; Paul E. Fields, *Studies in Concept Formation* (an ethological classic; if children's "verbal responses" show concept formation, so do rats' "jumping responses"!); N. R. F. Maier, *Reasoning in White Rats.*

[49] Dr. and Mrs. Gardner, for instance, in "Teaching Sign Language to a Chimpanzee," p. 666, explaining why they did not speak to each other in vocal language while they addressed Washoe in sign language, say: "We reasoned that this would make it seem that big chimps talk and only little chimps sign, which might give signing an undesirable status." This presupposes the whole social pattern in which the human nursery figures as a lowly stage of existence to be outgrown by children who long to be grown up; also, that little Washoe took her keepers for "big chimps."

strange, exciting quality betrays the fact—and then, not to the dreamer
—that the ordinary things hallucinated in sleep stand for something
not presented. The mechanism of symbol-making is there, but the
symbolic relation of the image to the concepts it could serve to express
is not evident yet.

Now, all these automatic processes of condensation, distortion, and
substitution of pictorial elements for unportrayable ones and, finally,
sensuous presentation of the cerebral products in dream are still apart
from waking life and its public, external world. At this juncture, however, another characteristic of dream may have played a crucial role in
the making of mind—as so often, a factor of no practical value: the
paradox already mentioned, that dream events are fugitive, but images
tend to be remembered and even to haunt us long after the action, the
dreamed story, is largely or wholly forgotten. In this way the image is
culled from its context and may occur in recollection without any context at all or in an incongruous one of waking perception. In animal
mentality, objects seem to figure essentially in situations, and derive
their characters from them and the acts they implement or hinder.[50]
Otherwise they may not be noticed, certainly not touched. Even such
visually inclined beasts as monkeys pay attention to new but clearly
inedible things only where stimulation by interesting ones is pathetically
low, as in captivity.[51] But the pure apparition of a memory image without its setting in actions and events is arresting; and since in human
memory it usually has some aura of its dream cathexis, this sudden
fantasy looms up as an abstracted form, usually with a "physiognomic"
appearance. Apart from action, albeit only the virtual action of dream,
its notable features are visual traits of shape, color, attitude and expres-

[50] See Chapter 13 above, esp. pp. 54–55, 61.

[51] The same thing seems to hold for lower primates. Allison Jolly, in her book,
Lemur Behavior, writes: "Lemur in partly adequate groups in barren cages may
turn their attention to objects, but in wild groups, their attention is directed elsewhere. The same is true of captive baboons when compared to wild ones" (pp.
78–79).

Schaller, in *The Mountain Gorilla—Ecology and Behavior*, p. 200, remarks that
"gorillas rarely handled anything for the sake of manipulation alone," and that they
"appeared to lack the inclination to investigate strange inanimate objects manually.
On one occasion," he says, "my rucksack lay in full view and within 15 feet of a
black-backed male. He glanced at it once and then ignored it." Kummer, in *Social
Organization of Hamadryas Baboons*, p. 171, says, "The hamadryas baboons rarely
handled any nonedible objects," except that juveniles turned over stones and sometimes knocked them down from the cliff, joined in this sport by other young ones;
and, further, on p. 172, he remarks, "No artificial objects thrown away by humans
were found in the area used by the White Rock troop."

sion. Even things and surroundings may be remembered with the peculiar intensity of dream images, while the story that involved them has left no trace of its passage.[52]

Once the pure form is abstracted and remembered, it may be suggested by actual perceptions of waking life; the identity of form is seen in all possible concrete instances, even such as depart somewhat from the model. That recognition of sameness or similarity is an intuition, as form perception itself is; but while the latter is first practiced in sleep, the logical intuition of similarity, which involves sameness and difference, seems to occur only in non-dreaming states. Yet it is intuitive, not learned from experience as the useful or hurtful properties of things are, and the whole development of logical thought and semantical insight to which it ultimately leads belongs to our waking hours. Originally, however, the material of such rational cognition stems from that more primitive deliverance of dream, the memorable image, to which real percepts are spontaneously assimilated if they fit it and from which they derive a more definite form than they are apt to have in animal-like empractic seeing. But in shaping them, the imaginary model also gives the new actual percept some of its emotional quality, the expression of central feeling it had to hold and finish in the dream or half-dream state; and some vestige of that feeling pervades all things seen to partake of that visual form. In this way the appearance abstracted by the paradoxical nature of dream memory carries the symbolic character of a dreamer's involuntary fantasies over into waking envisagement.

That is the momentous step, from form perception to the sense of significance—at this point probably not of the symbol but in the symbol, presenting, at first, more as a feeling of awe than as any real comprehension of meaning, yet marking the first, fleeting acts of ideation. Once the awareness of form had taken place, it would not take a dream episode to negotiate every further such abstraction; intuition, however it may have come into being, is a natural human function and, like Freud's "dream work" itself, once it is initiated it will seize on every possible material. But seeing expressions and symbolic values in physically presented things may have been involuntary and non-practical for millennia, impressive, sudden, without being available for autosuggestive use, i.e., symbolic thinking and systematic envisagement; more disturb-

---

[52] Just after writing these words, I found it a welcome corroboration to come across the following statement by F. Bremer, in a discussion following N. Kleitman's symposium paper, "The Nature of Dreaming": "Could it be that the objective impression of the dream process may be intense and vivid because it emerges from a blank background?" ("The Nature of Dreaming" [1961], p. 371).

ing than advantageous. There are some indications that apes tend, at least in captivity, to see some objects in this way.[53] That they see pictured objects as things seems quite certain, though often the observer may fail to understand how the ape sees a given form;[54] sometimes a form which to human eyes represents, say, a chair, being next to a picture of a small object like a spoon, may confuse the animal by the difference of scale, though in general size does not seem to matter. Also, the gestalt may be oddly divided as it often is in children's picture perception and in our dream formation. The Kelloggs reported that their infant chimpanzee, Gua, looking at a picture book that showed a brown-haired boy from the back, repeatedly tried to pick up his head from the page, apparently regarding it as a nut or a lozenge; indeed, she seemed to see even the simplest, uncolored outline drawings as three-dimensional tangible objects, and treated them not as representations but as the things themselves which they represented.[55] She even tried to pick

[53] This subject is discussed, with several examples, in *Philosophy in a New Key* (hereafter cited as *Phil. N.K.*), pp. 111 ff. I have come across no further materials since those were collected.

[54] Cf. K. J. Hayes and C. Hayes, "Picture Perception in a Home-Raised Chimpanzee" (1953), p. 470: "At about 18 months, Viki began to spend an increasing amount of time looking at books, magazines, catalogs, and newspapers, and this has continued to be a common play activity until the present time.... At three years, she leaned down and put her ear to a picture of a wrist watch in a magazine...."

"At three and one-half years, we tested her ability to imitate actions illustrated in pictures.... She performed fairly well from the first session on, and transferred readily through the various stages from movies to line drawings. She accepted the procedure as a game at first, and would often work without being rewarded for correct responses.... She seldom failed to imitate preferred actions (those which she often performs spontaneously in play), but she often made errors by performing such preferred actions in response to pictures of nonpreferred items. This type of error sometimes occurs when the demonstration is given by a real person and does not necessarily indicate poor picture perception" (p. 471) (nor imitation either, perhaps).

"It would have been surprising, in a sense, if Viki had proved completely lacking in picture comprehension. Pictorial items appear in human intelligence tests as early as 18 months, suggesting that this should not be a particularly difficult skill [for animals?]. Nevertheless, Viki made many mistakes, and it would be interesting to know what caused them" (p. 473).

[55] Kellogg and Kellogg, in *The Ape and the Child*, p. 92, tell how Gua "demonstrates a spontaneous interest in printed pictures in magazines and books even at as early an age as 10 months. This she indicates by pointing to various parts of them and usually attempting to pick them up with her lips. The sections which she touches with her lips are often vaguely similar to drawings of fruits or other edible objects. She consequently reaches toward the pictured back of a boy's head which is oval and brown like an acorn or a nut." Further on, p. 95, they relate that at sixteen months Gua evidently mistook a pictured cracker for a real one, and tried to seize it —at that age, with her hand.

up spilled liquids from her tray; and here the observers report an odd observation on their own child, whose nursery Gua shared, and draw what seems to me a questionable conclusion, as they say: "Everything, apparently, is at the start perceived as three-dimensional, and the quality of two-dimensionality is something new. This principle seems to apply to the reactions of both subjects. If Gua spills some milk upon the tray of her high chair during feeding-time she often tries to pick it up.... Donald also in numerous instances attempts to pick up spilled liquids as well as the woven designs on cloth. The conclusion appears inevitable from such behavior that although the subjects unquestionably observe printed forms, they do not at these young ages [Gua sixteen months, Donald eighteen and a half] distinguish two-dimensional from three-dimensional objects."[56] I have never seen a child of a year and a half try to pick up a puddle standing even quite high on a polished surface, nor read of such an observation anywhere else in the literature, and am led to wonder whether the "inevitable" conclusion, drawn from this single child's behavior, may not be ignoring the unusual condition imposed by the companionship of an ape in the place of a sister. The suggestion of picking up the flat deck of milk came from Gua's action and was given by her again and again. Babies usually put their fingers into such a puddle, and draw the liquid in lines over the bare parts of the surface; Donald followed his playmate's absurd example, but surely at his age he knew the milk was not a flat solid like an oilcloth mat.

The revealing aspect of these animal exhibits is that they give us at least a hint of the complexity and evolutionary growth of our own specialty, the intuition of symbolic meaning. For, all claims of animal psychologists to the contrary or not, animals do not have it; and how intuition could possibly have arisen and developed in just one type of primate, apparently without analogous functions or lower forms of the same talent in older or in parallel lines, presents a serious problem. But in these high non-human creatures, the chimpanzees, of which a number of randomly chosen individuals have received such special care and study as Vicki, Gua, more recently Washoe, and currently Sarah,[57] we find the same sort of rare opportunity to analyze a highly integrated phenomenon into some of its constituents as the observation of hypnagogic visions afforded in the study of dream imagery. In the brain of the ape, some intuitions evidently occur, while others never do, so one can gain some idea of the several intuitive functions, which ones seem

[56] P. 92.
[57] See David Premack, "The Education of Sarah" (1970).

to occur most easily, perhaps even in lower animals (though that would have to be determined for each species); and finally, in human mentation, which ones are elementary in that they are required in order to carry the crucial, humanizing intuition of meaning.

The recognition of forms is obviously spontaneous in infant chimpanzees, though it is a product of abstraction in them as in us, and some time in the long past of their race as of ours it must have had its beginning—perhaps in excess of vision, making pure shapes in the dark, as it does for us. Apes are predominantly visual animals. Form perception is an intuitive act, probably the lowest and earliest for primate mentality. But in Gua's case certainly, and apparently in Vicki's too, the distinction between the pictured object and the depicting image only asserted itself pragmatically when the infant tried to eat or handle the image as a real thing. Even in man this distinction is not perfect; in moments of vivid imagination it is lost, a story seems like a memory, a statue like a being, etc. Were that not the case, we would have no clue to the development of symbolic functions and the growth of mind.

One other intuitive perception which underlies the great human departure and shows at least a beginning in captive animals is physiognomic seeing, the immediate reception of expressive value in visual forms. In man it is stronger during childhood than in later years. Yerkes observed it in one of his little apes, Panzee,[58] and there are sporadic records of it from Koehler's ape station on Tenerife and the Yerkes primate colony formerly in Florida. But none of the observers of anthropoids in the wild have mentioned it, perhaps because it is most pronounced in early years, and they did not particularly observe the behavior of infants in such detail, and perhaps because it does not occur. Finding the semblance of gesture or power in the sheer configuration of objects, with or without true or suggested faces,[59] is an intuition of expressive form that goes beyond the function of form perception as such. In human life it has played a major part, I think, in the evolution of symbolic seeing and thinking, and has been, in fact, a preparatory step toward the emergence of speech.

The intuitive apprehension of symbolic import in sounds, movements, shapes and rhythmic changes like swinging, revolving, flowing[60]

---

[58] See *Phil. N.K.*, pp. 110–13.

[59] A striking instance from animal life is given by William Schiff, J. A. Cavines and J. J. Gibson, "Persistent Fear Responses in Rhesus Monkeys to the Optical Stimulus of 'Looming'" (1962).

[60] J. J. Gibson, in his two books already repeatedly referred to, as also the article "Visually Controlled Locomotion and Visual Orientation in Animals," has stressed the emotive value of effects produced essentially by movements.

may have had a long development, millennia at least, in prehuman natural history before such import became vaguely felt to belong intrinsically to some objects or phenomena: clouds, flames, fantastic rocks or huge trees and the places they defined, but also small articles with intriguing or suggestive shapes—smooth, hollow, serpentine, eye-like or what not. Their import was sensed without any further exegetics, as it is today by superstitious people who cherish amulets, *churingas* and other magical charms; their significance is felt as a power rather than a symbolic value, their intellectual potency as physical potency. That is a phase of symbol appreciation which probably preceded any real, conceptual use of symbols in thinking, and consequently any coherent thought. But in it we can see a step in the rise of true symbolism; for it may well have sprung from physiognomic seeing, which is rare and episodic in the highest animals but has developed in human mentality to a distinct kind of intuition, which begets at first the above-mentioned feelings of vague import, and finally leads to the development of a high symbolic form, the metaphorical symbol, discussed at some length in Part II of this essay.

The first startling effect of a proto-symbolic impression of emotional import received from an object would probably be a sense of awe in its presence. The more one looks at an expressive figure the more its expressiveness grows. Purposely constructed forms especially, set up in an open place for view, take on this aura of vague significance which embraces the whole place that belongs to them and evokes a primitive sense of "holiness." That is the first obvious gathering place of hominid hordes in a state of excitement, where any individual's emotional expression would be enhanced, seen and felt by others, but assimilated for them to the nature of the place rather than to the presence of the single being giving vent to his actual impulses. The figure commanding the place epitomizes the nameless value as an objective quality of its own, making it appear to the members of the horde as a fearsome power residing in that post, tree or devised bogey (this last may belong only to a later hominid stage than the pre-linguistic, pre-cultural beings here assumed).

At this point, again, a biological function we have already found operative in image-making affects the evolutionary process: the tendency to formalization, which seems to govern operant actions as well as vision and hearing.[61] This tendency imposes order and repetition on

[61] The spontaneous, subjective rhythmicizing of the sound of a ticking watch is a well-worn example in the auditory realm. Silberer's hallucination of deploying the squares of his hypnagogic sunlight mosaics in the rhythm sounded by the wheels of the train (see p. 287 above) was a case of formalized (though dreamt) movement.

bodily movements that are not guided by practical intent, but spring from emotional impulses. Such formalization is familiar from animal behavior, where our ethologists have given it entirely human designations—"ritual," "ceremony," "symbolic acts" and even "superstition." Here, at last, we reach the great divide where these terms become legitimate; and at this point we can see how the biological principles of repetition and formalization, which sometimes have spectacular effects in animal behavior, really enter into the etiology of the acts of human beings performing holy rites. As usual, the new mental phenomenon seems to have arisen on a complex substructure, a meeting of several coincident developments. The tendency to formalize non-practical movements, especially expressive, emotionally engendered ones, is certainly the first crucial physiological factor in the advance toward ritual action; another is the fact that probably all hominids, like most of the higher primates, are gregarious, suggestible and interested in each other's doings,[62] so any outwardly expressive, spectacular movement, such as wide-flung arms or top-like whirling on one foot, lifted hands, and vocal accompaniments would evoke imitative responses, perhaps long trains of them. Most of the elements of such behavior have simian parallels, not only in captive apes but in wild ones, at least in chimpanzees, though the formalizing tendencies in them are sparse, and the communal facilitation of example affects whole acts, which each animal "imitates" in its own way, rather than any sequence of moves.[63] The

[62] Cf. Étienne Rabaud, "Les hommes au point de vue biologique" (1931), pp. 695–96, who, after remarking on the gregarious habits of monkeys and apes, says: "Chez les Hommes, il y a plus. Les Hommes sont moins 'personnels'; chez eux, un certain altruisme apparaît, en ce sens que chacun d'eux s'occupe un peu du voisin et s'y 'intéresse': la création de signes de communication naît, justement, de cet intérêt. Les signes vocaux ont été utilisés, parce qu'ils étaient anatomiquement et physiologiquement possibles; des gestes manuels auraient aussi bien servi; sons ou gestes existent indépendamment de toute vie sociale.

"Quant à l'attention que tout Homme porte à son congénère, elle n'est en rien spécifique; elle ne l'est, du moins, que dans la mesure où elle marque une simple différence de degré par rapport à beaucoup d'autres animaux. Nombre d'entre eux, en effet, 'reconnaissent' la présence du voisin; mais l'attention ne va pas jusqu'à l'intérêt, sinon un intérêt fort rudimentaire et tel qu'il ne détermine aucun effet appréciable.

"L'augmentation de l'intérêt, suffisante pour provoquer une manifestation appréciable, semble liée au développement des états de conscience. Ceux-ci caractérisent vraiment les Hommes, en tant qu'il s'agit d'états de conscience claire.... A la conscience claire, correspond le désir de communiquer avec le voisin...."

[63] See Van Lawick-Goodall, *My Friends the Wild Chimpanzees*, pp. 76–77, for an account of purely excited behavior which she likens to a savage dance (and humorously calls a "rain dance," as it occurred chiefly during heavy storms); but it

kind of observation and stepwise following here attributed—purely hypothetically, of course—to prehuman hominids is shown by other, present-day primates not in wild excitement, but in sociable play, mainly among the young. But Schaller, watching gorillas in their native habitat,[64] and Carpenter, observing howler monkeys in theirs,[65] have seen them unmistakably playing what children call "follow the leader," where the action depends on noting the behavior of the animal just ahead and imitating his principal moves. The tendency to repetition which is often seen in play, both solitary and collective but especially the latter,[66] naturally produces some formalization of the repetitious act (most individual perseverative behavior springs from sexual excitement rather than play, and builds up elaborate forms under growing emotional pressure;[67] but it is communal formalized action that leads to genuine ritualization, though in itself it is not enough).

How genuine ritual actually began we shall never know; in the evolution of mind, it is the behavioral aspect of the past lives constituting our heredity that could really tell the story, but that aspect is irretrievably gone. Fragments of fossilized bones are all that remains of those men, "man-apes" or previous animals. A few stark mementos, chiefly stone artifacts of very ancient, yet approximately determinable, age, occur in the deposits that yield hominid bones, and bear witness to astoundingly early human activity. But apart from anthropological speculations on which there is no scientific agreement such exhibits do not tell us whether the beings who could fashion those crude spearheads, arrowheads, choppers and blades could also speak.

To ask when man began to speak is a bootless question, because

---

might just as well or better be likened to an athletic meet. The apes were noisy, but their utterances showed no formalization or imitation, though the performers clearly egged each other on, and the general action seemed to have been suggested by the first actor.

[64] *The Mountain Gorilla—Ecology and Behavior*, p. 250: "Most play included some form of wrestling and chasing, and games such as 'king of the mountain' and 'follow the leader.' "

[65] *A Field Study of the Behavior and Social Relations of Howling Monkeys*, p. 80: "I have observed as many as six young ones following each other over a definite circuit consisting of several kinds of supports. Sometimes young following each other will make a descending jump from one branch to another and then the action will be repeated again and again."

[66] Kummer, studying the play of baboons, remarks: "Ein charakteristischer Zug des Spiels ist auch die stetige *Wiederholung* derselben Szene" (*Soziales Verhalten einer Mantelpavian Gruppe*, p. 77).

[67] See Chapter 13, pp. 72–74, above.

speech itself has probably gone through so many phases that what one anthropologist might already honor with that name another might not. A system of vocal signals influencing the behavior of other members of one's own kind might satisfy one theorist as a criterion of speech, whereas his colleague would require the sound to be more than a signal in an actual situation, and to be a symbolic sign which would keep a fundamental conceptual meaning from any context to another. Also, the criterion of speech might or might not stipulate that the utterance be entirely analyzable into separate words. It is wiser, perhaps, to ask from what natural anlagen the process of speech as we know it in all men today can possibly have arisen and attained its unrivaled importance in the great evolutionary shift from animal existence to human estate.

Speech is a process which has created an instrument, language. These two phenomena present somewhat different theoretical problems; the existence of speech in all normal human beings after infancy is a biological trait, but the divergencies and interrelationships of languages, and the laws of language change and grammatical development (which have many characteristics of natural laws), defy all familiar biological canons and methods. Psychological factors abound in the acquisition of speech, and likewise in the history of language, but different factors operate in those two distinct fields of research. At present, it is the evolution of speech that concerns us. The subject has been treated many times, especially since the middle of the nineteenth century, then suffered something of an eclipse, but has been revived in recent years largely by virtue of the discoveries of "man-apes" in southeast Africa, on the one hand, and, on the other, at the incentive of the experimental training lately given to several young apes in the hope of leading them to speak. So far, however, our prehistorical speculations have not profited greatly from either source. These disappointments suggest that there is a fallacy in our approach rather than a deficiency in the new materials.

The fallacy, I think, is a principle which is sometimes avowed, often tacitly accepted, and sometimes—but very rarely, and then only casually —rejected: the assumption that because a cardinal function of speaking today is directive communication—i.e., warning, commanding and conveying information—the desire for such communication must have been the original motivation of the utterances which gave rise to speech.[68]

[68] John Dewey and George Herbert Mead naturally regarded the communicative function of language as paramount because of the extreme, almost exclusive value they placed on social relations. More recently, Charles Morris treated language entirely in terms of signs; and this approach is the one which shows the impact of the new "automation" industry in which communication is the sole aim, all effects

It follows as a corollary to this assumption that the precursor of speech was some cruder communicative system, perhaps pantomime accompanied by grunts, clicks of tongue and lips, or cries and variable, senseless babble.[69] The latter would merely have developed the articulating and phonetic capacities of the race, and furnished "phonemes" from which "roots," or primitive words, could be chosen. Some authors think of speech as something purposely invented, and adopted by agreement;[70] most scholars today, however, realize that such high intellectual

---

of recording, translating into code and reproduction are divided into "message" and "noise," and the former is the core of the designed procedure. The language and, of course, the basic categorizations of contemporary linguistics reflect this technological analysis. See Morris, *Signs, Language and Behavior* (1946); E. H. Lenneberg, *Biological Foundations of Language* (1967); C. F. Hockett, "The Origin of Speech" (1960); there are many other contemporary works which show the same influence.

Géza Révész, in *Ursprung und Vorgeschichte der Sprache*—a book which, despite some serious faults, is a mine of valuable ideas—declares: "Die Ursache der Sprache bzw. des Sprechens liegt meines Erachtens eben in der Tendenz, eine sprachliche Verständigungsgemeinschaft zu bilden" (p. 25n). This assertion recurs in many phrasings throughout the book.

[69] Raymond Dart, in "Cultural Status of the South African Man-Apes," wrote: "The Australopithecinae may not have talked about their works, their tools, and the actions performed with their aid; nor am I aware of any evidence that articulate speech ... was employed by any human type preceding *Homo sapiens*. There can, however, be little doubt that these australopithecine makers of osteodontokeratic tools, these followers of antelope-hunting techniques, these dissectors of animal bodies had a correspondingly adequate number of distinctive gestures and signals, manual, implemental and doubtless vocal, for communicating their intentions while assembling tools for, and employing those tools in, their hunting, and for designating their wishes in respect to those tools when dividing the spoils of the chase. In so doing they were laying the foundations upon which was erected the superstructure of articulate speech" (p. 337).

Only a few years later, in an article "On the Evolution of Language and Articulate Speech" (1958), he seriously supports Paget's proposal that "the original crude communicating system ... was perhaps gesture accompanied by cries and grunts and could have lasted for hundreds of thousands of years," that all this time mankind "remained in the stage of generalized pantomime and babbling," until a few advanced individuals—magicians—"acquired the mental trick of isolating the elements of shape, colour, number and so forth from their general impressions of the animals, over which they wished to exercise their magic, and of using words to describe those isolated elements." For this they produced the Aurignacian cave paintings! And, he adds, "Paget had thought too that the magicians probably kept their new way of thinking to themselves and thus maintained their authority over the gabbling tribe" (p. 158).

[70] Sir Richard Paget, in *Human Speech: Some Observations, Experiments and Conclusions as to the Nature, Origin, Purpose and Possible Improvements of Human Speech* (1930), p. 132, wrote: "What drove man to the invention of speech

acts would be beyond the reach of man-apes not already equipped with powers of language, and give special credit to theories which derive that amazing human attainment, the fulcrum of the "great shift" in pre-human zoological evolution, from animal beginnings and the special proclivities of one primate family in which coincident developments have repeatedly sparked fateful novelties.

Yet very few anthropologists seem to have studied general evolutionary principles enough to discover that most really new actions did not arise from older processes serving the same ends. They usually take shape in the course of quite unrelated activities which, perhaps, overgrow the agent's needs, and presently find a new use in the organism's economy.[71] The new function is unpremeditated, unintended, yet not accidental; it has been slowly building up with the development of all its elements in other quarters.

So, I think, it must have been with language, which involves so many elements of human specialization that no simple, pragmatic motivation (like that of nest-building, food-hoarding or many another complex instinctive performance) could have initiated it, and permitted the operation of "natural selection" to develop it. There could hardly have been any desire or felt need to communicate among prehuman beings before there were definitely symbolic utterances to evoke ideas, associated with them by their producer, in the similarly disposed brain of a hearer; that means that the utterance was already more than just a sound to both of them, but part of a remembered act in which they had

---

was, as I imagine, not so much the need of expressing his thoughts (for that might have been done quite satisfactorily by bodily gesture) as the difficulty of 'talking with his hands full.' It was the *continual* use of man's hands for craftsmanship ... that drove him to ... a specialized pantomime with the tongue and lips." Paget believed that word roots were imitations of gestures, and that the effect of blowing out air at the same time was *then discovered and found useful* to put over the pantomime at a distance or in the dark.

[71] It is generally agreed (with the exception of the experimenters cited in Chapter 16, n. 87) that the "dance" of a bee returned from a foraging trip gives the subsequent foragers their general direction and length of flight, as Karl von Frisch was the first to claim; but the origin of the "dance" does not seem to have been in any earlier sort of directive action, let alone "communication." Cf. p. 204, n. 103, above. Another example of the development of a function from another (or others) entirely differently motivated is presented by A. J. Marshall in *Bower Birds*, p. 64, where he describes the evident derivation of the blue male's display motions and postures from his threatening and fighting repertoire, with the comment: "It would seem that gestures originally evolved as part of a mechanism of aggression have become part of a display mechanism which is released during emotional excitement of a somewhat different kind."

both participated so that their memories converged sufficiently to have a common outside reference—that is, an objective, even if vaguely conceived, denotation, the same for both.

The source of such sounds is only in a secondary way the instinctive repertoire of *Homo* (probably *Homo* spp.), the "clicks" of tongue, lips and cheeks in sucking to which Van Ginneken tried to reduce consonants and primitive (he thought, non-vocalized) "root" words,[72] or even the vocalized cries and croons of early infancy which later beget lalling and babble. In such activities the young organism learns the production of distinguishable sounds and acquires the power of articulation —even, as has frequently been remarked, beyond the needs of the "mother tongue" it will learn;[73] but both "clicks" and formless vowel sounds, and even continued babble, belong to phases of babyhood which are passed through, and their manifestation dropped completely after their typical term is over. They do not persist unless they are reinforced at the crucial time by the enticement of adult speech. So the observation of infant learning in this regard seems to give us no clue to the origination of language in previously speechless creatures.

What may, however, have led to the formation of linguistic utterance and understanding was a prior sort of symbolic action, the vociferous accompaniment of the earliest communal expression of formalized feeling, ritual dance. Its motivation was not communication, but communion, though not the sheer desire for bodily contact or at least intimate nearness of ape and monkey bands; what found expression in the dance was the sense of a power residing in the horde as a single agent, pervading the holy place, and perhaps made visible in a fetish—a mysterious central tree or a nearby, terrible "bush-devil," made by nature as a chance form, or by primitive but fantasy-guided hands. The reason for formalizing the expression of group feeling was that in this

---

[72] J. van Ginneken, *La réconstruction typologique des langues archaïques de l'humanité* (1939). On p. 5 he says, "Il se pourrait très bien, qu'autrefois les mots lexicaux ne contenaient ordinairement qu'un seul phonème, d'une nature assez compliquée, comme les clics qui se forment par trois ou quatre occlusions du canal buccal." On this "very possible" condition of ancient speech sounds he builds up his whole evolutionary theory of language, which will be briefly sketched below (p. 304).

[73] Israel Latif, in "The Physiological Basis of Linguistic Development and the Ontogeny of Meaning" (1934), p. 60, speaking of the babbling or "lalling" period of infancy, cites many authorities to the effect that "many more sounds are produced by the infant during this period than are later used, at least in its own language," and adds, "Now, out of this astonishingly rich and varied repertoire of sounds, those which are used by the child's elders are reinforced, and become habitual; the others cease to be uttered."

way it was enhanced, sustained and upheld when subjectively it might have breaks and lapses. The sense of power it bestowed on each individual was a previous value, and to produce it an exhilarating act; to make men (or proto-men) enter into a dance undoubtedly required no persuasion. So it is not altogether surprising that, as Curt Sachs said in his *World History of the Dance*, "the history of the creative dance takes place in prehistory."[74]

The change from simian gregariousness to such organized assemblage as even the most savage true dance requires, though both, perhaps, were still equally based on wordless communion, was already part of the radical shift from animal mentality to mind; for it was the symbolic element—however vaguely sensed—that made dancing entirely different from prancing, and celebration from play, even if group play looks to the human observer like a rite. A playful act can be abandoned at any moment; even the lifting up of a baby animal and perhaps spinning around with it, which Hans Kummer reports in his observations on baboons,[75] has apparently no meaning beyond the rather rough, conjoint, athletic play of young monkeys with still younger ones. All animal acts which are repeated, whether for vital purposes, emotional release or in play, tend to become formalized; but to call this tendency "ritualization" is a grave mistake, ignoring the whole psychological aspect of such performance on the one hand and of ritual on the other. Any animal act in which an ethologist sees no sense is called a "rite";[76] but no non-human creature has ever performed a rite.

With the overgrowth of mental functions in hominid phylogeny, which seems to have led to fantasy and symbolic or proto-symbolic functions of the brain, the need of contact between individuals, found in all degrees in various animals, undergoes a change from bodily contact to mental contact.[77] Communion becomes an elaborate emotional need, in which the simple impulses to grooming, clinging or going to sleep in each other's arms are gradually replaced by symbolic collective acts: the expression of union with the horde in dance, and of the

---

[74] (1937), p. 62.

[75] *Soziales Verhalten einer Mantelpavian Gruppe*, p. 77.

[76] Even Paul H. Schiller, who recognized the deceptiveness of supposed "work" by apes and its real basis in play interest, referred to one animal's puzzling habit as a "measuring rite."

[77] It was Géza Révész who made interindividual contact the basis of all animal and human "communication," though he did not see the importance of physical contact for animals and the necessity to distinguish between this form and the mental form of contact before one could speak of "communication." This will be discussed below.

fear of outside powers—storm, earthquake, attack by real or fantastic dreaded creatures—in seeking refuge round a fetish or in a "holy" place. Gestures of devotion to visible or invisible superior beings are the hominid version of the baboons' frantic grooming of the "α-animal" in response to his own threats or bites.[78] All primitive divinities, or what goes before divinities in the way of mystic animals or dream figments, are terrible as well as protecting demons; and the mental contact among the proto-human beings which displaces the constantly needed physical contact of gregarious simians is most readily made by celebration, dance, choric shouts and gestures, centering around some symbol of potency. By such acts all the participants are joined in one performance and feel themselves as one.

By the time the pre-Adamites—whichever species may have existed at the time or times when language arose—had progressed to the point of symbolic expression, the physiological mechanisms for articulate utterance must have been fairly well complete.[79] The same may be said for the discriminative ear which takes in patterns of sound, the nervous structures that control utterance by coincident inner and outer hearing and the suggestibility of sociable primates that makes choric action the most natural behavior in a group concentrating on one intensely cathected symbol, whether an object or a progressive movement. In such a situation, both movement and shouted ululation would tend to become formalized and be precisely repeated, with more and more articulation at the recurrent high moments of the rhythmic round, which—in its emotional, proto-symbolic setting—was already genuine dancing. At these points, also, the excited brains of the actors are most likely to have generated images, probably visual-kinesthetic envisagements, reactivated by every repetition of the passage that had first inspired them—each dancer his own images, of course, but in a public framework, and perhaps the same crucial context wherein other participants had their private visions too.

These assemblies, if they existed at the dawn of human history (and

[78] See Chapter 15 above, pp. 167–71 *passim* and n. 50.

[79] E. L. Du Brul, in his dissertation, "Phylogenesis of the Speech Apparatus," pp. 59 ff, remarks that it is not the vocal organ but the mouth that makes human articulate speech possible. W. K. Gregory and M. Hellman, in "The Dentition of *Dryopithecus* and the Origin of Man," p. 110, note as one specialization of the human mouth "a great widening of the intercondylar diameter across the jaw associated partly with a great increase in the size of the brain and partly with a great increase in the width of the tongue." The latter made all lateral and velar consonants possible, the former made them and all other articulations desirable; the need and the means of its implementation developed together.

they are certainly very old, as cave paintings and traces of apparent "sacred places" show), were the first communal rituals, or rather, awesome aesthetic precursors of genuine ritual. This idea, especially of the humanizing importance of primitive dance and the vocalizations developed in connection with it, was propounded long ago by J. Donovan, in two articles entitled "The Festal Origin of Human Speech." No one ever paid much attention to them, possibly because they were published in a philosophical journal (*Mind*), where linguists were unlikely to see them, and at a time (1891–92) when philosophers were interested only in "isms"—materialism, idealism, empiricism, etc.—into which so factual a problem (no matter how elusive the facts) as the actual origins of speech did not fit. I adopted Donovan's hypothesis in *Philosophy in a New Key*, and it still seems to me fundamentally sound though today I cannot agree with his view of the nature of primitive dance as play,[80] nor with his treatment of so-called linguistic roots as the earliest real words (an assumption shared by many writers as the origins of speech).[81]

[80] The athletic play of chimpanzees which Van Lawick-Goodall called their "rain dance" had really no resemblance to a dance; the appellation indicates only that the exercise had no effective aim, but was a form of excitement to furious action (cf. n. 63, above). The repetitive procession of monkeys "following a leader," mentioned above, looks formalized, but does not suggest any spirit of dance. Such animal acts serve rather to show the difference between play and primitive dance than to identify them.

[81] One of the most distinguished linguists holding this view was Alfredo Trombetti, whose name is borne today by an active philological society. In his *L'Unità d'Origine del Linguaggio* (1905), pp. 59–60, having classified all language "roots" under three headings: interjective, demonstrative (pronominal) and predicative, he said: "Le radici predicative sono di gran lunga più numerose. Il loro monosillabismo fu affermato già a priori, per ragioni psicologiche. Si disse in sostanza che ad una impressione unica prodotta sull'uomo da una causa interna od esterna non può corrispondere che una sola emissione di voce, cioè una sillaba. L'esame dei fatti conferma questa teoria, poichè in tutti gruppi linguistici le radici sono di regola monosillabiche. Non mancano certo le radici bisillabe, ma il loro bisillabismo proviene semplicemente dall' aggiunta, in fine della radice, di una vocale omogenea a quella principale. . . ."

Dart, in his article cited above, "On the Evolution of Language and Articulate Speech," today takes the identity of "roots" and primitive words for granted, and searches this Aryan "vocabulary" to find the evidence for his curious doctrine that fishing was the great humanizing factor, so he ranks it on an equal footing with religion and social consciousness in the making of speech.

Van Ginneken set up the still more curious theory that language, arising from a desire to converse, originally consisted only of "click sounds" made with tongue and lips, then went through a phase of pure consonant structures audible only at close range, until the primitive speakers discovered that vowels made the sounds carry further, whereupon each "root" came to contain a vowel among the groups of

His own idea of the formation of speech makes the early reduction of separate words to fixed monosyllables improbable; far more likely, Jespersen made a sympathetic psychological guess when he wrote: "Primitive linguistic units must have been much more complicated in point of meaning, as well as much longer in point of sound, than those with which we are most familiar."[82]

It was Donovan's idea that words were not primitive elements in human utterance when it became symbolic, but that meaning first accrued to longer passages, which were gradually broken or condensed into separate sections, each with its own more and more special sense. But what he did not say was how conceptual meaning accrued to ·any vocal products at all. The symbolic function—in effect, conceptual meaning—begins with the occurrence of imagery; and by the time a particular image can be called up by some known means, imagination is coming under a degree, however slight, of voluntary control. In the fantastic development of tribal dance all individuals of the primitive horde became familiar with the vocal sounds that belonged to various sequences of steps and gestures, some perhaps mimetic, others purely expressive, working up to climaxes of excitement. The "song," or vocal part of the dance, became more and more differentiated with the evolution of the gestic patterns. At high points there were undoubtedly special yells or elaborate mouthed noises, like the "wa-wa-wa-wah" made by striking the mouth or the cheeks with one's hands while shouting; also elaborate halloos, with strings of articulated, repeated syllables, imitations of animal calls, etc.[83] Donovan suggested that renderings of the drum beat might have been an early motif. In the overstimulated brains of the celebrants, images must have been easily evoked at these points of action and special vocalization—images that tended to recur

---

consonants (usually in bunches of three consonants or clicks). These "roots" were the archaic words, succeeding—for communication at ordinary hearing range—to the gesture language that served when words were still without carrying power. See *La réconstruction typologique des langues archaïques de l'humanité, passim.*

[82] Otto Jespersen, *Language: Its Nature, Development and Origin* (1922), p. 425.

[83] Even today, in the "Bone Dance," or Monkey Dance, performed at fairly regular intervals at the Village of Bone on Bali, all the men in the ·village form the dance chorus while a few trained and costumed dancers enact the traditional episode from the Ramayana, in which Hanuman, King of the Monkeys, and his simian followers (the chorus) come to the aid of Rama to recover his kidnapped wife. The main theme of the "music" is a steady "how-how-how" voiced by the dancers, a formalized imitation of the langurs' cry; a primitive element in an otherwise civilized, highly developed balletic work with the serious purpose of inspiring a young clairvoyant to have a prophetic vision for the guidance of the village elders.

in that context, until for each individual his own symbolic images were built into the familiar patterns of tribal rituals. A dance passage takes time and energy, if not actually several persons, to perform, but the vocal ingredient can be reproduced with little effort and in a minimal time by any individual. To remember the festive occasion would probably bring the vocal element to his throat; as the memory or thought of a conventional wedding might make one hum the ineluctable Lohengrin march. Our lives are too individualized and various to relate the tune to the same memory for everyone, but in that most primitive, still speechless, barely human life, where the dance was a high and exciting occasion, the fit would be close and quite the same for all concerned. If the action at that point was, say, swinging a club, or even felt like that expansive act, the image may be of swinging, or of whirling clubs, lifted arms or what not; but whatever it is, it symbolizes the activity, the people and objects involved in it, and especially the emotional values of the event. The image with its whole cargo of feeling is the marginal effect of the sound pattern when it is intoned apart from the dance.

The image is a genuine conception; it does not signalize or demand its object, but denotes it. Of course, this conception itself is not communicable, for it is covert, purely private; but the things remembered are public and the sounds activating the private images are public; they evoke images in other persons, too, by arousing memories of roughly the same moments of dance action. Within a fairly wide range it does not matter how different the private images are. They are equivalent symbols for the act and the objects that mark those stations in the ritual where the vocal bits belong which may be uttered out of context by some individual; and suddenly the symbolic function shifts from the several private images to the vocal fragment that evoked them all concomitantly, so meaning accrues to the phrase, other beings understand, repeat the sounds or supplement them with a gesture that demonstrates their memory of the same act or thing awakened by the well-known utterance. If, then, the high ritual act involved a physical object such as a spear, this one element which is not transient like the action outlives the dance, and every so often, in mundane life, suddenly brings to mind the bit of chant, the syllables intoned, the melodious wail, or whatever vocal passage is associated with it. A proto-human being would possibly utter some bit of the chant that came into his head, without any further reason or any purpose, as he handled or suddenly noticed the spear.

The question has been raised more than once why a particular oral sign, attached to a particular object by one individual's whim, should be generally accepted as the name of that object, without interference by dozens of rival proposals. Donovan's notion, carried out as here suggested, offers an explanation: the choice was not whimsical, but logical under natural conditions, and the process of naming anything—acts, objects or feelings—went through a long preparation before the hominid celebrants were aware that their sounds had come to recall special acts or objects involved in them. No one chose a name at all; no one had any idea of what a name was. Very possibly, for centuries after genuine reference to ritual acts and objects apart from the actual ceremonies had come into practice, only such acts and objects had any symbols to represent them. But as savage dance is apt to draw all things from tribal life into its domain, those which were mentionable may have been a large moiety soon after the habit of using the voice in reference to special elements became established.

I suspect that the first meanings of such secularized vocalizations were so vague that the symbols could not really be called "words," let alone "names." Swing a club, hit a man, kill beast or man, whirl and hit, swing a club at the moon—such ideas, perhaps suggested or even mimed in the dance, may all have belonged by turns to one long utterance, in which the separate articulate parts need not have had any separable meanings.[84] But as some fragments were used more and more to call up ideas, perhaps combined with others from other dances to emphasize one possible meaning, as modern Chinese uses synonyms to fix one sense of a word above all possible homonymous ones[85] (e.g., reinforcing "swing a club" with a bit of abracadabra from a dance hailing the moon, to be sure of "swing a club at the moon"), the utterances themselves probably became merely suggested, hummed, rather than sung or roared as in the dance; and so they would be gradually reduced

[84] In the *Encyclopaedia Britannica*, 1957 ed., *s.v.* "language," Jespersen voices the same opinion.

[85] Bernhard Karlgren, in his little book *Sound and Symbol in Chinese* (1946; 1st ed., 1923), pp. 29–30, wrote: "The modern dialects all have a very meagre stock of vocables, with great numbers of homophones. The Mandarin dialect of Peking is one of the poorest, and, indeed, does not possess more than about 420 different syllables. . . .

". . . Of the common 4,200 words there are only two that are pronounced *jun*, but 69 that have the pronunciation *i*, 59 *shi*, 29 *ku*, and so forth. But . . . the inconvenience of the homophones is considerably alleviated by . . . the musical accents or 'tones.' Musical accent is a phenomenon that existed in the prehistoric Indo-European language, but it has not survived in the majority of the daughter languages. . . . In every Chinese word there is inherent a certain melody, and words otherwise phonetically identical can be distinguished by their different melodies."

to the speaking voice, even if they retained "tones" of inexact but distinguishable pitch as formal elements. That would encourage buccal articulation, i.e., the use of consonants and vowels, above musical and gestic elements.

Some excellent writers on the evolution of speech, Donovan among them, have hypothesized that originally all speech was sung: Jespersen, in the book already quoted, closes a discussion of voice inflections in passionate speech and the sing-song manner he attributes to "savages" (without further identification) by saying: "These facts and considerations all point to the conclusion that there once was a time when all speech was song, or rather when these two actions were not yet differentiated...."[86] But even if (as I find quite plausible) speaking was derived from chanting and shouting, the derivation was devious, and in the days before the two actions were distinct there was not really speech; the first communication of ideas might have been achieved, but there could have been nothing like conversation. The power of conversing could only have accrued to the symbolic utterances in a more manageable phase, when the vocables in combinations could be so freely and quickly produced that they attained the "transparency" they have today, conveying ideas without being themselves remembered in their precise order.[87]

The statement that the most ancient speech was sung has been made repeatedly, and has sometimes been supported by the claim that "savages" (usually unspecified) talk in a sing-song manner. The persons who make the claim, however, are often judging of a language they do not command, even to the extent of knowing whether it employs "tones" as semantic elements; Swedish has a "sing-song" character which is intrinsic to it, as it is to Chinese;[88] neither is a primitive language, nor are the speakers savages. And, furthermore, there are people and even whole populations, for instance, the Saxon in central Germany, who have a characteristic fluctuant intonation, but their speech

---

[86] *Language: Its Nature, Development and Origin*, p. 420.

[87] Paul Valéry observed this difference between the poetic and practical uses of language. In a lecture subsequently published as an essay, *Poésie et pensée abstraite* (1939), after discussing poetic expression—"ces discours si différents des discours ordinaires que sont les vers"—he says, "dans les emplois pratiques ou abstraits du langage, la forme c'est à dire le physique, le sensible, et l'acte même du discours ne se conserve pas; elle ne survit pas à la compréhension; elle se dissout dans la clarté; elle a agi; elle a fait son office; elle a fait comprendre; elle a vécu." Words are used and pass away. As he said shortly before, "Je vous parle, et si vous avez compris mes paroles, ces paroles même sont abolies" (pp. 12–13).

[88] Karlgren, *Sound and Symbol in Chinese*, pp. 29–30.

bears no relation to chant. A sing-song speaking voice is not a singing voice. Any incursion of spoken text in an opera, no matter how musical the speaking voices, is startlingly different from recitative, which is level in tone but held on a definitive pitch. Savage song is often full of shrieks, wails or other interpolations; these might have served originally to segment the sacred utterance into semantic units, but probably not for long after the units were borrowed for practical purposes. As soon as they had communicative functions, all utterances, no matter how they were derived, probably were quickly "verbalized"—spoken. Certainly household conversations, women's gossip and other such familiar exchanges were never sung, though public commands, men's boasts and all formal announcements might have been so for ages in a normally speaking society. Religious declarations still are chanted in many traditions.[89]

My only reason for giving so much weight to Donovan's old and purely hypothetical proposal concerning the rise and earliest development of human speech is that so far I have come upon no other notion that fits as well into the evolutionary theory of human origins conceived in the general frame of primate phylogeny: the adaptive radiation of lemuroid, simian and hominoid forms, and the long, mainly single-track history of the terrestrial Hominidae, perhaps terrestrial and bi-pedal longer than is generally believed. We have no real clue to give factual support to the "festal" thesis, which can only be classed with the familiar pictures of prehistoric scenes depicting dinosaurs in lakes and tree-fern jungles, sometimes conscientiously labeled "artist's conception." But it must be possible to set up other, equally plausible hypotheses concerning the earliest phases of that unique hominid trait, language. Perhaps the greatest stumbling block to original thought in

---

[89] There is an odd weakness among cultural prehistorians for ranging the distinguishable, perhaps separately derived and incorporated elements of language in a temporal order, and supposing each in its day to have furnished and ruled a complete communicative system before the next element was added. The fact that many people gesticulate when they talk and that "savages" are supposed to do so more than civilized peoples (a doubtful proposition) has frequently been taken to mean that a fully developed sign language preceded vocal speech. See, for example, J. M. Baldwin, *Mental Development in the Child and the Race* (1915; 1st ed., 1895), p. 492; Paget, *Human Speech*, p. 132 (this author claimed that oral speech was derived by using the mouth to imitate manual gestures); Latif, Dart and several other reputable scholars have followed the same lead. Van Ginneken furnished the most perfect example of the fallacious "priority principle" in ranging the successive phases of human language as "la dynastie des gestes et de la mimique," "la dynastie des clics," "la dynastie des groupes de consonnes," and finally the introduction of vowels to form the syllabic "roots" commonly regarded as the earliest words (cf. n. 81 above).

that domain is our present preoccupation with communicating devices and the analysis of factors "coded" in communicated information. This present fashion has led to a completely unpsychological and unbiological treatment of language in other connections than "computer" technology, translation schemes and techniques or (on a somewhat more intellectual level) comparative linguistics, all of which have good use for such systematizing procedures. But formal analyses of fully developed language, like Chomsky's currently influential work, throw no light on the beginnings of speech, which must have come with the gathering force of symbolic expression at a very early period of cultural life, really the period of *Menschwerdung*. There are so many elements interacting to make up language that some of them may be ancient and common to many animals, some peculiar to the Hominoidiae, some to mankind alone. So, for instance, the two quite separate elements of reference and of direct address to one or more persons may stem from different sources and have entered into language at different times. But surely the catalyst which precipitated the new and unique power of speech was symbolic conception, the intuition of meaning.

This intuition, too, must have gathered slowly and gone through bizarre, emotional, irrational stages. Unrealistic fantasy is probably more primitive than any intellectual grasp of causes and effects. If, then, we cast about for an alternative to the "festal" theory of the beginning of speech, we are not likely to find it in such practices as assigning names to objects, making statements of fact and directing the acts of other people. Géza Révész, in his *Ursprung und Vorgeschichte der Sprache* (1946), holds that all the essential functions of language reduce to three: command, declaration, and interrogation.[90] Since he admits nothing as even a forerunner of language that is not uttered with communicative intent,[91] the only possible antecedent of speech must be

---

[90] One of his principal sections is entitled "Die Dreifunktionstheorie." On p. 151 he defines language as follows: "*Unter Sprache wäre demnach jene Kommunikationsform zu verstehen, durch welche zum Zwecke gegenseitiger Verständigung— mit Hilfe einer Anzahl artikulierter und in verschiedenen Sinnverbindungen auftretender symbolischer Zeichen—Forderungen und Wünsche zum Ausdruck gebracht, Tatbestände der inneren und äusseren Wahrnehmung angezeigt und Fragen zur Veranlassung von Mitteilungen gestellt werden.*" In introducing this definition he said, on the previous page, "Diese drei sprachlichen Ausdrucksformen umspannen und erschöpfen alle Formen der *Verständigung* unter Menschen. . . . Denn tritt der Mensch zu seinen Artgenossen in sprachlichen Kontakt, so bestehen für ihn keine anderen Möglichkeiten, als ihnen etwas zu befehlen, sie zu einer Handlung aufzufordern bzw. anzuregen . . . oder ihnen etwas anzuzeigen, kundzugeben . . . oder sie um etwas zu fragen. . . ."

[91] This principle is treated at length and in many connections throughout the

either some animal communication or a human form of language not involving oral acts; but as he rejects the former because it shows no tendency to develop into any system of communicative signs,[92] and the latter as implausible,[93] it is hard to see where the elements of speech could have been found that were to implement the communicative purpose.

Although I cannot but reject many of Révész' assumptions and assertions, especially his cardinal principle that every element of language must have sprung from a desire for communication, and that this supreme human distinction presupposes the prior existence of minds capable of thinking, questioning and commanding, I do find in his book a key idea, though his treatment leaves too many immediately relevant problems not only unresolved, but as unillumined as ever. His key idea —which he sets up as such—is the need of contact between fellow creatures. That is what has largely shifted from actual to symbolic levels. In animals, there is usually a need of close, physical contact between mother and young until the latter can feed, groom and protect or hide themselves; in some species this need becomes extended and generalized so the parent-offspring relation changes by degrees to a relation between the individual and the herd (variously called flock, swarm, pack, in primates the horde) of familially connected or accepted other individuals.[94] In some animals, such as sheep, there remains a frequent demand

---

book, and is most clearly stated in an early section where he makes the distinction between proto-forms and early forms, but emphasizes that in order to count as either, a phenomenon such as an animalian luring call must have something akin to communicative intent to enter into the prehistory of language. See pp. 23–24, where he distinguishes between pre-linguistic forms (*Vorformen*) and early linguistic ones (*Frühformen*), and concludes: "Von diesem Gesichtspunkt aus wird man geneigt sein, den Lockruf entwicklungsgeschichtlich als Vorform der Sprache gelten zu lassen, vorausgesetzt, dass er prinzipiell demselben Bedürfnis dient und denselben Zweck verfolgt wie die menschliche Sprache."

[92] P. 47: "Ihrer äusseren Erscheinung wie ihrer inneren Struktur nach zeigen die Lautäusserungen der Tiere kein einziges Merkmal, das der menschlichen Sprache eigen ist." The entire passage, covering pp. 47–48, is relevant but too long to quote.

[93] P. 69: "Lebende Wesen geben, falls sie über ein klangerzeugendes Organ verfügen, von ihren inneren Erregungszuständen genau so durch Klanglaute wie durch Körperbewegungen kund.... Mit Rücksicht auf die *anatomischen und physiologischen Grundlagen* der Lauterzeugung und den Gebrauch der Klanglaute hat also der Primat der Gebärdensprache gegenüber der Lautsprache keine Wahrscheinlichkeit."

[94] "Accepted" here refers to the sporadic occurrence of adoptive members, like a *Lemur macaco* which Alison Jolly observed as a regular member of a troop of *Lemur catta* (*Lemur Behavior*, p. 119), or the occasional inclusion of newcomers, transiently or permanently, reported by observers of gorillas and chimpanzees in the wild.

for physical contact, body to body; in others the permanent need is satisfied by a sense of nearness. Between these two kinds of contact one may
find all degrees, such as the tendency in some species to crowd close and
seek real contiguity in case of alarm, or the apparent desire to reach the
utmost union by penetrating another animal's fur to the skin, although
ordinarily each individual goes its own way as far as it can without
losing sensory connection with the group as a whole.

Révész bases his study of language on what he has named the "contact theory," and draws the distinction, properly enough, between the
physical contacts of animals and the mental contacts which men strike
and maintain by symbolic communication. But how men ever began to
do so he does not say; on the contrary, he simply rules out the problem
of the biological origins of language altogether, on the ground that language is a purely human phenomenon, and a criterion of human status,
so that before language there were no men, and consequently no problems of language; and he reprimands scholars who overstep the bounds
of "their science," anthropology, to raise questions that belong neither
to it nor to zoology, where language has no place.[95]

It is, of course, precisely this problem, whereof Révész makes short
shrift by his decree that an issue which belongs to no recognized discipline should not be mooted at all, that is crucial in a phylogenetic approach to the uniquely human phenomenon of mind. Although his
"contact theory" is hardly a theory—consisting, as it does, of not much
more than the assertion that animals seek bodily contacts whereas men
seek symbolically negotiated, mental ones—the distinction he sets up
aptly narrows the field for an investigation like the present one. Contact
between individuals is a reality for all the higher animals, whether it is
limited to sexual and parental relations as in the arboreal sloths, slightly
exceeds that minimum as in the cats, which have agonistic encounters,
too, and in youth play with their littermates, or governs most of each
member's normal activities, as it does in truly gregarious kinds. In animals this relationship is almost a physiological condition, a felt communion of action and emotion and desire; in man that communion is
progressively weakened by the growing tendency to individuation which

[95] Pp. 33–34: "Sie schaffen eine künstliche Verbindung zwischen zwei wesens-
fremden Problemgebieten, die ihrem Stoff und ihren Methoden nach wenig Bezie-
hung zueinander haben. . . . Sieht man nämlich die Sprache als das wesentlichste
Merkmal des Menschen an, . . . so hat die Hypothese des sprachlosen Urmenschen
keinen Sinn. Denn die sprachlosen Menschen waren gemäss der Definition noch
keine Menschen, demzufolge wäre es widersinnig, den Anfang der Geschichte der
Sprache dort anzusetzen, wo eine Sprachschicht noch nicht vorhanden war."

comes with the increase of mental activity that eventuates in dream, fantasy, memory images and the mechanisms of symbolic transformation, the fateful specialty of the human brain.

But even as we lost the old empathic bonds, the symbolic function has moved into the place of our broken instinctive unity. Its development had to be high and intense before it could enter into ordinary life, and this high pitch was almost certainly reached in more concerted mental acts than enlisting help or directing another subject's practical behavior. All a man's (or man-ape's?) imaginative powers must have concentrated on a symbolic act to develop and hold the nascent conception at the heart of it, and to let other equally vague figments become entrained by its formulation in the course of its awesome, prerational, gestic and vocal expression. The possibility of festal excitement as such a source has been discussed, but it is not the only conceivable starting point. Even the symbolic celebration of communion, still on the instinctive level, might have developed without quite reaching the crisis of freeing a fragment of the vocal pattern for other uses and for a conscious extraneous application. But the next step in such conceptual and expressive indulgence comprises more elements of thought and envisagement: that is magic-making.

The earliest notions of magic probably were centered on objects that had some suggestive form, like the root of the mandrake, many naturally sculptured forms of stone or wood, physiognomic aspects of old trees, and things with mysterious properties, such as flints from which sparks can be struck and conch shells wherein the roar of the ocean sounds when they are held to one's ear. Without some *churinga*, talisman, amulet or concrete luck-piece of whatever sort to center on, the first magic-mongers could hardly have held to their fantasy steadily enough to develop the fixed, though autistic abracadabra of a spell-casting utterance. It may have been chanted or, in the interest of keeping private possession of it, mumbled *sotto voce*. But in any event the weird syllables were intoned, probably with equally weird gestures, over and at the objects which symbolized the power the magician sought to possess, and which consequently were imagined to contain the power.[96]

---

[96] It is characteristic of pristine symbolic expression that symbols are regarded not as meaning something apart from themselves, but as themselves the objects or facts presented. Silberer pointed this out some sixty years ago in his essay "Über die Symbolbildung" (1912), saying: "Das metaphorisch sprechende Volk empfindet das, was es spricht, durchaus nicht als metaphorisch; die Symbole, die es handhabt, sind ihm nicht Symbole, sondern Wirklichkeiten. . . . Ebenso hält der Träumende die Symbole, die ihm sein eigener psychischer Mechanismus vorzaubert, durchaus

In this way the element of address to another being, which Révész named as one of the criteria of language, would be inherent in the conjuring rite, and receive the cathexis of that imaginative performance. Not only that, but the power of the utterance, conceived as physical power to direct the course of events, is the essence of magic, only helped by the overt acts of witchcraft that carry the spell. The directive element, too, is contained in the great unrealistic performance, the enactment of a fantasy, in which feeling rises to a higher level than in any actual business of life.

One could undoubtedly make more guesses at the first sources of language, and still have no measure to apply to their relative probabilities. The only extreme improbability seems to me to be that language arose from some kind of previous communication by improvements that had survival value. Animal contact is not communication; animals may perform joint acts, even pick up an act one from another at some juncture, as bees seem to pick up the food-getting act in a round, without asking or telling anything. Suggestibility and a general community of feeling are enough. It is human mentality that does not remain in the animal pattern. The great individuation made by subjective activity, the symbolic finishing of excessive nervous impulses within the nervous system itself, breaks the system of instinctive responses and begets the first processes of ideation, which eventuate in wild expressions, dance, magic, then the wishing of curses and blessings on other creatures and investing implements such as arrows, fishhooks or weapons with potency and luck by solemn rites, and hallowing the places for dancing or feasting with sacrificial bloodshed. Speech was born, I believe, in such high reaches of proto-human activity, and gathered form when one individual knew by the symbolic utterance of another what that other was thinking about. For with such concentrated expression came real envisagement, the beginning of reflection, thought.

With that achievement, everything really was given. The intuition of meaning was no longer an elusive sense of import, giving emotional value to non-practical vocalizations and gestures, but became comprehension of the idea in the head of the utterer. Such insight probably

---

nicht für blosse Symbole, sondern für den wirklichen zusammenhang der Dinge" (pp. 665–66).

Ernst Cassirer, in *Sprache und Mythos* (1925) and at greater length in *Die Philosophie der symbolischen Formen* (1923–29), especially Vol. II, develops this idea of the mythic mode of thought; since I have presented it in some detail in *Phil. N.K.* I shall not repeat the discussion here. Cf. also Vol. I above, especially Chapter 4.

elicited an echoic answer; the accompanying act was understood, since the articulated phrase itself could be repeated faster than the overt gestures and manipulations; they were called up in imagination by the formula, instead of performed; and that is mentioning, naming. The name, or pseudo-name, may long have covered the magic action, the imagined effect, the sacred object addressed and adjured, perhaps even the magician. But once an idea of anything—act, agent, personage, magic power or symbol of it (e.g., the sun, the moon)—was communicated to someone by a syllabic complex, speech had begun.

After the inception of speech, the very first conveyance of personal ideas, the process may have grown and spread like wildfire; and what was communicated was not necessarily sober and useful information. That is not what a dawning mind, a rapidly evolving individuating brain, would be likely to live on and live for. But with communication a change would also come over the human imagination, recording and amassing its intangible products, instead of leaving each dreamer to find the bogeys and wraiths to embody his own terrors and desires, so that the vertiginous dances, drums and vocalizations of pre-Adamite sacraments really celebrated a different dream for every individual. Strange ideas which nothing but speech would realize and hold could now be shared, and those which appealed to many members of the horde would be accepted, perhaps modified by fusion with others, and taken as realities. None of these hominid creatures in the heyday of fantasy is likely to have suspected any difference between imagination and fact.

One change, however, occurred so quietly that it has seldom been remarked; the change from animal memory to human recollection of past events, which made the time dimension of the mind. But this change is so great that it requires many-sided consideration of its effects on the human ambient as well as on the organism itself, so it belongs more properly to the next chapter and will be treated there.

With the development of language came, of course, its quotidian uses, which most theorists speculating on its origins and elementary forms take for granted as its earliest phase (most of them are convinced that primitive man was entirely realistic and knew nothing but material nature).[97] Certainly those uses became its essential ones: it was in everyday, realistic situations that various degrees of precision became

---

[97] Requests for help, which some writers regard as the earliest kind of communication (e.g., A. S. Diamond, *The History and Origin of Language* [1960], p. 7; G. Baumann, *Ursprung und Wachstum der Sprache* [1913]; also Paget, and many others, old and new), Révész classes as command, i.e., direction of another person's acts. See *Ursprung und Vorgeschichte der Sprache*, pp. 261 ff.

necessary; times, numbers, relations had to be specified and, above all, the use of language tended to become more economical and speedy. The elaborate syllabic formulae with omnibus meaning were more and more broken into smaller semantic units, until speech consisted very nearly or wholly of words with separable, limited (though not always strict) meanings. Relations were implicitly given by suffixes, prefixes and other modifiers, some of which became inflexions, where they were not expressed by actual differences of words used in different typical situations (as "go" and "went," or, for nouns, "cow," "bull," "ox," "calf," "heifer"). The burgeoning of vocabulary and proliferation of grammatical and syntactical forms which must have been very rapid in early periods are mainly products of ordinary practical intercourse, argument, gossip, transactions. Such alteration still goes on in any living language and reflects the cultural changes that are the real movement of history. It belongs pre-eminently to the common idiom; only religious, legal, and in some societies theatrical languages are conservative, sometimes archaic to the point of being incomprehensible except to people steeped in the linguistic tradition.

The rise of language in the Hominidae marked the completion of the "Great Shift" from animal to man. The power of speech transformed the genus *Homo* and every aspect of its ambient; for with speech came thought and remembrance, intuition, conception and reason. With words—in dim, distant and very long ages—some strange, unimaginable ancestors of ours built up the human world.

18

Symbols and the Human World

THE importance of verbal communication for human society is widely recognized; few, indeed, are the sociologists who would belittle it, or even the ethologists who would claim really social organization among animals without imputing something like language to the members of the flock or troop. Yet the imputation is shallow and easily proved specious, because whatever interaction may hold animal aggregates together has nothing like the psychical functions of language. Language makes every speaker, and even every deaf-mute who has some equivalent for speech and its reception, a thinker; ideas of things, of moves to make, and of possible events fill his mind, and things, acts and happenings which realize or contradict his ideas fill his senses. Words designating things carve out and fixate our objects, quite apart from the acts in which they figure, giving them a defined status they probably do not have for animals, for which they seem to be built into acts so they are parts of acts and may not keep their identity from one situation to another. How animals see objects we cannot know, but we know that among human beings not all thinking and perceiving is as firmly centered on physical things as ours, which is governed by Indo-European, Semitic, Indo-Chinese and other mainly Asiatic forms of speech. Students of Australian indigenous languages have repeatedly pointed out that verbs—words of action—are more frequent and more important in those tongues than nouns or adjectives, and their various forms usually express what substantives or properties of things and events are involved in the acts they mention.[1] Human thinking, in the frameworks of such

---

[1] Alf Sommerfelt, in *La langue et la société: Caractères sociaux d'une langue de type archaïque*) (1938), p. 184, says of the language of the Aranta in Australia: "La langue n'exprime . . . que l'action et l'état; la notion de l'objet n'y existe pas." Cf. also Van Ginneken, *La réconstruction typologique des langues archaïques de l'humanité*, p. 128: "la nature primordiale du verbe est prouvée une fois pour toutes; et tous les noms ne sont formés que postérieurement, comme des formes de participe, dérivées d'un verbe. . . ." This opinion, though in Van Ginneken's case a pure speculation based on his own theory, is shared (on various grounds) by several anthropological evolutionists and also by Géza Révész.

languages, is different from that which rests chiefly on concepts of objects as the fixed items of experience, designated by nouns, which are further elaborated by adjectives and related to each other by verbs. In this way, the influence of language on human life goes much deeper than communication; it is intrinsic to thinking, imagining, even our ways of perceiving. Conception, far from being abstracted from sensory experience, has grown up in constant interaction with the latter, and often—by spurts—in advance of it. A concept is born of words, its exemplification found in the perceptible world. But those Baconian methodologists who think one should simply check a hypothetical concept against direct observation don't know what a help in that business a lively imagination can be! The part played by imagery in the formation of concepts shows the intimate relation of perceptual and intellectual processes at all levels of human mental action.

From the beginning of each dawning mind its humanization starts not only with communication or even with the desire for it, but with the first identification of any items of experience evoking expectation or interest. How early distinction of things from each other or from persons occurs we cannot tell with any certainty, nor even at what point those substantive elements stand out from the acts and events in which the infant normally encounters them;[2] children born in societies speaking European or the main Asiatic languages, however, are ready to order their percepts by categories implicit in those languages before they begin to use words. The learning of speech seems to meet with no logical difficulty, whatever oral limitations may appear in "baby talk." This predisposition within a language group (taken in its largest scope) affects the whole mentality of each individual, making him the human being that he is, somewhat as in the physical make-up of any higher animal the repetition of the entire genome in every cell of its body makes its individuality so pervasive that its uniqueness and unity are intrinsic to its chemical composition, and continue with its growth.[3]

Animals do not have a continuous world in which one or more coherent orders are to be found. In our so-called objective or outside world, there is a predominant order, the basic classification of things according to kinds, big general classes subsuming more specifically defined ones which, however, first meet the general definitions; that is, an order of genera and species, in which every object which is designable

[2] For a preliminary experimental treatment of this subject see Stephan Baley, "Le comportement des enfants et des singes inférieurs en présence des objets placés sur un support" (1935).

[3] Compare the reference to R. Schoenheimer's work in Vol. I, p. 320 and n.

by a common noun is a member of the class defined by that noun. In a very interesting article going back to the beginning of our century, "De quelques formes primitives de classification," Emile Durkheim and Marcel Mauss remarked: "For us, to classify things is to divide them into distinct groups set apart from each other by clearly discernible, definite lines of demarcation. . . . Underlying our concept of 'class' is the idea of a precise circumscription setting exact boundaries. Yet one might almost say that this concept of classification does not go back beyond Aristotle."[4]

Classification, however, is much older than Aristotle; not the particular mode he systematized, but the notion that every individual object, act, being, condition (e.g., sickness, luck, heat) or event such as rain, lightning, earthquake is at the same time a kind of thing, act, event, etc. There are many possible ways of classifying, but the people using any particular way do not know that; to them it seems that categories are part of nature, given in direct experience. That is because no one, originally, consciously imposed them; they are ways of thinking and seeing that express themselves in language, in the process of naming acts or agents, objects or places. Alf Sommerfelt pointed out that Aristotle could formulate his logic of substance and attribute, relation, assertion and negation, because these categories were implicitly given in the Greek language;[5] to all speakers of Indo-European languages the classical syllogism seems to be a logic of "natural inference," because they speak and think in subject-predicate forms.

So much for ways of thinking; but the influence of language goes even further, for it extends into people's ways of perceiving what meets their senses.[6] Those of us who have grown up with subject-predicate languages see self-identical objects with all sorts of properties; the properties may change, but if their bearers disappear we stand confounded: "They have made themselves air!" We can see a cat with or without a grin, but not a grin with or without a cat, for "a grin" really denotes an act, and in all European languages an act points to an agent or several agents, who are permanent entities. The function of nouns is hypo-

---

[4] (1901), pp. 2–3.

[5] *La langue et la société*, p. 9: "Quand Aristote, dans sa logique, operait avec les catégories de la substance, du nombre ou de la relation, il pouvait le faire parce que ces catégories étaient représentées dans la langue grecque. Notre logique repose sur les catégories des langues indo-européennes."

[6] *Ibid*. The passage quoted in the note above goes on, after a brief further discussion: "Il n'est pas ici question seulement des catégories fondamentales de la pensée, mais de toutes les façons de nommer et de concevoir les êtres, les objets et les phénomènes qui l'entourent, que l'homme a imaginées."

static; whatever is designated by a noun becomes a thing, a substance with properties; and for speakers whose vocabularies consist as largely of nouns as ours do, the world consists mainly of physical objects. Next in importance is the category of property words, adjectives,[7] and verbs which assign the named properties to named entities; especially the form of the verb "to be" known as the "copula" in Aristotelian logic, often symbolized by "ε," and read "is a." The pure structural business of a verb is to serve as a kind of "logical glue," literally a "copula," joining words into propositions.

But verbs are very interesting elements in our essentially static conceptual frame of entities and properties, because they have the further function of referring the propositional complexes to the actual world of events, and therewith creating the entirely new dimension of truth and falsehood. Truth and its negative, falsehood, are not logical concepts, but basically metaphysical. The fact that they can be treated like properties of propositions has led to the most far-reaching, systematic confusions logicians have ever encountered, probably in any age and any advanced culture.[8] But the epistemological problems these confusions have revealed and sometimes created belong to the last part of the present essay.

Meanwhile, the early students of Australian languages, who still had the pure and whole material to work on—Spencer and Gillen,[9] Howitt,[10] Durkheim and Mauss—were amazed to find that the words of these exotic tongues did not denote fixed objects, as their own principal words did, but actions in which agents and means of action (i.e., things) were implicitly involved. There were no "parts of speech" comparable to ours, expressing relations that held among things, people or animals, and no inflections, but short words of wide denotation strung together to describe series of related acts. As in Indo-European languages nouns

---

[7] In syllogistic logic these are often replaced by nouns denoting classes defined in terms of the adjectives; i.e., "all men are mortal" becomes "all men are mortals."

[8] The classical statement of these difficulties as a whole, made at the time when they were becoming apparent, is in the introduction to the second edition of the great *Principia Mathematica* of A. N. Whitehead and Bertrand Russell, Volume I. It was the shift from the logic of language to that of mathematics which suddenly showed how many problems of meaning—logical, semantical problems—lie buried in the Indo-European linguistic forms we take for granted.

[9] W. B. Spencer and F. J. Gillen, *The Native Tribes of Central Australia* (1899); also *Northern Tribes of Central Australia* (1904). A later book by these two authors, *The Arunta; A Study of a Stone Age People* (1927), still pictures the native Australians as they had found them three decades before.

[10] A. W. Howitt, *Native Tribes of South East Australia* (1904).

are the anchors of discourse, in Australian the main words are more like our verbs, though grammatically they function quite differently.[11] To epitomize the findings of linguists in such an unfamiliar field by a brief summary of their statements would, of course, be useless; the mention of them here is intended only to call attention to the fact that the categories of our thinking might be different under the influence of a different mode of speech—that a grin might be grinned by many Cheshire cats, or by none at all, if we thought in Arunta instead of the King's English, but a cat of no kind, neither Cheshire, Siamese, alley, nor of any sort or totem, and doing absolutely nothing, would be inconceivable. "Cat" is not a separable concept.

No society known from observation or historical records is primitive in the sense of showing us man in transition from a prehuman phylogenetic phase to full humanity.[12] Often the most complicated ideas and institutions of savages, if they differ from ours, are called "primitive,"

---

[11] One does not need to go as far as Australia, nor always back to the Stone Age, to find languages differently organized from Indo-European ones; M. Cohen, "Aspect et temps dans le verbe" (1927), stated that in some languages, e.g., Hebrew and some Negro tongues of Africa, the conjugations of the verb express the state of completion of an act, not the time of its performance. This makes verb forms relative to the act, not—like ours—to the time of speaking of it.

An entirely different principle of conjugation is adduced by Dorothea Lee in an article on the speech of the Wintu tribe of Californian Indians, "Conceptual Implications of an Indian Language" (1938). Dr. Lee says: "The Wintu speaker divides his predicative statements into two categories: that of the subjective or experiential, and that of the objective. He has two ablaut stems to choose from, for every verb. He uses one stem to express a state or action in bringing which about the grammatical subject can or does participate, another for the state or action that is irrespective of the agency of the subject. Correlatively, the speaker himself participates in the event or state of the first category (I), in so far as he perceives or apprehends it; but that of the second category (II), is the object of his belief: in speaking of it, he asserts a truth which is beyond experience" (p. 89). Thereupon she lists five suffixes, and explains: "The distinctions made by the five suffixes so far given correspond to subjective differences in the speaker, not the grammatical subject. Other affixes, added to the stem and preceding any personal or temporal suffixes there may be, indicate differences of attitude on the part of the grammatical subject" (p. 92).

[12] Ralph Linton, in an essay, "Primitive Art" (1941), p. 35, says: "Actually, there is no culture extant today to which the term primitive can be applied legitimately. There are cultures of greater or less complexity and cultures which have many or few features in common with our culture, but every one of them is a product of its own evolutionary sequence." And J. Paliard, in "Les deux sources de la connaissance. Notes sur la pensée implicite" (1953), p. 74, speaking of early thought and its expression, said much the same: "le 'primitif indistinct' est à jamais dépassé et irretrouvable en lui-même."

merely on the assumption that anything such people think and do must be relatively childish, cruder and simpler than our ways, and exhibiting a stage of culture we have already passed through. Similarly, any language built on different principles from ours is often deemed "primitive" and even supposed to be inadequate for communication,[13] but no language that has ever been studied by linguists has borne out this assumption.[14] It seems rather that—as true scholars, from Wilhelm von Humboldt to some of our own contemporaries, have realized and declared—a spoken language grows with the intellectual needs it has to meet and is always adequate to the thinking of the public that uses it, though not always to the most advanced individual thought.[15] In this way language exhibits a principle of mind which has been remarked by psychologists and pathologists, namely, that the mind tends always to work as a unit, and after localized or specialized impairment restores the balance of functions as a whole even though it has to operate on a lower level generally, developing potentialities in structures which possess them but do not usually realize them in action, so many nervous

---

[13] So, for example, Durkheim and Mauss, in "De quelques formes primitives de classification," p. 7, wrote: "Les systèmes de classification les plus humbles que nous connaissons sont ceux que l'on observe dans les tribus australiennes." But totemic classification is actually anything but simple; it is a highly complicated system that extends to other things than marriage groups, even to the ordering of seasons, stars and on the earth almost all animate and inanimate things. L. Frobenius called his book on savage culture *Aus den Flegeljahren der Menschheit* (1901) (mistranslated as *The Childhood of Man*; "*Flegeljahre*" means specifically the preadolescent years of boyhood, and "*ein Flegel*" is a naughty boy, not any other child).

[14] This topic has been sufficiently discussed in *Phil. N.K.*, chap. v, esp. pp. 102–3 and the extensive first footnote (New American Library ed., pp. 94–95) to need no reiteration here.

[15] Von Humboldt, in his *Sprachphilosophische Werke*, p. 42, proposed that anthropologists and linguists should study the speech of truly wild tribes, "um wenigstens die unterste Stufe der Organisationsleiter der Sprachen aus Erfahrung zu kennen. Meine bisherige aber hat mir bewiesen, dass auch die sogenannten rohen und barbarischen Mundarten schon Alles besitzen, was zu einem vollständigen Gebrauche gehört, und Formen sind, in welche sich . . . im Laufe der Zeit das ganze Gemüth hineinbilden könnte, um, vollkommener oder unvollkommener, jede Art von Ideen in ihnen auszuprägen."

Révész, in his *Ursprung und Vorgeschichte der Sprache*, p. 82, makes the statement: "Die Sprachen primitiver Völker sind Vollsprachen, die verschiedene Wortarten, lexikalen Reichtum, grammatische Kategorien . . . usw. aufweisen." This is the more surprising as in *Die Menschliche Hand*, published only a few years earlier, p. 100, he lends full credence to the popular belief, based on the reports of one or two early travelers, that some African tribes have to supplement their inadequate speech with gesture language for purposes of ordinary practical discussion. It seems to depend on whether the tongue or the hand is to be glorified.

mechanisms do wholly or largely substitute work. As the late Lord Brain has written: "Where the left cerebral hemisphere is damaged early in life, the right hemisphere usually takes over the speech functions of the left. Hence infantile right hemiplegia is not as a rule associated with aphasia."[16] Where such a complete changeover is not possible, the constituent elements of the lost function may be divided among several agencies according to their respective potential abilities, so that no one mechanism stands in for the lost one, but the system as a whole still performs without it. Sir Henry Head, more than half a century ago, remarked the unity of mental life in spite of losses in sensation, powers of speech, reasoning, envisagement and other capacities by organic lesions, saying: "Each such local disturbance is associated with some specific psychical loss of function. But ... the field of consciousness remains continuous as before; it closes over the gap as the sea leaves no trace of a rock that has crumbled away."[17]

All the products of human minds show this holistic tendency. In another article Lord Brain noted its functioning in severe disorders of the "body image" (which is not so much an image as a total sense of one's own body)—in his example, a loss of awareness of the whole left half of the body—and he noted that his patient had lost not only the perception of that large part, but all memory of ever having experienced it. "The remaining half of the body image," he said, "seems to constitute itself a new Gestalt, and consciousness, having lost the memory of the left half of the body, is unaware of the incompleteness of what remains."[18] Similarly, a damaged sculpture, a temple ruin, a partly obliterated drawing can maintain its appearance of organic form, letting physical insults go to astounding lengths before it loses its implicit unity. It seems to reorganize its appearance after every mutilation, as a living creature reorganizes its functional pattern on a smaller or simpler scale. One is reminded of Thorner's truncated snakes which thenceforth moved in curves characteristic of shorter normal snakes.[19] Walter Börnstein, who made investigations on traumatized auditory mechanisms and their subsequent functioning comparable to Kurt Goldstein's work on visual impairments,[20] set up what he called the "law of concentric

---

16 W. R. Brain, "Speech and Handedness" (1945), p. 839.

17 "The Conception of Nervous and Mental Energy" (1923–24), p. 141.

18 "The Cerebral Basis of Consciousness" (1950), p. 478.

19 See above, Chapter 12, pp. 11–12.

20 See especially Goldstein, "Die konzentrische Gesichtsfeldeinschränkung als eine Folge organischer Schädigung" (1918); also Goldstein and Adhémar Gelb, "Über eigentümliche 'ringförmige' Gesichtsfelddefekte" (1922).

reduction," which is "that in case of destruction of any part of an auditory cortex, the remainder of that cortex takes over the function of the whole, but suffering a reduction in total strength, according to a fixed principle: the range in which hearing is normally keenest and most important—that wherein speech has been developed—suffers the least; the ranges increasingly far from this center are pre-eminently affected. . . ." And apropos of this "law" he remarks that it seems to him to rest on the same principle of organic action as the development of a mutilated sea urchin egg into a normal-shaped but subnormal-sized sea urchin.[21]

Nothing could indicate more clearly that language is not a code invented as a signaling device or, indeed, for any other purpose, but is a biological trait of mankind, than its constant adequacy to the mental needs and capacities of the society in which it prevails. Another sign pointing the same way is the relative autonomy with which separate languages diverge from a common root and undergo series of alterations such as vowel changes, typical changes of word endings (as Latin *"universitas"* becomes *"università"* in Italian and *"universidad"* in Spanish, quite predictably for anyone who knows the respective language patterns), nasalization, suppression of some phonemic combinations, etc., independently of the ways in which other languages change or continue. Still a further aspect which makes an essentially pragmatic motivation of this paramount human activity implausible is that language draws so many other mental functions into its orbit—very deep and phylogenetically ancient processes of emotive and instinctive character—and lifts them from their animalian state to a new, peculiarly human level. It also engages all sorts of higher, largely cortical mechanisms, producing distinct forms of memory, sequences of recall, logical contradiction, logical entailment, the propositional structure of ideas that is inherent in the conception of fact, and the correlative, largely emotional disposition of the whole mind, belief. The depth to which the influence of language goes in the organization of our perception and apperception becomes more impressive the further one pursues it; com-

---

[21] "Der Aufbau der Funktionen in der Hörsphäre" (1930), p. 120. The passage quoted above continues (pp. 120–21): "Das Auftreten der 'konzentrischen Einengung' der Hörfähigkeit bei Verletzung der Hörrinde . . . ist m.E. völlig gleich zu setzen mit dem Prinzip der Entwicklung eines verstümmelten Seeigeleis zu einem ganzen (verkleinerten) Seeigel (*Driesch*), mit dem Auftreten von Ringskotomen bei Läsion des optischen Sektors (*Goldstein-Gelb*), mit der Änderung des Bewegungstypus bei Käfern mit Beinverstümmelungen (*Bethe*): das . . . Prinzip der konzentrischen Einengung ist . . . eine Erscheinungsform des grossen Gesetzes . . . das *Bethe* als *Gesetz der Plastizität* beschrieben hat."

munication, no matter how great its role in human society, is only one of the functions of language, and probably one which became more and more important as speech developed. But to stipulate, as Révész does, that nothing can be a proto-phenomenon of language that does not spring from the intent or desire to communicate is certainly misdirecting. The phylogenetic precursor of language in our history probably was not any means of communication, nor its purpose to convey commands, information or requests for information to fellow creatures, as Révész holds.

What, then, was its source, and what its motivation? What led to its beginning—that "beginning" which different evolutionists have placed at such different junctures in the course of our supposed departure from the ancestry of modern apes?[22]

It may have had no true "beginning" at all. The elements of language may have lain in genes which expressed themselves in quite differently motivated acts before the time was ripe for them to converge in that strangest of all primate attainments; and some of them may go back so far in the unbroken history of the hominid stock that they might have been met with not only before Adam but before Hanuman, the mythical King of the Monkeys (divine progenitor, no doubt). One of these elements is the trait of vocalizing in the course of some well-formed, repetitious actions. Man is certainly not alone in that. Many birds utter characteristic calls in flight, especially on their migratory flights, of such regular character that the utterance seems to be part of the wingbeat. This is strikingly noticeable in wild geese, where honking accompanies every long flight and seems to play some part in concatenating and sustaining the basic movements (a single goose or even a pair, if not alarmed, may fly silently across a lake). Dogs digging in earth or snow usually utter short repetitious growls timed by their motions and compounded by throaty noises, constant snuffing to clear their noses, and little repressed barks of excitement or self-stimulation, as if egging themselves on. Such accompaniments of physical movements, however, are entirely stereotyped, probably unintentional and certainly very simple vocal elements in habitual behavior. The bipedal, semi-arboreal primates that lived millions of years ago may have been much more

---

[22] Lord Brain, in "Speech and Handedness," p. 840, said: "we may guess [from the evidence he had presented in that lecture] that when human culture first developed man was already both able to speak and predominantly righthanded." In sharp contrast, R. A. Dart, in his speculative article "On the Evolution of Language and Articulate Speech," dates the invention of language only from Aurignacian times —in the measures of phyletic history, a modern innovation!

vociferous and especially much more versatile in their vocal supplements to action than any other animal living then or now.[23]

Whenever an ability develops beyond the current needs of its possessors it is apt to be used for the realization of some other impulse or impulses, sometimes quite unrelated to its original use. So the noises emitted as parts of strenuous acts, incidental to the sympathetic contractions of chest and throat muscles as an act grows and takes over the whole body, make it audible, as well as inwardly felt and perhaps outwardly visible. The sounds come back as part of it and expand the act itself in a sensory way. Every act tends to expand, and the ability to enlarge a pleasant act by prolongation or obvious effectiveness (whether good or bad for the agent) is an animal value which is often pursued for its own sake. So, if the ancient animal stock that eventuated in human generations had an unusual repertoire of vocal elements, these might have been put to wide and habitual use to accompany all sorts of acts, not by accidental production as groans of effort and joyful exclamations of success and relief,[24] but more as supplementary elements of even quite effortless doings, drawn into the total acts simply to elaborate and expand them. Such utterances would have no organically determined forms, but be open to the free play of spontaneous feelings, fleeting impulses to accentuate steps or moments in larger processes: the moment of seizing food, breaking the expectation of it, the reaction to a taste or

[23] The elaborate use of the voice in mankind rests on some unique traits even on the level of crude sound emission, due to neural peculiarities. In a discussion following the reading of a symposium paper, Dr. Wilder Penfield remarked: "The appearance in man of vocalization control from the cortex is a rather extraordinary thing. In no other animal that I know of does stimulation of the cortical motor area produce vocalization. . . . In man there is not one area but there are four areas . . . of vocalization. The response to stimulation is the same no matter whether it is right or left supplementary motor, or the right or left classical motor area. . . . Vocalization requires the action of the whole mechanism, including diaphragm, lips, mouth, everything, so that it is quite clear that the cortex is utilizing a neuron mechanism which is in the brain stem lower down. I suppose it is that upward migration of the bark representation that makes possible the extraordinary voluntary performance during speech" (C. G. Phillips, "Changing Concepts of the Precentral Motor Area" [1966], p. 412).

[24] Karl Bücher, *Arbeit und Rhythmus* (1924; 1st ed., 1896), derives musical and poetic rhythms from sources of this general kind. See esp. chap. vii, "Der Ursprung der Poesie und Musik," where he says (p. 379): "Bei schwerer Arbeit stösst der Mensch naturgemäss Atmungs- und Erleichterungslaute aus, die den Ausrufen in Schifferliedern, Holzhackerliedern, etc. treffend ähnlich sind. Diese Laute mögen dann in ähnlich-klingende Worte umgewandelt worden sein, woraus die oft sinnlosen Kehrreime entstanden sind die bei Arbeitsliedern oft den Rahmen des ganzen Liedes darstellen."

a texture, haste for more, or satisfaction (which usually closes a subact at least), or disappointed stop. Tame occupations, like gathering mushrooms, nursing a baby, whittling and filing objects, may have had their vocal elements.

Those elements, however, may have been peculiar to each individual being, some distinctly broken into phonemes, others much less articulated; as some bird species—song sparrows, for instance—have a wide range of individual patterns, though one can always assign the singer to its kind. The utterances of early hominids or proto-hominids might have evolved most of the sounds of human language in the instinctive process of elaborating, filling and enhancing ordinary quotidian behavior, as the increasing cerebral hemispheres developed in that phyletic line above all others and favored the potentialities of speech. The best vocalizers, in this phase, may have had special forms to complete characteristic acts. Yet such "language" may have been entirely autistic for a long evolutionary age, while our worthy ancestors were animals— perhaps not even very big ones, but certainly very special ones.

We have no hominid brains from ancient times, before speech could have existed, but today it is correlated with a structural peculiarity of the human brain, which may be a specialization evolved by a speaking stock, or an older oddity which underlies the development of the linguistic functions: a noticeable asymmetry in the right and left temperolateral cortices, where one hemisphere, usually the left, normally develops the so-called speech center. This structure is visible to the naked eye in happily chosen levels of coronal section in adult brains, as Geschwind and Levitsky have shown—adequately, I think—on a basis of large numbers of preparations. In a brief prefatory abstract of a paper which is itself a summary report, they say: "We have found marked anatomical asymmetries between the upper surfaces of the human right and left temporal lobes. The planum temporale ... is larger on the left in 65 percent of brains; on the right it is larger in only 11 percent. The left planum is on the average one-third larger than the right planum. This area makes up part of the temporal speech cortex. . . ."[25]

The diagram of such a section, here shown, illustrates the difference (which is unusually pronounced in this specimen). In conclusion of their article they say, "These studies support earlier assertions in studies lacking quantitative data or based on small samples, that the supratemporal plane showed marked right-left asymmetries in man. Pfeifer

[25] Norman Geschwind and Walter Levitsky, "Human Brain: Left-Right Asymmetries in Temporal Speech Region" (1968), p. 186.

and von Economo and Horn found by contrast no asymmetries in the same region in anthropoid apes."[26]

It has been widely reasoned and asserted that the development of "speech areas" (for there are several, though all connected, involving also the parietal lobe and the insula, as lesions and ablations have shown) is a purely ontological process, without any anatomical predispositions.[27] The factual basis of this tenet is that in young persons, severe injury to the areas usually concerned with linguistic functions— speech, understanding, reading and writing and other related actions— does not cause permanent aphasic symptoms. The other hemisphere seems to take over without difficulty.[28] In older people restitution may be slower, but even at fairly advanced ages lost speech (e.g., after a "stroke") is usually somewhat restored by the intervention of other possible mechanisms. If the injury occurs early enough in life, a normal speech area is likely to develop on the intact side which was not really pre-formed to have it. But recent researches have revealed the asymmetrical anlage even in newborn infants' brains.[29]

An interesting parallel to these findings is that a similar specialization, apparently peculiar to man, determines his preference of one hand, more commonly the right, over the other. The great skill of the human hand as against any animal paw may be exaggerated; some simians might rival an awkward, clumsy-fingered man's dexterity.[30] The great,

[26] P. 187. The reference is particularly to a long article by C. von Economo and L. Horn, "Über Windungsrelief, Masse und Rindenarchitektonik der Supratemporalfläche, ihre individuellen und ihre Seitenunterschiede" (1929).

[27] Edward Sapir, in his excellent book *Language, an Introduction to the Study of Speech* (1921), pp. 8–9, flatly denies the possibility of a "speech center" in the brain; but Sapir was not a neurologist, and had the usual layman's simplistic conception of what such a "center" would be. Perhaps the age of his book also helps to excuse his naïve judgments on a subject which really received its first scientific investigation in the decade following World War I.

[28] Cf. above, p. 323.

[29] Geschwind, "The Organization of Language and the Brain" (1970), says: "It is widely stated in the literature that the human brain is symmetrical, and this had led . . . even to the assumption that speech dominance is somehow acquired as the result of postnatal experience. . . . Walter Levitsky and I . . . found that some earlier authors had claimed that there were in fact anatomical differences between the hemispheres. We demonstrated that such differences exist. . . . More recently Wada has confirmed our results. He has, in addition, studied this region in the brains of infants and has found that these differences are present at birth." (His reference is to a paper read by J. Wada at the Ninth International Congress of Neurology held in New York in 1969, and apparently unpublished as yet.)

[30] Consider, for example, Bernhard Grzimek's observations on a young chimpanzee: "Eines Tages sass sie an der Schreibmaschine und drückte vorsichtig die Tasten herab. Bleistifte wurden gern zum Kritzeln auf Papier benutzt, noch öfter

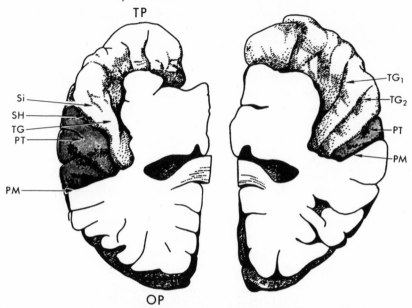

Figure 18–1. Left-Right Asymmetry of the Human Brain

a structural peculiarity of the human brain ... a noticeable asymmetry in the right and left temperolateral cortices

(Norman Geschwind, "Language and the Brain," *Scientific American*, CCVI [1972], copyright © 1972 by Scientific American, Inc., somewhat modified from a figure in Norman Geschwind and W. Levitsky, "Human Brain: Left-Right Asymmetries in Temporal Speech Region," *Science*, CLXI [July 12, 1968], 186–87, copyright 1972 by the American Association for the Advancement of Science.)

The posterior margin (*PM*) of the planum temporale (*PT*) slopes backward more sharply on the left than on the right, so that end *y* of the Sylvian fissure lies posterior to the corresponding point on the right. The anterior margin of the planum formed by the sulcus of Heschl (*SH*) slopes forward more sharply on the left. In this brain there is a single transverse gyrus of Heschl (*TG*) on the left, but two on the right (*TG₁*, *TG₂*). TP, temporal pole; OP, occipital pole, Si, sulcus intermedius of Beck.

species-specific superiority of the hand lies less in its prehensile uses than in its epicritical sensibility and its expressive power, both of which are said to have some sporadic occurrences in subhuman life,[31] but a

---

aber zerbissen.... Besonders nachhaltig und lange bemühte sie sich, eine grosse Teppichnadel mit Faden durch harte Borte zu stechen, was sie bei einem Teppichnäher gesehen hatte. Es kam ihr offensichtlich nur auf das Durchstechen an sich an, keineswegs auf das Ergebnis ihrer ausgesprochen angestrengten Tätigkeit" ("Beobachtungen an einem kleinen Schimpansenmädchen" [1940], p. 299). His account shows plainly the euphemism of his term "Schimpansen*mädchen*," for a girl is exactly what the ape was not. But her skill was that of a child of comparable age.

[31] Hans Kummer, in *Soziales Verhalten einer Mantelpavian Gruppe*, presents gestures of grooming as a purely expressive abreaction of emotion following a fright; see p. 37.

real development only in man. These higher functions belong to his intellectual heritage. Lord Brain, in the lecture to which I have referred before in this chapter, "Speech and Handedness," pointed out the perfectly comprehensible, though indirect, relationship between handedness and the complex language functions, i.e., utterance, comprehension, logical concatenation, reading, writing, repeating words or statements, etc. Linguistic and manual development usually both occur in the dominant hemisphere. It is hemisphere dominance that seems to be uniquely human,[32] and although there is at present no explanation of this tendency (which has slight parallels in simian and other, even non-primate brains, e.g., paw preferences in some rats, without trophic or behavioral consequences), Lord Brain did remark its essential character in human evolution, as he wrote: "What is speech, and how does it differ from mere vocalization? Many living creatures utter sounds under the stress of feeling. . . . This is vocalization. . . .

"The emotional noises are simply involuntary performances both in man and the animals. Vocalization in the monkey persists in a simple form after decortication. In the human infant . . . crying is mainly an affair of subcortical centres directly connected with the muscles of vocalization. . . . Such relatively simple reactions can utilize symmetrical and bilateral pathways. In contrast to this, speech calls for articulation, the precise integration of the small muscles of the lips, tongue, palate, and larynx besides the respiratory muscles, so that these contract synchronously on the two sides with such delicacy that a variety of sounds can be differentiated through a range of fine gradations. This motor integration seems to require that the motor cortex of both cerebral hemispheres should be under the control of a higher 'centre,' the motor speech 'centre,' and that such a 'centre' must be single. Speech, in other words, necessitates Broca's area. . . .

"Why should Broca's area be associated with handedness . . . ? . . . Is it not . . . probable that it was the appearance of a motor speech 'centre' in the left hemisphere in man that made that the dominant hemisphere, and the right hand the dominant hand,[33] in contrast to the ape,

---

[32] Cf. Geschwind, "The Organization of Language and the Brain," p. 944: "The phenomenon of cerebral dominance . . . occurs, as far as we know, in no mammal other than man. The dominance of the left side of the brain for speech is the most striking example of this phenomenon."

[33] B. Naunyn, in Die organischen Wurzeln der Lautsprache des Menschen (1925), p. 24, speculated that the development of the hand "centers" in the left hemisphere led to its general dominance and prepared it for the implementation of speech, so the "speech centers" subsequently developed there.

in which right- and left-handedness develop with equal frequency? ...
the dominance of one hemisphere involves many other functions than
speech. Not only symbolic thinking but also the purposeful manipulation of objects depends on pathways in the dominant hemisphere. In
gesture and manipulation the hand represented in that hemisphere
takes the lead, and it is the dominant hand which converts thought
into symbols in writing. Thus handedness connotes a much richer series
of functions in man than in the ape. It is, as it were, raised to a higher
power and is an integral part of the activity of the dominant hemisphere" (p. 840).

If such a physiological condition underlies the psychical specialization
of man, particularly the use of speech in every human population, it is
no wonder that the influence of language pervades his entire mentality,
even shaping his percepts as he imposes his worded ideas on them. By
means of words, any events and objects, no matter how incompatible,
may be brought together in thought; they may be connected by the
linguistic particle "and," which expresses this most general of all relations. It is this same limitless, potential togetherness in thought that
makes a human being's ambient a world. The power of language not
only to designate things and communicate facts, but to formulate and
establish what is a thing or a fact and define what perception hence-
forth is to illustrate, gives the human world entirely different dimensions from those of any animal's ambient.[34] An evolutionist may wonder

[34] The formative, conceptually creative work of language was apprehended by a
few philosophers even in the eighteenth century, and some psychologists early in our
own, but received its first serious treatment in Ernst Cassirer's *Philosophie der
symbolischen Formen*. See Vol. I, p. 20: "So zeigt etwa der Progress der Sprach-
bildung, wie das Chaos der unmittelbaren Eindrücke sich für uns erst dadurch lichtet
und gliedert, dass wir es 'benennen' und es dadurch mit der Funktion des sprachlichen Denkens und des sprachlichen Ausdrucks durchdringen. In dieser Welt der
Sprachzeichen gewinnt auch die Welt der Eindrücke selbst einen ganz neuen
'Bestand.'. . ." And further, Vol. III, p. 475: "Was wir ein Faktum nennen, muss
immer schon in irgendeiner Weise theoretisch orientiert, muss in Hinblick auf ein
gewisses Begriffssystem gesehen und durch dasselbe implizit bestimmt sein. Die
theoretischen Bestimmungsmittel treten nicht nachträglich zum bloss-Tatsächlichen
hinzu, sondern sie gehen in die Definition des Tatsächlichen selbst ein."

Recently, in the present-day frame of code-and-signal approaches to animal and
human communication, J. Bronowski and U. Bellugi have reasserted the basic intellec-
tuality implicit in any real language. Reflecting especially on the Gardners' experiences with the young chimpanzee Washoe, they observe that "the human practice
of naming parts of the environment presupposes and rests on a more fundamental
activity, namely, that of analyzing the environment into distinct parts and treating
these as separate objects. That is, there is implied in the structure of cognitive sentences a view of the outside world as separable into things which maintain their

how and when the transformation from the highest animal mentality to mind took place. The answer, I believe, is that it never did. There was no transformation from a previously well-developed system of mental functions, but a very ancient specialization of nervous structures, and consequently of unprecedented mental potentialities, which followed a deviant line of development from their earliest inception. In other respects, meanwhile, the hominid stock could have continued for some millions of years to evolve in the general primate pattern, except for one skeletal oddity which may have been still older and is altogether without a parallel among mammals—the bipedal stance and walk, making for a constant upright carriage of the head, which permitted and possibly induced the cerebral specialization. There was probably never a time when language was an entirely new achievement, nor ever a first word spoken, nor any agreement on what things were to be called; before anyone intentionally used his utterances as signals, they unintentionally served as such, for other members of the proto-human community understood them, as all gregarious warm-blooded animals treat each other's acts as parts of the changing situation. Acts and sounds may be common or highly personal, but close companions understand them, though they be characteristics of just one individual; mothers understand their babies' particular tricks of behavior and entirely autistic expressions, and animals seem to be alerted by the so-called warning cries of their fellows, which are in all probability not uttered as warnings at all, but are unintended vocal reactions to big or little alarms. Communication among instinctively vociferous familiars would have grown up as imperceptibly as the complicated utterances themselves, to varying degrees according to conditions in different places (such as the state of development of communal dance and its vocal elements, the prevalence of sorcerers articulating charms, also talented individuals making up or interpreting speech sounds).

Some anthropologists concerned with the origin of language have claimed that the problem must be treated in the context of the means of communication in general.[35] That it has its place in this context is

---

identity and which can be manipulated in the mind, so that even actions and properties are reified in words. In this philosophical sense, predication is not merely putting together words in syntactical patterns, nor even the manipulation in the mind of ready-made objects and categories. Rather, predication is in the first place a way of analyzing the environment into parts, and only after that can they be regrouped in new arrangements and new sentences" ("Language, Name and Concept" [1970], p. 627).

[35] See, e.g., Joseph H. Greenberg, *Essays in Linguistics* (1957), pp. 61–62: "The

true enough, but that does not make the communicative function a necessary point of departure for research on every aspect of the subject; it may, in fact, slant inquiry so strongly toward one aspect that it obscures other, less obvious ones of real importance, such as the symbolic functions which make communication—and much more than communication—possible through speech. The word, or whatever phonetic usage preceded it, traditional or novel, public or individual and ephemeral, is what holds a concept, while percepts change and leave nothing but a conceptual trail of successive phases of an over-all event, symbolized by the "word." By being expressed in one symbol the phases belong together, as the many moves involved in an act belong together in the realization of a single impulse. And like the subacts in a complex act, many of the perceptual impressions composing a witnessed event occur in a strict, continuous order. Others do not; when an object is given to our vision, our eyes pass in unfixed, saccadic movements over its presented surfaces (though within these passages there is a continuum of effects from point to point). The elements of a visual impression are simultaneous in what William James called a "specious present"—that is, they are psychically co-present, because the perceptual subacts overlap in their cerebral completions if not their retinal inceptions. In the case of auditory percepts, however, this integration is less assured. The tempo of sound reception and impression is much slower than that of light; speech sounds pass away as fast as new ones occur. So, as soon as articulate patterns of sound are to have symbolic value, they have to be held conceptually as units in a greatly extended "specious present"; and this extension is not in space, but in time.

Time is the new dimension which verbalizing and its mental consequence, symbolic thinking, have imposed on the human ambient, making it a world, with a homogeneous spatial frame and a history. The influence on man's mentality has been as great as that on his environment. The two are, of course, correlative. Since the spectacularly and uniquely evolved human organism is more amenable to study than its counterpart, the vastly enlarged ambient in which it lives, we had better deal directly with the former, and with the latter by implication. The part played by time in the human world, for instance, escapes our analy-

---

basic function of language is communication. This leads us to place language in the total frame of the evolution of the means of communication. . . . To ask the question regarding language alone is like discussing the evolution of the bow without regard to its position among other weapons." Such a separate study might well be called for; it might stem from research on the uses of wood and knowledge of its different properties, or many another context besides weapons in general.

sis. The temporal aspect of that world is a completely integrated, essential element in historical thinking, and the historical world of any period is seen through modern eyes, for history, as an aspect of the world, i.e., as an objective datum, is a late discovery—so late that the development of the general concepts of world history or even national history, reaching beyond local chronicles and traditional legends, belongs to ages of literacy, and in European learning is recent even in that epoch (in China it goes back farther, but not in all older literate cultures). Our sources for reconstructing stages of human life in the past and assembling a record of man's relations to his world since it had a temporal dimension at all are infinitesimal, and such a "history" is not worth undertaking. In the evolution of mind, however, the influence of symbolic presentation, whereby a behavioral act is projected as a passage from its inception to an external effect, may be logically analyzed and evaluated though we do not know just when each element in the process emerged and what developmental changes it has undergone.

The first radical effect of the symbolizing functions of the hominid brain, human or prehuman, was to initiate the whole complex faculty of memory, which seems to have pre-empted a number of brain structures for its diverse operations. We do not even know whether the neural linkages which negotiated them were primitive physical peculiarities of our kind or arose with the enlarging brain under the encouragement of increasing use. Very possibly both; there is usually an anlage and a motivating condition for its development. The physiology of memory is practically unknown as yet; pathological losses, so far, have revealed the existence of several relatively independent mnemonic processes, and also some brain areas where they may be selectively interrupted by lesions, but on the whole we know next to nothing of the mechanisms implementing these all-important mental activities. Although the distinction between "short-term" and "long-term" memories has been known for some time, the possibility of their resting on different cerebral activities is a notion of recent date; F. C. Bartlett, in 1956, at the very end of his Croonian Lecture delivered to the Royal Society of London made bold to say, "it might be that the neural basis of immediate, short term memory is different from that of long term memory," but added quickly: "this, however, is, on my part, obviously nothing more than a guess."[36] The empirical distinction, however, has been made in many quarters, so we have a fair literature speculating on its neurological implications, offering models of hypothetical processes or

---

[36] "Some Experiments about Thinking," p. 451.

reporting clinical findings in illustration of the psychological phenomenon, chiefly by way of differential pathological losses. But the dichotomy itself is rough and general, as may be seen at once from the fact that in today's increasing literature short-term memory already goes by several names: "immediate memory," "primary memory," "current memory," "recent memory" are often used in place of it. J. J. Gibson speaks of "primary or immediate memory," using these two terms synonymously, and defining them in a way that makes them further identical with "current memory."[37] Yet some of these variants are not synonymous; for instance, "current" and "recent" memory are not; though both are of short term, there are cases of pathological loss of one without the other.[38]

Current memory seems to come nearest to the animalian pattern of hysteretic retention, the fact that each successive move in a total act changes the motivating conditions in the matrix just enough to induce the next advance, so the organism is influenced by its own past in the enactment of a complex impulse at least to consummation, or—failing in that—to preparing a new internal situation with subsequent potentialities. The difference between such cumulative effects of action, and "short-term memory" of an act in its development, that is to say, step for step, is that in the latter case the act as a whole has been realized as a conception before, during or immediately upon its passage. If that conception cannot be held there is failure of "current memory."[39] The act may be one of hearing and understanding a piece of discourse, even a sentence; in that, or any other case of cumulatively realized

[37] *The Perception of the Visual World*, pp. 158–59: "Successive excitations of the retina must be integrated by memory.... The kind of memory required to explain perception is not, of course, that commonly understood by the term. It is often called primary or immediate memory. It is the kind of memory which makes possible the apprehension of a melody [of which many birds are capable].... Although the concept of primary memory has been derived from the study of auditory perception, it must apply with even greater force to visual perception, where successive integration is so complete that the observer can be wholly unconscious of his fixations."

[38] See, for instance, a report by W. H. Sweet, G. A. Talland and F. R. Ervin, "Loss of Recent Memory Following Section of Fornix" (1959), of a case in which the trauma did not affect immediate recall, but memories five or ten minutes old, showing the selectiveness of functions in the interrupted neural paths.

[39] Gibson, in the passage already quoted (see n. 37 above), does not refer to the conceptual aspect of current retention, so his account applies to perception with or without conception—to hysteretic biological motivation as well as to human current memory. He may have been dealing with animal action, for all that his discussion lets us know.

action, it is essential that each subact be remembered at least to the extent of psychically retaining its contribution to the advancing conception of the whole.

Such cumulative retention, though perhaps the simplest of all our mnemonic talents, already exhibits the radical departure of *Homo* from the rest of the primate order; for it constitutes the primitive conceptual activity that is the substructure of mind, as the matrix of vital acts is the substructure of the organism. It is a subjective version of the unity of the act, which normally can extend over a long and complex mental performance, continually entraining perceptions that record the progressively changing relevant situation. Such memory of what has just been said and done, what has been happening and is still going on, and especially of the agent's own intentions and how far they have been realized is the background of human behavioral action, the basic pattern of what is usually meant by "consciousness"; where that pattern is impaired, "consciousness" falls apart.[40] There still is feeling, even simple, familiar response to questions and instructions, but the specious present shrinks to a minimum, the only extension of acts is by repetition, intentions are forgotten before any act requiring several steps is completed, and habit largely replaces the normal adaptation to circumstance, so the agent may continue in a task when its purpose has long been fulfilled.[41] Superficially this condition may resemble animal mentality, but not truly; for the hereditary, pre-formed source of impulses which supports the animalian life of instinct has no systematic counterpart in us, so the impaired human being cannot fall back on the watchfulness and elaborate direct responses of a fully competent animal.

---

[40] In a thoughtful article, "Untersuchungen über Aufbau und Störung der menschlichen Handlung" (1930), based mainly on a detailed study of one patient suffering from loss of current memory, Stephan Krauss wrote: "Dieses psychophysische Ganze [viz., the patient] ist wie 'hingeworfen,' es 'befindet' sich überhaupt nicht, sondern ist 'verloren.' Wir nehmen bei diesem Zustand eine verhältnismässige *Entleerung* des Bewusstseins an.... Gemeint ist die fehlende Ausgeprägtheit der Gefühls-, Vorstellungs- und Gedankenbildung, vorhanden ist aber der dumpf sich dahinwälzende Gefühlsstrom" (pp. 655–56).

[41] *Ibid.*, p. 666: "[Eine] vollgültige Handlungsgesamtheit ist ja dadurch charakterisiert, dass sie mit ihrer Spitze sich dauernd *in etwas* W*erdendes hineinbewegt* ... das für das Individuum W*ert* und *Bedeutung* hat." His patient could perform simple chores, such as paring potatoes, but showed no sign of understanding the purpose of his act or knowing when it was completed. When he was asked to cut fringes out of paper strips he continued to cut long after the fringes were made, and finally cut the paper into little pieces; Dr. Krauss points out that what the man's action lacks is "der *Prägnanzcharakter* in der besonderen Weise, dass die *Prägnanzkontinuität* nicht möglich ist, es bleibt vielmehr nur ein diffuser Tätigkeitsdrang übrig, der zunehmend *amorphisiert*."

The most primitive sort of conceptual memory is enough to give the human world something which the ambients of other creatures do not have—a time dimension, which extends backward into the past as well as forward to a future. Animal acts are all forward-directed; the influence of the past upon them is physiological, and though it enters constantly and systematically into subsequent motivations of reflex movements and of fears, desires and expectations, it is those immediacies that are felt, not any image or idea of the bygone events which "conditioned" them. Just as animal life is lived "here," "there" and en route from one place to the other, but not in a geometric space, so its "time" is a present always heading into a future, but not a homogeneous temporal dimension in which earlier and later events are ranged. Dimensions are conceptual principles, which require symbolic presentation to let them emerge as spontaneous elementary abstractions. This is probably one of the greatest steps dividing man from the rest of the animal kingdom, although it is also one of the earliest.

"Short-term" or "current" memory was apparently the phenomenon which suggested the theory of "circulating messages" in the brain as the neurological explanation of remembering,[42] and is still the best empirical support of that hypothesis. But it seems, also, to be the simplest mnemonic process; there are other kinds of memory which cannot be regarded as reverberations of an activity starting from a main, comprehensive impulse to an act with several successive stages. They are sometimes lumped together as "long-term memory,"[43] but the first attempts to find a neurological hypothesis to account for such a general category soon revealed that it subsumes several fairly unrelated forms.

[42] It was propounded in 1947 by Norbert Wiener in his *Cybernetics: Or Control and Communication in the Animal and the Machine,* and used to liken the brain to a digital computer, which had already been developed to the extent of preserving a message by repeating its formulation within the machine over and over until halted or switched. D. O. Hebb, who started from a similar assumption but with a more physiological and, therefore, more complex idea of the mechanism to which the cyclic process was attributed, said in *The Organization of Behavior:* "A simple closed circuit may reverberate for perhaps 0.001 to 0.05 sec.; the cell-assembly . . . for periods as great as 1/2 sec.; a phase cycle . . . 1 to 5 or 10 seconds (the apparent duration of conceptual processes in man)" (p. 142). Obviously both authors were dealing with short-term retention.

[43] As, for instance, in an interesting article, "Short-Term Memory" (1964), by John Brown, on the possible existence of two separate mechanisms for holding long-term and short-term memories, respectively. Unfortunately that article is so filled with the metaphors taken from our present calculating and recording machinery that it is sometimes hard for the reader to maintain his biological orientation against all the talk about "storage" of "traces" (even "a store with about seven compartments"), "accessibility," etc.

The differences between some of them seem, at least on first inspection, to be more than deviations from a common pattern—differences of kind rather than varieties of one function. For instance, a poem "committed to memory" is remembered in a way quite unlike the recollection of an event, such as exterminating a nest of hornets or watching the finish of a sailing race.[44]

There are, furthermore, notable differences in the phenomena of recall: we have faint bits of memory of very old impressions, sights which were called to our attention in early childhood but would not have been registered otherwise, which are retrievable as fleeting images now, perhaps distorted; and, on the other hand, sudden intense and detailed recollections that come involuntarily like a "flash-back" to some actual experience, sometimes only to the place of its occurrence or a completely present but momentary feeling of the event, like a telescoped reality.[45] Normal long-term memories can often be pieced together to vouch for the actual historicity of stories largely "filled in" with circumstantial evidence, probability, hypothesis and other constructive elements. That is the sort of memory one is asked to produce on the witness stand. Its dangers are well known,[46] yet it is indispensa-

[44] Dr. Penfield, in his Epsilon Psi lecture at Yale University in 1963, "Neurological Mechanisms of Speech and Perception," remarked that there seems to be a different mechanism of word memory from that of conceptual or "abstracted" memory, and suggested that the latter develops in the hemisphere not used for speech, as also does interpretation. Yet in laboratory investigations of long- or short-term memories no attention is usually paid to any other distinctions between memories than "short" and "long," and possibly sensory modalities; the materials are meaningless items, i.e., numbers, letters or nonsense syllables. See, for example, L. R. Peterson, "Short-Term Memory" (1966); all "remembering" tested in the experiments there reported was pure memorization, not retention of detailed facts, verbatim speech, etc. There are obvious reasons for such a procedure, but it may be testing only one very special mechanism. One may wonder whether the simplifications required for an unambiguous result may not call the status of "laboratory science" for psychology in question; though, like history, psychology is a discipline which can well use many findings of scientific experimentation.

[45] In The Excitable Cortex in Conscious Man (1958), p. 31, Dr. Penfield used the term "flash-back" in speaking of this sort of eidetic memory incurred by electrical stimulation, and also as a part of the aura heralding an epileptic fit. Also H. G. Beigel, experimenting with dreams and their hypnotically induced repetitions, speaks of "flash-back to a new fact of the original dream problem in a completely different set-up" ("Mental Processes during the Production of Dreams" [1959], p. 182).

[46] One of the earliest psychologists, if not the first, to realize those dangers was Hugo Münsterberg. See his On the Witness Stand: Essays on Psychology and Crime (1912; 1st ed., 1908).

ble in human life, because it is what carried the time dimension beyond the single act that is its limit in even the most advanced animal mentality.[47] So we have really at least five kinds of memory which seem, offhand, to be distinct and possibly of different derivation. (1) Old childhood memories, usually very circumscribed, a single act or scene such as a person entering through a door, a caught fish jumping, the dusk and smell in a firelit room, or sitting in a deep, motherly lap in a rocking chair that made the room dip and rise. Such memories usually come as intense, very brief flash-backs, and may be classed with later flash-backs. (2) Biographical memory, recollection of what one has heard and seen, which is apt to be somewhat incomplete, but to have enough elements strongly tinged with the psychical quality of "pastness" to admit no doubt as to their actual occurrence in one's own history. (3) Factual memory, or acquired knowledge that something is the case, where the occasion of learning and the source of information may be vaguely known or quite forgotten; this is the memory tested in examinations. (4) Inductive memory, the power of memorizing, generally regarded as a somewhat special endowment, very unevenly distributed among people and apparently with little relation to general intelligence; it seems to be largely limited to words or tunes, and certainly to involve the peculiar mechanism whereby each new unit—word or tonal element— is like a step in a pre-formed progression, being induced by its predecessor in the framework of a phrase, statement or poem (which may have no real linguistic sense, Révész to the contrary notwithstanding), or, in music, a melody. This sort of memory may extend to (or stem from?) concatenated steps, building up ritual movements, and at a much higher level of evolution, but still on the same principle, the use of hands and fingers in the deft playing of keyed or plucked instru-

---

[47] L. A. White, in an article, "On the Use of Tools by Primates" (1942), p. 372, corroborates this limitation even for the chimpanzee (despite the fact that elsewhere he credits apes with more conception than I would attribute to them), saying: "There is some foresight and some hindsight in the ape. But the characteristic feature of their mental life is the 'extremely narrow limits' of the temporal world in which they live; this, according to Köhler, is 'the chief difference ... between anthropoids and even the most primitive human beings.'... On the inner, subjective side, the ape's tool experience is thus a discontinuous psychological process subjectively as well as objectively." And further, summing up his reflections (p. 373): "In the ape, ... the inner experience begins and ends with the overt act. In man, tool experience is a continuum. Though the overt expression of this experience is disconnected and episodic, the inner experience is an uninterrupted flow. And it is the symbol, the word-formed idea, that makes this continuity of experience possible."

ments. And finally, (5) there is the primitive sort of memory based on something that is probably common to all the higher animals, though it takes its own subjective form in hominid cerebral evolution: object memory, the basis of recognition. In animals this may be felt more as familiarity versus strangeness than as identity of an object in disconnected situations; in human mentation it holds such diverse situations together and, so to speak, ranges them on a temporal string, making each recognized object an orientation mark to organize its situation. None of these versions of memory grow up alone, though some—for instance, the last-mentioned and the first—may have a somewhat precocious start; but in general all our mental functions interact in their growth, and each has some infantile phase which heralds it.

Yet I think it most likely that several, if not all, the distinct kinds of memory arise from different mental functions, and consequently involve different mechanisms. The fact is that the human specialty, the cortical activity of conception, starting in an early phylogenetic stage, has been invading every cerebral function that progressed to a psychical phase, and in the course of that progress somehow imprints it with an image that symbolizes it and revives it. It is the symbol—whatever it may be— that can be envisaged, thought, and thought again. So perhaps the best way to understand the great variety of mnemonic forms is to trace each one to the felt aspects of the sensory or impulsive action which the imaginative, conceptual procedure has seized upon for its own implementation. By this rather crudely practical method, one is led to the highly diverse sources of the fabric of memorable events which constitutes each human individual's own past, and there is nothing amazing about the conglomerate of elements which enter into it.

The most elementary sort of memory, giving rise to what Bertrand Russell, many decades ago, called "knowledge by acquaintance,"[48] is formed on a cerebral function which has been little understood, so far, in physiological terms, but has recently received a suggestive sidelight from an experimental study in animal neurology, which reveals something of the mechanism whereby an act of perception, when stimulated by one object or motion, automatically isolates its stimulus from rival impingements.[49] Such concentration of vision, hearing, smell or any

[48] "Knowledge by Acquaintance and Knowledge by Description" (1910).
[49] See Gabriel Horn, "Physiological and Psychological Aspects of Selective Perception" (1965), p. 164: "Nerve fibers from the visual cortex pass, in the monkey and the cat, to the lateral geniculate body ... and in the monkey, from the frontal lobes to the somesthetic relay nucleus in the thalamus ... and from the auditory cortex to the medial geniculate body.... In some animals and in some

senses together on one stimulus may be supposed, then, to occur without any added voluntary act of "paying attention"; it is the act of attention itself, and takes place in some way at least wherever there is a forebrain to guide animal behavior. In man, however, it incidentally provides a "servomechanism" for another evolving function, for it abstracts a percept from the whole sensuous array, and this percept promptly takes on the character of an image, without requiring much spontaneous imagination. Very soon, however (we have no way of knowing how soon), the percept is a hybrid of sense impression and dreamlike image; and it is probably in this state that it is remembered and recognized, at least for short times, in infancy. How early in the history of mankind this departure from animal memory began is a matter of guesswork. Whenever it did, that was the mental beginning of our humanization.

Evolutionary advances, as several scientists and scholars have pointed out,[50] do not keep close step with each other; and apparently the species-specific function of imagination at some early period outruns the other

---

sensory systems, centrifugal fibers pass to even more peripheral structures. In the cat, for example, fibers arising in the medulla pass along the auditory nerve toward the cochlea.... Electrical stimulation of these fibers is followed by a reduction in the response of the auditory nerve to an acoustic stimulus....

"There is nothing inherently improbable in the hypothesis that these centrifugal fibers play an important role in selective perception...."

[50] See E. C. Olson, *Origin of Mammals Based upon Cranial Morphology of the Therapsid Suborders* (1944): "The very advanced ictidosaurs suggest that they possessed accelerated development of mammalian trends, a process which might be anticipated in the ancestry of the marsupials and placentals and their probable predecessors, the pantotheres. Certain of the very primitive characters of the monotremes suggest origin from a stock, which, though it passed the mammalian threshold, did not progress as rapidly as others" (p. 125).

Tilly Edinger, likewise, has repeatedly remarked this unevenness of evolutionary progressions. In "Paleoneurology versus Comparative Brain Anatomy" (1949) she pointed out that in the earliest birds the whole skeleton was birdlike while the brain was still reptilian rather than avian. Even though birds today appear so harmoniously functional in construction, she said: "*Actually, the recent avian level of evolution was attained in the different features at different times; of those we know, the brain was slowest in evolution*" (p. 10). In another paper, "Frontal Sinus Evolution (Particularly in the Equidae)" (1950), she said that sinuses are not, and apparently never were, functional structures, but accidental results of disharmonious growth of the various bones of the skull.

In the realm of human history Meyerson observed a similar diversity in the rates of intellectual and social developments, which led him to say: "il faut toujours penser que l'histoire n'est pas unilinéaire. Elle est une polyphonie. Chaque série a son régime et son rythme propre qu'il faut pouvoir suivre" ("Discontinuités et cheminements autonomes dans l'histoire·de l'esprit" [1948], p. 274).

mental powers of man, though they all seem to grow like mushrooms as the upright spine rising through the central *foramen magnum* encourages the upward and lateral expansions of the cranium. Certainly in our history, presumably for long ages—eons, lasting into present times—the human world has been filled more with creatures of fantasy than of flesh and blood. Every perceived object, scene, and especially every expectation is imbued with fantasy elements, and those phantasms really have a stronger tendency to form systematic patterns, largely of a dramatic character, than factual impressions. The result is that human experience is a constant dialectic of sensory and imaginative activity—a making of scenes, acts, beings, intentions and realizations such as I believe animals do not encounter. In fact, it is only in human life that I think one can really speak of "experience." And it is experiences that make up human memory, a psychical background of each normal person's current consciousness and future envisagement. It is this structure that constitutes what we mean by the "life of the mind."

The dialectic which makes up that life is a real and constant cerebral process, the interplay between the two fundamental types of feeling, peripheral impact and autonomous action, or objective and subjective feeling. As fast as objective impingements strike our senses they become emotionally tinged and subjectified; and in a symbol-making brain like ours, every internal feeling tends to issue in a symbol which gives it an objective status, even if only transiently. This is the hominid specialty that makes the gulf between man and beast, without any unbiological addition, and probably goes back as far as any possible division between our kind and other primates.

In the early stages of human or prehuman existence, with all the crucial hominid traits already present in some degree, the excess of imagery over sober sense perception may have been really dangerously great. It must have been in such phases that the hordes of ghosts, monsters, spirits and the primitive divinities—gods of high places and of sun and moon, animal gods such as Jane Harrison found to have been the forerunners of the anthropomorphic Olympians, and the divine beings that are hard to classify distinctly as gods or devils, powers that may appear in all sorts of incarnations—were produced as tribal symbols and fearsome mysteries simply by being imagined. Once their images had been dreamed or invented they were easy enough to impose on actual constellations of visual data or on the voices in water and wind. There may have been periods when the unrealism of man presented a real hazard to his survival; and as there seem to have been several human genera which have not survived, it is interesting—though of little other value—to speculate whether magic, sacrifice and ritual self-abuses may not have been weakening influences on a stock departing so radically from the normal primate pattern.

To the average civilized person today, the uncontrolled welter of nightmarish conceptions belongs to childhood, and to a period of intense emotional feeling. It is largely from such early phases of mental life, when the subjectification of all sensory material tended to hold sway over the dialectic of inner and outer feeling, that "flash-back memories" arise later in life. But different temperaments, different religious and intellectual standards prevail all over the world, so the balance between emotional, subjective, creative impulses and analytic perception and symbolic objectification, which constitutes actual personal experience, can vary between very wide extremes. With maturity, the vividness that marked early impressions and still tends to make their memories eidetic, like immediate reality, in sudden flash-back experiences gives way to a new characteristic of biographical recollection, which has been referred to by several authors as a "sense of pastness."

That designation, of course, does nothing but give the phenomenon a name; I have never seen any analysis or even theoretical suggestion to account for its subjective aspect, despite the fact that objectively all personal responsibility, all factual records, and even all that we have of history rest somewhere on biographical memory. The "sense of pastness" distinguishes such memory from two related mental actions, (1) the eidetic type of sudden, effortless, perfectly convincing "reliving," and (2) sheer imagination, invention, *poesis*, which may also be recalled and rehearsed, but does not normally seem like something that has happened to the subject in his actual, external world. The fact is that a quality, like "a sense of pastness," gives us no clue to understanding anything in even the most tentative, speculative terms; only events, processes, can be factually or hypothetically construed. A quality is a phenomenon to be understood in terms of what is going on in the organism.

The problem of biographical memory, then, is the problem of how current experiences are relegated to memory in a more or less constant, automatic way, lose their feeling of present impact and emergence, and acquire the "sense of pastness" in a normal and steady flow that is the subjective passage of time. Unfortunately, at present, we know too little of the neurological processes involved in memories of any type to hope for a physiological theory to emerge from the existing literature. Empirical description of psychological observations is the best we can expect to construct; and biographical memory is about the most complex mental function of ordinary human life, running like a spine through each individual history, and concatenating the human agent's mental acts into a life of the mind.

There are several phenomena involved in the process of relegating an experience to memory; one is, of course, the "presentational immediacy" of the momentary experience itself, which is the felt dialectic of sensory impact and conceptual interpretation. This dialectic is a transient act at any moment of life, but it involves something more than its own passage; for the interaction of peripheral and central felt processes begets the sense of reality, which holds over from the experience itself to the elements of memory that stem from its actual occurrence. Our conceptual formulation of sensory impacts is generally so smooth and prompt and rhythmic that we are not aware of taking any active part in it at all; yet impacts are remembered with a "sense of reality" that anchors biographical memory to experience, and makes the great difference between such recall and the recall of fantasies entertained before, stories read or heard and other non-actual elements in the background of our mental life.

But our knowledge of our own past experiences is by no means an unbroken flow of memory. The relatively certain recollections are items, held together by conceptual assumptions of what must lie between them to account for their sequences and their deployment in clock-and-calendar time. History is a fabric of memories, convergent circumstantial evidence (i.e., records, chronicles) and rational construction; it is like a fine, strong, woven web in which there is hardly a single thread that could bear much of any sharp pull on itself alone without breaking.

The formative element of biographical memory is verbal conception. I doubt that any creature without some sort of speech has a sequential memory of its own life, or the possibility of constructing its own past. Language, propositional thinking and everything that goes with speech is such a special development in the hominid brain that it is not surprising to find verbal memory exhibiting quite different forms and procedures from any other type of recollection. Its chief characteristic is that if a series of words is recollected, the main elements are rhythm, sound combinations, flow and length of phrases, stops and emphatic starts (such as vocative forms and their accents—"O Captain, my Captain!"), with the so-called message often serving as a secondary or even dispensable support. Many people can learn verbal formulae, long poems, even orations in languages they do not understand. Each phrase induces the next; this sort of recollection might be called "inductive memory," and is what we generally mean by "committing something to memory" or "learning by heart."[51] Very similar processes seem to be involved in memorizing music and possibly ritual movements, elaborate gestures as in dance and other essentially rhythmic actions.

The whole mental shift of the Hominidae away from the rest of the primates is epitomized in the evolution of symbolic activity;[52] and this, in turn, reaches its highest development in the uniquely human function of language. There is so much mentation involved in language that to think of it as a "signaling system" or a social habit encouraged by survival value is worse than superficial, it is simplistic, not to say silly. Language, despite the fact that its development requires the influence of a speaking society during the early years of each individual life, is not only acquired for communal purposes, but even as it is learned penetrates the entire system of cerebral activities, so that perception and fantasy and memory, intuition and even dreaming take their special human forms under its continual and increasing influence. Its complexity is shown quite spectacularly in the pathology of language, the various forms of aphasia, by the peculiar losses of separate elements which, apart from such demonstrations, common sense would never have regarded as isolable. The elements which may fall apart certainly suggest some possible ways this exceedingly complex phenomenon may have taken shape in its long history. There are cases on record of focal cerebral lesions causing inability to name and apparently to recognize animate beings, while maintaining recognition of inanimate objects, and contrariwise, lesions which make such ordinary things as a bottle of milk or a glass, or an automobile, nameless and strange, while the patient calls persons by name correctly, remembers absent associates, and can identify any organic objects, birds and even plants, alive or dead, and recognizes parts of bodies—hands, hair, etc.[53] Since in some cases a doll may be recognized as an "animate object" and in another case recognized (or unrecognized) as something inanimate, and the

[51] Another distinguishing feature of verbal memory is that its products usually carry no sense of pastness.

[52] J. N. Spuhler, in an article entitled "Somatic Paths to Culture" (1959), wrote that "there is a gap between cultural behavior and non-cultural behavior. The two sides of the gap are defined in terms of symbol and lack of symbol" (p. 1). The gap is that which divides animals and men.

[53] The first collection of these rare but spectacular cases was published in J. M. Nielsen's *Agnosia, Apraxia, Aphasia* (1946; 1st ed., 1936). The same author, in his "Epitome of Agnosia, Apraxia and Aphasia with Proposed Physiologic Anatomic Nomenclature" (1942), p. 114, wrote: "From the stand point of cerebral localization it is necessary to distinguish between recognition of animate and inanimate objects because one function is not infrequently lost without the other."

[345]

same ambiguous status may be given to false teeth, it appears that some process of classification goes on before any conscious conceptual identification of objects.[54] The basic perceptual distinctions and imposition of categories on experience, though apparently peculiar to humanity and therefore, in evolutionary terms, higher processes based on general primate mentation, seem to pervade and modify the elementary functions on which they have grown up. This is, in fact, typical of superposed activities: instead of remaining distinct, separable, advanced forms which might be lost again or destroyed without seriously affecting their older substructures, they so deeply alter their own very roots that their destruction jeopardizes the whole organic system. In schizophrenia, for instance, there is certainly a diminution of the patient's intellectual range and sometimes an appearance of childishness in overt action, yet he cannot really revert to childhood thought, emotion and other activity, because a child is a growing and developing person, and the schizophrenic is the opposite; he is not immature, but impaired in depth as well as deprived of his late-acquired skills and habits.[55] There is, as far as I know, at present no trustworthy theory to explain this influence of every new advance on the entire forebrain, but there is a suggestion of an underlying neural mechanism of integration in the finding of V. B. Mountcastle that the functional patterns of cortical action are vertical rather than—as generally supposed—topologically "layered" like the cortex,[56] and some other casual discoveries of interactions among superimposed structures and their more primitive supports.

[54] A similar, preconscious activity has been fairly well demonstrated with regard to valuation, which affects the comprehension of words, and consequently must precede their intellectual reception. As this phenomenon has already been discussed in another connection, see above, Chapter 14, pp. 113–16, and references there.

[55] Norman Cameron, in an article, "Experimental Analysis of Schizophrenic Thinking" (1944), remarked on the fairly common error of regarding schizophrenia as a reversion to a childhood pattern of thought. "It is quite true," he wrote, "that the child is in the process of developing adult social language and thought organization, whereas the schizophrenic is in the process of losing it. But one process is not, as often erroneously implied, simply the reverse of the other. It is hardly more correct to assert that as the schizophrenic loses his adult organization he becomes a child in his thinking, than it is to say of normal children that as they grow up they recover from schizophrenia" (pp. 59–60).

[56] See his paper, "The Neural Replication of Sensory Events in the Somatic Afferent System" (1966), p. 89: "Single neuron studies have revealed that at least through the cortical input stage the specificity for place and quality is preserved. They have also indicated what the plan of functional organization there may be. It appears that this is not one related transversely in accord with the layers of classical cytoarchitecture. The functional unit is a vertical column of cells extending

The elements of language which may be separately impaired or even completely lost certainly suggest that this apparently simple and single, universal human ability has actually been built up from a great number of mental traits, entrained in the course of a long cerebral evolution by the basic process of finishing excessive neural impulses in the brain itself as symbolic images and utterances.[57] In various aphasic conditions, such as are often brought on by war injuries, accidental skull fractures or concussions, or else by internal lesions like tumors, the patient may lose the fluency of speech, though he can still find the key words and combine them in comprehensible sentences, but without articles, connectives, dependent clause structures or other formal elaborations;[58] or,

---

across the cortical layers. . . ." Another suggestion that new, "high" cerebral functions tend to mesh with older ones of lower order comes from an observation contributed by Stephen Polyak to a discussion of a paper by P. Bailey, W. S. McCulloch and G. von Bonin, "Long Associational Cortico-Cortical Pathways in the Cerebrum of the Chimpanzee as Revealed by the Method of Physiological Neuronography" (1942). Dr. Polyak remarked: "The observation . . . that the impulses generated in the oculomotor center of the frontal lobe reach directly the parastriate area or field 18 which we know to be the occipital center for the conjugate eye movements . . . seems to indicate the linking of widely separated foci having similar function into functional units of a higher order" (p. 76). An even more striking illustration of this principle is given by F. W. Jones in *The Principles of Anatomy, As Seen in the Hand*, pp. 342–43: "The peripheral sensory nerve . . . can inform the central nervous system of sensations of touch, heat, cold, pain, etc. . . . In order to sort impressions travelling to the brain there must, therefore, be a readjustment of the myriad streaming stimuli of one definite kind carried by the lowest sensory axon in a variety of channels. It is this readjustment which is effected in the cord. In the cord the regrouping consists of an integration of all the stimuli of one kind, no matter what their source. All the fibers subserving pain, touch, heat, and cold, no matter if their source be superficial or deep, epicritic or protopathic, are isolated into separate groups travelling upward in the cord."

57 This general view of language was expressed long ago by A. Heveroch in an article entitled "Amerisia" (1915), where he declared: "*Unsere Sprache ist bedingt durch die Fähigkeit, Sätze und Worte zu finden, ferner durch die Fähigkeit sie auszusprechen und sie niederzuschreiben, aber ausserdem noch durch eine dritte, zwischen beiden liegende Fähigkeit: die Fähigkeit, das wachgerufene Wort zur Sprache oder zur Schrift zu gliedern. Dass die angeführten Fähigkeiten in gewissem Masse selbstständig sind, beweist der Umstand, dass sie selbstständig erkranken können, die Funktionen werden zu Afunktionen oder Dysfunktionen*" (p. 329). Loss of the third of these essential linguistic abilities he has named "Amerisia."

58 For instances of this disability, see especially M. Isserlin, "Über Agramatismus" (1922), one of the first extensive studies (i.e., with long follow-up records) of head injuries received by soldiers in World War I. One of his patients, after two years, recovered a fair ability to speak, but always in the "agrammatic" form which Isserlin denoted as "telegraph style" ("*Depeschenstil*"). K. Kleist has recorded similar cases

contrariwise, chiefly in schizophrenia, he may keep the ability to chatter in a fluent fashion, but lose command of word meanings. In the first case he will speak in so-called "telegraph style," in the second, opposite case the result is a "word salad," which sounds like conversation but really contains no comprehensible statements. So, evidently, the rhythm and continuity of communicative speech and the conceptual use of words are distinct elements, which may be of different origin. This suggests the possibility that Donovan's "festal origin" of speech (if that source really existed) might have contributed only one factor—the rhythmic flow and elaborate sound structure of talking—while most of the conceptual content came from other sources, less excited, the daily round of activity accompanied by characteristic patterns of audible, more or less articulated utterance noted above (pp. 326–27).

Another extraordinary fact is that when language is used covertly, i.e., as an instrument of thought, words do not seem to be simple, "assigned" elements of a code, but to mark the center of a wider range of related ideas; so that in case the exact word for a concept is somehow blocked, and another word presents itself in its place, that other word is not a completely arbitrary substitution, but usually denotes something in the same conceptual range.[59] Like all failures of verbal expression, this sort of slip is most apparent in pathological disturbances of speech; but its common occurrence in normal as well as abnormal speakers shows that the cerebral mechanism whereby the correct word for a con-

---

in "Gehirnpathologische und lokalisatorische Ergebnisse. 4. Mitteilung. Über motorische Aphasien" (1930).

Another experienced and systematic investigator of aphasic disorders was Kurt Goldstein, whose work, often in collaboration with Dr. Adhémar Gelb, goes back to World War I and continued through and after World War II. In *Language and Language Disturbances* (1948) we have his last case histories and theoretical reflections; most of the case records deal with the loss of nouns, the loss of "small words"—prepositions, connectives, etc.—and the consequent tendency to save words by speaking in "telegraph style."

[59] Isserlin, "Über Agrammatismus," pp. 366–67, says of one patient who regularly used wrong words: "Spricht mit ganz falschen Flexionen und oft falschen Worten; so 'gehört' statt 'gesehen.' " And somewhat later (p. 369), "Besonders Präpositionen werden schlecht verstanden. Verwechselt z.B. *in* und *aus*, *über* und *unter*." The words this aphasic confused were words belonging to the same category; and in the case of the prepositions, of opposite, not simply unrelated, sense.

This phenomenon had been noted earlier; Arnold Pick cited a case of Messer's, whose patient called it *"Sphärenbewusstsein,"* and said of it, "eigenartiger Zustand, in dem man genau weiss, in welchen *Bereich* von Gedanken das Wort gehört." Pick himself gave several examples of such "near hits" on the desired words (*Über das Sprachverständnis* [1909], p. 38).

cept is, as a rule, promptly produced is much more complex, the process more deeply started and built up, than its usual case and largely automatic progression would lead one to believe.[60]

There are other surprising indications of the scattered and, perhaps, anciently independent sources of what today seems a coherent system of words all used according to rather simple grammatical and syntactical rules. So, for instance, it is not unlikely that proper names did not originally function as "nouns," or terms for designating objects,[61] but may have been purely means of addressing individuals—an ancient function of which there is still a trace in some languages, the existence of a "vocative case." The social significance of names in several highly developed cultures also bears witness to their special, perhaps independent symbolic functions in the distant past, and their entrainment by language in the course of its irresistible growth and intellectual dominance.[62]

Another anomalous character of speech which is revealed in many cases of aphasia is the fact that both naming and reading of numbers often remain unaffected where other words, spoken or written, can no longer be produced at will.[63] Numbers seem to have a special status; their symbolic expression by numerals, which every reader verbalizes according to his own language, shows that number concepts are not ordinary elements of vocabulary, but may long have been conceived and conveyed by non-linguistic symbols, and perhaps had a history of their own in our cerebral evolution. But whatever was their prehistoric mode of symbolization, it has become associated, at least among civilized men,

[60] For a typical example from normal life see T. P. Bailey, "Snapshot of a Hunt for a Lost Name" (1907), mentioned by Pick, *Über das Sprachverständnis*.

[61] E. R. Guthrie notes, incidentally, that "nouns and verbs apply only to classes of events or objects. Proper names are not material for science" ("Association by Contiguity" [1959], p. 177).

[62] See, e.g., J. S. F. Garnot, "Les fonctions, les pouvoirs et la nature du nom propre dans l'ancienne Egypte d'après les textes des pyramides" (1948).

[63] S. P. Goodhart and N. Savitsky, in a short paper, "Alexia Following Injury of the Head" (1933), report the case of a man of forty-five, hit by an automobile, who lost and did not recover his ability to read words, though he never lost the ability to read numbers.

In an early and more detailed article, "Über einen Fall von sogenannter Leitungsaphasie mit anatomischem Befund" (1915) H. Liepmann and M. Pappenheim describe a case of internal (tumorous) damage which greatly impaired the patient's spontaneous speech by constant paraphrastic slips and distortions, but left him able to count smoothly to 29; and they report, furthermore, that in trying to recite any other well-known series such as the alphabet or the order of months, he always slipped into the natural number series again.

with vocables that finally displaced and replaced any gestic or other means, and assimilated numbers and numerical relations to language, though not to the exclusion of all their conceptual independence. A similar distinction sometimes appears in the apprehension of musical form and the ability to read musical notation despite verbal aphasia and alexia.[64] Such notation belongs to no alphabetical writing, i.e., renders no words of any language, and heard or read musical forms have no linguistic meanings, so (like numbers) they may escape the influence of disease affecting the capacity to use words, or written symbols for spoken words.

From all these oddities of speech and literacy and especially their pathology we may gather an idea of the complexity and spread of the origins from which man's ability to talk has arisen. Its sources are really as broad as the whole range of conception, personal or communal; elements of language have come from practically all cerebral functions that involved symbolic activity. Its principal achievement is, of course, communication—so much so that people quite naturally regard that as its whole purpose and earliest motivation. Very probably the practice of verbal communication, i.e., exchange of ideas, proposals, claims and presentation of fantasies and sentiments, go back to the beginnings of any group acceptance of articulate utterance; and as it served for intellectual contact it penetrated and formed the mind of every user. Listening to sounds with meanings is not simply hearing and remembering a collection of distinguishable noises and associating them with acts or objects; as Jarvis Bastian said (in an essay which otherwise suffers all the effects of the present "signal code" conception of language and of animal sounds), "A much more cogent conceptualization of the processes of phonemic identification ... has been developed in the research of the Haskins Laboratories ... and ... extended to the design of phonemic recognition devices in the work of the Electronic Research Laboratories at the Massachusetts Institute of Technology. The central idea of this conceptualization is that the phonemic identification of a linguistic signal is decided by the listener in terms of the articulatory controls by which he would repeat the signal when acting as a speaker."[65]

[64] There is one old article by J. G. Edgren, "Amusie (musikalische Aphasie)" (1895), concerned directly with this syndrome, but in the wider literature on aphasia there are many incidentally reported instances.

[65] "Primate Signaling Systems and Human Languages" (1965), p. 596. This is not the only case in which the physicists who aim to make mechanical models of organic actions have discovered the weakness of psychological and neurological concepts based on their own tentative experimental mechanisms and have challenged the simplistic biological view, to the advantage of biology and the furtherance of their own technological ambitions.

This is an interesting view, in that it shows listening, too, as an activity involving more than auditory reception, namely, a play of impulses which reach the speech apparatus without coming to overt expression, but which fuse with the cochlear stimuli that served in their motivation, to be inseparably consummated as symbolic elements in the conceptual work of the cortex.

The depth to which the influence of language goes in the formation of human perception, thought and mental processes generally is as amazing as its evolution from human feeling, peripheral and central, in all corners and reaches of man's overtaxed psyche. The formation of separate languages does not stem from the variability of semantical codes and deliberate choices of terms and rules of combination, but bears all the marks of organic process:[66] the unplanned growth of grammatical inflections to a stage of high elaboration, often followed by periods of gradual simplification, popular misuse and loss of forms, and in the course of such decline a tendency to generate entirely new languages, much as hereditary taxonomic lines produce intricate forms up to a turning point where these begin to degenerate again, and the stock, temporarily "defeated," tends to speciate, i.e., to initiate various phylogenetically new departures. At such junctures each speech community is apt to develop its own words and usages, until people who have been separated only a few hundred years can no longer understand each other. Also, in every tongue there are metaphorical words and expressions which are understood as readily as literal designations and statements (for instance, calling a language a tongue); whether they originated as poetic images or as slang, they give the language its richness and vivid quality long after their metaphorical status is no longer noticed. In its totality, its sound and rhythm and especially its figurative expressions, it reflects the tempo and emotional base line of the population that speaks and thinks in it; and thought which rises far above that level is apt to employ unusual words and metaphors. Many religious institutions use an archaic or even foreign language in their observances, prayers, chants and recitations. Throughout the Middle Ages Latin was the language of the church, long after the common people anywhere had ceased to speak it; in India Sanskrit, no longer understood by the laity, is still the holy script, and the Greek Orthodox church in Yugoslavia holds its services in an old form of Bulgarian. The archaic diction does more than moralists and modernizers realize to remove religious thought from the realm of commonplace interest, exalt the sense

---

[66] This fact was remarked in 1852 by Jakob Grimm in *Über den Ursprung der Sprache*.

of holiness of the worshippers, and hold it at a sustained high tension throughout the celebration.

With a more personal need for conservatism, many middle-aged or old people who have emigrated from their native country and adopted a new language in their later home insist on having church services held in their mother tongue, and often try to make their children, who do not speak the old language, still use it liturgically. This is essentially an emotive value somewhat apart from the "distancing" quality of a special church language, though it is related to that practice for the congregation demanding it: the idiom of the new country is usually learned entirely in a secular, practical setting and seems to the immigrant like a strictly vernacular, unpoetic kind of speech, without cherished associations or fine degrees of seriousness and lightness.

Many of the deeper effects of language on mental life are revealed only by the subjective experience of polyglot persons. Where the possession of more than one language is deeply ingrained (a complete command for thinking and poetic imagination rarely goes beyond bilingualism), several neurologists have held that special "speech centers" in the brain form with the use of an alternative system of speech; others reject that hypothesis because there is really no decisive evidence for it.[67] Usually, in aphasia due to a sudden lesion (injury or "stroke"), it is the later-acquired language that is lost;[68] but there have been enough cases in which the earliest is lost and a subsequently, even academically, learned one partly or wholly retained to lead Otto Pötzl to the conclusion that one cannot even call this order of recoveries a rule, still less a law of psychology. Pötzl, studying the exceptions, discovered that in all those anomalous cases which he was able to study there was always a special condition to account for predominance of the second language; either that it was the language the patient was using at the time of the disaster, or was in the forefront of his interest because he was in process of learning it under emotional, professional or social pressure.[69] Quite

[67] In Otto Pötzl's article, "Über die parietal bedingte Aphasie und ihren Einfluss auf das Sprechen mehrerer Sprachen" (1925), it appears that the author subscribed to some form of this theory, for he went into some detail to support it and controvert objections to it; yet he candidly declared (p. 122) that there was, at the time of his writing, "kein Anhaltspunkt für die Existenz getrennter zentraler Apparate für jede einzelne Sprache."

[68] In *ibid.*, p. 100, Pötzl attributed to Pitres the first statement of the "law" that the language most familiar to the aphasic patient is always the first to be recovered, while other languages are repressed by its revival; and to Ribot the further "law," known as the "law of regression," that the later a language is acquired, the more easily it is lost (p. 117).

[69] Pp. 101 ff.

generally an act in progress, involving a particular language, seems to give that vocabulary an advantage even over a much more familiar one.[70]

Normally, persons who command more than one language find that they think in one or the other according to what they are doing or thinking about. A language fully possessed is a system of conception; its figures of speech are figures of thought. That is the main condition for one's shifting (sometimes momentarily) from one tongue to another without any external motivation such as talking to a person who prefers one over the other, or being addressed and naturally giving reply in the same language regardless of one's inward verbalization a moment ago. The mind is so largely formed and its higher functions sustained by words and ways of wording ideas that the linguistic influence is not limited to cortical, rational and semi-rational processes, but reaches far into the emotional sphere, coloring fantasies and wishes and even perceptions; some moods dispose a polyglot individual to favor his earliest, babyhood language, some a later-acquired one if, for instance, it seems more adult and public.

Perhaps the most powerful and also most surprising fact revealed by the use of two or more languages is the entirely unconscious part played by language in the formation of dreams. I happen to be bilingual myself; I did not learn English until I went to school. Then, of course, it became my conversational and intellectual language, and finally my poetic one, too. So it is from personal experience that I say, every dream is dreamt in a language, even if not a word is spoken in the dream; indeed, speeches in a dream may be in another language than the one in which the dream is constructed, which operates at the level of what Freud designated as the "dream work." That is the same level at which images are formed, and often stand proxy for words. It is usually by tracing images to their verbal meanings that the language of the dream work is revealed; yet without any such analysis I usually know in which language I dreamt a perfectly wordless dream. It seems that whatever the dream work is, it begins with emotional processes, probably deeply subcortical, and passes through many parts of the brain, entraining recent memories here and very old, buried ones there, before it reaches the visualizing areas of the cortex; and that somewhere along its course all dream material passes through the speech apparatus, where the "dream thought" is sub-verbally formed; which means that those illustrated narratives, our dreams, are something thought.

[70] This impetus reminds one of that which physiologists find in the somatic sphere, where a mitotic act will often run to its finish even after death; cf. Vol. I, p. 379, n. 41.

The linguistic elements in the construction of dreams become most evident in the rare cases where the "dream thought" shifts from one language to another, but the same elements undoubtedly take part where no such special circumstance allows us to see them. Punning is a common practice in dream construction, often hiding the basic dream thought by visually illustrating the ostensible, not the secret sense of the word played upon; but perhaps as often the image rests on the secret meaning; and where the pun is not recognized the incursion of language into the process of dreaming is not apparent at all.

The life of the mind is so complex and so many-faceted that practically no categorizing or systematizing principle holds without qualification. Even the elementary distinction between impulses to action felt as impacts, usually starting peripherally, and those felt as autogenic acts arising within the organism, and taking shape more slowly before they are overtly consummated, has some exceptions. A thought, a recollection of some forgotten fact or intention, though centrally produced, may break in on the rest of one's thinking with a suddenness and force that can only be classed as impact. As peripheral feeling keeps us generally and quietly aware of what we call "external reality," except when it is intensified and stirred up by special events, so our autogenic mental acts usually run their normal courses, unless suddenly a thought from an entirely different line of thinking breaks in on them with a shock much like that of a real, external blow delivered to the organism. Such a thought is a "realization," which clashes with the rest of the brain's work and is felt as impact. The human brain is so elaborate, and functionally so departmentalized, that one act may impinge on a whole system of other processes; and one word may be the symbol that triggers such a mental and even physical emergency.

In this chapter I have dwelled especially upon the intraorganic influences of man's unique trait, symbolic conception and expression, because their importance and depth have been misjudged by a great number of psychologists and anthropologists who deem the communicative function of speech not only its paramount value, but its entire *raison d'être*, and consequently class it, on the one hand, with technological signal codes, and on the other with animal signs of intention and disposition. But animal values are only incidental to human life, and the techniques of intercourse a constant by-product of conceptual contact among men. Communication is, indeed, the driving force in language-making; but it is communication of ideas, beyond the realm of a present situation, that builds up the human world. The first cerebral finish of a mental act, the first discovery of the unreality of figments created in dream, beget the concept of reality. When the sense of reality embraces events and dangers, the world of time and space becomes the theater of natural powers, all seen in imaginary forms, felt to be actual but incomprehensible denizens of that world. The enormous potency of speech lies in the fact that it can transmit such intangible conceptions to all members of a human group, familial or congregated, and make it a society. Language can grow up only in communicative use, which for human beings is the typical process of contact with one another; Révész was surely right when he pointed out that interindividual contact is the principle which holds every group of gregarious beings together, and that in mankind communication—mental contact—has replaced the physical contact needed by other sociable creatures.[71]

It is in society, and more particularly in the verbal intercourse called conversation, that men have acquired what the most intelligent other animals have never developed—intellect. Animal mentation and human intellect rest on different principles. The most organized animal community is not comparable to human society, for only the latter is based on intellectual and moral values—personal responsibility, standards of justice, honor and loyalty to a social order. Society, like the spatiotemporal world itself, is a creation of man's specialized modes of feeling—perception, imagination, conceptual thought and the understanding of language. The rise of his typical way of life as a member of a continuous, recognized society, built up on the ancient and gradual separation of the evolving Hominidae from all other, differentially evolving primate lines, in its advance constantly epitomizes the great shift from beast to man.

[71] Révész, *Ursprung und Vorgeschichte der Sprache*, esp. pp. 165–70.

Bibliography

ALEXANDER, R. D. "Sound Communication in Orthoptera and Cicadidae," in *Animal Sounds and Communication*. Edited by W. E. Lanyon and W. N. Tavolga. Washington, D.C.: American Institute of Biological Sciences, 1960, pp. 38–92.

ALLEN, M. D. "Observations on Honeybees Attending Their Queen," *British Journal of Animal Behaviour*, III (1955), 66–69.

ALLEN, W. H. "Bird Migration and Magnetic Meridians," *Science*, CVIII (1948), 708.

ALTMANN, STUART. "Primates," in *Animal Communication*. Edited by T. A. Seboek. Bloomington: Indiana University Press, 1968, pp. 466–522.

ANDERSEN, H. (ed.). *The Biology of Marine Mammals*. New York: Academic Press, 1969.

ARDIS, J. A., AND McKELLAR, PETER. "Hypnagogic Imagery and Mescaline," *Journal of Mental Science*, CII (1956), 22–29.

ARDREY, ROBERT. *The Territorial Imperative: A Personal Inquiry into the Animal Origins of Property and Nations*. New York: Atheneum, 1966.

ARMSTRONG, E. A. *The Wren*. London: Collins, 1955.

ARNHEIM, RUDOLF. *Art and Visual Perception: A Psychology of the Creative Eye*. Berkeley: University of California Press, 1954.

ASTIC, LILIANE, AND JOUVET-MOUNIER, DANIÈLE. "Mise en évidence du sommeil paradoxal *in utero* chez le cobaye," *Comptes Rendues des Séances de l'Académie des Sciences*, D, CCLXIX (1969), 2578–81.

ATTNEAVE, FRED. "Some Informational Aspects of Visual Perception," *Psychological Review*, LXI (1954), 183–93.

BAERENDS, G. P. "Fortpflanzungsverhalten und Orientierung der Grabwespe *Ammophila campestris* Jur.," *Tijdschrift voor Entemologie*, LXXXIV (1941), 68–275.

BAILEY, P., McCULLOCH, W. S., AND BONIN, G. VON. "Long Associational Cortico-Cortical Pathways in the Cerebrum of the Chimpanzee as Revealed by the Method of Physiological Neuronography," *Transactions of the American Neurological Association*, LXVII (1942), 73–78.

BAILEY, T. P. "Snapshot of a Hunt for a Lost Name," *Journal of Philosophy, Psychology and Scientific Method*, IV (1907), 337–42.

BALDWIN, J. M. *Mental Development in the Child and the Race*. 3d ed.; 1st ed., 1895. New York: Macmillan, 1915.

Bibliography

BALEY, STEPHEN. "Le comportement des enfants et des singes inférieurs en présence des objets placés sur un support," *Acta Psychologica,* I (1935), 30–38.

BARBOUR, THOMAS. *Reptiles and Amphibians.* Boston: Houghton Mifflin, 1926.

BARCROFT, SIR JOSEPH. *Researches on Prenatal Life,* Vol. I. 1st British ed., 1946. Springfield, Ill.: Charles C Thomas, 1947.

BARLOW, J. S. "Inertial Navigation as a Basis for Animal Navigation," *Journal of Theoretical Biology,* VI (1964), 76–117.

BARTHOLOMEW, G. A. "The Role of Behavior in the Temperature Regulation of the Masked Booby," *The Condor,* LXVIII (1966), 523–35.

———. "Temperature Regulation in the Macropod Marsupial, Setonix brachyurus," *Physiological Zoology,* XXIX (1956), 26–40.

BARTLETT, F. C. "Some Experiments about Thinking," *Proceedings of the Royal Society of London, Series B,* CXLV (1956), 443–51.

BARTLEY, S. J., NELSON, T. M., AND RANNEY, J. E. "The Sensory Parallel of the Reorganization Period in the Cortical Response in Intermittent Retinal Stimulation," *Journal of Psychology,* LII (1961), 137–47.

BASTIAN, JARVIS. "Primate Signaling Systems and Human Languages," in *Primate Behavior.* Edited by I. DeVore. New York: Holt, Rinehart and Winston, 1965, pp. 585–606.

BAUCHOP, T., AND MARTUCCI, R. W. "Ruminant-like Digestion of the Langur Monkey," *Science,* CLXI (1968), 698–99.

BAUMANN, G. *Ursprung und Wachstum der Sprache.* Munich and Berlin: R. Oldenbourg, 1913.

BEACH, F. A., AND JAYNES, J. "Effects of Early Experience upon the Behavior of Animals," *Psychological Bulletin,* LI (1954), 239–63.

BEATTY, R. T. *Hearing in Man and Animals.* London: Bell and Son, 1932.

BEEBE, B. F. *African Elephants.* New York: David McKay, 1968.

BEECHER, W. J. "On Coriolis Force and Bird Navigation," *Scientific Monthly,* LXXIX (1954), 27–31.

BEIGEL, H. G. "Mental Processes during the Production of Dreams," *Journal of Psychology,* XLVII (1959), 171–87.

BELLROSE, FRANK C. "Orientation in Waterfowl Migration," in *Animal Orientation and Navigation.* Edited by R. M. Storm. Corvallis: Oregon State University Press, 1967, pp. 73–99.

BENOIT, J. A. A. "États physiologiques et instinct de reproduction chez les oiseaux," in *L'Instinct dans le comportement des animaux et de l'homme.* Edited by P. P. Grassé. Paris: Masson, 1956, pp. 177–260.

BESSERER, INGEBURG, AND DROST, RUDOLF. "Ein Beitrag zum Kapitel 'Vogelzug und Elektrizität,'" *Vogelzug,* VI (1935), 1–5.

BEST-MAUGARD, ALPHONSO. *A Method for Creative Design.* New York: A. A. Knopf, 1926.

BETHE, ALBRECHT. "Dürfen wir den Ameisen und Bienen psychische Qualitäten zuschreiben?" *Archiv für die gesamte Physiologie des Menschen und der Tiere,* LXX (1898), 15–100.

BIERENS DE HAAN, JOHAN A. *Die tierischen Instinkte und ihr Umbau durch Erfahrung: Eine Einführung in die allgemeine Tierpsychologie.* Leiden: E. J. Brill, 1940.

[358]

Bibliography

BILLS, A. G. "Blocking: A New Principle of Mental Fatigue," *American Journal of Psychology*, XLIII (1931), 230–45.

BLEST, A. D. "The Evolution, Ontogeny and Quantitative Control of the Settling Movements of Some New World Saturniid Moths, with Some Comments on Distance Communication in Honey-Bees," *Behaviour*, XVI (1960), 188–253.

———. "Interaction between Consecutive Responses in a Hemileucid Moth, and the Evolution of Insect Communication," *Nature*, CLXXXI (1958), 1077–78.

BOGERT, CHARLES M. "Thermoregulation in Reptiles, a Factor in Evolution, *Evolution*, III (1949), 195–211.

BOLK, LOUIS. *Das Problem der Menschwerdung.* Jena: G. Fischer, 1926.

BONNER, J. T. *Size and Cycle: An Essay on the Structure of Biology.* Princeton: University Press, 1965.

BÖRNSTEIN, WALTER. "Der Aufbau der Funktionen in der Hörsphäre," *Abhandlungen aus der Neurologie, Psychiatrie, Psychologie und ihren Grenzgebieten*, LIII (1930), 1–126.

BRAIN, W. R. "The Cerebral Basis of Consciousness," *Brain*, LXXIII (1950), 465–79.

———. "Speech and Handedness," *Lancet*, II (1945), 837–41.

BRONOWSKI, J., AND BELLUGI, URSULA. "Language, Name and Concept," *Science*, CLXVIII (1970), 666–73.

BROWN, JOHN. "Short-Term Memory," *British Medical Bulletin*, XX (1964), 8–11.

BRUNER, J. S., AND POSTMAN, L. "Perception, Cognition and Behavior," *Journal of Personality*, XVIII (1949), 14–31.

———. "On the Perception of Incongruity: A Paradigm," *Journal of Personality*, XVIII (1949), 206–23.

BUCHANAN, J. W. "Intermediate Levels of Organismic Integration," *Biological Symposia*, VIII (1942), 43–65.

BÜCHER, KARL. *Arbeit und Rhythmus.* 6th ed.; 1st ed., 1896. Leipzig: Hirzel, 1924.

BUCKLEY, W. *Big Game Hunting in Central Africa.* London: C. Palmer, 1930.

BUDDENBROCK, W. VON. *Vergleichende Physiologie.* Vol. I: *Sinnesphysiologie.* Basel: Birkhäuser, 1952.

BUETTNER-JANUSCH, J., AND ANDREW, R. J. "The Use of the Incisors by Primates in Grooming," *American Journal of Anthropology*, n.s., XX (1962), 127–29.

BULLOCK, T. H. (ed.). *Physiological Triggers and Discontinuous Rate Processes: Papers Based on a Symposium at the Marine Biological Laboratory, Woods Hole, Mass., September 1955.* Washington, D.C.: American Physiological Society, 1956.

BUSNEL, R. G., GIBAN, J., GRAMET, P., AND PASCHINELLY, F. "Absence d'action des ondes du radar sur la direction de vol de certains oiseaux," *Comptes rendus hebdomadaires des séances et mémoires*, CL (1956), 18–20.

CALDWELL, D. K. "Notes on the Spotted Dolphin, *Stenella plagiodon*, and the First Record of the Common Dolphin, *Delphinus delphis,* in the Gulf of Mexico," *Journal of Mammalogy,* LVI, (1955), 467–70.

CALDWELL, M. C., AND CALDWELL, D. K. "Epimeletic (Care-Giving) Behavior in Cetacea," in *Whales, Dolphins and Porpoises.* Edited by K. S. Norris. First International Symposium on Cetacean Research, Washington, D.C., 1963. Berkeley: University of California Press, 1966, pp. 755–89.

———. "Vocalization of Naive Captive Dolphins in Small Groups," *Science,* CLIX (1968), 1121–23.

CAMERON, NORMAN. "Experimental Analysis of Schizophrenic Thinking," in *Language and Thought in Schizophrenia.* Edited by J. S. Kasenin and N. D. C. Lewis. Berkeley: University of California Press, 1944, pp. 50–62.

CARPENTER, C. R. *A Field Study of the Behavior and Social Relations of Howling Monkeys.* Comparative Psychology Monographs, X. Baltimore: Johns Hopkins Press, 1934.

———. "Territoriality: A Review of Concepts and Problems," in *Behavior and Evolution.* Edited by Anne Roe and George Gaylord Simpson. New Haven: Yale University Press, 1958, pp. 224–68.

CARR, ARCHIE. "Adaptive Aspects of the Scheduled Travel of *Chelonia,*" in *Animal Orientation and Navigation.* Edited by R. M. Storm. Corvallis: Oregon State University Press, 1967, pp. 35–55.

CASSIRER, ERNST. *Die Philosophie der symbolischen Formen.* (Translated by Ralph Manheim as *Philosophy of Symbolic Forms,* 1953–57.) 3 vols. Berlin: Bruno Cassirer, 1923–29.

———. *Sprache und Mythos.* Leipzig: B. G. Teunber, 1925.

CHILD, CHARLES MANNING. *Senescence and Rejuvenescence.* Chicago: University of Chicago Press, 1915.

CHURCH, R. M. "Emotional Reactions of a Rat to the Pain of Others," *Journal of Comparative and Physiological Psychology,* LII (1959), 132–34.

CLARK, W. E. LeGROS. *The Antecedents of Man.* 2d ed.; 1st ed., 1959. New York: Harper and Row, 1963.

COHEN, M. "Aspect et temps dans le verbe," *Journal de Psychologie,* XXIV (1927), 7.

CRAIG, W. "Appetites and Aversions as Constituents of Instinct," *Biological Bulletin,* XXXIV (1918), 91–107.

CRAWFORD, M. P. *The Cooperative Solving of Problems by Young Chimpanzees.* Comparative Psychology Monographs, XIV. Baltimore: Johns Hopkins Press, 1937.

DANIELSON, R. N. "The Melanophore Responses of Fishes in Relation to Contrast in the Visual Field," *Physiological Zoology,* XIV (1941), 96–102.

DART, RAYMOND A. "Cultural Status of the South African Man-Apes," *Annual Report of the Smithsonian Institution, Washington, D.C.* Washington, D.C.: By the Institution, 1955, pp. 317–38.

———. "On the Evolution of Language and Articulate Speech," *Homo,* IX (1958), 154–58.

DE BEER, GAVIN R. *Embryos and Ancestors.* Oxford: Clarendon Press, 1940.

Bibliography

DEMENT, W. C. "The Effect of Dream Deprivation," *Science*, CXXXI (1960), 1705-7.

———. "An Essay on Dreams: The Role of Physiology in Understanding Their Nature," in *New Directions in Psychology*, Vol. II. New York: Holt, Rinehart and Winston, 1955, pp. 137-257.

———, AND WOLPERT, E. A. "The Relation of Eye Movements, Body Motility, and External Stimuli to Dream Content," *Journal of Experimental Psychology*, LV (1958), 543-53.

DIAMOND, A. S. *The History and Origin of Language*. London: Methuen, 1960.

DIXON, N. F., AND HAIDER, M. "Changes in Visual Threshold as a Function of Subception," *Quarterly Journal of Experimental Psychology*, XIII (1961), 229-35.

DONOVAN, J. "The Festal Origin of Human Speech," *Mind*, XVI (1891), 498-506; XVII (1892), 325-39.

DORST, JEAN. *The Migrations of Birds*. Translated by Constance D. Sherman from the orig. Fr. ed., 1956. London: Heinemann, 1962.

DROST, RUDOLF. "Zugvögel perzipieren Ultrakurzwellen," *Vogelwarte*, XV (1949), 57-59.

DU BRUL, E. L. *Evolution of the Speech Apparatus*. Springfield, Ill.: Charles C Thomas, 1958.

———. "Phylogenesis of the Speech Apparatus." Ph.D. dissertation, University of Chicago, 1955.

———, AND LASKIN, D. M. "Preadaptive Potentialities of the Mammalian Skull: An Experiment in Growth and Form," *American Journal of Anatomy*, CIX (1961), 117-32.

DUNBAR, I. K. "Observations on Visual Activity in Birds," *The Kingbird*, XI (1961), 32.

DUNBAR, M. J. "The Evolution of Stability in Marine Environments. Natural Selection at the Level of the Ecosystem," *The American Naturalist*, XCIV (1960), 129-36.

DURKHEIM, ÉMILE, AND MAUSS, MARCEL. "De quelques formes primitives de classification: Contribution à l'étude des représentations collectives," *L'Année sociologique*, VI (1901-2), 1-72.

DYE, J. A., AND KINDER, F. S. "A Prepotent Factor in the Determination of Skull Shape," *American Journal of Anatomy*, LIV (1934), 333-46.

EBERT, J. D. *Interacting Systems in Development*. New York: Holt, Rinehart and Winston, 1965.

EDGREN, J. G. "Amusie (musikalische Aphasie)," *Deutsche Zeitschrift für Nervenheilkunde*, IV (1895), 1-64.

EDINGER, TILLY. "Frontal Sinus Evolution (Particularly in the Equidae)," *Bulletin of the Museum of Comparative Zoology of Harvard College*, CIII (1950), 411-96.

———. "Paleoneurology versus Comparative Brain Anatomy," *Confinia Neurologica*, IX (1949), 5-24.

EIBL-EIBESFELDT, I. "Angeborenes und Erworbenes im Verhalten einiger Säuger," *Zeitschrift für Tierpsychologie*, XX (1963), 705-54.

———. "Beiträge zur Biologie der Haus- und Ährenmaus nebst einigen

Bibliography

Beobachtungen an anderen Nagern," *Zeitschrift für Tierpsychologie*, VII (1950), 558–87.

———. "Der Kommentkampf der Meerechse (*Amblyrhynchus crystatus* Bell.) nebst einigen Notizen zur Biologie dieser Art," *Zeitschrift für Tierpsychologie*, XII (1955), 49–62.

ELDRED, E., GRANIT, R., AND MERTON, P. A. "Supraspinal Control of the Muscle Spindles and Its Significance," *Journal of Physiology*, CXXII (1953), 498–523.

ETKIN, WILLIAM. "Social Behavioral Factors in the Emergence of Man," in *Culture and Direction of Human Evolution*. Edited by S. M. Garn. Detroit: Wayne State University Press, 1964, pp. 81–91.

EVANS, WILLIAM E., AND BASTIAN, JARVIS. "Marine Mammal Communication: Social and Ecological Factors," in *The Biology of Marine Mammals*. Edited by H. Andersen. New York: Academic Press, 1969, pp. 425–75.

EVANS, W. F. *Communication in the Animal World*. New York: Thomas Y. Crowell, 1968.

FERGUSON, D. E. "Sun-Compass Orientation in Anurans," in *Animal Orientation and Navigation*. Edited by R. M. Storm. Corvallis: Oregon State University Press, 1967, pp. 21–34.

FIELDS, PAUL E. *Studies in Concept Formation*. Baltimore: Johns Hopkins Press, 1932.

FISHER, CHARLES. "A Study of the Preliminary Stages of the Construction of Dreams and Images," *Journal of the American Psychoanalytic Association*, V (1957), 5–60.

FISHER, J., AND HINDE, R. A. "The Opening of Milk Bottles by Birds," *British Birds*, XLII (1949), 347–57.

FONTAINE, MAURICE. "Analyse expérimentale de l'instinct migratuer des poissons," in *L'Instinct dans le comportement des animaux et de l'homme*. Edited by P. P. Grassé. Paris: Masson, 1956, pp. 151–75.

FOPPA, KLAUS. "Motivation und Bekräftigungswirkungen im Lernen," *Zeitschrift für angewandte Psychologie*, X (1963), 646–59.

FOSSEY, DIAN. "Making Friends with Mountain Gorillas," *National Geographic*, CXXXVI (1970), 48–67.

FOULKES, D. "Dream Reports from Different Stages of Sleep," *Journal of Abnormal and Social Psychology*, LXV (1962), 14–25.

FRÄDRICH, HANS. "Zur Biologie und Ethologie des Warzenschweines (*Phagochoerus aethiopicus* Pallas), unter Berücksichtigung des Verhaltens anderer Suiden," *Zeitschrift für Tierpsychologie*, XXII (1965), 328–74.

FREUD, SIGMUND. *Gesammelte Werke*, Vol. IV: *Zur Psychopathologie des Alltagslebens*. Orig. pub. 1901. (Translated as *The Psychopathology of Everyday Life*.) Frankfurt-am-Main: S. Fisher, 1958.

———. *Gesammelte Werke*, Vols. II–III: *Die Traumdeutung*. Orig. pub. 1900. (Translated by A. A. Brill as *The Interpretation of Dreams*.) Frankfurt-am-Main: S. Fisher, 1961.

FRIEDMANN, HERBERT. *The Cowbirds: A Study in the Biology of Social Parasitism*. Springfield, Ill., and Baltimore: Charles C Thomas, 1929.

———. *Host Relations of the Parasitic Cowbirds*. Washington, D.C.: Smithsonian Institution, 1963.

Bibliography

FRINGS, HUBERT, AND FRINGS, MABEL. "The Language of Crows," *Scientific American*, CCI (1959), 119–31.

FRISCH, KARL VON. *Bees: Their Vision, Chemical Senses, and Language.* Ithaca, N.Y.: Cornell University Press, 1950.

———. *The Dancing Bees: An Account of the Life and Senses of the Honey Bee.* Orig. pub., 1927. Translated by Dora Ilse from the rev. German ed., *Aus dem Leben der Bienen*, 1948(?). New York: Harcourt, Brace, 1955.

———. "Über den Gehörsinn der Fische," *Biological Reviews of the Cambridge Philosophical Society*, XI (1936), 210–46.

FRITH, H. J. "Breeding Habits of the Family Megapodidae," *The Ibis*, XCVIII (1956), 620–38.

———. "Incubator Birds," *Scientific American*, CCI (1959), 52–58.

FROBENIUS, L. *Aus den Flegeljahren der Menschheit: Bilder des Lebens, Treibens und Denkens der Wilden.* Hanover: Jänecke, 1901.

FULTON, J. F. *Physiology of the Nervous System.* 2d ed. London: Oxford University Press, 1943.

GAFFREY, GÜNTER. "Ortsgebundene Scheinjagd bei einer afghanischen Windhündin," *Zeitschrift für Tierpsychologie*, XI (1954), 144–46.

GARDNER, R. A., AND GARDNER, B. T. "Teaching Sign Language to a Chimpanzee," *Science*, CLXV (1969), 664–72.

GARNOT, J. S. F. "Les fonctions, les pouvoirs et la nature du nom propre dans l'ancienne Egypte d'après les textes des pyramides," *Journal de psychologie normale et pathologique*, XLI (1948), 463–73.

GARSTANG, WALTER. *Larval Forms, with Other Zoological Verses.* Introduction by Sir Alister Hardy. Oxford: Basil Blackwell, 1962.

———. "The Morphology of the Tunicata, and Its Bearings on the Phylogeny of the Chordata," *Quarterly Journal of Microscopical Science*, LXXII (1928), 51–187.

———. "The Origin and Evolution of Larval Forms," *Report of the British Association for the Advancement of Science, Section D* (1928), pp. 77–98.

———. "The Theory of Recapitulation: A Critical Restatement of the Biogenetic Law," *Journal of the Linnean Society of London*, XXXV (1922), 81–101.

GEHLEN, ARNOLD. *Der Mensch: Seine Natur und seine Stellung in der Welt.* 4th ed.; 1st ed., 1940. Bonn: Athenäum, 1950.

GESCHWIND, NORMAN. "The Organization of Language and the Brain," *Science*, CLXX (1970), 940–44.

———, AND LEVITSKY, WALTER. "Human Brain: Left-Right Asymmetries in Temporal Speech Region," *Science*, CLXI (1968), 186–87.

GESELL, ROBERT. "A Neurobiological Analysis of the Innate Behavior of Man," in *L'Instinct dans le comportement des animaux et de l'homme.* Edited by P. P. Grassé. Paris: Masson, 1956, pp. 561–75.

GIBSON, J. J. "Observations on Active Touch," *Psychological Review*, LXIX (1962), 477–91.

———. *The Perception of the Visual World.* Boston: Houghton Mifflin, 1950.

————. "Visually Controlled Locomotion and Visual Orientation in Animals," *British Journal of Psychology*, XLIX (1958), 182–94.

GINNEKEN, J. VAN. *La réconstruction typologique des langues archäiques de l'humanité.* Verhandelingen der koninklijke Nederlandsche Akademie van Wetenschappen, n.s., XLIV. Amsterdam: Nederlandsche Akademie van Wetenschappen, 1939.

GOLDBY, F., AND GAMBLE, H. J. "The Reptilian Cerebral Hemispheres," *Biological Reviews*, XXXII (1957), 383–420.

GOLDSTEIN, KURT. "Die Konzentrische Gesichtsfeldeinschränkung als eine Folge organischer Schädigung," *Deutsche Zeitschrift für Nervenheilkunde*, LIX (1918), 199–216.

————. *Language and Language Disturbances.* New York: Grune and Stratton, 1948.

————. "Über die Plastizität des Organismus auf Grund von Erfahrungen am nervenkranken Menschen," *Handbuch der normalen und pathologischen Physiologie*, XV (1930), 1131–74.

————, AND GELB, ADHÉMAR. "Über eigentümliche 'ringförmige' Gesichtsfelddefekte," *Archiv für Ophthalmologie*, CIX (1922), 387–403.

GOODHART, S. P., AND SAVITSKY, N. "Alexia Following Injury of the Head," *Archives of Neurology and Psychiatry*, XXX (1933), 223–24.

GOODWIN, BRIAN C. "A Statistical Mechanics of Temporal Organization in Cells," *Symposia of the Society for Experimental Biology*, XVIII (1964), 301–26.

GOULD, EDWARD. "Orientation in Box Turtles *Terrepene c. carolina* Linnaeus," *Biological Bulletin*, CXII (1957), 336–48.

GREENBERG, JOSEPH H. *Essays in Linguistics.* Chicago: University of Chicago Press, 1957.

GREGORY, W. K., AND HELLMAN, M. "The Dentition of *Dryopithecus* and the Origin of Man," *Anthropological Papers of the American Museum of Natural History*, XXVIII, Pt. 2 (1926), 1–117.

GRIFFIN, DONALD R. *Listening in the Dark: The Acoustic Orientation of Bats and Men.* New Haven: Yale University Press, 1958.

————, AND GALAMBOS, ROBERT. "Obstacle Avoidance by Flying Bats," *Anatomical Record*, LXXVIII (1940), 95.

————. "The Sensory Basis of Obstacle Avoidance by Flying Bats," *Journal of Experimental Zoology*, LXXXVI (1949), 481–506.

GRIMM, JAKOB. *Über den Ursprung der Sprache.* Berlin: F. Dimmler, 1852.

GRZIMEK, BERNHARD. "Beobachtungen an einem kleinen Schimpansenmädchen," *Zeitschrift für Tierpsychologie*, IV (1940–41), 295–306.

————. "Einige Beobachtungen an Wildtieren in Zentral-Afrika," *Zeitschrift für Tierpsychologie*, XIII (1956), 143–50.

————. "Ein merkwürdiges Verhalten von afrikanischen Elefanten," *Zeitschrift für Tierpsychologie*, XIII (1956), 151–52.

GUDGER, E. W. "Fisherman Bats of the Caribbean Region," *Journal of Mammalogy*, XXVI (1945), 1–15.

GUGGENHEIM, LOUIS. *Phylogenesis of the Ear.* Culver City, Calif.: Murray and Gee, 1948.

GUILLAUME, P. *La formation des habitudes.* Paris: Alcan, 1936.

GUTHRIE, E. R. "Association by Contiguity," in *Psychology: A Study of a*

Science, Vol. III. Edited by S. Koch. New York: McGraw-Hill, 1959, pp. 158–95.

HAHN, EMILY. "Chimpanzees and Language," *The New Yorker*, December 11, 1971, pp. 54–98.

HALL, K. R. L. "Observational Learning in Monkeys and Apes," *British Journal of Psychology*, LIV (1963), 201–26.

HAMBURGER, VICTOR. "Some Aspects of the Embryology of Behavior," *Quarterly Review of Biology*, XXXVIII (1963), 342–65.

HAMILTON, JAMES A. "Intelligence and the Human Brain," *Psychological Review*, XLIII (1936), 308–21.

HAMILTON, W. J. *American Mammals: Their Lives, Habits, and Economic Relations*. New York: McGraw-Hill, 1939.

HARA, T. J., UEDA, K., AND GORBMAN, A. "Electroencephalographic Studies of Homing Salmon," *Science*, CXLIX (1965), 884–85.

HARDY, A. C. "Change and Choice: A Study in Pelagic Ecology," in *Evolution*. Edited by G. R. de Beer. Oxford: Clarendon Press, 1938, pp. 139–59.

———. "Escape from Specialization," in *Evolution as a Process*. Edited by J. Huxley, A. C. Hardy and E. B. Ford. London: George Allen and Unwin, 1954, pp. 122–42.

HARRISON, C. J. O. "Open-Billed Probing by the Princess Stephanie Bird of Paradise," *The Condor*, LXVI (1964), 162–63.

HASLER, A. D. "Underwater Guideposts for Migrating Fishes," in *Animal Orientation and Navigation*. Edited by R. M. Storm. Corvallis: Oregon State University Press, 1967, pp. 1–20.

HAYES, K. J., AND HAYES, C. "Picture Perception in a Home-Raised Chimpanzee," *Journal of Comparative and Physiological Psychology*, XLVI (1953), 470–74.

HEAD, HENRY. "The Conception of Nervous and Mental Energy," *British Journal of Psychology*, (Section, General), XIV (1923–24), 126–47.

HEATH, R. G. "Motor Activity and Inhibition from Identical Subcortical and Cortical Points," *Transactions of the American Neurological Association*, 77 (1952), 248–51.

HEBB, D. O. *The Organization of Behavior: A Neuropsychological Theory*. New York and London: John Wiley and Chapman and Hall, 1949.

HEDIGER, H. "Die Bedeutung von Miktion und Defäkation bei Wildtieren," *Schweizerische Zeitschrift für Psychologie und ihre Anwendung*, III (1944), 170–82.

———. "Vom Traum der Tiere," *Ciba Zeitschrift*, IX (1945–47), 3558–66.

HELD, R., AND HEIN, A. "Adaptation of Disarranged Hand-Eye Coordination Contingent upon Reafferent Stimulation," *Perceptual and Motor Skills*, VIII (1958), 87–90.

———. "Movement-Produced Stimulation of Visually Guided Behavior," *Journal of Comparative and Physiological Psychology*, LVI (1963), 872–76.

HERRNSTEIN, R. J., AND LOVELAND, D. H. "Complex Visual Concept in the Pigeon," *Science*, CXLVI (1964), 549–51.

HESS, ECKHARDT H. "The Effects of Meprobamate on Imprinting in Water-

Bibliography

fowl," *Annals of the New York Academy of Sciences*, LXVII (1957), 724–33.

———. "Imprinting," *Science*, CXXX (1959), 133–41.

HEVEROCH, A. "Amerisia," *Zeitschrift für die gesamte Neurologie und Psychiatrie*, XXVII (1915), 321–56.

HEWES, G. W. "Hominid Bipedalism: Independent Evidence for the Food-Carrying Theory," *Science*, CXLVI (1964), 416–18.

HILDEMANN, W. H. "A Cichlid Fish, *Symphysidon discus*, with Unique Nurture Habits," *American Naturalist*, XCIII (1959), 27–34.

HINDE, R. A. "Factors Governing the Changes in Strength of a Partially Inborn Response, as Shown by the Mobbing Behaviour of the Chaffinch (Fringilla coelebs). I. The Nature of the Response, and an Examination of Its Course. II. The Waning of the Response," *Proceedings of the Royal Society of London, Series B*, CXLII (1954), 306–58.

———. "Rhesus Monkey Aunts," in *Determinants of Infant Behaviour III*. Edited by B. M. Foss. Proceedings of the Third Tavistock Seminar on Mother-Infant Interaction, London, 1963. London: Methuen, 1965, pp. 67–75.

HINSCHE, G. "Ein Schnappreflex nach 'Nichts' bei Anuren," *Zoologischer Anzeiger*, CXI (1935), 113–22.

HOCKETT, C. F. "The Origin of Speech," *Scientific American*, CCIII (1960), 89–93.

HOESCH, W. "Über ziegenhütende Bärenpaviane (*Papio ursinus raucana* Shortridge)," *Zeitschrift für Tierpsychologie*, XVIII (1961), 297–301.

HOFER, GUSTAV. "Zur motorischen Innervation des menschlichen Kehlkopfes," *Zeitschrift für die gesamte Neurologie und Psychiatrie*, CLXXVII (1944), 788–96.

HOFF, HANS. "Die zentrale Abstimmung der Sehsphäre," *Abhandlungen aus der Neurologie, Psychiatrie, Psychologie und ihren Grenzgebieten*, LIV (1930), 1–96.

HOFFMANN, KLAUS. "Die Einrechnung der Sonnenwanderung bei der Richtungsweisung des sonnenlos aufgezogenen Stares," *Naturwissenschaften*, XL (1953), 148.

HOLST, ERICH VON. "Quantitative Messung von Stimmungen im Verhalten der Fische," *Symposia of the Society for Experimental Biology*, IV (1950), 143–72.

———, AND SAINT PAUL, URSULA. "Vom Wirkungsgefüge der Triebe," *Naturwissenschaften*, XVIII (1960), 409–22.

HOLZWORTH, J. M. *The Wild Grizzlies of Alaska*. New York: G. P. Putnam's Sons, 1930.

HOOKER, DAVENPORT. *The Prenatal Origin of Behavior*. Porter Lectures, Series 18. Lawrence: University of Kansas Press, 1952.

HOREL, J. A., TREICHLER, F. R., AND MEYER, D. R. "Coercive Behavior in the Rhesus Monkey," *Journal of Comparative and Physiological Psychology*, LVI (1963), 208–10.

HORN, GABRIEL. "Physiological and Psychological Aspects of Selective Perception," in *Advances in the Study of Behavior*. Edited by D. S. Lehrman, R. A. Hinde and E. Shaw. New York: Academic Press, 1965.

HOROWITZ, N. H. "On the Evolution of Biochemical Syntheses," *Proceed-*

ings of the National Academy of Sciences (1945), pp. 153–57. Reprinted in *Great Experiments in Biology*. Edited by Mordecai L. Gabriel and Seymour Fogel. Englewood Cliffs, N.J.: Prentice-Hall, 1955, pp. 297–300.

————, BONNER, D., MITCHELL, H. K., TATUM, E. L., AND BEADLE, G. W. "Genic Control of Biochemical Reactions in Neurospora," *The American Naturalist*, LXXIX (1945), 304–39.

HOWELLS, W. W. "Origin of the Human Stock," *Cold Spring Harbor Symposia on Quantitative Biology*, XV (1950), 79–86.

HOWITT, A. W. *Native Tribes of South East Australia*. New York: Macmillan, 1904.

HOYLE, GRAHAM. *Comparative Physiology of the Nervous Control of Muscular Contraction*. Cambridge: University Press, 1957.

HUMBOLDT, WILHELM VON. *Sprachphilosophische Werke*. Berlin: F. Dimmler, 1884.

HUME, DAVID. *Treatise on Human Nature*. 1740.

HUNTER, J., AND JASPER, H. "Reactions of Unanaesthetized Animals to Thalamic Stimulation," *Transactions of the American Neurological Association*, LXXIII (1948), 171–72.

HUNTER, RUTH R. "Symbolic Performance of Rats in a Delayed Alternation Problem," *Journal of Genetic Psychology*, LIX (1941), 331–57.

HYMAN, LIBBIE. "The Transition from the Unicellular to the Multicellular Individual," *Biological Symposia*, VIII (1942), 27–42.

ILSE, D. R. "Olfactory Marking of Territory in Two Young Male Loris, *Loris tardigradus lydekkerianus*, Kept in Captivity in Poona," *British Journal of Animal Behaviour*, III (1955), 118–20.

ISSERLIN, M. "Über Agramatismus," *Zeitschrift für die gesamte Neurologie und Psychiatrie*, LXXV (1922), 332–410.

JACOBSON, A., KALES, A., LEHMANN, D., AND ZWEIZIG, J. R. "Somnambulism: All-Night Encephalographic Studies," *Science*, CXLVIII (1965), 975–77.

JANDER, R., AND WATERMAN, T. H. "Sensory Discrimination between Polarized Light and Light Intensity Patterns by Arthropods," *Journal of Cellular and Comparative Physiology*, LVI (1960), 137–60.

JESPERSEN, OTTO. "Language," *Encyclopaedia Britannica*, 1957 ed.

————. *Language: Its Nature, Development and Origin*. London: G. Allen and Unwin, 1922.

JOHNSON, D. L. "Honey Bees: Do They Use the Direction Information Contained in Their Dance Maneuver?" *Animal Behavior*, XIV (1967), 261–65.

JOLLY, ALISON. *Lemur Behavior. A Madagascar Field Study*. Chicago: University of Chicago Press, 1967.

————. "Lemur Social Behavior and Primate Intelligence," *Science*, CLIII (1966), 501–6.

JONES, FREDERICK WOOD. *The Principles of Anatomy, as Seen in the Hand*. 2d ed.; 1st ed., 1920. Baltimore: Williams and Wilkins, 1942.

JOUVET, M. "Étude de la dualité des états du sommeil et des mécanismes de la phase paradoxale," in *Aspects anatomo-fonctionnels de la physiologie du sommeil.* Edited by M. Jouvet. Paris: Centre National de la Recherche Scientifique, 1965, pp. 397–449.

————, MICHEL, F., AND MOUNIER, D. "Analyse electroencephalographique comparée du sommeil physiologique chez le chat et chez l'homme," *Revue Neurologique,* CIII (1960), 189–205.

KARLGREN, BERNHARD. *Sound and Symbol in Chinese.* 2d ed.; 1st ed., 1923. London: Oxford University Press, 1946.

KATZ, DAVID. "Der Aufbau der Tastwelt," *Zeitschrift für Psychologie und Physiologie der Sinnesorgane,* Suppl. Vol. XI (1925), xii–270.

KAVANAU, J. L. "Compulsory Regime and Control of Environment in Animal Behaviour. I. Wheel-Running," *Behaviour,* XX (1963), 251–81.

KELLEHER, R. T. "Concept Formation in Chimpanzees," *Science,* CXXXIII (1958), 777–78.

KELLOGG, W. N. *Porpoises and Sonar.* Chicago: University of Chicago Press, 1961.

————. "Superstitious Behavior in Animals," *Psychological Review,* LVI (1949), 172–75.

————, AND KELLOGG, L. A. *The Ape and the Child.* New York and London: McGraw-Hill and Whittlesey House, 1933.

KENDEIGH, S. C. *Parental Care and Its Evolution in Birds.* Illinois Biological Monographs, XII. Urbana: University of Illinois Press, 1952.

KING, J. A. "Closed Social Groups among Domestic Dogs," *Proceedings of the American Philosophical Society,* XCVIII (1954), 327–36.

KLEIN, MARC. "Aspects biologiques de l'instinct reproducteur dans le comportement des mammifères," in *L'Instinct dans le comportement des animaux et de l'homme.* Edited by P. P. Grassé. Paris: Masson, 1956, pp. 287–344.

KLEIST, K. "Gehirnpathologische und lokalisatorische Ergebnisse. 4. Mitteilung. Über motorische Aphasien," *Journal für Psychologie und Neurologie,* XL (1930), 338–46.

KLEITMAN, N. "The Nature of Dreaming," in *The Nature of Sleep.* Edited by G. E. W. Wolstenholme and Maeve O'Connor. Ciba Foundation Symposium on the Nature of Sleep, London, 1960. Boston: Little, Brown, 1961, pp. 349–74.

KLINGEL, HANS. "Soziale Organisation und Verhalten freilebender Steppenzebras," *Zeitschrift für Tierpsychologie,* XXIV (1967), 580–624.

KLOTS, A. B., AND KLOTS, E. B. *Living Insects of the World.* Garden City, N.Y.: Doubleday, 1959.

KLÜVER, HEINRICH. "The Equivalence of Stimuli in the Behavior of Monkeys," *Journal of Genetic Psychology,* XXXIX (1931), 3–27.

KNORR, A. O. "The Effect of Radar on Birds," *The Wilson Bulletin,* LXVI (1954), 264.

KOEHLER, O. Review of H. G. Schmitt, "Abnormes Umweltbild eines Grünfinks," *Behaviour,* II (1950), 319.

————. "Sprache und unbenanntes Denken," in *L'Instinct dans le comportement des animaux et de l'homme.* Edited by P. P. Grassé. Paris: Masson, 1956, pp. 647–75.

KÖHLER, WOLFGANG. *The Mentality of Apes.* Translated by Ella Winter from the 2d rev. German ed.; 1st German ed., 1925. New York and London: Harcourt, Brace and Kegan Paul, Trench, Trubner, 1931.

Bibliography

KOENIG, OTTO. *Kif-Kif. Menschliches und Tierisches zwischen Sahara und Wilhelminenberg.* Vienna: Wollzeilenverlag, 1962.

KRAUSS, STEPHAN. "Untersuchungen über Aufbau und Störung der menschlichen Handlung," *Archiv für Psychologie*, LXXVII (1930), 649–92.

KROEBER, A. L. *Anthropology.* 2d ed.; 1st ed., 1923. New York: Harcourt, Brace, 1948.

———. "Sign and Symbol in Bee Communication," *Science*, XV (1952), 483.

KROTT, PETER, AND KROTT, GERTRAUD. "Zum Verhalten des Braunbären (*Ursus arctos* L., 1758) in den Alpen," *Zeitschrift für Tierpsychologie*, XX (1963), 160–206.

KÜHME, WOLFDIETRICH. "Freilandstudien zur Soziologie des Hyänenhundes (Lycaon pictus lupinus Thomas 1902)," *Zeitschrift für Tierpsychologie*, XXII (1965), 495–541.

KUMMER, HANS. *The Social Organization of Hamadryas Baboons.* Chicago: University of Chicago Press, 1968.

———. *Soziales Verhalten einer Mantelpaviangruppe.* Bern: Huber, 1958.

KUNKEL, PETER. "Zum Verhalten einiger Prachtfinken (*Estrildinae*)," *Zeitschrift für Tierpsychologie*, XVI (1959), 302–50.

LACEY, J. I., AND LACEY, B. C. "The Relationship of Resting Autonomic Activity to Motor Impulsivity," *Proceedings of the Association for Research in Nervous and Mental Disease*, XXXVI (1958), 144–209.

LAMY, J.-C. "The Beauty and the Beasts of East Africa," *Réalités*, CCIII (1967), 42 ff.

LASHLEY, K. S. "Notes on the Nesting Activities of the Noddy and Sooty Terns," in *Homing and Related Activities of Birds.* Edited by John B. Watson and K. S. Lashley. Papers from the Department of Marine Biology of the Carnegie Institution of Washington, VII. Washington, D.C.: Carnegie Institution of Washington, 1915, pp. 61–83.

———. "The Problem of Cerebral Organization in Vision," in *Visual Mechanisms.* Edited by Heinrich Klüver. *Biological Symposia*, Vol. VII. Edited by Jacques Cattell. Lancaster, Pa.: Jacques Cattell, 1942, pp. 301–22.

LASIEWSKI, R. C., AND BARTHOLOMEW, G. A. "Evaporative Cooling in the Poor-Will and the Tawny Frogmouth," *The Condor*, LXVIII (1966), 253–62.

LATIF, ISRAEL. "The Physiological Basis of Linguistic Development and the Ontogeny of Meaning," *Psychological Review*, XLI (1934), 55–85, 153–76, 246–64.

LAZARUS, R. S., AND MCCLEARY, R. A. "Autonomic Discrimination without Awareness," *Psychological Review*, LVIII (1951), 113–22.

LEACH, W. J. *Functional Anatomy, Mammalian and Comparative.* New York: McGraw-Hill, 1961.

LEE, DOROTHEA. "Conceptual Implications of an Indian Language," *Philosophy of Science*, V (1938), 89–102.

LEHRMAN, D. S. "On the Organization of Maternal Behavior and the Problem of Instinct," in *L'Instinct dans le comportement des animaux et de l'homme.* Edited by P. P. Grassé. Paris: Masson, 1956, pp. 475–520.

LENNEBERG, E. H. *Biological Foundations of Language.* New York: John Wiley, 1967.

LEYHAUSEN, PAUL. "Über die Funktion der relativen Stimmungshierarchie dargestellt am Beispiel der phylogenetischen und ontogenetischen Entwicklung des Beutefangs von Raubtieren," *Zeitschrift für Tierpsychologie*, XXII (1965), 412–94.

LIEPMANN, H., AND PAPPENHEIM, M. "Über einen Fall von sogenannter Leitungsaphasie mit anatomischen Befund," *Zeitschrift für die gesamte Neurologie und Psychiatrie*, XXVII (1915), 1–41.

LILLY, JOHN C. *Man and Dolphin*. Garden City, N.Y.: Doubleday, 1961.

———. *The Mind of the Dolphin: A Nonhuman Intelligence*. Garden City, N.Y.: Doubleday, 1967.

LIND, HANS. "The Activation of an Instinct Caused by a Transitional Action," *Behaviour*, XIV (1959), 123–35.

LINDEGREN, C. C. "The Role of the Gene in Evolution," *Annals of the New York Academy of Sciences*, LXIX (1957), 338–51.

LINSENMAIR, K. E. "Konstruktion und Signalfunktion der Sandpyramide der Reiterkrabbe *Ocypode saratan* Forsk. (Decapoda Brachyura Ocypodidae)," *Zeitschrift für Tierpsychologie*, XXIV (1967), 403–56.

LINTON, RALPH. "Primitive Art," *The Kenyon Review*, III (1941), 34–51.

LORENZ, KONRAD Z. "The Comparative Method in Studying Innate Behavior Patterns," in Society for Experimental Biology, *Physiological Mechanisms in Animal Behavior*. Society for Experimental Biology Symposia, IV. New York: Academic Press, 1950, pp. 221–68.

———. *King Solomon's Ring*. Translated by M. K. Wilson from the German, *Er redete mit dem Vieh, den Vögeln, und den Fischen*, ca. 1952. London: Pan Books, 1957.

———. "The Objectivist Theory of Instinct," in *L'Instinct dans le comportement des animaux et de l'homme*. Edited by P. P. Grassé. Paris: Masson, 1956, pp. 51–76.

———, AND TINBERGEN, N. "Taxis and Instinct: Taxis and Instinctive Action in the Egg Retrieving Behavior of the Greylag Goose," in *Instinctive Behavior: The Development of a Modern Concept*. Edited by Claire H. Schiller. Orig. pub., 1938. New York: International Universities Press, 1957, pp. 176–208.

LOWE, PERCY R. "Some Additional Anatomical Factors Bearing on the Phylogeny of the Struthiones," *Proceedings of the Zoological Society of London*, B, CXII (1942), 1–20.

MACHIDA, H., PERKINS, E., AND GIACOMETTI, L. "The Skin of Primates XXIX: The Skin of the Pygmy Bushbaby (*Galago demidovii*)," *American Journal of Physical Anthropology*, XXIV (1966), 199–204.

MAIER, N. R. F. *Reasoning in White Rats*. Comparative Psychology Monographs, VI. Baltimore: Johns Hopkins Press, 1929.

MALAMUD, WILLIAM, AND LINDER, F. E. "Dreams and Their Relationship to Recent Impressions," *Archives of Neurology*, XXV (1931), 1081–99.

MALGAUD, W. *De l'action à la pensée*. Paris: Alcan, 1935.

MARSHALL, A. J. "Bower Birds," *Scientific American*, CXCIV (1956), 48–52.

———. *Bower Birds. Their Displays and Breeding Cycles*. Oxford: Clarendon Press, 1954.

MARSHALL, N. B. *The Life of Fishes*. 2d ed.; 1st ed., 1966. New York: Universe Books, 1970.

Bibliography

MARSHALL, W. H., AND TALBOT, S. A. "Recent Evidence for Neural Mechanisms in Vision Leading to a General Theory of Sensory Acuity," in *Visual Mechanisms.* Edited by Heinrich Klüver. *Biological Symposia,* Vol. VII. Edited by Jacques Cattell. Lancaster, Pa.: Jacques Cattell, 1942, pp. 117–64.

MATTHEWS, G. V. T. *Bird Navigation.* Cambridge: University Press, 1955.

———. "The Orientation of Untrained Pigeons: A Dichotomy in the Homing Process," *Journal of Experimental Biology,* XXX (1953), 268–76.

MAXWELL, MARIUS. *Stalking Big Game with a Camera in Equatorial Africa.* New York: Century Co., 1924.

McBRIDE, A. F., AND KRITZLER, H. "Observations on Pregnancy, Parturition, and Postnatal Behavior in the Bottlenose Dolphin," *Journal of Mammalogy,* XXXII (1951), 251–66.

MELLAND, FRANK. *Elephants of Africa.* New York: Scribner's, 1938.

MENG, MATHILDE. "Untersuchungen zum Farben- und Formensehen der Erdkröte *(Bufo bufo L.),*" *Zoologische Beiträge,* n.s., III (1958), 313–63.

MEYERSON, IGNACE. "Discontinuités et cheminements autonomes dans l'histoire de l'esprit," *Journal de psychologie normal et pathologique,* XLI (1948), 273–89.

MILLER, H. A. "The Buccal Food-Carrying Pouches of the Rosy Finch," *The Condor,* XLIII (1941), 72–73.

MOLTZ, H. "Imprinting: Empirical Basis and Theoretical Significance," *Psychological Bulletin,* LVII (1960), 291–314.

———, AND ROSENBLUM, L. A. "The Relation between Habituation and the Stability of the Following Response," *Journal of Comparative and Physiological Psychology,* LI (1958), 658–61.

MONNIER, A.-M. "Élaboration du message lumineux au niveau de la rétine," in *Problèmes de la couleur.* Edited by Ignace Meyerson. Paris: S.E.V. P.E.N., 1957, pp. 15–27.

MONTAGNA, WILLIAM. *The Structure and Function of Skin.* 2d ed. New York: Academic Press, 1962.

MONTGOMERY, K. C., AND HEINEMANN, E. G. "Concerning the Ability of Homing Pigeons To Discriminate Patterns of Polarized Light," *Science,* CXVI (1952), 454–56.

MOORE, ARTHUR RUSSELL. *The Individual in Simpler Forms.* Eugene: University of Oregon Press, 1945.

MOORE, J. C. "Bottle-Nosed Dolphin Supports Remains of Young." *Journal of Mammalogy,* XXXVI (1955), 466–67.

MORGAN, CLIFFORD T. "Physiological Mechanism of Motivation," in *Nebraska Symposium on Motivation.* Edited by M. R. Jones. Lincoln: Nebraska University Press, 1957–58, pp. 1–35.

MORLEY, DEREK W. *The Ant World.* Baltimore: Penguin Books, 1953.

MORRIS, CHARLES. *Signs, Language and Behavior.* New York: Prentice-Hall, 1946.

MORRIS, CHARLES W. *The Nature of Mind.* Houston, Tex.: Rice Institute, 1929.

MORSE, ROGER A. "Swarm Orientation in Honeybees," *Science,* CXLI (1963), 357–58.

MOUNTCASTLE, V. B. "The Neural Replication of Sensory Events in the Somatic Afferent System," in *Brain and Conscious Experience*. Edited by J. J. Eccles. New York: Springer, 1966, pp. 85–115.

MÜNSTERBERG, HUGO. *On the Witness Stand: Essays on Psychology and Crime*. 2d ed.; 1st ed., 1908. New York: Doubleday, Page, 1912.

NAPIER, JOHN. "The Antiquity of Human Walking," in *Human Variations and Origins: An Introduction to Human Biology and Evolution. (Readings from Scientific American)*. San Francisco: Freeman, 1967, pp. 116–26.

NAUNYN, B. *Die organischen Wurzeln der Lautsprache des Menschen*. Munich: J. F. Bergmann, 1925.

NIELSEN, J. M. *Agnosia, Apraxia, Aphasia*. 2d ed.; 1st ed., 1936. New York: Paul B. Hoeber, 1946.

————."Epitome of Agnosia, Apraxia and Aphasia with Proposed Physiologic-Anatomic Nomenclature," *Journal of Speech Disorders*, VII (1942), 105–41.

NOBLE, G. K., AND BRADLEY, H. T. "The Mating Behavior of Lizards; Its Bearing on the Theory of Sexual Selection," *Annals of the New York Academy of Sciences*, XXXV (1933), 25–100.

————, AND SCHMIDT, A. "The Structure and Function of the Facial and Labial Pits of Snakes," *Proceedings of the American Philosophical Society*, LXXVII (1937), 263–88.

NORRIS, K. S. (ed.). *Whales, Dolphins, and Porpoises*. International Symposium on Cetacean Research, Washington, D.C., 1963. Berkeley: University of California Press, 1966.

————, AND PRESCOTT, J. H. "Observations on Pacific Cetaceans of Californian and Mexican Waters," *University of California Publications in Zoology*, LXIII (1961), 291–402.

OLSON, E. C. *Origin of Mammals Based upon Cranial Morphology of the Therapsid Suborders*. Geological Society of America Special Papers, No. 55. New York: The Society, 1944.

ORGEL, A. R., AND SMITH, J. D. "Test of the Magnetic Theory of Homing," *Science*, CXX (1954), 891–92.

OSWALD, IAN. "After-Images from Retina and Brain," *Quarterly Journal of Experimental Psychology*, IX (1957), 88–100.

————. *Sleeping and Waking. Physiology and Psychology*. New York: Elsevier, 1962.

PAGET, RICHARD. *Human Speech: Some Observations, Experiments and Conclusions as to the Nature, Origin, Purpose and Possible Improvements of Human Speech*. London: K. Paul, Trench, Trubner, 1930.

PALIARD, J. "Les deux sources de la connaissance. Notes sur la pensée implicite," *Revue Philosophique*, CXLIII (1953), 60–75.

PANTIN, C. F. A. "Behavior Patterns in Lower Invertebrates," *Symposia of the Society for Experimental Biology*, IV (1950), 175–95.

PARDI, L. "Beobachtungen über das interindividuelle Verhalten bei *Polistes gallicus*. (Untersuchungen über die Polistini, no. 10)," *Behaviour*, I (1947), 138–71.

PARKER, G. H. "The Prolonged Activity of Momentarily Stimulated Nerves," *Proceedings of the National Academy of Sciences*, XX (1934), 306–10.

Bibliography

PARSONS, FRANCES T. *How To Know the Ferns*. Orig. pub., 1899. New York: Dover Publications, 1961.

PAVLOV, I. P. *Lectures on Conditioned Reflexes*, Vol. I. Translated by H. Gantt. New York: International Publishers, 1928.

PENFIELD, WILDER. *The Excitable Cortex in Conscious Man*. Springfield, Ill.: Charles C Thomas, 1958.

―――. "Neurological Mechanisms of Speech and Perception," Epsilon Psi lecture delivered at Yale University, 1963.

PENROSE, LIONEL S. "Self-Reproducing Machines," *Scientific American*, CC (1959), pp. 105–14.

PETERSON, L. R. "Short-Term Memory," *Scientific American*, CCXV (1966), 90–95.

PETRINOVICH, L., AND BOLLES, R. "Delayed Alternation: Evidence for Symbolic Processes in the Rat," *Journal of Comparative and Physiological Psychology*, L (1957), 363–65.

PHILLIPS, C. G. "Changing Concepts of the Precentral Motor Area," in *Brain and Conscious Experience*. Edited by J. C. Eccles. New York: Springer, 1966, pp. 389–421.

PICK, ARNOLD. *Über das Sprachverständnis*. Leipzig: Barth, 1909.

PIERON, HENRI. "L'Évolution du comportement dans ses rapports avec l'instinct," in *L'Instinct dans le comportement des animaux et de l'homme*. Edited by P. P. Grassé. Paris: Masson, 1956, pp. 677–704.

POMPEIANO, O., AND MORRISON, A. R. "Vestibular Origin of the Rapid Eye Movement during Desynchronized Sleep," *Experientia*, XXII (1966), 60–61.

PÖTZL, OTTO. "Experimentell erregte Traumbilder in ihren Beziehungen zum indirekten Sehen," *Zeitschrift für die gesamte Neurologie und Psychiatrie*, XXXVII (1917), 278–349.

―――. Über die parietal bedingte Aphasie und ihren Einfluss auf das Sprechen mehrerer Sprachen," *Zeitschrift für die gesamte Neurologie und Psychiatrie*, XCVI (1925), 100–124.

PRECHTL, H. F. R. "Problems of Behavioral Studies in the Newborn Infant," in *Advances in the Study of Behavior*. Edited by D. S. Lehrman, R. A. Hinde and E. S. Shaw. New York: Academic Press, 1965, pp. 75–98.

PREMACK, DAVID. "The Education of Sarah," *Psychology Today*, September, 1970, pp. 55–58.

RABAUD, ÉTIENNE. "Les hommes au point de vue biologique," *Journal de psychologie*, XXVIII (1931), 673–704.

RAISTRICK, HAROLD. "Reflections on Some Present Tendencies in Microbiological Chemistry," in *Perspectives in Biochemistry*. Edited by J. Needham and D. E. Green. Cambridge: University Press, 1939, pp. 263–73.

RASHEVSKY, NICOLAS. "Learning as a Property of Physical Systems," *Journal of General Psychology*, V (1931), 207–29.

REID, M. J., AND ATZ, J. W. "Oral Incubation in the Cichlid Fish *Geophagus jurupari* Heckel," *Zoologica*, XLIII (1958), 77–88.

RÉVÉSZ, GÉZA. *Die Menschliche Hand: Eine Psychologische Studie*. Translated from the Dutch, *De menschelijke Hand*, 1941. New York: Karger, 1944.

———. *Ursprung und Vorgeschichte der Sprache*. Bern: A. Francke, 1946.

RIBBANDS, C. R. "The Defence of the Honey-Bee Community," *Proceedings of the Royal Society of London, Series B*, CXLII (1954), 514–24.

ROEDER, KENNETH. *Nerve Cells and Insect Behavior*. Cambridge, Mass.: Harvard University Press, 1963.

ROFFWARG, H. P., MUZIO, J. N., AND DEMENT, W. C. "Ontogenetic Development of the Human Sleep-Dream Cycle," *Science*, CLII (1966), 604–19.

ROWELL, THELMA. "Some Observations on a Hand-Reared Baboon," in *Determinants of Infant Behaviour*. Edited by B. M. Foss. New York and London: John Wiley and Methuen, 1965.

RUSSELL, BERTRAND. "Knowledge by Acquaintance and Knowledge by Description," *Proceedings of the Aristotelian Society*, n.s., XI (1910–11), 108–28. Reprinted in *The Problems of Philosophy* (New York, 1912) and in *Mysticism and Logic and Other Essays* (New York, 1918).

RYAN, T. A. "Interrelations of the Sensory Systems in Perception," *Psychological Bulletin*, XXXVII (1940), 659–98.

SACHS, CURT. *World History of the Dance*. Translated by B. Schönberg from *Eine Weltgeschichte des Tanzes*. New York: W. W. Norton, 1937.

SAINT PAUL, URSULA. "Nachweis der Sonnenorientierung bei nächtlich ziehenden Vögeln," *Behaviour*, VI (1953), 1–7.

SAPIR, EDWARD. *Language, an Introduction to the Study of Speech*. New York: Harcourt, Brace, 1921.

SCHAEFER, KARL ERNST. "Physiologische Anpassung bei Meeressäugetieren," in *Ueberleben auf See, 2. Marinemedizinisches Symposium in Kiel*. Kiel: Schiffahrtmedizinisches Institut der Marine, 1968, pp. 183–91.

———, et al. "Pulmonary and Circulatory Adjustments Determining the Limits of Depths in Breathhold Diving," *Science*, CLXII (1968), 1020–23.

SCHALLER, G. B. "The Behavior of the Mountain Gorilla," in *Introduction to Primate Behavior: Field Studies of Monkeys and Apes*. Edited by I. DeVore. New York: Holt, Rinehart and Winston, 1965, pp. 324–67.

———. *The Mountain Gorilla—Ecology and Behavior*. Chicago: University of Chicago Press, 1965.

SCHIFF, WILLIAM, CAVINES, J. A., AND GIBSON, J. J. "Persistent Fear Responses in Rhesus Monkeys to the Optical Stimulus of 'Looming,'" *Science*, CXXXVI (1962), 982–83.

SCHILLER, PAUL H. "Innate Motor Action as a Basis of Learning. Manipulative Patterns in the Chimpanzee," in *Instinctive Behavior: The Development of a Modern Concept*. Edited by Claire H. Schiller. New York: International Universities Press, 1957, pp. 264–87.

SCHINDEWOLF, OTTO H. "Das Problem der Menschwerdung, ein paläontologischer Lösungsversuch," *Jahrbuch der preussischen geologischen Landesanstalt*, XLIX (1928), 716–66.

SCHLOETH, R. "Zur Biologie der Begegnung zwischen Tieren," *Behaviour*, X (1956–57), 1–80.

Bibliography

SCHMID, BASTIAN. "Zur Psychologie des Treibens und Hütens: Beobachtungen am Appenzeller Sennenhund und am deutschen Schäferhund," *Zeitschrift für Tierpsychologie*, I (1937), 241–58.

SCHMITT, H. G. "Abnormes Umweltbild eines Grünfinks," *Zeitschrift für Tierpsychologie*, VI (1949), 271–74.

SCHNEIDERMAN, H. A. "Onset and Termination of Insect Diapause," in *Physiological Triggers and Discontinuous Rate Processes. Papers Based on a Symposium at the Marine Biological Laboratory, Woods Hole, Mass., September 1955.* Edited by T. H. Bullock. Washington, D.C.: American Physiological Society, 1956, pp. 46–59.

SCHOENHEIMER, R. *The Dynamic State of Bodily Constituents.* Cambridge, Mass.: Harvard University Press, 1942.

SCHULTZ, A. H. "The Specializations of Man and His Place among the Catarrhine Primates," *Cold Spring Harbor Symposia on Quantitative Biology*, XV (1950), 37–53.

SETON, ERNEST T. *The Biography of a Grizzly.* New York: Century Co., 1899.

SEWARD, J. P. "The Sign of a Symbol: A Reply," *Psychological Review*, LV (1948), 277–96.

SHAPIRO, ARTHUR. "Dreaming and the Physiology of Sleep. A Critical Review of Some Empirical Data and a Proposal for a Theoretical Model of Sleep and Dreaming," *Experimental Neurology*, Suppl. Vol. IV (1967), 56–81.

SHOOP, C. R. "Orientation of *Ambystoma maculatum*: Movements to and from Breeding Ponds," *Science*, CXLIX (1965), 558–59.

SILBERER, HERBERT. "Bericht über eine Methode, gewisse symbolische Halluzinations-Erscheinungen hervorzurufen und zu beobachten," *Jahrbuch für Psychoanalytische und Psychopathologische Forschung*, I (1909), 513–25. Translated in *Organization and Pathology of Thought.* Edited by David Rapaport. New York: Columbia University Press, 1951, pp. 195–207.

———. "Über die Symbolbildung," *Jahrbuch für Psychoanalyse und psychoanalytische Forschung*, III (1912), 661–723.

SIMPSON, GEORGE GAYLORD. *Tempo and Mode in Evolution.* New York: Columbia University Press, 1944.

SINCLAIR, F. G. "Myriapoda," in *The Cambridge Natural History*, Vol. V. Cambridge: University Press, 1922.

SINNOTT, EDMUND W. *The Problem of Organic Form.* New Haven: Yale University Press, 1963.

SKINNER, B. F. " 'Superstition' in the Pigeon," *Journal of Experimental Psychology*, XXXVIII (1948), 168–72.

SLUCKIN, W., AND SALZEN, E. A. "Imprinting and Perceptual Learning," *Quarterly Journal of Experimental Psychology*, XIII (1961), 65–77.

SOMMERFELT, ALF. *La langue et la société; caractères sociaux d'une langue de type archaïque.* Oslo: Aschenhoug (W. Nygaard), 1938.

SONNEBORN, T. M. "Beyond the Gene," *American Scientist*, XXXVII (1949), 33–59.

SPARKS, J. H. "Allogrooming in Primates: A Review," in *Primate Ethology.* Edited by D. Morris. Chicago: Aldine, 1967, pp. 148–75.

Bibliography

SPENCER, W. B., AND GILLEN, F. J. *The Arunta; a Study of a Stone Age People*. London: Macmillan, 1927.

————, AND GILLEN, F. J. *The Native Tribes of Central Australia*. New York: Macmillan, 1899.

————. *Northern Tribes of Central Australia*. New York: Macmillan, 1904.

SPIEGEL, MELVIN. "The Reaggregation of Dissociated Sponge Cells," *Annals of the New York Academy of Sciences*, LX (1955), 1056–78.

SPUHLER, J. N. "Somatic Paths to Culture," in *The Evolution of Man's Capacity for Culture*. Edited by J. N. Spuhler. Detroit: Wayne State University Press, 1959, pp. 1–13.

STEBBINS, G. L. *Variation and Evolution in Plants*. New York: Columbia University Press, 1950.

STENUIT, ROBERT. *The Dolphin, Cousin to Man*. Translated from the French by C. Osborne. New York: Sterling Publishing Co., 1968.

STRAUS, WILLIAM L., JR. "The Riddle of Man's Ancestry," *Quarterly Review of Biology*, XXIV (1949), 200–223.

SUDD, JOHN H. *An Introduction to the Behavior of Ants*. London: St. Martin's Press, 1967.

SUTHERS, R. A. "Optomotor Responses by Echolocating Bats," *Science*, CLII (1966), 1102–4.

SUTTON, G. M., AND GILBERT, P. W. "The Brown Jay's Furcular Pouch," *The Condor*, XLIV (1942), 160–65.

SWEET, W. H., TALLAND, G. A., AND ERVIN, F. R. "Loss of Recent Memory Following Section of Fornix," *Transactions of the American Neurological Association*, LXXIV (1959), 76–82.

TAVOLGA, M. C. "Behavior of the Bottlenose Dolphin (*Tursiops truncatus*): Social Interactions in a Captive Colony," in *Whales, Dolphins and Porpoises*. Edited by K. S. Norris. First International Symposium on Cetacean Research, Washington, D.C., 1963. Berkeley: University of California Press, 1966, pp. 718–30.

————, AND ESSAPIAN, F. S. "The Behavior of the Bottle-Nosed Dolphin (*Tursiops truncatus*): Mating, Pregnancy, Parturition, and Mother-Infant Behavior," *Zoologica* [N.Y.], XLII (1957), 11–31.

TEUBER, HANS-LUKAS. "Alterations of Perception after Brain Injury," in *Brain and Conscious Experience*. Edited by J. C. Eccles. New York: Springer, 1966, pp. 182–216.

THORNDIKE, E. L. *Animal Intelligence*. Orig. pub., 1898. New York: Macmillan, 1911.

THORNER, HANS. "Die harmonische Anpassungsfähigkeit des verkürzten Nervensystems, untersucht an Schlangen," *Pflügers Archiv für die gesamte Physiologie des Menschen und der Tiere*, CCXXX (1932), 1–15.

THORPE, W. H. "The Evolutionary Significance of Habitat Selection," *Journal of Animal Ecology*, XIV (1945), 67–70.

————. "The Language of Birds," *Scientific American*, CXCV (1956), 128–38.

————. *Learning and Instinct in Animals*. Cambridge, Mass.: Harvard University Press, 1956.

————. "Some Problems of Animal Learning," *Proceedings of the Linnean Society of London*, CLVI (1944), 70–83.

————, AND ZANGWILL, O. L. (eds.). *Current Problems in Animal Behaviour.* Cambridge: University Press, 1961.

TINBERGEN, NIKOLAAS. *The Herring Gull's World: A Study of the Social Behaviour of Birds.* London: Collins, 1953.

————. *The Study of Instinct.* Oxford: Clarendon Press, 1951.

TITCHENER, E. B. *A Textbook of Psychology.* New York: Macmillan, 1911.

TROMBETTI, ALFREDO. *L'Unità d'Origine del Linguaggio.* Bologna: Beltramini, 1905.

TSCHANZ, BEAT. "Zur Brutbiologie der Trottellumme (*Uria aalge aalge* Pont.)," *Behavior*, XIV (1959), 1–100.

TUMARKIN, A. "On the Evolution of the Auditory Conducting Apparatus: A New Theory Based on Functional Considerations," *Evolution*, IX (1955), 221–43.

TWITTY, V. C. "Influence of the Eye on the Growth of Associated Structures, Studied by Means of Heteroplastic Transplantation," *Journal of Experimental Zoology*, LXI (1932), 333–74.

UEXKÜLL, JAKOB VON. "A Stroll through the Worlds of Animals and Men: A Picture Book of Invisible Worlds," in *Instinctive Behavior: The Development of a Modern Concept.* Translated by Claire H. Schiller from *Streifzüge durch die Umwelten von Tieren und Menschen*, 1934. New York: International Universities Press, 1957, pp. 5–80.

————, AND SARRIS, E. G. "Das Duftfeld des Hundes. (Hund und Eckstein)," *Zeitschrift für Hundeforschung*, I (1931), 55–68.

VALENTA, J. G., AND RIGBY, M. K. "Discrimination of the Odor of Stressed Rats," *Science*, CLXI (1968), 599–601.

VALÉRY, PAUL. *Poésie et pensée abstraite.* The Zaharoff Lecture. Oxford: Clarendon Press, 1939.

VANDERPLAS, J. M., AND BLAKE, R. R. "Selective Sensitization in Auditory Perception," *Journal of Personality*, XVIII (1949), 252–66.

VAN LAWICK-GOODALL, JANE. "Chimpanzees of the Gombe Stream Reserve," in *Introduction to Primate Behavior: Field Studies of Monkeys and Apes.* Edited by I. DeVore. New York: Holt, Rinehart and Winston, 1965, pp. 425–73.

————. *My Friends the Wild Chimpanzees.* Washington, D.C.: National Geographic Society, 1967.

VAN TYNE, JOSSELYN, AND BERGER, ANDREW J. *Fundamentals of Ornithology.* New York: Wiley, 1959.

VIAND, G. "Taxies et tropismes dans le comportement instinctif," in *L'Instinct dans le comportement des animaux et de l'homme.* Edited by P. P. Grassé. Paris: Masson, 1956, pp. 5–49.

VOEKS, VIRGINIA. "What Fixes the Correct Response?" *Psychology Review*, LII (1945), 49–51.

VOLKELT, HANS. *Über die Vorstellungen der Tiere: Ein Beitrage z. Entwicklungspsychologie.* Leipzig: Engelmann, 1912.

VOWLES, D. M. "Neural Mechanisms in Insect Behaviour," in *Current Problems in Animal Behaviour.* Edited by W. H. Thorpe and O. L. Zangwill. Cambridge: University Press, 1961, pp. 5–29.

WALKER, E., *et al. Mammals of the World.* Baltimore: Johns Hopkins Press, 1964.

WALLON, HENRI. *De l'acte à la pensée. Essai de psychologie comparée.* Paris: Flammarion, 1942.

WALTER, W. GREY. "The Functions of Electrical Rhythms in the Brain," *Journal of Mental Science,* XCVI (1950), 1–31.

WANDELER, IRENE, AND PILLERI, GEORG. "Weitere Beobachtungen zum Verhalten von *Aplodontia rufa* Rafinesque (Rodentia, Aplodontoidea) in Gefangenschaft," *Zeitschrift für Tierpsychologie,* XXII (1964), 570–83.

WARREN, E. R. *The Beaver.* Monographs of the American Society of Mammalogists, No. 2. Baltimore: Williams and Wilkins, 1927.

WASHBURN, S. L. "The Analysis of Primate Evolution with Particular Reference to the Origin of Man," *Cold Spring Harbor Symposia on Quantitative Biology,* XV (1950), 67–78.

WATSON, A. J. "The Place of Reinforcement in Behaviour," in *Current Problems in Animal Behaviour.* Edited by W. H. Thorpe and O. L. Zangwill. Cambridge: University Press, 1961, pp. 273–301.

WATSON, JOHN B., AND LASHLEY, K. S. (eds.). *Homing and Related Activities of Birds.* Papers from the Department of Marine Biology of the Carnegie Institution of Washington, VII. Washington, D.C.: Carnegie Institution of Washington, 1915.

WEBER, N. A. "Fungus-Growing Ants," *Science,* CLIII (1966), 587–604.

WEBSTER, D. B. "A Function of the Enlarged Middle-Ear Cavities of the Kangaroo Rat, Dipodomys," *Physiological Psychology,* XXXV (1962), 248–56.

WEIDENREICH, FRANZ. "The Trend of Human Evolution," *Evolution,* I (1947), 221–36.

WEISS, PAUL. "Tierisches Verhalten als 'Systemreaktion.' Die Orientierung der Ruhestellung von Schmetterlingen gegen Licht und Schwerkraft," *Biologia Generalis,* I (1925), 167–248.

WEISZ, P. B. "Morphogenesis in Protozoa," *Quarterly Review of Biology,* XXIX (1954), 207–29.

WELLS, G. P. "Worm Autobiographies," *Scientific American,* CC (1959), 132–42.

WENDT, G. R. "An Interpretation of Inhibition of Conditioned Reflexes as Competition between Reaction Systems," *Psychological Review,* XLIII (1936), 258–81.

WENNER, ADRIAN M. "Honey Bees: Do They Use the Distance Information Contained in Their Dance Maneuver?" *Science,* CLV (1967), 847–49.

———, AND JOHNSON, D. L. "Simple Conditioning in Honey Bees," *Animal Behaviour,* XIV (1966), 149–55.

———, WELLS, P. H., AND ROHIF, F. J. "An Analysis of the Waggle Dance and Recruitment in Honey Bees," *Physiological Zoology,* XL (1967), 317–44.

WHITE, L. A. "On the Use of Tools by Primates," *Journal of Comparative Psychology,* XXXIV (1942), 369–74.

WHITTEN, W. K., BRONSON, F. H., AND GREENSTEIN, J. A. "Estrus-Inducing

Pheremone of Male Mice: Transport by Movement of Air," *Science,* CLXI (1968), 584–85.

WHITEHEAD, ALFRED NORTH, AND RUSSELL, BERTRAND. *Principia Mathematica,* Vol. 1. 2d ed.; 1st ed., 1910. Cambridge: University Press, 1935.

WIENER, NORBERT. *Cybernetics: Or Control and Communication in the Animal and the Machine.* New York: John Wiley, 1948.

WOLF, WERNER. "Der archäische Sprachorganismus," *Zeitschrift für Psychologie,* CX (1929), 113–34.

WOODRUFF, L. L. "The Protozoa and the Problem of Adaptation," in *Organic Adaptation and the Environment.* Edited by M. R. Thorpe. New Haven: Yale University Press, 1924, pp. 45–66.

YEAGLEY, H. L. "A Preliminary Study of a Physical Basis of Bird Navigation. Part I," *Journal of Applied Physics,* XVIII (1947), 1035–63.

———. "A Preliminary Study of a Physical Basis of Bird Navigation. Part II," *Journal of Applied Physics,* XXII (1951), 246–60.

YERKES, R. M. *The Mental Life of Monkeys and Apes.* New York: Henry Holt, 1916.

YOUNG, J. Z. "The Evolution of the Nervous System and of the Relationship of Organism and Environment," in *Evolution.* Edited by Gavin R. de Beer. Oxford: Clarendon Press, 1938, pp. 179–204.

———. *The Life of Vertebrates.* 2d ed.; 1st ed., 1950. Oxford: Clarendon Press, 1962.

———. *Patterns of Substance and Activity in the Nervous System.* London: H. K. Lewis, 1946.

YOUNG, STANLEY P., AND GOLDMAN, EDWARD A. *The Wolves of North America.* Washington, D.C.: American Wildlife Institute, 1944.

ZALOKAR, MARKO. "Ribonucleic Acid and the Control of Cellular Processes," in *Control Mechanisms in Cellular Processes, a Symposium.* Edited by David M. Bonner. New York: Ronald Press, 1961, pp. 87–140.

ZOTTERMAN, YNGVE. "The Nervous Mechanism of Taste," *Annals of the New York Academy of Sciences,* LXXXI (1959), 358–66.

———. "Studies in the Neural Mechanism of Taste," in *Sensory Communication.* Edited by W. A. Rosenblith. Cambridge, Mass., and New York: M.I.T. Press and John Wiley, 1961.

ZUBEK, JOHN P. (ed.). *Sensory Deprivation: Fifteen Years of Research.* New York: Appleton-Century-Crofts, 1969.

Index

Index of Names

Index of Subjects

Mind: An Essay on Human Feeling
Volume II
by Susanne K. Langer

Designed by Edward King

Type set by Monotype Composition Company, Inc., in
Electra text and Palatino display

Printed on S. D. Warren Sebago paper and bound in
Joanna Buckram cloth by The Maple Press Company

Manuscript edited by Jean Owen